The Americas in the Age of Revolution

The Americas in the Age of Revolution
1750–1850

Lester D. Langley

Yale University Press   New Haven and London

Published with assistance from the foundation established in memory of Philip Hamilton McMillan of the Class of 1894, Yale College.

Designed by Rebecca Gibb.

Set in Walbaum type by The Composing Room of Michigan, Inc.

Printed in the United States of America.

Library of Congress Cataloging-in-Publication Data

Langley, Lester D.

    The Americans in the age of revolution, 1750–1850 / Lester D. Langley.

      p. cm.

    Includes bibliographical references and index.

    ISBN 0-300-06613-9

    1. Revolutions—America—History—18th century. 2. Revolutions—America—History—19th century. 3. United States—History—Revolution, 1775–1783. 4. Haiti—History—Revolution, 1791–1804. 5. Latin America—History—Wars of Independence, 1806–1830. I. Title.

E18.82.L36 1996

973.3—dc20
                                    96-11598

                                        CIP

A catalogue record for this book is available from the British Library.

The paper in this book meets the guidelines for permanence and durability of the Committee on Production Guidelines for Book Longevity of the Council on Library Resources.

10 9 8 7 6 5 4 3 2 1

For Walter LaFeber

If everything occurred at the same time there could be no *development*. If everything existed in the same place there could be no *particularity*. Only space makes possible the particular, which then unfolds in time. Only because we are not equally near to everything; only because everything does not rush in upon us at once; only because our world is restricted for every individual, for his people and for mankind as a whole can we in our finiteness endure at all. . . . Particularity is the price of our existence. . . . To let this space-conditioned particularity grow without letting the whole run wild—that is political art.
August Lösch, Economics of Location

It is always necessary to watch out for something, a little beneath history, the break with it, that agitates it; it is necessary to look, a little behind politics, for that which ought to limit it, unconditionally.
Michel Foucault, "Is It Useless to Revolt?"

When change (truly fundamental change) is unavoidable, everyone or virtually everyone embraces it, and this is the dangerous moment. The breakdown of order becomes simultaneously the breakdown of ideology. When everyone talks about the language of change, it is hard to distinguish the sheep from the goats, the tenants of old privilege from their opponents, the heralds of more egalitarianism from the proponents of less egalitarianism.
Immanuel Wallerstein, Geopolitics and Geoculture

Contents

Maps

Acknowledgments

My greatest debt in writing this book is to the hundreds of scholars who have written about virtually every aspect of the revolutionary age in the Western hemisphere and whose work is a continual reminder that those of us who attempt a synthesis such as this must proceed cautiously. The citations to every chapter attest to my reliance on their scholarship. But I am also indebted to those comparativists whose work prompts an instinctively suspicious historian to move beyond the particular to the universal. The latter may not be satisfied by my reluctance to provide a singular explanation for the causes of these revolutions; the former may be irritated by my insistence that the choices confronting a generation of revolutionaries were never so clear-cut as we would like to believe. Both will demur at my preference for what is contemptuously referred to as *histoire événimentielle* or my insistence on the critical importance of personality. The age was no less complicated than our own; certainly it was more hazardous for anyone taking up arms in defense of a cause. Those who did may not have provided us with a satisfactory explanation of *revolution, liberty,* or *equality,* but their understanding of these words was more than a matter of linguistic convention.

Others contributed in a more direct way. Three colleagues in the Department of History at the University of Georgia—Early American historians Peter Hoffer and Michael Winship, and Latin Americanist Thomas Whigham—read portions of the manuscript, alerting me to monographs and articles I would otherwise have missed and gently prodding me to rethink some of my arguments. Fredrick Pike (emeritus, University of Notre Dame) and Ralph Lee Woodward, Jr. (Tulane University) provided a thorough assessment of the completed work.

Through words and deeds, Charles Grench of Yale University Press sustained my commitment following a justifiably critical reader's report on an early version of the manuscript. Jane M. Zanichkowsky provided a thorough copyediting of the manuscript. Jane Hedges guided the final draft through the production process with a professional attentiveness and skill that would please even the most demanding author. To all I am deeply appreciative.

My thanks also go to Julian Bach, my literary agent, who retains a gentlemanly style in what must be a mean business; to David Roberts, chair of the Department of History at the University of Georgia, an intellectual historian whose work has received international recognition and who maintains a refreshing commitment to ideas in an era when ideas seem to matter less than ideologies; and to Joe Key, Vice-President for Research, whose office has provided much-needed support.

The maps were prepared by Xueling Hu, Brian Davis, and Jim Ingram (Director) of the University of Georgia Office of Cartographic Services.

Finally, my deepest appreciation to Wanda Langley for two readings of the manuscript.

A Note on Usage

I have defined Spanish and French words in the text rather than attach a separate glossary. Spanish surnames ordinarily include the father's name followed by the mother's family name, even if the same, as in Fernando Díaz Díaz, which might be abbreviated as Fernando Díaz D. Place names have been modernized. Thus, I refer to Bogotá, *not* Sante Fe de Bogotá, and Veracruz, *not* Vera Cruz. In the text and especially in the endnotes, I have used Mexico City, *not* México, D.F.; Havana, not La Habana. It is common in English usage to drop the accent from Panamá, México, and Perú.

The most troublesome contemporary names are *America* and *American.* Even today, and certainly in the eighteenth century, *America* as a geographical term referred to the entire New World. When the British, the French, and especially the Spanish scribbled *America,* they usually meant *British America,* *French America,* and *Spanish America,* respectively. When referring to themselves, George Washington and Thomas Jefferson used *American* with less assurance than they did *Virginian.* The Haitian revolutionary leader Toussaint-Louverture thought of himself as French until his death at the hands of the French. In the Spanish-American struggles for independence Miguel Hidalgo, José María Morelos, and especially Simón Bolívar employed *America* and *American* to distinguish not only place but cultural identity. By the 1820s, if not earlier, United States leaders systematically used *America* and especially

American as references to the United States and its people. The reason had less to do with the awkwardness of saying "United Statesian" than the perception among national political leaders that the credibility of government depended on their ability to identify the abstract beliefs about *America* with their expansive notions about the United States. In other words, United States leaders "nationalized" *America* and *American.*

Throughout Spanish, Portuguese, French and even British dominions, sexual unions among Europeans, Africans, and Amerindian peoples had produced by the mid-eighteenth century a bewildering variety of names to designate those of mixed-race ancestry. (Colonial Mexico had fifteen such terms; French Saint Domingue, perhaps as many as sixty!) I have tried to be precise without burdening the reader with an unnecessarily large number of these terms.

Unless otherwise noted, translations from French or Spanish are mine. Where emphasis appears within a quotation, the emphasis is from the source. In other instances, the emphasis is mine, unless otherwise noted. The epigraphs of contemporaries are identified by author and date; those of twentieth-century persons are identified by author and source.

The Americas in the Age of Revolution

Introduction

By common agreement among historians and social scientists, revolution is a rewarding but complicated topic for comparative study. For one thing, the definition of *revolution* is elusive.[1] One indisputable certainty is that revolutions are the work of humans, and their coming depends on the calculations of both ruling groups and those who seek to bring them down. As John Dunn observes, "revolutions . . . have to be considered as very complex series of actions initiated in highly particular circumstances and at particular points in time."[2] Thus, situation can be as important as cause in arriving at a definition of revolution. Robert R. Palmer, the distinguished historian of the late eighteenth-century revolutions in Europe and America, has described a "revolutionary situation . . . [as] one in which confidence in the justice or reasonableness of existing authority is undermined; where old loyalties fade, obligations are felt as impositions, law seems arbitrary, and respect for supervisors is felt as a form of humiliation; where existing sources of prestige seem undeserved, hitherto accepted forms of wealth and income seem ill-gained, and government is sensed as distant, apart from the governed and not really 'representing' them."[3]

Both of these descriptions of *revolution* are quite properly tentative. It is the absence of an empirically based definition that makes them more persuasive.

Nineteenth-century social science provided more precise classifications of phenomena, its twentieth-century heirs with complicated models for explaining causation. Neither, lamentably, provides the appropriate intellectual inspiration for capturing the meaning of a revolution, mostly because there is no satisfactory methodology for that task. Walter LaFeber astutely observed in what was indisputably the most widely read book on Central America published in the 1980s that the biggest mistakes the United States has made in confronting revolutions in the isthmus have been its stubborn refusal to accept their inevitability and its unwillingness to "work with these revolutionaries to achieve a more orderly and equitable society."[4] LaFeber required none of the theoretical social science models to arrive at this sensible conclusion.

The Americas in the Age of Revolution is a comparative history of the revolutionary age that commenced with the American Revolution in 1776, continued with the slave revolt that erupted in Saint Domingue (the French colony that became Haiti at independence) in 1791, and culminated with the prolonged Spanish-American struggle for independence that officially ended a half-century later. Chapter 12 offers an interpretive overview of the Americas at 1850.

I propose a portrait of hemispheric political culture in an epoch spanning three wars in the Americas, each of which left a powerful legacy for the new states that took form in their aftermath. In a half-century, three European empires fell to independence movements. The origins of these struggles, as interpreted in traditional historical accounts, have been explained as a protest against imperial measures that led to revolution and ultimately to a war for independence in British North America; a political struggle among whites and colored in French Saint Domingue that collapsed into racial conflict and slave revolt and culminated in the creation of the second independent nation-state in the Americas; and a prolonged, devastating conflict in Spanish America that brought about independent but severely weakened republican states.

Even when they concede the appropriateness of the word *revolution* to describe these wars, modern scholars often measure their impact by the degree of social change that occurred. Undeniably, no assessment of their origin, character, or legacy can ignore their social impact. But I have chosen to take a political rather than a social measure of these revolutions for two reasons. First, though the involvement of popular forces in these struggles indicated the existence and, it is sometimes contended, the centrality of powerful and divisive social issues, they cannot be extrapolated from the fundamental political strains of the age. The radicalism of these wars may be measured by the dynamics of social change, but the violent overthrow of legitimate authority and the creation of independent states largely defined the revolutionary meaning of the age.[5]

Second, though debates over their meaning occasionally precipitated bitter disputes among contemporaries, few could deny their role as fundamental historical references in the formative years of political cultures in these states. A rebellion may lead to an adjustment of relationships between ruler and ruled or inspire central authority to accommodate the grievances of those in a remote portion of the empire or nation. Revolution provides a dynamic environment for a restructuring of that relationship. Rebellions may last longer and may even be more destructive. If successful, rebellions are sometimes transmuted into revolutions in popular mythology, but a triumphant rebellion does not make a revolution. Something more fundamental has to happen. Rebellions conform to linear processes: their beginnings, crucial turning points, and ends are easily recognized. Revolutions exhibit the characteristics of nonlinear dynamics: their origins, patterns, and finalities are never very clear. They are simultaneously simple and complex, easily comprehensible and equally baffling. Rebellions may precipitate repression or reform; revolution provides opportunity for destruction or creativity or both.

Undeniably, each of these wars of independence and the revolutions subsumed within them possessed an international character of political, economic, ideological, social, and even cultural dimensions, but they cannot be understood without an assessment of the political and social tensions reverberating throughout British America, French Saint Domingue, and Spanish America in the late eighteenth century. What made these upheavals distinctive was not only the demand from colonial elites for equality within empires but also the often reluctant choices they made in order to mobilize populations in their cause; the consequences of popular involvement; and, especially, the racial and spatial dimensions of these struggles. Put somewhat differently, in an age when political, economic, and social dynamics profoundly shook transatlantic empires, colonial elites wanted a different relationship with the home country and risked treason and war to achieve it. What they did not anticipate was the changes in their relationship with those who participated in these conflicts.

These factors by themselves do not necessarily set these revolutions apart from the fundamental questions comparativists have asked about twentieth-century revolutions, such as the Russian or the Chinese, and especially the French Revolution, which profoundly affected the colored revolt and slave rebellion in Saint Domingue, indirectly influenced Spanish-American rebels, and inspired or frightened the revolutionary generation in the United States. Indeed, historians of revolutions are more likely to compare the American and the French Revolutions than to measure either by the standards of the Haitian or the Spanish-American struggle. The American, Haitian, and Spanish-American revolutions, though comparable to the French, Chinese, or Russian in many ways, nonetheless are different in a crucial respect: in the former, revolutions not only brought new political groups to power and altered social relationships but also were subsumed within a struggle for independence. The often confusing distinction between revolution and war of independence and its consequences is a central focus of this book.

The reader may be understandably perplexed with the titles I have chosen to describe these three wars. In identifying the American war of independence as "the revolution from above," I am alluding to the articulation of colonial grievances by British American leaders in the years before the first battle, their creativity in adjusting to unexpected and often divisive forces once the conflict was under way, and, more than anything, their refusal to create a dominating revolutionary central government. The republic they crafted may have effectively excluded all save white males from the realistic prospect of full enjoyment of the benefits of independence, and the first postrevolutionary generation lived with the apprehension that the republic would not survive. Some spoke of the blessings of monarchy and comported themselves in the monarchical tradition, yet they never seriously considered restoring monarchy. They excluded women and minorities from any meaningful participation in political life, and for a generation some resisted granting the suffrage to anyone but property holders. They may have failed to address the "social question" and they could be privately contemptuous of "the people," but they articulated a revolutionary mythology with its vaguely defined but inspirational nationalism. Frustrated, occasionally embittered, and fearful over what they had brought about, they did not undermine the revolution. The incipient military coup in the last years of the revolution was the counterrevolution, not the Constitutional Convention, and it collapsed when George Washington refused to countenance a movement to address what he acknowledged were legitimate grievances.

I have incorporated the Haitian struggle for independence into this book for a reason that has less to do with the recurring debates over "Eurocentric" history than with the meaning of the Haitian Revolution in the late eighteenth and early nineteenth centuries. Occurring after the American Revolution but before the Latin American war of independence, the slave uprising on French Saint Domingue has often been relegated to a few pages in the modern historical surveys of the age of revolution in the Americas. But it preoccupied and frightened contemporaries. Indeed, the Haitian Revolution and its meaning are essential for understanding the revolutionary age in the Americas. Haiti was at once an affirmation of the *universality* of such revolutionary credos of liberty and equality and a denial of that contemporary ideology, which subsumed slavery in the revolutionary cause. The reach of European and U.S. power into French Saint Domingue and independent Haiti is well documented; less appreciated but no less consequential for the age was the impact of the slave rebellion and the creation of the second independent state in the Americas. Though his comments pertain to modern Haiti, Sidney Mintz underscores this importance when he writes, "What makes Haiti unique is that no other nation in world history has ever been created by slaves. Those slaves wrested their weapons from the hands of their masters and then threw the masters out."[6] This was the "revolution from below," expressed in the nineteenth-century Haitian constitution as the right of a people to take to the streets to bring down a government they no longer considered legitimate.

Finally, I have characterized the Latin American wars of independence as the "revolution denied" not for any failure of rebellious Spanish-American Creoles to articulate grievances, to mobilize a patriot army, or to craft new political institutions to replace those they had toppled but for their lack of faith in those institutions, their seeming unwillingness to fashion a necessary revolutionary mythology and tradition, and, most important, their efforts to reverse many of the democratic achievements of the revolutionary era. Explanation of the revolution denied has been variously attributed to the devastation of a fifteen-year war—not only in its environmental and economic but also in its emotional and racial impact—and to the enormous obstacles confronting the first generation of Latin American leaders and their fratricidal politics. Conservatives stand condemned for their refusal to accept the revolution (or, as in Mexico, for their efforts to restore monarchy), liberals for the price they imposed on the people in their schemes of economic growth.

Clearly, there was no lack of political ability in the new republics. During fifteen years of war, Creole elites had not only learned how to lure mixed-race peoples to join their armies but had accepted them in positions of authority. They had enlisted rural peoples in the cause of disaffected urbanites but never without apprehending their behavior or what they might demand. In the early years of these wars, particularly in Mexico, fears of a violent social and racial dimension of the struggle, with chants of "death to whites," prompted some Creoles to join royalist authorities in suppressing the rebellion. For at least a generation after the wars of independence, elites recalled wartime savagery and unpredictable behavior they identified with those from below, reconfirming their conviction that the first purpose of government was preservation of social control through the restoration of older social relationships and the cloning of European or North American models onto the political corpus. This was the revolution denied.

This book also deals with the putative triumph of liberalism and the controversial issue of modernization (what nineteenth-century observers called progress) and state-making in an age of international conflict and revolution. In the late eighteenth and early nineteenth centuries, monarchies succumbed to republics; corporatist societies where one had identity in the group (usually the family) presumably gave way to notions of identity based on individual wealth or achievement; and traditional ways relinquished their grip on the human spirit as new ways of thinking replaced them. In this era, newly independent states took on an economic and political character that reflected their cultural preferences and profoundly shaped what each ultimately became. Where the new political order did not unshackle the new state from the past, most assessments of these wars hold, entire peoples were left behind. By the mid-nineteenth century, liberalism was everywhere imperiled; its contradictions, particularly in the social costs of progress, had deeply scarred national politics and fragmented societies. This crisis was not unique to the Americas; Europe experienced deceptively similar patterns of social and political convulsion, but its dynamics and legacy were different. Paradoxically, the mid-nineteenth century proponents of liberalism correctly sensed that resolution of some fundamental political quarrels would make possible the crafting of a modern state and a modern economic order. In several Western states, notably the United States and Mexico, civil war, not political compromise, provided the opportunity to create this new order.

Though I recount the chronological unfolding of these revolutions and recapitulate their inception and their legacy, I am less concerned with addressing matters of causation, assessing the motives of revolutionary leaders, or determining if the revolutionary experience in the Americas resolved the social question than with exploring the particularity of these struggles. Thus, the questions "Why were they fought?" or "What did they achieve?" have generated a rich and often contentious scholarship. Just as valuable for understanding the revolutionary heritage of the Western hemisphere, I believe, are the impact of place or location on the course of revolution, the dynamics of race and color as well as class, the strength of counterrevolutionary movements, and the unexpected patterns of violence, among others. Most accounts of these revolutions, especially studies of the American Revolution, concentrate on achievement or, as a generation of social historians has pointed out, the failure to address manifest social inequities. I evaluate these issues, but I am more concerned with what these revolutions were able (or unable) to avoid—the militarization of society, for example—and other fundamental questions challenging the first generation of postrevolutionary leaders.

Among these, the most important included governance and the parallel factor of legitimacy. Most linear accounts of these struggles presume that there could be no turning back or that the explanation for the frustrations and failures of postrevolutionary governments lay in the refusal of elites to incorporate marginal groups into the new society or their determination to use military force to suppress those raising legitimate grievances against the new order. The experience of waging a revolution and creating a new political order was much more problematical, and the only way of getting at the meaning of these revolutions for the generations that led and fought them is to emphasize their particularity. The character of the American Revolution was so ambiguous and complex that the inevitability of U.S. independence was a reality only when the war was over, yet the prevailing sentiment of revolutionary accomplishment was probably stronger at the outset than at the end. Ambiguity and complexity in different forms characterized the Haitian and the Spanish-American struggles as well. In each there existed a manifest tension between universalism and particularism, where the dictates of a world-system economy, the appeal to reason, and the interstate system collided with the separatist and divisive forces inherent in the racial, religious, and political dynamics of the age. Despite the validity of these generalizations, they persuade only when each revolution is studied in its particularity and, indeed, when differences attributed to location—the spatial and ecological dimensions—are considered.[7]

An inquiry uninformed by theory, I concede, may contribute little more than a narrative account. A study oblivious to the nuances of the particular and to the parallel complexities that an awareness of place can inspire, however, can be sadly lacking in explanatory power. Historians and social scientists often make understandable but simplistic judgments about motivation or behavior. Two examples from the revolutionary age in the Americas suffice to make this point. In each of these revolutions, slaves fought on both sides. The prospect of obtaining freedom was ever present, but so were other motives—getting away from the harsh regimen of plantation life or simply wanting the status that comes with carrying a weapon *in* as much as *for* a cause. Simón Bolívar, the great liberator of northern South America, argued for the arming of slaves and the reward of freedom for their participation. His motives were infuriatingly complex, as were the circumstances. Bolívar the strategist wanted to counter the Spanish tactic of arming slaves; Bolívar the tactician rejuvenated a faltering struggle by freeing his own slaves in order to obtain Haitian aid; Bolívar the modernist believed in the eventual abolition of slavery; Bolívar the racist informed doubtful whites that if white people did most of the fighting they would do most of the dying and would live in a republic dominated by people of color; and Bolívar the social philosopher spoke eloquently of a "new people" born of miscegenation. Within him burned every passion and complexity of the revolutionary age.

What is lacking in many modern accounts of these revolutions is an appreciation of the dynamics of the age, where events did not unfold in a linear process of gradually or suddenly escalating power but in chaotic patterns that took differing forms in different places; of the social explosiveness generated not by class but by perceptions of color; of the infuriating complications generated when liberating ideas and traditional values interact; and of the ability of presumably traditional peoples—Indians, slaves, mixed-race progeny, among others—to adapt. Twentieth-century analysts have gone a long way in ridding the literature of many of the nineteenth-century postulates about revolution, but they have sometimes substituted equally rigid methodological constructs that diminish the critical role of people on the margins. Whether describing a revolutionary process, as the natural-history school of revolution undertakes, or providing a systemic or structural analysis, as its successors postulate, events and personalities are fitted into a scheme. History is reordered and restructured to explain the simultaneous existence of contradictory evidence or unanticipated consequences. In the process, aperiodic and nonlinear patterns are undervalued or excluded altogether.[8]

These revolutions exhibited a commonality that can best be understood by going beyond the deceptive similarities of colonial experience or grievance or republican destiny or how well each revolutionary movement addressed the social question. What they had in common was chaos and complexity. Those who led these wars experienced the simultaneous opportunity for and uncertainty of violence, at once destructive and creative, and the dilemmas and contradictions these opportunities imposed. And they had to adapt to the infuriating complexity of these struggles, to ever-shifting patterns of violence in different places, where people behaved in ways inexplicable to twentieth-century social science but comprehensible and even rational for contemporaries. The successful must adapt and respond, a simplistic view of leadership posits—leaders must have followers, and followers, leaders. If at every level people adapt and respond to events according to their own beliefs, self-interests, or predicaments, then the dilemmas confronting those who lead become far more complicated.[9]

Such complex systems have a capacity for adaptation because of their spontaneous self-organization. At every level, the local disorder and the often random violence accompanying revolution require contingent action, but the human responses are not simply an instinctive reaction to events but an expression of creative adaptability. Chaos theory is inadequate to explain the dynamism of this process or to mark that point where complex systems bring chaos and order into a precarious equilibrium—a balance where there is order and creativity, the reasurrance of tradition and inspiration for change. Complexity provides a theoretical model to assess what happens at the "edge of chaos."[10]

The chaos of revolution creates as it destroys. Instability and probability are partners in creativity as well as in destruction. What is often troublesome in the calculation of probability is that the slightest deviation in the route of revolutionary instability can have enormous impact on its trajectory. Revolution may rid the political culture of archaic forms such as monarchy or of evils such as slavery, but it may leave in its wake a more frightening and inhuman state or may tighten the bonds of enslavement. A suggestive metaphor for revolution is the weather. The variables can be identified, but their dynamics can be either complicated and unpredictable or readily measured and predicted. As in a hurricane, those at the eye of the revolutionary storm may experience little inconvenience while those in the swirling periphery are buffeted in the violent winds.

What these revolutions also shared was irony. Explaining the postrevolutionary frustrations of U.S. leaders, Gordon Wood writes: "This democratic society was not the society the revolutionary leaders had wanted or expected. . . . The founding fathers were unsettled and fearful not because the American Revolution had failed but because it had succeeded."[11] Toussaint-Louverture, the liberator of Haitian slaves, thought of himself as French and with the best intentions imposed an economic plan that for the liberated seemed distressingly similar to their lives as slaves. In a sweeping statement, Jorge

Domínguez generalizes about the collapse of the Spanish empire: "The empire broke down because it was both too traditional and too modern."[12] In addressing the paradox of revolution in Mexico, Luís Villoro notes that the revolution was begun by one group but consummated by its enemies. Some viewed the revolution as reaction to innovative liberal reforms from afar; others responded to a contradictory impulse. "What is significant is that both viewpoints may be validated by the evidence. The revolution of independence incorporated both antagonistic aspects."[13]

In the 1830s the "America" Alexis de Tocqueville extolled as the "democratic society" and Bolívar bemoaned as "ungovernable" offered sharply contrasting examples of the revolutionary legacy: the first born of political creativity and liberal imagination, the second forged by victors more interested in preserving tradition and privilege than in breaking the shackles of a debilitating past. The character of society, not political institutions, provided the most determining features of government. This contrast was perhaps too sharply drawn. When Tocqueville warned about the "tyranny of the majority" or the inevitability of conflict over the issues of slavery in the United States, he wrote in apocalyptic tones disturbingly similar to those Bolívar had evoked to describe Spanish-American society a few years earlier. By mid-century, the arrogant views U.S. leaders of the 1820s had voiced about the new republics in Latin America had lost some of their sharpness. Victory over Mexico produced not unity but bitter division and the collapse of the American democracy. The fratricidal civil war that followed appeared to confirm Bolívar's somber prognosis about the legacy of revolution—despair for those who lead a revolution and chaos for those who try to rule in its wake.

Part 1   The Revolution from Above

All that part of Creation that lies within our observation is liable to change. Even mighty States and Kingdoms are not exempted.
John Adams (1755)

The use of force alone is but *temporary*. It may subdue for a moment; but it does not remove the necessity of subduing again: and a nation is not governed, which is perpetually to be conquered.
Edmund Burke, "On Conciliation with America," speech in Parliament (March 2, 1775)

The American is a new man, who acts upon new principles; he must therefore entertain new ideas, and form new opinions. From involuntary idleness, servile dependence, penury, and useless labour, he has passed to toils of a very different nature, rewarded by ample subsistence.—This is an American.
J. Hector St. John de Crèvecoeur (1782)

The characteristic difference between your revolution and ours, is that having nothing to destroy, you had nothing to injure, and labouring for a people, few in number, incorrupted, and extended over a large tract of country, you have avoided all the inconveniences of a situation, contrary to every respect. Every step in your revolution was perhaps the effect of virtue, while ours are often faults, and sometimes crimes.
Mme. d'Houdetot to Thomas Jefferson (1790)

I

The Tense Society

In 1762 the last major battle of a war for trade in the Caribbean occurred, a massive British assault on the fortified Spanish city of Havana, the third largest in the Americas after Lima and Mexico City. Cuba was the second major conquest of the Spanish in the New World. From its shores, expeditions had sailed for Panama, Mexico, and Florida. Havana had suffered periodic raiding by buccaneers in the past (children still heard fearful stories of "Draques, el terrible," Sir Francis Drake, and the raids of his Elizabethan privateers), but not since a band of French pirates had seized the city in the sixteenth century had it fallen victim to foreign occupation. Forty years earlier, as British contraband traders—important suppliers for many of the isolated towns of the Spanish Main—sailed the Caribbean, the Spanish threw their efforts into making Havana an impregnable fortress in their New World dominion. Now it fell to a conquering army of soldiers, slave traffickers, and aggressive English traders. Alert to the growing carping among English colonials about these imperial conflicts, the young King George III emphasized the importance of including men from North America in the invading army so that they might recognize the larger purpose of the mission. Before the occupation ended, one-quarter of the British force of 22,000 were men from Britain's North American colonies.[1]

The seizure of one of Spain's most heavily fortified cities was a moment of high triumph for the British. From the beginning of the seventy-five-year conflict with France and its reluctant ally, Spain, two generations of English merchants had sought to channel the nation's imperial energies toward opening the lucrative market in the Indies. In 1713, in the Peace of Utrecht, England had won the *asiento*, the coveted Spanish slave trade; in the 1730s, English smugglers had plied the Caribbean, and English goods found their way into Spanish America via Portugal (after 1702 a British ally), Brazil, and the North American colonies. The Dutch and the French, longtime rivals of the English in the pursuit of the coveted Spanish market, rapidly fell behind as these eighteenth century wars for trade progressed. British North American commerce with the Spanish colonies and even Iberia accelerated dramatically.

Heightened sentiments about Britain's mission and grandeur were severely tempered by distressing tales, disseminated through private letters or in newspapers, about the suffering of ordinary British Americans in these conflicts. In the Caribbean phase of the third Anglo-French imperial war in the 1740s, British Americans served in the calamitous campaign against Cartagena and fought in the strike against Guantánamo. Ninety percent perished in these tropical ventures. The survivors returned home with bitter memories of ill treatment: British officers had compelled them to work alongside slaves or to labor as ordinary deckhands on ships—or, if wounded, had denied them equal treatment with soldiers from the home islands.[2]

The fourth war, the French and Indian War (called the Seven Years' War in Europe), involved even larger numbers of mainland British Americans. In this presumably decisive struggle for a continent, some British Americans were fired with grand designs. The experience subtly altered British Americans' feelings about their place within the empire. John Adams imagined an imperial future in the first year of the war that would have deeply troubled George III: "If we remove the turbulent Gallicks, our people, according to the exactest computations, will in another century become more numerous than England itself. Should this be the case, since we have . . . all the naval stores of the nation in our hands, it will be easy to obtain the mastery of the seas; and the united force of all Europe will not be able to subdue us."[3]

Empire and Economy

Though in the peace settlement of 1763 it had emerged victorious in the great war for trade, the British empire began to experience the strains that often follow war. The first was the strategic economic role that British North America assumed in imperial calculations in the postwar years, which had to do with the political economy of British North America and its place in the transatlantic economic order. Completion of the economic goals of empire, the more radical imperial reformers argued, required not only new endeavors but a different way of looking at the role of *colonies* within the world economy.

Regrettably, this view was politically untimely for a generation of British leaders who confronted a different kind of problem in the colonies. To encourage the colonies to take greater responsibility for their defense, as the imperial rationalists were arguing, would promote intercolonial cooperation, to be sure, but it would also require greater dependence on colonial volunteers in time of crisis. The British experience with volunteers in King George's War (1744–1748) had been disappointing, as evidenced by a near-fiasco in Virginia, where the governor had tried to mobilize the colony to undertake wartime measures and then had had to appeal for regular troops from Britain. Despite British-American protestations, regulars, not colonial auxiliaries, had determined the victory in the French and Indian War. A considerable portion of the regular army remained in British America at the end of the war. What was unsettling to British officials was the *experience* of these peacetime forces, especially at those times when governors had employed troops to maintain control. For policing, British Americans looked to their militias, not to regular British troops.[4]

The debilitating legacy was indecisiveness and irresponsibility in the critical formative years of postwar imperial policy. Two diverse examples illustrate the degree of damage. The first has to do with ambitious postwar British plans for the Indians of North America. In their expansive notions about the territorial rewards of victory, most colonials believed the conquered "inner domain" of New France must be opened for settlement and exploitation. The war in the colonies had in fact begun two years before it had erupted in Europe because of the precipitous actions of Virginians who coveted the Ohio country. In the colonials' estimation, Indians of the western country were allies of the French and, just as damnable, stood in their way.

A different view of the Indian problem prevailed in Britain. During the war, British strategy was to wean the Indians from their French alliance with promises of assistance and, especially, pledges that the acquisitive whites from east of the Appalachians would be contained. Colonial governments had never handled Indian affairs in a responsible manner, it was generally agreed in London, and the Proclamation of 1763 (discussed below), which decreed a halt to such overland migration, appeared to be a justifiable measure. Given the need to avoid a costly Indian war, fulfilling the wartime promises made sense. Circumstances in British America, however, created a different scenario: the migrations into Indian domain continued, and an Indian war erupted.[5]

It occurred almost simultaneously with the apparent collapse of the wartime coalition that had orchestrated the British victory over France. An invigorated sense of British-American identity prompted some colonial leaders to express a very different, and threatening, imperial vision—not as sharply defined as that of British imperial planners but with strong roots in provincial culture, reflecting the aspirations of a generation of colonials (Franklin was the most articulate of this group) who sensed that the colonies had become self-reliant and deserved a rank of equality within the empire. This view of "empire with autonomy" had adherents in England, men who believed that the old empire that had depended on military force—what Stephen Saunders Webb has characterized as the "garrison state"—must yield to modernizing forces. By 1750 "it was apparent that the anti-imperial forces of acquisitive capitalism, individual liberty, provincial autonomy, and Anglo-American oligarchy had won lasting social and political influence for the local elites who were the eventual authors of the American Revolution."[6]

These beliefs about the transatlantic relation were contradictory but did not precipitate an open break until the imperial crisis of midcentury. Both views derived from the colonial experience. One was integrative, gaining its strength from a gradual but perceptible incorporation of the Atlantic colonies within the empire and calling upon them in the expansion and defense of that empire. The second definition of empire was inherently divisive. Even as British Americans professed their anglophilia, adopted British cultural fashions, and boasted of their prosperity within the colonial family, they sensed that the old rhythms of empire were giving way to a modern notion of empire, one less expressive of the sentiments of Greater England than of the calculations of economic policy and market opportunity. Montesquieu's *lois fundamentales de l'Europe* had extolled European mercantilism and British colonial policy, but during the last of the imperial wars British leaders, who grumbled about colonial profiteering and preoccupation with provincial interests, had begun to worry about the problems of defending and administering an empire without relying on the colonies. Such a policy required greater control and more efficient imperial administration.[7]

Just as important for our understanding of British America on the eve of revolution is the uneven economic development within the Atlantic colonies.

These years saw the emergence of *Homo oeconomicus* in a colonial society of individualistic, entrepreneurial farmers determined to promote their own interests by taking advantage of the expanding transatlantic market. The pace of economic change accelerated, and with it the realization that economic benefit carried an unexpected price. A demand-driven market required the staple colonies to export more wheat and flour to southern European markets and caused New Englanders to depend on the West Indian commerce to pay for British manufactures. The consequence was "Americanization through Anglicization," but its political legacy was a more acute sense of dependence and revolutionary nationalism. As British North Americans indulged their consumer appetites for English goods, they not only went deeper into debt but also expressed nostalgia for an imagined era of self-sufficiency. There was no realistic hope of turning back the clock, of course, but colonials now viewed imported goods as a symbol of their growing dependence and the reach of metropolitan power. "An expanding market," observes T. H. Breen in commenting on these changes, "linked frontiersmen to city dwellers, colonists living on the periphery of empire to the great merchants of the metropolis."[8]

The parallel legacy of this expanding marketplace was the consumer revolution of the age, a revolution whose social impact was uneven and uncertain because its pervasiveness both united and divided backcountry yeomen, pretentious country gentry, urban merchants, artisans, and propertyless migrants. Tied to the same economic marketplace of material rewards and labor demands, rich and poor participated inequitably in its benefits, yet the *prospect* and *opportunity* offered by the consumer revolution permeated the collective psyche. In the economic arena, consumers, especially women, discovered they had individual choice and economic clout. The marketplace not only dictated economic priorities and social choice but also subtly altered the political culture as small landholders with voting privileges recognized they shared with social elites a passion for the pursuit of gain. They became less deferential for their "participation in a developing economy permitted [them] to extend their powers and turn their practical accomplishments into claims for greater esteem."[9]

The consumer revolution presumably mitigated the fragmentation of British North American society, because the remotest settlers and even the Indians were drawn into the market economy, but it did not produce the integrated society that modernization theorists occasionally stipulate must happen. On its effects, historians sharply differ. If one argues that the market was an eighteenth-century creation that was the basis for the modern liberal, capitalist society of individualist producers, laborers, and consumers, then the presumption is that colonial British North America must have been traditional, self-sufficient, and communal. On the other hand, if it is presumed that colonial society exhibited *both* an entrepreneurial market orientation *and* a self-sufficient communal ethos, then the historiographical either-or dispute turns on which was the more determining factor in explaining social change on the eve of revolution.[10] Put another way, which values—those of *Homo oeconomicus* or *Homo republicanus*—would shape the character of a revolutionary culture?

The Peopling of Empire

The presumably unshakable British-American sense of identity and community was strained as well. Disparate but related forces now intruded; a wave of postwar immigrants with heightened expectations of a better life; uncertainty about the social and political complications identified with slavery and, especially, miscegenation; changes in religious identity associated with evangelicalism; the intrusion of religion into the transatlantic political debate, specifically the rise of civic millenialism; restlessness and violence; and a gnawing sense among colonial elites that those beneath them in the social order no longer accepted the patriarchal community and its unwritten rules of deference to their betters.

From the earliest settlements until about 1760, more than 50 percent of colonists entering British North America south of New England were in bondage, usually as servants. African slaves augmented this involuntary labor force considerably, particularly in the Chesapeake and the Lower South, where the plantation economy had already taken hold. Economic historians persist in their debates over the preferences for indentured, free, or slave laborers and why slave labor appeared more suitable for plantation agriculture. The social and political implications of this shift to a predominantly white free labor and predominantly colored slave labor population, particularly in Virginia, were profound and, to southern patriarchs, unsettling. In the late seventeenth century, the mingling of white and colored bonded laborers was not uncommon. Its racial product was successive generations of mulattoes, "new people." Its disturbing social and political legacy was the understandable anomaly of a revolutionary generation who believed that freedom for whites depended on the enslavement of people of color.[11]

The post-1760 wave of immigration to British North America profoundly shook the empire. This last and most significant of the great colonial migrations—from the North British borderlands—got under way after the Peace of Utrecht in 1713 and lasted until the American Revolution. More ethically diverse than their predecessors, these were peoples whose social condition was often precarious and who were, to exploit a modern phrase, pursuers of the American dream. They carried their boisterousness and instinctive passion for "natural liberty" from the borderlands of North Britain to the frontier of British North America.[12]

And it was the movement of peoples, within British North America and from Britain and Europe, that initially befuddled British planners as they laid out in the Proclamation of 1763 a grand scheme for reorganizing the interior of North America (see map 1). The intent was to separate Indian domain west of the Appalachians from white settlements east of the mountains. It was an act of bureaucratic expedience necessitated by the desire to maintain the Franco-Indian interior trade under metropolitan control, and it was virtually unenforceable. There seemed no practical way of dealing with the western question—not by proclamation nor by the circulation of tales about Indian atrocities in the western country. Pessimistic reports of the disruption of the Indian trade recommended force as the only realistic way of preserving order on the frontier. A trading concern in Philadelphia described traders as "the most debased banditti that ever infested a government, the greater part gaol gleanings and the refuse of Ireland"; and a British soldier in South Carolina, where a ferocious war between colonists and Cherokees had broken out in 1759, called the traders "a shame to Humanity, and the Disgrace of Christianity. . . . The Savages daily saw themselves cheated in Weight and Measure; their Women debauched, and their young Men corrupted."[13]

There were other challenges to imperial control. To the white settlers east of the mountains and the Indians west of the mountains, the central issue was not the Indian trade but land. The war with France had commenced with the intrusion of Virginians into New France. British Americans had supported the war in large part because of the immediacy of the French threat to their security in the interior and because they coveted the land; some of France's Indian allies had changed sides because they believed the lands claimed by the French would eventually pass to them. During wartime negotiations, British representatives had pledged to draw a line between white and Indian jurisdictions and to keep white settlers from pushing onto lands claimed by Indians. Before the war's end, it had seemed apparent to the Indians that the promise would not be kept: British troops had seized Detroit, and Virginia speculators had dispatched agents and settlers into the interior. The immedi-

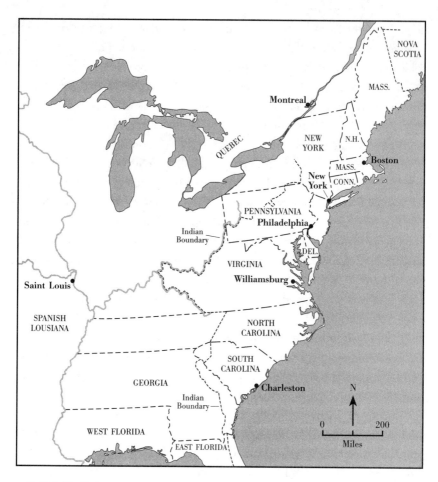

1. British North America, 1775.

ate response had been an uprising of Iroquois Senecas and Mohawks under Pontiac, an Ottawa, whose war had launched the initial phase of a thirty-year struggle between white and Indian in the Old Northwest. When it was over, the British held onto the forts but offered the defeated Indians a mollifying gesture—the Proclamation of 1763, with its prohibitions against further white encroachment.[14]

British officials were not unprepared for the Indian uprising. Indeed, they had discussed such a prospect months beforehand, and they did so in the context of the more important issue of the day—control over the colonies. As one wrote: "The apprehension which the People have of those savages, will always induce them to look on the Station of Troops amongst them as necessary for their safety. And Troops, and Fortifications will be very necessary for Great Britain to keep up in her Colonys, if she intends to secure their Dependence on Her."[15] But they felt ensnared by the circumstances: having to manage many diverse and conflicting groups in a place where none of these groups dominated. Doing nothing was risky. The inability to manage affairs or anticipate what might happen if they pursued a more aggressive policy made such a course even riskier.[16]

What the British confronted on the North American frontier was chaos. The situation was "chaotic because no power could control it. . . . Power was in fact local and unstable, often applied opportunistically quite outside of traditional or formal systems."[17] By the mid-1770s, as many as 50,000 whites had penetrated the interior beyond the Appalachians. The British military had largely abandoned any expectation of controlling them, as Thomas Gage recognized, for they were "too Numerous, too Lawless and Licentious ever to be restrained."[18]

The Proclamation of 1763 could not stem the great internal and transatlantic migration. Whole families picked up and moved, dreaming of possibilities more imagined than real. Others, speculators and organizers, formed companies to move peoples into the vast interior. The migration was not solely from the eastern seaboard across the mountains; there were also powerful regional migrations from present-day Massachusetts to the Connecticut and Hudson river valleys and north into what is now Maine and New Hampshire. But it was the West that galvanized the attention of the migrants—southwestern Pennsylvania, western Virginia, northwestern North Carolina, and eastern Tennessee. In London, the earl of Hillsborough, president of the Board of Trade, had calculated that the proclamation would not only stem this internal flow but would also address another problem: a diminishing agricultural labor supply worsened by the emigration of Protestant Irish, Scots, and English to British America.[19]

They came to a British America undergoing a different kind of change: an unsuspected transformation in social relationships. Its roots lay in the Great Awakening in the eighteenth century, which paralleled the imperial wars and stirred British Americans as deeply because its effect reached throughout the population. Among slaves, who had resisted the incorporation of African forms into established Anglicanism, the evangelicals encouraged religious activities with their missions and brought African music into their liturgy. In Virginia, Baptists exercised social control over blacks by accepting them as "brothers and sisters" and subsequently disciplining them if they strayed from the orderly life. Denounced from Anglican pulpits for their disruptive influence, they had little interest in political power and certainly no desire to bring about a social leveling. Yet they constituted a threat to the gentry, for theirs was a "different and more inclusive model for the maintenance of order in society."[20]

This wave of revivalism sweeping the colonies, dividing churches and entire communities, was a milder form of the Protestant Reformation, which had undermined Catholic unity. In British America, this second Reformation occurred in an era of secularism, when common folk had come to believe that the established churches had become too formal and ritualized and educated people too rational. Inspired by revivalist sermons, laymen became less deferential to clergymen and more responsive to the dictates of inner religious consciousness. But they did not become more obedient. Evangelists were agitators, not healers. "The Great Awakening shook people as well as churches. It drove deeper into the grain of American life the principle of lay choice and lay decision and in this sense it was a quintessential expression of Protestantism."[21]

Political Choices and Social Realities

Revolutions, it is said, are not made; they come. The reality is more complicated. Often the revolutions that come are not the ones that are made or even anticipated. What occurred in the decade before the onset of revolution in British North America was a transformation of colonial identity with a parallel realization by ordinary people of the relation between events and their own lives. Perceived arbitrariness of a government far away made them more aware of the functioning of their own local governments; as their commitment to Anglo-American political community diminished, they looked increasingly to provincial and especially local political institutions. For the radicals and pamphleteers trumpeting in the coffeehouses, the fundamental conflict lay between power and liberty. In this historic struggle, power was pernicious, always threatening liberty. Such political thinking drew inspiration from the opposition rhetoric and literature of Georgian England, where a determined assemblage in Parliament stood ready to check the erosion of liberty at the hands of a corrupted monarch.[22]

The link between colonial policy and colonial protest, on the one hand, and the virulently divisive politics of George III's first decade, on the other, appeared to be a favorable portent for those in British America who believed that traditional liberties were under siege. What was not anticipated, however, was the intrusion of politics into the considerations for maintaining a large peacetime army in the colonies. The rationale for this scheme blended the strategic agenda for the vast territory acquired from France, the tentative designs for dealing with the Indian question, and the vaguely defined issue of security in the colonies, but its acceptance was dependent on the dynamics of British politics. As political economists crafted their arguments for reducing the costs of empire, opportunists were clamoring for military commissions. In these commissions lay an important source of power and patronage, certainly for the king but also for the scores of political opportunists who gained influence or a seat in Parliament because of such appointments. In Parliament, ordinarily suspicious of any effort by the monarch to exert greater control, the king's men pushed through the measure for a peacetime garrison army in North America with scarcely any outburst of indignation. There was neither conspiracy nor benevolence in this decision.[23]

Where institutions lacked the strength to nourish beliefs that life would be better, as in British North America, those who presumed to lead depended on their ability to channel the violent passions of local people in the service of the community. And violence was endemic in the countryside and in the cities. It began before the revolution, continued among civilians during the conflict, and resumed after the war had ended. Violence assumed an institutional role in the community because there was no police force, and city folk refused to allow an army or militia to act as one. In emergencies, such as fires, crowds mobilized to save property; they also gathered to keep out press gangs, close down bordellos, and harass merchants who wanted to ship out foodstuffs. Even Governor Thomas Hutchinson acknowledged that "mobs, a sort of them at least, are constitutional."[24]

In the 1760s urban violence came to play a more disturbing role in urban life, attributed to something rather fearful: the heightened awareness of a generation of discontenteds that it had concerns more immediate than the reach of royal authority into colonial political life. This sentiment was not so much an expression of class consciousness and solidarity as a collective grievance on the part of the dispossessed about the visible inequities about them and, in a few places, a determination to organize. They demanded public galleries in the assemblies and called for the publication of votes, public meetings to discuss issues, and the election of their own to local and provincial government. In words frightening to their betters, they called for price controls, condemned wealth, and decried social inequities.[25]

Assessed from the perspective of almost two centuries, the prerevolutionary strife in British-American cities has been traced to myriad conditions: land concentration and the dwindling size of plots available to small farmers in the tidewater regions of the colonies, compelling a move to the frontier, a shift to tenancy, or a migration into the city; the economic uncertainty identified with indentures and the propertyless; unruliness among free persons of color and the unskilled; and the general inability of urban institutions to adapt to the larger numbers of transients, newly arriving immigrants, and ordinary soldiers and seamen competing for jobs with locals. Like the farmers, these people became tenants, migrated to the frontier, or moved into town. Many of the newcomers were people with no roots. What they had in common was poverty. They often held temporary jobs, endured forced reduction in consumption of food and clothing, and acquired the drinking habits and sexual vices eighteenth-century English philanthropists bemoaned in London's poor. They joined milling urban crowds, sometimes as angry dispossessed venting their grievances, at other times as aimlessly bored people looking for excitement. When it took the form of rebellion against lawful authority or property, the reaction of government and social elites was often swift and punitive.[26]

Rural violence was different. Country people were accustomed to having weapons and displayed no reluctance to use them against legal authority. They broke into jails and freed their comrades, kidnapped judges and sheriffs, and challenged social and political authority. Their motives have been variously described as class-conscious, ethnocultural, religious, or even tribal. Pennsylvania's Scots-Irish were politically inactive until galvanized by two issues— the denial of the vote by the Quakers, which meant overtaxation and inadequate representation in the assembly, and insufficient protection against Indians. During the war with France, they bore much of the fighting on the Pennsylvania frontier and showed little remorse in their treatment of Indians. Nor did they apologize for their illegal encroachments on Indian land, invoking the laws of God and nature in their dismissal of the Indians as savages.[27]

Rural violence sometimes took the form of a direct assault on authority. Back-country South Carolina Regulators were vigilantes who posed no direct threat to planter society but organized to police a region infested with ruffians and outlaw gangs. North Carolina Regulators organized white farmers who fought with the colonial government from 1766 to 1771 over title to land and political power. That they threatened North Carolina's plantation system, as far as the planters were concerned, was another way of saying that they were enemies of civilized society.[28]

A Changing Political Culture

Whatever their provenance, the urban and rural troubles of the 1760s alerted ambitious men. James Otis, Jr., John Adams, Samuel Adams, Alexander

McDougal, Isaac Sears, John Lamb, Patrick Henry, and others sensed opportunity in the volatile political climate of prerevolutionary British America.
These "patriot" Whigs came from what Benjamin Franklin called middling
stock and were the leaders of the war for independence and the creators of the
United States. They understood the rapidly changing political culture of the
tidelands and the cities, sensed the restlessness of a new generation of city
dwellers, especially young professionals eager to challenge the older social
elites, and, early in the colonial debate, recognized the explosive power in the
crowds of sailors, petty clerks, and dock laborers ready to burn a British revenue cutter or the house of a compliant merchant. Their followers did battle
on the streets and the docks. In Boston, Otis led the "popular" party and filled
the *Gazette* with denunciations of his enemy, Governor Thomas Hutchinson.[29]

Elsewhere, the radicals exchanged inflammatory rhetoric with their Tory
neighbors. By protesting and boycotting British goods during the Stamp Act
crisis of 1765, the Marylander Daniel Dulany wrote during the crisis, common
people would be able to comprehend what was at stake: "Instead of moping,
and puling, and whining to excite compassion; in such a situation we ought
with spirit, and vigour, and alacrity, to bid defiance to tyranny, by exposing its
impotence, by making it as contemptible, as it would be detestable."[30] More
than a threat to liberty, the Stamp Act signified a direct assault on the historic
power of the assemblies to exercise control over governors by preventing the
diversion of public monies to their personal uses. In Massachusetts such parliamentary taxation undermined the historic role of the assembly by taking
money directly from the people and dispensing it without the approval of their
representatives.[31]

Had the debate over British policy from the Stamp Act crisis to about 1770
(years when successive pieces of economic legislation fell before colonial resistance) not given way to more forceful measures, leaders on both sides might
have chosen a conciliatory path. What made that less likely was the ritualistic
violence of the decade, a public theater of defiance by ordinary people. Their
striking anti-British animus stood in sharp contrast to the uncomplicated nationalism of the war years. This was only partially attributable to the incendiary political climate, however. Relieved of the French menace by the British
victory, colonists' anti-Catholic fanaticism, widely prevalent during the war,
diminished, but the emotions explaining it were now directed at the British.[32]

Uncertainty about motive ran even deeper. Indeed, the complexity and ambiguity of colonial purpose during these years belies the description of a people resolved to resist parliamentary encroachment. The course of events after 1763 had brought both expected and unanticipated results within British

North America. In the outburst over the Stamp Act, disaffected elites everywhere in the colonies had demonstrated an unappreciated strength in their appeals to the populace. When merchants called for nonimportation of British goods, they were able to rid themselves of large stockpiles of inventory. The benefit was short-lived, however; three years later, another glut of imports from abroad precipitated another merchant outcry for nonimportation.[33]

Chesapeake planters, especially in Virginia, also displayed a disquieting ambivalence toward British policy. Large planters enjoyed the access to easier credit made available by Scots factors, which permitted deferment of debt for imported goods and allowed the planters to use their cash to purchase slaves and land. A parallel development was disturbing: the Scots traders exploited their financial power to intrude into tobacco markets, regulate currency, and even deal directly with the small planters, heretofore economically and socially dominated by the large planters. In the northern neck of Virginia, particularly, wealthy Virginians sensed diminished influence. They spoke expansively of "new inland empires," agricultural diversification, and, especially, of economic sovereignty; they began to fashion patriotic alliances with small farmers against the Scots factors. The members of South Carolina's ruling social elite built their wealth on plantation economies and slave labor. Prosperity enabled them to idealize a society of material accomplishment and refinement; British economic policy did not threaten their wealth so much as their economic sovereignty and future prosperity.[34]

Both merchants and planters were alerted to two groups, the urban "lower sorts" and small farmers, who were very different in social profile and attitudes toward property but who expressed a common frustration about the intrusion of the "better sorts" into their lives. Uncertainty about what the lower classes would do in a volatile situation offers a partial explanation of the dilemmas confronted by Whig patriot leaders throughout the revolutionary era and the decision of social conservatives to side with the loyalists. Involvement of the urban poor began with the making of common cause in nonimportation and nonconsumption with the more socially prominent colonials, who tried to manipulate them and then grew more fearful as these groups began to organize among themselves, calling for a democratization of society. Because they operated in the revolutionary crucible—the cities—the elite's fears of what this portended for the structure of society were justifiable, if exaggerated.

Small farmers were latecomers to the prerevolutionary discontent, but their participation was crucial. Ninety percent of British North Americans were engaged in agriculture. Though scattered and presumably more con-servative in their social and political outlook than their urban counterparts, predictions of what the farmers wanted and what they would do in a crisis were hedged with uncertainties. Most northern and Appalachian farmers seemed indifferent to the economic quarrels raging between colony and metropole. Isolation, religious pacifism, and protection from the vagaries of a market economy explained much of this detachment. After about 1774, however, pa-triot Whigs, especially in the Chesapeake, began to cultivate small farmers and win them over to the cause. But their unpredictability remained. The only certainty was that no war against Britain could be possible without their par-ticipation.[35]

Defiance of British colonial legislation was not new; what was different about the colonial situation was the incendiary political climate and the dy-namics it created for both British officials *and* the outraged (and calculat-ing) Whig spokesmen in the colonies. The Stamp Act crisis was the seminal event of the prerevolutionary decade. Serving as a forum for a collective state-ment of British-American grievances, the crisis also portended the social volatility of the era. Leaders of the protesting crowds were sometimes from among the middling ranks, sometimes from the working classes. What was striking was their divergent sense of purpose. Merchants and shopkeepers railed against British policies; those from below decried not only the tax but also the economic grip of the new social elites, especially in the port cities of Boston, Philadelphia, and New York. A protesting crowd in New York watched three members of the Sons of Liberty, the best known of the organized protest groups, burn stamps and vilify merchants who used them. This was insuffi-cient punishment, many in the crowd roared, and they marched off to the res-idences of the offending merchants. Only by fervent pleas were the leaders able to contain them. The Sons of Liberty needed such gatherings to drama-tize their protest when they stomped aboard a ship to look for stamps or to in-timidate or harass officials. But they were never sure how the crowd would behave. Whig architects of the riots in New York, General Thomas Gage noted sarcastically, "began to be terrified at the Spirit they had raised [and] to per-ceive that popular Fury was not to be guided, and each individual feared he might be the next Victim to their Rapacity."[36]

Colonial politics had been turned upside down. Until the Stamp Act, popu-lar forces had been able to resist royal measures by waging a war of words in the assemblies. Before 1765 (except for commercial regulations, which might be followed or evaded), imperial governance operated through instructions to governors, who depended on their approval by the assemblies, in order to be enforced. Without that approval, noncompliance would not be upheld by any court. If a governor balked at carrying out a royal directive, the king could replace him with someone who would. The assemblies would inevitably frustrate even the most determined governor. Parliamentary legislation, by contrast, was law before it arrived in the colonies. Assemblymen could rail against the injustice of such laws, but they could not prevent their enforcement unless the battle was taken to the streets. There British officials might be able to arrest noncomplying individuals, but without troops they would not be able to discipline crowds.

Certainly the power of the executive in most of the colonies (Rhode Island and Connecticut were the exceptions) in fundamental areas, such as the veto or the authority to dissolve the assembly, was greater than that of the British monarch, and it grew stronger in the eighteenth century. But influence actually weakened under the cumulative pressures of disparate conditions: the loss of patronage (because British America, unlike the home islands, had no "rotten boroughs"); the forty-shilling freehold requirement for voting, which effectively curtailed the British but not the British-American electorate; and the tenuous hold of the aristocracy in the colonial political culture, which made for uncertainty, especially in times of discord.[37]

The Survival of Empire

In England, the social turbulence accompanying political disputes between the Crown and Parliament appeared to follow a course similar to that in the colonies. As economic issues coupled with the vigorous enforcement of parliamentary legislation drew the thirteen colonies toward a political consensus, the heated exchanges within Parliament between the king's men (those who ruled) and those Whigs who denounced executive privilege persuaded colonial spokesmen that they were kindred spirits. There were other indicators of common cause: popular rumblings, both on the Continent and, especially, in London. Agitation was not uncommon, but in Britain the crowd had a leader, John Wilkes, member of Parliament, who had libeled George III, been thrown in the Tower of London, and released to the cheers of his followers. Declared an outlaw, Wilkes fled the country but returned, precipitating yet another riotous celebration. Again incarcerated, he emerged from jail in 1770 and immediately plunged into London politics, often leading crowds in protest marches.[38]

This agitation took place during the parliamentary debate over colonial policy, further complicating the issues. Wilkes had admirers throughout British America and among members of Parliament, but the latters' notion about the role of Parliament was very different from that of their transatlantic counterparts. To English Whigs, parliamentary supremacy was dogma. Cleansed of the corrupting influence of Crown politics, they believed, Parliament was more truly representative of the people's interests than any of the town meetings that had sprung up in support of Wilkes in Middlesex or in Massachusetts to denounce British policy. Those British Americans who railed against parliamentary supremacy could be as irritating to an English Whig as some of the sycophants who spoke of royal privilege. Edmund Burke, whose denunciations of parliamentary corruption inspired radical Whigs in British America, most succinctly expressed classic Whig thought when he wrote in *Thoughts on the Cause of the Present Discontent* (1770), "The power of the crown, almost dead and rotten as Prerogative, has grown up anew under the name of Influence."[39]

Burke was among those who took their complaints into a public forum in an effort to rouse the people against the king's mischief, defended Wilkes, and encouraged colonial defiance. But the parliamentary Whigs had little in common with British reformers and no sympathy for British Americans who decried parliamentary supremacy. Their rhetoric, however, signaled a breakdown of consensus about the viability of a mercantilist empire and augured well for those who championed the American cause. But the king's opponents in Parliament offered no realistically acceptable alternative to the colonial dilemma. On the eve of the revolution, Burke spoke of a federation, but this concept seemed no more feasible in the mid-1770s than it had fifteen years earlier. Reluctant to press the colonies on issues they believed were unnecessarily arbitrary exercises of royal power, the parliamentary Whigs were nonetheless a loyal opposition.[40]

More precisely, British officials had become more fearful about their ability to direct the course of history in British America. They began to talk less about the functioning of empire and more about the threats against it. Government had to be authoritative as well as credible. Its legitimacy derived not only from its willingness to safeguard rights but also from its duty to shield society against the excesses of liberty. In such perilous circumstances, government had to act more purposefully, especially if denunciation of its laws meant public disorder, harassment of public officials, and destruction of property. Was this no less than a "conspiracy" against the constitutional balance, so destructive that it "would lead to mob rule, and that, in turn, to independence"?[41]

The justness of parliamentary legislation was one thing; the authority and the willingness to enforce it, whether deemed just or unjust, was another. The former was a philosophical question, as far as the parliamentary Whigs were concerned. They had few qualms about the Declaratory Act of 1766, which reaffirmed Parliament's supreme authority to legislate for British America, and they understood the intent of Chancellor of the Exchequer Charles Townshend's legislative program, which imposed external taxes on lead, tea, glass, and several other imports into British North America. Intent, of course, meant less to British Americans than to Townshend's *Whig* colleagues in Parliament, who were less attuned to colonial political philosophy than to the minds of the English ruling classes.[42]

Execution of the law was another matter. To collect the duties required not only conscientious commissioners but accompanying legislation authorizing them to seize prohibited or smuggled goods in colonial warehouses, shops, cellars, or even homes. Further, carrying out the law ultimately required placing troops, revenue cutters, and customs officials among people unaccustomed to so much scrutiny of their behavior. They resisted by tarring and feathering British agents who dared to enforce the law. In Boston, the defiance was particularly widespread, prompting the stationing of troops in the city, which only worsened matters. In March 1770, youths threw stones and snowballs at a squad of British soldiers, who fired into a gathering crowd, killing five and wounding others. Throughout the colonies, the event was immortalized as the Boston Massacre, a tragic reminder of Parliament's putatively oppressive reach. A jury packed by a Tory sheriff acquitted the commanding officer and all but two of his men, who were convicted of manslaughter. Governor Hutchinson was more sanguine about the violent course of affairs. "The Boston people are run mad," he wrote. "The frenzy was not higher when they banished my pious great grandmother, when they hanged the Quakers, when they afterwards hanged the poor innocent witches."[43]

Later in the year, Lord North befuddled even his supporters with his expressions of uncertainty about what to do toward resolving the colonial dispute with the Atlantic colonies. George Grenville, now among his critics, had queried North about a plan "for establishing a government in the colonies, over which such laws as England shall think fit to be insisted upon may be exercised and enforced." To this North had lamely replied: "Everyman tells how desirable it is that the authority of this country should be resumed in those parts. The want of a strong government is obvious; but to effect that requires great abilities, great experience, great knowledge."[44]

In these circumstances, a strong government meant a government whose laws had to be enforced with troops. In Boston, it required something more— the willingness of a people to accept militarization of society as the alternative to social disorder. Indeed, as the number of soldiers had grown, the problem had been exacerbated. Their commander, Thomas Gage, had alerted his superiors to the precarious situation in the aftermath of the Boston Massacre: "The Occasion which brought the Regiments to Boston," he wrote, "rendered them obnoxious to the People, and they may have increased the Odium themselves." They lacked "Military Authority, and no Person in Civil Authority would ask their aid."[45]

"Revolution in the Hearts and Minds of the People"

The world had turned upside down: the cause of disorder was the government. Informed that if the six hundred British troops were not withdrawn, they would be confronted with an opposition of thousands, Governor Hutchinson reluctantly asked for their removal. Had they remained, he wrote Hillsborough, "the people of this town would have taken to their arms . . . and it is most probable the confusion would have continued until the troops were overpowered."[46]

In such a volatile social climate, violent behavior assumed a significant political meaning. The Boston Tea Party of 1773, the celebrated destruction of British property by outraged Bostonians, prompted the imposition of harsh countermeasures, culminating in the Intolerable Acts of the following year. In the minds of Bostonians, North's response to the city's challenge of British power was the substitution of force for law. Officials closed down the port of Boston until the tea was paid for, permitted trials in England for offenses committed in Massachusetts, and transferred all governing power in the colony to the executive. A quartering act (valid in all the colonies) permitted British officials to seize public or private buildings for housing troops. Another law extended the boundaries of Quebec southward to incorporate territories claimed by Connecticut, Massachusetts, and Virginia. Anglicans in Virginia often maligned New Englanders as bigots, but their common interest in western lands now made them allies, for the Quebec Act threatened to make permanent what had been seen as a temporary measure, the Proclamation of 1763. In his *Summary View of the Rights of British America*, Thomas Jefferson transformed a material interest into a political principle when he wrote that a people retained the right to set their geographical boundaries.[47]

The effect of imposing parliamentary law and enforcing it with troops was to tear British America asunder. Massachusetts resisted, and from the other colonies came aid. Committees of correspondence formed to relay information, and from coastal cities people dispatched aid to Boston's poor. By summer 1774, the political agitation had prompted the calling of a continental congress to decide on the proper course of action. Some of its members appeared to be as fearful of internal commotion as of British countermeasures, proposing what came to be derided as the "olive branch" resolution. Massachusetts and Virginia were strongest for retaliation, and they succeeded in pushing through a measure calling for the boycotting of British goods, collective sacrifice and readiness, and the forming of local committees to ensure compliance. When the discussions ended, the delegates agreed that a second convention should be called for the following spring to determine how effective these measures had been.

By the time it met, events had altered the agenda. A rebellious spirit swept the colonies. Committees to enforce the association sprang up, threatening naysayers and intimidating men of property. "The people," wrote the lieutenant governor of South Carolina, William Bull, "have discovered their own strength and importance and are not now so easily governed by their former leaders."[48] Patriot leaders spoke of rights and the necessity of taking their arguments to "the people" when appeals for justice had been scorned. They had fashioned committees of correspondence to articulate the grievances against parliamentary legislation and, more important, to remind royal governors of the power they commanded among the people. But when they presumed to call for action, they realized that the people had their own local agendas. When the Boston committee of correspondence called upon the provincial towns to urge compliance with a resolution not to consume British-made goods, it encountered reluctance.[49]

More unsettling was the patriot leaders' realization that people they presumed to guide made little distinction between justice and retribution, right and righteousness. In early 1774, a Boston crowd made up mostly of sailors seized a customs official, accused him of "venality and corruption as well as . . . extortion in office," and turned down pleas from patriots to turn him loose.[50] John Adams grew so vexed over the tarring and feathering of officials or the mindless ransacking of houses by "rude and insolent Rabbles, in Resentment for private Wrongs or in pursuance of private Prejudices and Passions," that he countenanced obedience of misdemeanor laws and joined with other patriot spokesmen in publicizing rules for popular action.[51]

The First Continental Congress had given its blessing to a defensive war in the protection of American liberties. For both Gage and the popular leaders of Boston, the congress's decision was a virtual incitement to act. Minutemen began to organize and stockpile military supplies, waiting for word from committees in the city on the movement of British troops. Women supplying them with provisions for the militias, wrote a man who rode along the road into Boston, "surpassed the Men for Eagerness & Spirit in the Defense of Liberty by Arms." He remembered seeing "at every house Women & Children making Cartridges, running Bullets, making Wallets, baking Biscuit, crying & bemoaning & at the same time animating their Husbands & Sons to fight for their Liberties."[52] There was a spiritual earnestness to these endeavors: seditious clergymen referred to the king as the Antichrist and railed against Lord North, occasionally ending their sermons by passing out weapons.

Gage may have been a social dullard, but he was sufficiently alert to these doings to hire spies, including one in the Massachusetts assembly who dutifully kept him informed about the seditious actions of that body. He knew he would have to move his soldiers, grown increasingly restless and irritable, into the countryside around Boston to enforce the Coercive Acts, to throw fear into the colonists, to demonstrate British resolve by action. He threatened New Englanders, saying "by the living God, that if there was a single man of the King's troops killed in any of their towns he would burn it to the ground." But he wrote gloomily to his superiors about the weakness of his army: "If you think ten Thousand Men sufficient, send Twenty, if one Million is thought enough, give two; you will save both Blood and Treasure in the End."[53]

A decade of protest and defiance could not have unfolded into such a desperate situation without a parallel weakness of the institutions of law and order. England and France experienced popular rage and violence during these years, and in their makeup and purpose European mobs seemed little different from those in British America. What made the latter different was the "almost total absence of resistance by the constituted authorities, with all that this absence may signify in explaining the nature of the society and the consequence of the outburst."[54]

But something more fundamental than the willingness to use force confronted British commanders in the colonies in 1775. The army possessed neither the physical nor the moral strength required to deal with the obstacles to governance in British America. The reasons for this debility could not be explained by neglect; indeed, imperial planners in 1763 had skillfully rationalized army strategy and organization in order to meet the new tests of dominion. What this imperial reordering had bequeathed, however, was a montage of unanticipated problems that not even a modernized army could resolve—obstacles that required a capacity to survive in a continually changing environment where good will toward the army rapidly dissipated after 1770. Josiah Quincy, who had defended British soldiers after the Boston "massacre" because they had preserved order in the streets, spoke defiantly against their presence four years later. The British resort to force had nullified the social contract.

By then, a retrospective judgment about the imperial restructuring in 1763 brought reminders of the demurrals against the plan offered by a few who made the commonsensical observation that to deal with the colonies collectively would prompt colonials to react collectively, however well intentioned the policy. The naysayers recognized that the basic problem in British America was not military but political. And benevolent men who were reluctant to use force could not avoid a confrontation if they determined that parliamentary sovereignty was unquestionable—unless, of course, they were willing to withdraw the military.

The declaration that the British army was in the colonies to provide defense collapsed when troops arrived in Boston. Their appearance demonstrated that British officials had been duplicitous; it also persuaded British Americans that the government remained uncertain about what to do with the army. British Americans did not require such a force for their defense; they did not want garrison troops in Boston. But they hated neither the soldiers nor the government that had dispatched them. Theirs was a more ominous sentiment—alienation.[55]

2

A People at War

City and country dwellers exhibited differing behavior toward the intrusive British troops. In Boston, where soldiers tried to provoke the militiamen, there was a brief but dangerous encounter during the Boston Massacre Oration in March 1775, but the militiamen did not initiate battle in the city. Congress had forbidden offensive action. Had the Bostonians commenced the revolution under the pretext that they were wrongfully attacked, few of their comrades in other colonial cities would have supported them.

But sentiments in the Massachusetts interior had dramatically changed with the coming of British troops. Even in socially conservative towns, radicals and hotheads had found a following. Here, a rebellion against the injunctions laid down by the Intolerable Acts would have ensued without the urging of Boston's patriot Whigs. In the course of a century, Massachusetts towns had assumed supremacy in the political and social life of the colony. When Parliament declared the illegality of town meetings (except for one annual gathering to elect officers) held without the governor's permission, the defiance of the towns reverberated throughout the province. In the 1680s, a similar prohibition had prompted angry New Englanders to take up arms against the harsh regime of Governor Edmund Andros and to oust him from power.[1]

"A Shot Heard Round the World"

On the night of April 18, 1775, British troops marched into the seditious Massachusetts countryside, where once-insulated towns were now systematically undermining royal government by refusing financial and even moral support. Their purpose was to apprehend two patriot firebrands, Samuel Adams and John Hancock, reported to be in Lexington, and to seize a cache of arms at Concord. The primitive but effective patriot intelligence network had already learned of Gage's plans. Though two men sounded the warning, only one of them—Paul Revere—was immortalized in American Revolutionary folklore. The British advance, which brought on the battles of Lexington and Concord, is famed as the "shot heard round the world."

Thomas Gage dismissed the fight as "nothing but an affair," but John Adams perhaps best captured the somber portent of the battles when he scribbled, "When I reflect and consider that the fight was between those whose parents but a few generations ago were brothers, I shudder at the thought, and there's no knowing where our calamities will end." Shortly after the fighting, Adams rode his horse over the short distance between Braintree and Lexington in order to assess this "affair." There was, he recalled later, "great confusion and distress." Adams returned from his brief and unsettling tour of the American Revolution's first battlefield persuaded that "the Die was cast, the Rubicon crossed."[2]

The suddenness of these events did little to clarify choices for the majority of colonials and Britons who retained a fleeting hope for some kind of accommodation. As expected, radicals exploited news of the conflict in the escalating propaganda war. In tracts and broadsides, they called for revenge against "British butchers." In Boston, the committee of correspondence equated the first volley at Lexington with the onset of the American war of independence and the defense of liberty. News of the battle swept the colonies in a firestorm of protest that prompted Marylanders to sport the revolutionary cockade, Virginia frontiersmen to don hunting clothes and carry tomahawks, and South Carolinian officers to resign their royal commissions. In May, Philadelphians exhibited a martial spirit and flew the Liberty or Death banner as they greeted delegates to the Second Continental Congress.

The Second Continental Congress promptly resolved that the colonies be put into a "state of defence," assumed control of the Massachusetts militia, called for an army of twenty thousand, and named George Washington as its commander. Its *Declaration on Taking Arms* was militantly defiant: "Our cause is just, Our Union is perfect. Our internal resources are great, and, if necessary, foreign assistance is undoubtedly attainable."[5] The congress authorized the printing of paper money. In July, Benjamin Franklin presented his Articles of Confederation and Perpetual Union, a proposal too controversial to be entered into the journal but widely discussed by the delegates. What had commenced was a struggle of colonies that "differed in Religion, Customs, and Manners, yet in the great Essentials of Society and Government," John Adams solemnly wrote, "they are all alike."[4]

New Englanders had already taken the offensive with the dramatic seizure of Crown Point and Ticonderoga, strategically placed British forts along the Hudson–Lake Champlain waterway. In the fall came the invasion of Canada, undertaken to prevent a British assault from the north and, John Hancock declared, to "open a Way for Blessing of Liberty, and the Happiness of well-ordered Government to visit that extensive Dominion."[5] A thousand volunteers from the Continental Army landed at Newburyport, Massachusetts, to join New Englanders for the invasion. They marched gloriously through the town and into church, stacked their arms in the aisles, and listened as the minister quoted Moses: "If thy spirit go not with us, carry us not up hence."[6]

Inspired by revolutionary slogans, the invaders expected to garner the support of presumably disaffected French Canadians. In 1774, in a "message to the Canadian people," the continental congress denounced the undemocratic character of the Quebec Act and suggested the Swiss example of Protestant and Catholic confederations as the model of government it would adopt if French Canadians rallied to the American cause. Congress, however, undermined whatever good intentions its members may have harbored by dispatching an anti-Catholic Address to Great Britain; moreover, the ideology and political goals of the revolution from the south ill suited the French Canadians. George Washington tried to reassure them by declaring that the Americans came not to plunder but to protect, but the invading American troops comported themselves in a scandalous manner. One of Washington's generals casually described the French Canadians as "little removed from savages."[7]

The governor-general of Canada, Sir Guy Carleton, who had persuaded Parliament to accept the Quebec Act's provisions respecting French civil law, seigneurial land tenure, and religious tolerance for Catholics, conveyed the congressional message to the French-speaking *habitants*. New England's invaders were liberal and Protestant. They denounced as authoritarian a state that practiced religious toleration. When Carleton called on the habitants to fight, however, they resisted. Not even the Catholic clergy was able to persuade them to do battle with the invading Protestants. A few fought on both sides, but most remained sullenly neutral throughout the conflict. This was not their war. They feared forcible exile, as had happened to the Acadians. "Only fifteen years had passed since the Conquest, and the treatment they had received had not been so harsh that they would support the Americans, but it had been sufficiently abrasive to render them incapable of supporting the cause of their foreign masters."[8]

Within a year much of the anticipated support from English radicals also collapsed. In February 1775, the London Common Council had declared that Americans were justified in resisting government measures. When fighting erupted at Lexington and Concord, the Council appealed to the Crown not to make war on them. John Wilkes, the hero of London's milling crowds in the 1760s and now Lord Mayor of the city, defended the colonial cause in Parliament. Wilkes secretly provided valuable assistance for the Americans by acting as an intermediary between Arthur Lee (the first American agent in Europe) and the French playwright Beaumarchais, who played a critical role in obtaining French aid for the rebellion. George III was outraged by the expressions of sympathy. In August 1775 he condemned "traitorous correspondence, counsels and comfort of divers wicked and desperate persons within this realm" and appealed to his subjects throughout the empire "to use their utmost endeavors to withstand and suppress . . . rebellion, and to disclose . . . all treasons and traitorous conspiracies which they shall know to be against us, our crown, and dignity."[9]

A more critical factor in the dissolution of political bonds between disaffected English Whigs and radicals was the persuasiveness of an argument that made such a coalition impossible—independence. The word and certainly the notion had appeared early in the colonial debate, but it had gained little currency. Not until the publication of Thomas Paine's *Common Sense* in January 1776 did colonial spokesmen possess such a powerful articulation of the arguments for separation. Paine's message was intended for both ideologue and commoner—union with Britain was stupid, irrational, and "repugnant to reason, to the universal order of things; to all examples from former ages."[10]

The Rage Militaire

In the preceding year, colonial actions had prompted the British to take firmer measures. In the uncertain months of spring 1776, stories of retaliatory and threatening measures taken by British officials galvanized congressional sentiment in favor of a declaration of independence. The British, it was rumored, were scurrying about Europe looking for mercenaries. Patriots now denounced moderates and conciliators as fools. Radicals called for appeals to the French as a counterploy. And throughout the colonies, the cumulative grievances and social stresses endured by a generation of British Americans, high and low, defined how people behaved in this year of decision. Their mythical resolve in pushing for a formal declaration of independence was, in fact, less a manifestation of their leadership than a hurried response to public opinion in the colonies, where committees and conventions had grown impatient with the congress's hesitancy. Sam Adams received a somber warning from Massachusetts: "The People are now ahead of you and the only way to prevent discord and dissension is to strike while the iron is hot. The Peoples blood is too Hot to admit of delays."[11]

When John Adams spoke of a "revolution in the hearts and minds of the people" before the war commenced, he contributed as much to American Revolutionary mythology as he did to a recounting of history. Such words belied the doubts of radicals in the continental congress as they plunged ahead with one retaliatory measure after another. The congress declared American ports (some of them wasted by British raids) open to all except British ships. It sent an advisory directive to colonies to establish republican governments. It joyously celebrated the British withdrawal from Boston. A revolutionary army had invaded Canada; the countryside was in a state of rebellion. The secret committee of correspondence sent Silas Deane to solicit aid from the French foreign minister, the Comte de Vergennes. A formal declaration of independence, the radicals argued, guaranteed French support. Delay, they warned, gave the British time to confuse and thwart the cause.

What befuddled those at Philadelphia debating the issue of independence was the *emotional* commitment to the patriot cause. To measure this sentiment required going beyond the philosophical debates about the British constitution or natural rights. A revolutionary agenda presumed commitment and a willingness to demonstrate it, by word or deed or both. Yet individual choices were often as much responses to the social dynamics of the community as the collective wrath of thirteen disparate colonies. In Massachusetts, committees defied legal authority and created another social order in its stead. Judges and officers competed with them for the people's loyalty. Those who presumed themselves better suited to rule the people appealed to custom and tradition and vied with others who declared that all men were equal.

Subsumed in this discourse were widespread fears, especially among country people, that with taxes came debt, financial ruin, and loss of freehold.

The role of rural peoples in the coming of the American Revolution appeared peripheral until the crises of 1774–1775. Afterward, particularly in the northern colonies, they participated in a special way. "Their direct social concerns were not those of crowds in either rural England and France or urban America . . ., [b]ut by their very existence they helped to add to the atmosphere of general crisis."[12]

New York's case was especially complicated. In the Mohawk Valley (a rural county west of Albany), a band of committeemen, inspired by events in Massachusetts, waged a vendetta against a landlord who dominated Indian trade. This manner of settling quarrels indicated class warfare. Similar examples cropped up throughout the interior, in New York and other colonies. But such a cataloging of loyalty or patriotism in New York (whose social elites were often holders of baronial estates) on the basis of rivalry between upstarts and old money or between gouging landlord and suffering tenant sometimes misses the mark. The De Lanceys and the Livingstons wound up in opposite camps in the revolutionary age, but their choice had less to do with ideological conviction or economic interest than personal calculation about which side would win. The ambiguities of revolutionary New York frustrate any deterministic economic analysis. Yeomen and small-town "middling sorts" were whiggish but less enthusiastic about the cause than the Albany Sons of Liberty, many of whom were large landholders. Freehold farmers overwhelmingly supported nonimportation. Tenants vacillated between loyalism in their politics and radicalism in their social agenda. Patriot Whigs seemed so indifferent to their situation that royal emissaries promised them Whig lands if they would fight for the king.[13]

The Continental Association inspired commitment to the patriot cause with broadsides, fiery oratory, and public condemnations of Loyalists. When these measures proved inadequate, the association (imitating a British practice) encouraged the revival of oath-taking. Canvassers conducted house-to-house audits of commitment. In New York City, committees of inspection formed to ascertain compliance with the call for nonimportation and nonconsumption of British goods. Those who refused to swear were considered in contempt. In such perilous times, the dual terror of social collapse and impending British invasion prompted thousands to flee. Continental soldiers took over their houses. News of the Declaration of Independence inspired a mob to pull down the statue of George III on Bowling Green. One former committeeman roared against the mobocracy: "Those Enemies to Peace and good Order shall not rule over me; I despise their threats."[14]

In Philadelphia, where the Quaker elite had been ill prepared to command the disaffected "lower sorts," conservatives and even moderates warned of a provincial collapse into the putative "social anarchy" they identified with Massachusetts. Pennsylvania's Anglican gentry, unlike that of Virginia, was not ready to chart a political agenda. Independence, they feared, boded ill for their place in society, a self-attributed aristocracy; yet to profess loyalist sentiment was to equivocate. John Dickinson, the moderate of the continental congress, who had strong ties with all social groups in the province, was typical of Pennsylvania's hesitant and divided upper class. From 1774, when he had championed strong responses to parliamentary legislation, until spring 1776, when he was yet laboring for reconciliation, his role became that of martyr. A friend warned him of the price of disarray among those who presumed to rule: "I cannot help regretting that [through] a perseverance which you were fully convinced was fruitless, you have thrown the affairs of this state into the hands of men totally unequal to them."[15]

In Virginia, whose gentry solemnly acknowledged the threat of evangelicals to their social pretensions, the high administrators were loyalists, but the planter elites chose the patriot banner and manifested their grievances in the assembly. They demonstrated their commitment by organizing committees and militias. In April 1775 the British governor, Lord Dunmore, had infuriated the patriots by removing Williamsburg's powder supply to a British ship. Fearing he would try to run, Patrick Henry led a band of Virginia patriots, most of them buckskin-shirted volunteers, in surrounding the capital. Lacking sufficient forces to put up a fight, the desperate governor called on slaves to take up arms, promising them emancipation, inspired by a proposal in the House of Commons to humble "the high aristocratic spirit of Virginia and the southern colonies." Dunmore was initially tentative about such a radical proposal. The appearance of the volunteers, however, so alarmed him that he threatened to "declare freedom to the slaves and reduce the City of Williamsburg to ashes."[16]

Farther south, in the Carolinas, the low country planters had not yet acquired the common touch of their Virginia compatriots. If they professed to speak for the people in their incendiary diatribes against king and Parliament, and the people did not rally, then what of sustaining the cause? South Carolina's "inland civil war" persisted. The British governor wrote in 1775: "The loyalty of those poor, honest, industrious people in the back part of this and neighboring provinces discontents [Charleston's Whigs] greatly."[17]

The inspired patriot Whigs took more forceful measures to persuade the doubters. Backcountry Germans who came into Charleston with wagonloads of goods had to show proof they had joined the association. When this did not work, the radicals turned to more punitive means of persuasion in dealing with Tories. The royal governor, alert to antiradical notions among the up-country people, boldly declared that with war supplies he could maintain royal control in the western country. The British dispatched a shipload of weaponry to him in early 1776, but before it could be delivered, the Whigs quickly re-grouped and won a battle against the Tories at Widow's Moore Creek Bridge. They jubilantly threw loyalists in jail and seized their property. Undeniably, the revolution in backcountry South Carolina appeared to be another phase of the Regulator conflict of the early 1770s, but it was not so much a sectional or class struggle as a war in the shadows in which patriot Whigs ultimately pre-vailed, "as much by default as by design . . .; [they] strengthened their position within a divided frontier and furthered the interests of aspiring inland planters."[18]

Even in the *rage militaire* the "people" were as divided as those who put claims on their consciences or called them to action, but in such circum-stances those who make revolution cannot reveal their doubts nor convey their true intentions to those who follow. To do so is to show uncertainty about the probable course of the revolution, about the things it will change and the things it will leave unchanged. The true revolutionary can never admit of am-biguity or contradiction in the waging of the cause. British America's revolu-tionaries were not exempt from this consideration because they fought the "just war." Of one thing they were certain: Power could not be made into Right. King and People were separated in 1776, but not Law and People. "A sovereign people," John Adams recognized, "must become the sovereign lawmaker, binding themselves and later generations."[19]

Inevitably, some would see the removal of the king's laws and courts as a chance to advance their own interests. Years after the revolution, Adams per-haps best conveyed the dilemma confronted by the advocates of popular sov-ereignty and the rule of law in a story about his meeting in 1775 with a former client ("a common horse jockey"). The man thanked him for ridding the province of its royal courts of justice, thus removing a legal impediment faced by him and like-minded opportunists. Adams rode away from "this wretch" ruminating about the social consequences of his professional endeavor. "If the power of the country should get in such hands, and there is great danger that it will, to what purpose have we sacrificed our time, health, and everything else?"[20]

British Miscalculations

Most North Americans have little sense of the ambiguities of their war of independence. They remain unaware that it was less a struggle won by the enlightened leading the valiant in a conventional war for the purpose of securing their freedoms than a protracted irregular war that has much in common with the "wars of national liberation" of the twentieth century. Americans won because the British lost, but the British defeat is explained less by American military superiority than by the *way* each fought the war.

Early on in the struggle, for example, the British alertly recognized that they were confronting a traditional war between conventional armies, much like the conflicts their armies had fought in Europe. But they did not respond by dispatching large numbers of troops to fight it. Instead, they decided to shift their operations from New England to the port of New York and to New Jersey, where public sentiment for the rebellion rapidly diminished. Three thousand residents (including a signatory to the Declaration of Independence) took an oath of allegiance to the Crown. British strategy called for victory over Washington's retreating army and simultaneous restoration of royal authority in the province.

But the policy of leniency, which had worked well in the beginning of the war, suddenly and dramatically collapsed. Geography favored the rebels. At Trenton and at Princeton the British appeared helpless before the sudden American assault. In the southern campaign, in pursuit of Nathaniel Greene's retreating force in the Carolinas and in Virginia, the British were continually befuddled and ultimately "doomed in the face of American willingness to use the space at their disposal to keep their armies intact rather than attempt to decide the issue in a single positional engagement."[21]

Particularity of place was often a better indicator of revolutionary dynamics than grand strategy. Unintentionally, the British inspired loyalists who had suffered rebel intimidation to exact their revenge. In Bergen County, New Jersey—a gallimaufry of religious, political, and ethnic rivalries—prewar familial feuds revived with destructive fury. A British observer commented: the "licentiousness of the troops, who committed every species of rapine and plunder," combined with British inability to live off the countryside to shift the balance in favor of the rebels. When the war moved to the south, patriot and loyalist fought a guerrilla war in the countryside.[22]

Although the observation that one-third of the population of British America joined the rebellion, one-third remained loyal, and one-third stood by indifferent to the outcome suggests a range of possibilities for most British

Americans, only in a narrow sense did they realistically have a choice in the matter. The character of the American Revolution was a paradoxical meshing of *both* political and social causes, crafted in such a manner as to divide people at every level of society. "Nabour was against Nabour, Father against Son and the son against the Father," bemoaned a New England Tory, "and he that would not thrust his one blaid through his brothers heart was cald an Infimous villon."[23]

Early on, British leaders miscalculated. Colonial society, they were persuaded, replicated that of England—a privileged elite grown prosperous and a middling class of artisans and farmers ill disposed to fight on their behalf. The British view of colonial martial capability and commitment derived from the colonial wars, in an age before newspapers became a powerful force in shaping public opinion. This was a costly analysis, but it explains why the British adopted such punitive measures in Massachusetts and undertook a conventional military campaign in 1776 and 1777. At times, the British appeared to be waging the kind of war they had carried out in Europe and in Ireland. In 1778, British leaders altered their strategy, striving to capitalize on the weaknesses and tensions within revolutionary society and to build a loyalist British America.

By then, however, it was too late. Revolutionary leaders had turned the struggle into a world war and signed two treaties with the French and were obtaining secret aid from several European courts. For three years, their scattered and presumably inferior armies had comported themselves well enough in the fight to persuade doubters that the British might lose. As the British moved to restore loyalists to positions of authority, they often found themselves allied with those motivated less by principle than by a determination to seek revenge for rebel mistreatment. British policies did not restore the loyalists to power, however, but revived the civil war within the colonies. This led to a longer war, one that British Americans—loyalist or patriot—would settle in their own way, one that the British could not win.[24]

The parallel considerations among British and American commanders concerning Indian allies (or, at least, Indian neutrality) in the war offers another example of British miscalculation. By any realistic assessment, most of the Indians, especially in the trans-Appalachian country and in the *pays d'en haut* of the Great Lakes, should have joined the British cause or remained neutral. In this region, the war was local and imperial in scope—a contest among Indian, French, and Anglo-American villagers in which Indians proved as calculating as the British who organized them into raiding parties or plied them with gifts and promises. Indians proved unreliable allies. They waged a fierce battle in Kentucky in order to keep intruding Americans from their lands, not to abet the British cause.

In 1776 the congress tried to mitigate the understandable Indian suspicions of patriot designs on their lands by dispatching commissioners to Pittsburgh to reassure the Delawares, the Senecas, the Munsees, and the Mingos. "We call God to Witness," the commissioners solemnly pledged, "that we desire nothing more ardently than that the white & red Inhabitants of this big Island should cultivate the most Brotherly affection, & be united in the firmest bands of Love & friendship." But their listeners had witnessed and often suffered from white intrusion for a generation. They had lived through the imperial struggles for the continent and the furtive alliance fashioned in Pontiac's Rebellion. And they certainly knew the deepest sentiments of white westerners concerning Indians, for the west was a place where, as one chronicler wrote, "every child . . . learns to hate an Indian. . . . With persons thus reared, hatred towards an Indian becomes a part of their nature, and revenge an instinctive principle."[25]

Beliefs about "ignoble savages" reversing progress and civilization permeated European thought but were strongest among Americans. In *Common Sense,* Paine referred to "that barbarous and hellish power" that roused Indian and slave against American liberties, and one of Jefferson's indictments against George III in the Declaration of Independence held that the king had instigated attacks by these "merciless Indian savages" on helpless frontier people. Such notions initially prompted both Britons and Americans to pause when considering the issue of seeking Indian alliances, but the shift of the conflict to the countryside and, especially, the impact of local conditions on the war soon changed matters. Indians may have professed neutrality, but they had been involved in the fighting among whites for years, and their participation in the American Revolution was probable. Save for Oneidas, Tuscaroras, and some Creek and Cherokee factions, they fought for the British. As the war progressed, however, Indian belligerents made it apparent that they intended to fight according to their own ways.[26]

Except for those Indians who were economically independent, neutrality was impossible. Caught in a conflict not of their making, the Indian tribes found themselves both wooed and warred upon by intruding British and American troops. For most, survival dictated choosing the British side. The trans-Appalachian "middle ground," though remote from the major theatres of war, offered no sanctuary, as both British and American agents intruded.

Washington dispatched into the region a force under George Rogers Clark, a Kentucky land speculator who despised Indians and vowed "for his part he would never spare Man woman or child of them on whom he could lay his hands." Driving his men like a conqueror obsessed with liberating an empire, he soon discovered that advancing American interests in the Illinois country depended on making alliances with the Indians. Their approach, he wrote, "must be preferable [to] ours, otherwise they could not possibley [*sic*] have such great influence among them."[27]

His remark was a reluctant admission of the unappreciated strengths of and links among Indian villages in the western country. Indians could not only "think continentally" but could also recognize their common interests. Even as most of the British armies were surrendering in 1781, Indians from the Great Lakes to the Gulf of Mexico appeared to be getting stronger, united in their opposition to white encroachment. At the peace settlement in 1783, the British abandoned them, but for twenty years after the onset of the American Revolution, the nativists and accommodationists among the trans-Appalachian Indians managed to overcome many of their intertribal differences. The older habits of negotiation and accommodation with white intruders were momentarily subsumed in a militant determination to resist.[28]

A Respectable Army

Given the antipathy of Americans to standing armies—a hostility that had driven Massachusetts farmers and militiamen to fight a presumably superior force—few Britons supposed that even the intractable would readily commit themselves to sustain the *kind* of army needed to fight the *kind* of war in the offing. These sentiments presupposed an army led by professional soldiers capable of sustaining discipline in the ranks through long months of sacrifice, an army supported not only in word but in deed by government and society because it was fighting for legitimate and unassailable goals. Only in nineteenth-century mythology did such a belief describe the condition of revolutionary British North America. In actuality, the struggle was replete with uncertainty about the commitment and capability of even the vaunted citizen soldiers. In September 1776, during the British landing on Manhattan, George Washington rushed to the scene and watched as New England troops fled before British regulars and Hessian mercenaries. He threw his hat to the ground, declaring, "Are these the men with whom I am to defend America?"[29]

He harbored a parallel suspicion of militiamen. More than a year earlier, having arrived at Cambridge to assume command of the newly formed Continental Army, Washington had expressed dismay about his task of commanding an army to "defend American liberties" with New England officers who quarreled endlessly about status and soldiers indifferent to order and discipline. An exemplar of the imperial officer cadre, Washington remembered with distaste the record of the citizen-soldier in the French and Indian war: "To place any dependence upon militia is assuredly resting upon a broken staff."[30]

One choice—a professional army of hirelings devoid of any commitment to citizenship—was out of the question. There remained three possibilities to address the unavoidable issue of discipline. The first was a rigorous imposition of discipline and force without reliance on the emotional appeal of revolutionary ideals. The second called for modification of those ideals out of respect for military discipline in the common interest of achieving them. Finally, a soldier might acknowledge the need for discipline, but with the understanding that revolutionary ideals envisioned a society in which the traditions of military rank and privilege had little place. All three existed in the Continental Army, but the third ultimately prevailed. Disavowal of a hireling army as unworthy for a republican society meant, inevitably, frustration for those who tried to mobilize an army in the face of widespread evasion of service and corruption in that society. This frustration was compounded when individual soldiers were called on to fight on behalf of a revolutionary society unwilling to acknowledge that their voluntary service and commitment were essential for victory.[31]

In the end Washington got his professional army, but its social makeup offered little comfort to his Virginia sensibilities. As the British offensives in Canada and in New York got under way in 1776, the continental congress appeared to acquiesce in his assessment of the reliability of the militia. It authorized eighty-eight battalions for a projected revolutionary army of seventy-five thousand (a number representing less than one-fourth of the potential white male soldiers in the population) drawn from state quotas based on population. To meet the problem of short-term service, the congress provided for three-year enlistments. Acknowledging that patriotic appeals were insufficient for the kind of war the revolutionaries confronted, the congress voted bounties (the initial sum was twenty dollars), a yearly clothing allowance, and (for those who served for the duration) a hundred acres of land. Within a few years, as morale diminished and departures increased, the bounty was raised and the land grant increased, but this was not enough to maintain an army of proper-tied freeholders and artisans, of "men possessed" with the fire of republican liberty.[32]

The revolution's first Continental Army was an undisciplined constabulary of small property holders willing to fight a short war. Their commitment to community was undeniable but often seemed to relate more directly to their individual predicament than to the larger issues at stake. The collective spirit of this army collapsed in the British offensive against New York in 1776. What remained of it formed part of the Continental Army Washington commanded for the remainder of the war, a military force presumably more committed to fighting away from home and drawn from all social strata. To sustain the army's numbers, the congress took what civilians it could get, expanding the definition of "able-bodied and effective" to permit the hiring of substitutes or the enlistment of indentures and slaves by their masters. Maryland impressed vagrants, Massachusetts and Rhode Island raised black battalions, and two slave states (Virginia and Maryland) allowed slaves to serve in the place of whites. Social misfits and the dispossessed enlisted or were impressed into the service of a cause offering the survivor not a materially better life but differ-ent social circumstances. In these respects, the Continental and invading British armies were similar.

A conflict in which slaveholders invoked revolutionary slogans created fur-ther ambiguity. Undeniably, on the eve of the war, those who proclaimed the libertarian cause grasped the significance of their words and their irreconcil-ability with slavery. For black slaves, the prospect of a change in status was a powerful incentive regardless of the contradictions of fighting to sustain the liberties of those who enslaved them. "Whoever invoked the image of liberty, be he American or British, could count on a ready response from the blacks."[33] In the southern colonies, the matter was unambiguous. A South Carolinian ob-served that to abolish slavery was to "complete the ruin of many American provinces, as well as the West Indian islands." Few Virginians shared Jeffer-son's estimation, which he sent to the Virginia delegation to the continental congress, that "the rights of human nature are deeply wounded by this infa-mous practice" and that slavery's abolition was "the great object of desire in those colonies where it was unhappily introduced in their infant state." They found more comforting the opinion of Patrick Henry. The Virginia firebrand was distressed when he considered the "general inconvenience of living here without [slaves]," but he reconciled these contradictory impulses with the prospect of a time "when an opportunity will be offered to abolish this lamentable evil."[34]

By the third year of the war, the problem of replacing the dwindling numbers in the Continental Army prompted several northern states (and, ultimately, Virginia and Maryland) to enroll black soldiers. Washington himself recognized that since a war in the defense of slavery provided the British with an advantage, victory depended "on which side could arm the Negroes the faster."[35] In Georgia and South Carolina, which had large slave populations, legislatures resisted the call to mobilize slave troops even when the fighting moved into the south. Some five thousand blacks welcomed the chance to fight, fought on land and sea, and performed capably. Persuaded of a new era, they petitioned individually for freedom and collectively urged several state legislatures to abolish slavery. They fought at Monmouth, the North's final significant battle, and were at Yorktown in the summer of 1781. In the American victory, those slaves who had served gained their freedom and, in a few instances, a grant of land. One by one, state legislatures in the North began abolishing slavery. Others won their freedom by fighting for the British, whose military commanders confronted a shortage of troops.

Officers and men came from differing social ranks, a division blurred during the war, but the line separating poor white and black (whether slave or free) remained. The sense of identify forged among ordinary soldiers did not extend to blacks, utilized rather than welcomed into the ranks. "In this regiment," wrote a young Pennsylvanian camped near Boston, "there were a number of Negroes, which, to persons unaccustomed to such associations, had a disagreeable, degrading effect."[36]

The result of all this was an army with an unsettlingly high proportion of poor people and misfits—indentures, substitutes, farm workers, unemployed persons, transients, British deserters, foreigners, and (save in the lower South) black slaves—who had lived at the margin of colonial society. It is now easy to see why Washington privately anguished in his command of them. The social morphology of the army that wintered at Valley Forge was similar to that of the men he faced on the battlefield. These were not people from *his* America, yet they were the cannon fodder of the professional army he had insisted was vital to the cause. His officers spoke contemptuously of their haggard and unkempt troops as "food for worms—miserable sharp looking Caitiffs, hungry lean fac'd Villains."[37]

These were the outcasts and ne'er-do-wells who persevered through the harshness of revolutionary campaigns and endured years of fighting while more socially acceptable Americans bought their way out of service or retired to more comfortable duty in the militias. The continentals were not the revolutionary soldiers of American myth, but they fought for a society that offered the hope of social advancement if they survived; they were willing to suffer and perhaps die for a cause that had little meaning for them. They were not citizen-soldiers defending their homes and communities. They had little property and no community accepted them as members. They were not professionals. One officer bemoaned this "strangest mixture of Negroes, Indians, and whites, with old men and mere children . . . [whose] nasty lousy appearance made the most shocking spectacle."[38]

Expressed ideals, civilian behavior, and military strategy seemed as contradictory to the revolutionary generation as they do to us. Two factors, I believe, are crucial to explaining how revolutionary British America reconciled these contradictions. First, civilian patriots believed they had accomplished a revolution with the Declaration of Independence. Their revolution was a collective battle cry on behalf of freedom but not a war on behalf of the revolutionary state. The defense of freedom, they knew, might require voluntary or even involuntary service in the cause of the nation, but revolutionary ideology called for vigilance in defense of personal freedom, a freedom as compelling to one who fights as to another who strives to keep the war from intruding. What divided revolutionary soldier and civilian was that inevitable mutual disdain between one who surrenders personal freedom to fight in the service of a noble cause and one who believes that retaining personal freedom is a nobler cause. What united them was a belief, often disproved by the facts, that the British would give up the fight and leave.[39]

But the reality was that the war did not end, even after the French alliance of 1778 and the Spanish assault on British Florida the following year. In 1780, the British launched a major offensive in the South, where loyalist sentiment was widespread. A succession of defeats in the southern theatre sapped revolutionary morale and prompted more derelictions among the civilian population. But these reverses, paradoxically, seemed to strengthen the determination to achieve independence and to spur vendetta wars between loyalist and revolutionary, a southern reprise in the Carolinas and Georgia of the civil conflicts that had raged in New York and New Jersey in earlier years. The British strategy of manipulating the slave population in order to placate white southerners collapsed in a campaign of destructive pacification in the course of which the British impressed slaves as laborers for the army or for loyalist planters. Though slavery was effectively preserved, the British practice heightened prospects for eventual emancipation if the British won the war. More than four thousand followed the British army of Cornwallis into the Upper South and the final disaster at Yorktown.[40]

In the southern theatre, the formalities of eighteenth-century warfare degenerated into cruel familial vendettas. General Nathaniel Greene, dispatched by Washington to command the Continental Army's southern campaign, wrote disconsolately of "desolation, bloodshed and deliberate murder. . . . For want of civil government the bands of society are totally disunited, and the people, by copying the manners of the British, have become perfectly savage." The victorious British general was similarly perplexed when he obtained professions of loyalty to the king only to meet violent resistance when he tried to compel loyalists to fight in the king's cause. Behavior was often a poor indicator of sentiment. Collaboration with British troops, for example, sometimes signaled a pursuit of self-interest or survival. Other times, it concealed a fearfulness about struggle. But the prospect that one could be subjugated if apathetic or selfish and thus lose the capability to struggle aroused even deeper fears and goes far in explaining how revolutionaries were able to alternate their rhetoric and behavior from accommodation and moderation to fiery oratory and unspeakable violence. "Perhaps only the fear of deserving a tyrant could exceed the fear of fighting one."[41]

Second, the war was fought in the countryside between armies with a similar strategy—winning civilian support—but different tactics in achieving that goal. Washington and his generals put more emphasis on keeping the army intact than on taking posts or holding territory, the British, on controlling cities and venturing into the surrounding countryside to intimidate neutrals and to rally loyalists. One effect of this Fabian strategy, of course, was to lower civilian morale, momentarily rejuvenated by Washington's victorious campaign against the Hessians at Trenton in December 1776 and a subsequent engagement with British regulars at Princeton. The rejoicing just as quickly lessened in the following year, when Fort Ticonderoga and Philadelphia fell, and in 1780, when the British seized Charleston.[42]

Ambiguities peculiar to a war in the countryside remained, as the revolutionary struggle in Pennsylvania after the fall of Philadelphia to British forces demonstrated. Continental soldiers complained about the indifference of Pennsylvanians to the cause and about their willingness to sell their produce to the British, calling the province a "Tory labyrinth" and vilifying its Quaker pacifists. When Washington suspended his policy of forbidding large confiscations of produce from civilians, detached soldiers carried out their assignments with such forcefulness and personal abuse that the countryside was thrown into a protracted guerrilla war involving civilians, soldiers, brigands, looters, and marketeers. Ultimately, both Washington and Howe did business with the locals, but Howe paid with specie. The effect was to drain the countryside of desperately needed provisions, despite the imposition of martial law by militias. Continental soldiers sometimes collaborated with the farmers by allowing them to pass along the roads into the city in exchange for favors.

Both Washington and Howe accommodated local interests to the point of securing material supplies. Each floundered in efforts to nurture a loyal constituency, which required a large detachment of troops to police a fractious and divided populace. Washington grasped the problem when he reluctantly dispatched regular troops to aid New Jersey Whigs embroiled in a local conflict precipitated by a foraging expedition of detached continentals. "A few hundred Continental troops quiet the minds and give satisfaction to the people of the Country," he wrote, "but considered in the true light, they rather do more harm than good. They draw over the attention of the Enemy and . . . are obliged to fly and leave the Country at the Mercy of the foe. But . . . the people do not view things in the same light, and therefore they must be indulged, tho' to their detriment."[43]

A Dispirited Military

Some of the most troubling manifestations of the revolutionary experience occurred early in the war, in the relationship between the continental congress and the professional military taking shape under Washington's command. Continental officers may have sensed the need to prove their fitness for command to ordinary soldiers, but they differed measurably in their material stake in the coming republican political order and the role of the military in sustaining it. As the war dragged on and the cause became more uncertain, civilian-military relations sharply deteriorated. Irritation over inadequate supplies grew to resentment of a "niggardly Congress" that dined sumptuously, continental officers complained, while yielding to political pressures and denying those who led the army of independence their rightful claim to pay and rank. "I despise my countrymen," Lieutenant Colonel Ebenezer Huntington wrote in 1780. "I wish I could say I was not born in America. . . . The insults and neglects which the army have met with from the country beggars all description."[44]

As such, officers expected not only deference but proper treatment in return for their sacrifice. Deprived of opportunities to capitalize on the rising demand for goods and foodstuffs, their financial status diminished by the rampant inflation, and compelled to clothe and equip themselves, they were understandably angered by tales of civilians who had rapidly grown rich. During the winter of Valley Forge, they resolved to follow the British example and demand half-pay lifetime pensions, with payments to begin at the end of the war. Washington was initially suspicious about such "unrepublican" notions but heartened to the plan when his officers began to desert. In Congress, irate delegates spoke of a "patriotic war" and the inevitable collapse of "virtue" that would obtain if they funded a "privileged class" of military pensioners. In May 1778, however, they acquiesced, approving seven-year pensions and, in addition, providing $80 bonuses to those enlisted soldiers who agreed to fight until the end of the war. It was a minor victory for the continentals and, more important, for Washington himself, whose resolve in this matter apparently persuaded a suspicious congress that the war could not be won without his leadership. He successfully countered the efforts of a band of republican ideologues in congress to advance the cause of several subordinates.

But the bitterness over the pensions lasted and, in the final years of the war, nearly brought on a military coup when disaffected officers demanded lifetime half-pay. In the aftermath of this affair, the reputation of the regulars among the general population deteriorated. Officers spoke angrily about civilians "sauntering in idleness and luxury, despis[ing] our poverty and laugh[ing] at our distress."[45] Acting in concert, military historians of the American Revolution have acknowledged, officers and rank-and-file members of the Continental Army could have imposed their will on a tight-fisted Congress, demanding better treatment and, more frightening, threatening the nation's republican future by the menace of their armed presence, justifying their choice by the arguable logic that the "virtuous" professional soldier must save the "corrupt society." That they held back from this course has been variously attributed to seemingly unrelated issues: Washington's reluctance to lend his name to any conspiracy; his seeming public indifference to accusations among jealous officers (most notably Brigadier General Thomas Conway, who was denied a top command and retaliated by conducting a smear campaign); the financial skills of Robert Morris, who reassured the generals with his reorganization of the army; and the ratification of the Articles of Confederation in 1781.[46]

In the end, the differing and often ambiguous motivations of those fighting the war provide a clue to why the United States escaped a military coup in these troublesome years. Although officers and men came from different social strata, they shared a bond of *experience* forged by deprivation and ingratitude. Yet they acted separately from the "vulgar herd" beneath them in their protest against public indifference to their plight. They were determined to preserve not only the military but also the social hierarchy of the republic. Some talked of a military takeover. Though sharing their anger, others harbored a deeper fear: the revolution required not only competent but virtuous officers. Replacing a bickering and ineffectual congress with a praetorian guard would doubtless make for a more efficient campaign against the enemy, but it would exact a heavy political price. Nathaniel Greene perhaps best expressed the most persuasive rationale for civilian control of the military: "With our government compact, a Dictator might draw out the forces and resources of the Country with greater dispatch than any other mode that can be adopted, . . . [b]ut as the Government is wide, and as the people are jealous and will be more and more so if the Miltary departments get the reins of civil government, I am in great doubt whether there would be as prompt obedience from the people at large under a Dictator as under a Congress with full and ample powers."[47]

In 1783 a discontented cadre joined in the Newburgh conspiracy, the culmination of two years of plotting by officers fearful that demobilization would wreck their influence and relegate them to public shame as half-pay pensioners. The army became politicized. A few nationalists in the congress urged them to mutiny. Meeting at Newburgh, disaffected generals wrangled over the issues, then decided against punitive measures. Their leader explained: "I consider the American Army as one of the most immaculate things on earth. . . . We should . . . suffer wrongs and injuries to the utmost verge of toleration rather than sully it in the last degree. [Our cause can] only exist in one point, and that . . . is a sharp point which I hope in God will never be directed than against the Enemies of the liberties of America."[48]

To Americans flushed with pride in the bicentennial, his remark reaffirmed the soldier's faith in the higher purpose of the U.S. war for independence and a parallel conviction about civilian superiority over the military. In retrospect, had the Newburgh conspirators pushed ahead with their plan and perhaps seized power, they would have set a pattern that most Latin Americanists concede was one of the more regrettable legacies of the long struggles for Latin American independence; militarism, symbolized by the general on horseback who is persuaded that only by his forceful unseating of a spineless or ineffectual civilian authority will the nation survive and the people prosper.

In the aftermath, however, public distrust of the military deepened. When

General Henry Knox and a group of officers founded the Society of the Cincinnati, intended as a fraternal organization for continental officers and their descendants, it was denounced as yet another example of aristocratic pretensions. Matters worsened when a virtually bankrupt congress, ignoring Washington's pleas for three months' pensions to riotous troops, sent them home without a financial settlement or even an expression of thanks for their services. In Philadelphia, two hundred angry soldiers held hostage several members of congress and the Executive Council of Pennsylvania. The threat ended when the congressmen emerged and bullied their way through the shouting assemblage. Congress moved to the more peaceful ambiance of Princeton, but public apprehensiveness over the perceived threat to civilian authority remained.[49]

Revolutionary Governance

This incident, among others, was a symptom of what congressional malcontents identified as a fundamental weakness in revolutionary governance—vulnerability to external pressures. But the congress bore a responsibility for this debility. At the onset of the American Revolution, revolutionary leaders were less inclined to tamper with the structure of government—governors, bicameral legislatures, judicial systems, and local governments, all of which had existed in the colonial era—but were determined to alter how these functioned. The powers of government in the colonies, the continental congress decreed in May 1776, were now carried out by those chosen by the people. Jefferson articulated this sentiment in the memorable phrases about equality, sovereignty, and the right of rebellion he included in the Declaration of Independence. Under the Articles of Confederation, the states remained sovereign, which made for legislative dominance in both the central and the state governments and for democracy at every level. This may not have been intended, but it was one of the results of the revolution.[50]

Patriots did not need the reminders of Tory pamphleteers such as Jonathan Boucher to persuade them of the perils in urging an aroused populace to resist *British* authority. Hortatory pronouncements might unleash popular animosity toward authority whether identified with the appointed or the elected. In the beginning of the war, John Adams expressed a conviction that "there must be a Decency, and Respect, and Veneration for Persons in Authority, of every Rank, or We are undone," but believed that "love and not fear will become the spring of their obedience." As did other patriot leaders, Adams recognized the continuity of colonial experience in the structure of revolutionary state governments—colonial voters, after all, had elected their magistrates—but retained classical Whig apprehensions about the nature of power and the origins of despotism. The experience of war and, particularly, the internal bloodletting over the character of state constitutions sobered the earlier faith in the survival of republicanism and reminded some of the patriots of Tory warnings about "intestine quarrels." Put another way, such a lament was tantamount to an admission that the experience of war and the fashioning of revolutionary state governments had failed, as Adams put it, "to purge away the monarchical impurity we contracted by laying so long upon the lap of Great Britain."[51]

What he missed, of course, was the revolution in governance that had taken place. In the early years of the war, the continental congress had assumed extraordinary powers to direct affairs, assuming the character of a de facto national government. The sense of unity accompanying the rage militaire persuaded several delegates to lay the foundations of a "lasting confederacy," as one of them put it, to "hand down the blessings of peace and public order" to later generations and to serve as a model of union to the world.[52]

What delayed its creation were the parallel demands of managing the business of conflict and dealing with the persistently divisive issues among the rebellious colonies, and, ultimately, the isolation of the congress from both the Continental Army and the wartime state governments. It may be an exaggeration to argue that the congress became so preoccupied with the continental war and the winning of international support that its early determination to create a strong confederation simply withered. What actually occurred was more complicated. Within the congress there was a gnawing fear that the civil conflict within the states made more imperative a short war that would assure independence. When neither the victory at Saratoga nor the French alliance prompted a British withdrawal, both the character of the war in the states and the responses of respective state governments changed.

The congress had not shrunk from its commitment to independence. Indeed, the radicals were able to persuade moderates that conciliatory measures taken in Parliament and the peace commission dispatched in the spring of 1778 were ruses to confuse the people. In the aftermath the congress's preoccupation lay with the army and the reorganization of revolutionary finance. The latter involved transfering much of the cost of the war to the states, a matter of considerable significance for understanding the conflicts of the eighties. It meant, too, that the states and not the congress would determine their revolutionary political—and, by implication, social—character. Such was a disturbing prospect for moderates, who responded favorably to the complaints of landowners and merchants expressing doubts about the new state constitutions in New York, Maryland, and Pennsylvania, and who prompted reconsideration of British peace offerings. Rejecting this opportunity for peace, Charles Carroll of Maryland wrote in the fall of 1776, meant probable ruin, "not so much by the calamities of war, as by the intestine divisions and the [likelihood] of bad govern[men]ts: ... simple Democracies, of all govern [men]ts the worst, will end as all other Democracies have, in despotism."[53]

By dispersing so much power and responsibility to the states, the congress may have unwittingly shackled the revolution's first national government with such debilitated authority that its demise with the Constitution was inevitable. Clearly, the Articles of Confederation, not formally established until 1781, when the war was nearing its end, undergirded a weaker government than that established later in the decade. A properly apposite reference for the Articles of Confederation is not the Constitution but the structure and processes of governance in monarchical British America and, especially, the widespread apprehension about the intrusion of government from afar and from above. "What is truly remarkable about the Confederation," observes Gordon Wood, "is the degree of union that was achieved."[54]

Of more importance than the grumblings and calculated maneuvers of the congressional nationalists, who declared political war on the states in 1780, are the convictions of their colleagues who understood popular sentiment and recognized that centralization of authority was a wartime expedient with little prospect of taking hold in the public imagination. The revolution had been inspired from above, but those who articulated it ultimately relied on the states to finance the war and to oversee local military operations. Strapped for funds in the desperate years of 1779 and 1780, the congress pressed the states to impose higher taxes, collect supplies, prosecute allegedly derelict officials, confiscate property, and even pay military salaries. Such a transfer of authority symbolized not only an admission of the congress's administrative failure but also its dependence on the states. That such a dependence may have weakened the revolution's first national government may seem plausible in retrospect, but it accurately reflected commonly held beliefs about the nature of confederation.[55]

In transferring power, those who had inspired the revolution from above recognized not only their dependence on the states and, more fundamentally, on the people, but also their unspoken acknowledgment that they had neither the intention nor the desire to create a revolutionary state that assumed total power under the pretext of fulfilling the revolutionary purpose.

Some of those who had called for revolution and nourished the "contagion of liberty" that swept the colonies during the rage militaire of 1775–1776 came to regret to what ends their ideas and beliefs were put. They despaired over the civil conflict that persisted throughout the revolution and, indeed, survived it; railed against the generation of upstarts and opportunists who presumed to share power with them; and took grim satisfaction when the Articles of Confederation collapsed. They had not schemed to replace a corrupt and chaotic Old World society with another in the new. As skillful propagandists, they had effectively, and occasionally brilliantly, stated the case for rebellion; they had tried George III and Parliament in a public forum.

In both public affairs and business, a generation of opportunists and unprincipled men had risen out of obscurity to join the creators of the revolution. The intent of the revolutionaries of 1775 had been to assume their rightful place in the political order when the king's ministers and lackeys departed. They had not expected the many new faces joining them at the republican governing table. John Adams, snubbed by Tories in his early days as a lawyer, had sorely resented it. Now, in the aftermath of the revolution, he resented the lack of deference of the upstarts. "When the pot boils, the scum will rise," James Otis had prophesied in the early years of the revolution. A decade later, James Madison lamented in *Federalist No. 62* about the debilitating social legacy of the democratization of political life: "Every new election in the States is found to change one half of the representatives, men without reading, experience, or principles."56

These "old revolutionaries" anticipated the political crisis of the early 1770s, but they grew ever more fearful of the social disorder and the political calamities it wrought in the following decade: distrust, indebtedness, the weakness of the Articles of Confederation in dealing with foreign governments, and the general decline in civility and deference. Amid the uncertainties of the postwar years, those who bemoaned the decline of virtue and civility and those who advocated a market economy characterized the emergence of new political alliances among lower-status urban organizers as a menace. The economic battle lines had been drawn in wartime as merchants and commercial farmers had opposed subsistence farmers and urban artisans over price controls. In the depression that followed, debt-ridden farmers looked to state legislatures for easier credit and tax relief. In several states, political in-fighting enabled elites to fend off attempts to form hard currency policies.

Yet the manifest insecurity of the republic's first national government did not prompt civilian leaders to defer to a disgruntled soldiery or to create a privileged place for its alienated officer corps. In victory, the soldiers, especially the continentals, suffered further humiliations. Washington's most persevering troops received little in either gratitude or compensation. They left for home with their weapons, the clothes on their backs, furlough papers, and land warrant certificates. The prospect of a new life in the western country was for most of them a dream never realized, as land speculators took advantage of desperate soldiers who traded their certificates for food or money. Impoverished when they joined the Continental Army, many returned to a life of poverty. Considering their social position before the war, the greatest beneficiaries among them may have been those slaves and felons who had been committed to servitude or imprisonment before the war and had obtained freedom by fighting. For many continentals, however, civilian life was an unrelenting struggle to extract pensions from state governments and to stave off penury. One, Joseph Plumb Martin, wrote: "When the country had drained the last drop of service it could screw out of the poor soldiers, they were turned adrift like old worn-out horses, and nothing said about land to pasture them upon."[57]

Officers, of course, fared better, but even they found it difficult to exploit their military experience in the political culture of the postrevolutionary era. Correctly sensing the public's deeper affections for the militia, Washington attempted to reconcile the nationalists' desire for a regular military with the spirit of the age in his proposal for enlisting militiamen into a preparedness force to guard against invasion and internal threats to republican institutions. His arguments collapsed before indifferent and suspicious congressmen, who saw the dual use of militias and regular troops in the winning of the war as a contradictory mix of rivalrous military traditions. The fact that the war had been won by exploiting both seemed irrelevant to a postwar generation that no longer regularly equated social and military rank. Just as people had discovered that religious leaders could be found below the "better sort," they had hesitated to subscribe to the axiom that the military officer from the established family was any more suitable for the role of influential than someone from the middling social ranks who had proved himself in war.[58]

3

The Dilemmas of Victory

The American revolutionary experience created uncertainties, doubtless, but few contemporaries recognized that the young republic possessed an advantage that Haiti and Latin America lacked. A people had been mobilized for war, but the experience had not militarized society. North Americans had been perilously close to a military coup in the final years of the revolution. In the fractious politics of the 1780s, some would call for military solutions to the social strife they believed threatened the survival of the republic. The contradiction they inherited from the revolutionary experience—the fighting of a war with a professional army *and* citizens in arms—would prove problematical throughout the history of the United States, but this was a minor issue compared with the militarism that plagued Latin America in the aftermath of independence.[1]

Old Revolutionaries and Political Upstarts

In one of the many effusive congratulations that swept the country on July 4, 1783, the New Englander John Warren spoke somberly about the prospects for despotism among a people who failed to remember why they had fought. In such circumstances his words doubtless seemed unduly pessimistic, but they were reminders of the social transformation at work in the revolution. A few of the aging revolutionary elites sank into bitter despair over what they had wrought. As they aged, their pessimism deepened. The departure of those loyalists who had possessed an inordinate power and influence in British America had broken old ties and familial connections and created opportunities for newcomers. Resentment was inevitable. "Fellows who would have cleaned my shoes five years ago," one of the old revolutionaries had complained in 1779, "have amassed fortunes, and are riding in chariots."[2]

It was at this conjuncture of conflicting interest groups in public affairs that Otis's "scum"—what Linda Grant DePauw has called the "lesser denominators" of the revolutionary era—performed a critical role. The "great disseminators," the revolutionary elites—broadened to include not only merchants and lawyers but also artisans and yeomen—had taken their rightful place in the continental congress and the state legislatures. They were more politically visible but not more numerous than the lesser denominators, local activists who organized committees of safety and formed local "militias." These were rough-hewn people indisposed to deference toward their betters. During the *rage militaire,* they had driven not a few fence straddlers over to the loyalist camp. "If I must be enslaved," roared Boston's Reverend Samuel Seabury, "let it be by a King at least, and not by a parcel of upstart lawless committeemen. If I must be devoured, let me be devoured by the jaws of a lion, and not gnawed to death by rats and vermin."[3]

In the politics of the postwar era, some of the former loyalists figured prominently in state politics. New Jersey Whigs were aghast at their numbers in the state government. This generosity toward the losing side existed in a country whose revolutionary settling of accounts had resulted in a greater percentage of exiles and more widespread confiscation of property than had the French Revolution. What happened in New Jersey was another indicator of the dual character of the revolution, whose victor meted out punishment *and* tolerance. In the South, where the irregular war of loyalist and patriot militias had devastated rural communities, postwar extralegal societies and political clubs sprang up in an apparent challenge to the Whig elites, who spoke fearfully of street agitators and mobs taking revenge on their loyalist neighbors. In Charleston, anti-Britannic political agitation was particularly unsettling to the low-country Whigs, but the leaders of the political clubs were quick to reassure them. In 1784, the Marine Anti-Britannic Society declared "that all *mobs, riots,* and *tumults* (so far from being abetted or promoted by the society) are, and always have been considered by them as *odious, abominable,* and *destructive* of the peace, prosperity, and population of this infant country."[4]

Nowhere was the subtlety of the social transformation wrought by the revolution expressed more unmistakably than in postwar Virginia. In perhaps the most fervent political squabble in the assembly between 1776 and 1785—the disestablishment of the Anglican Church—Thomas Jefferson and James Madison persuaded a legislature dominated by Anglicans to accommodate religious dissenters. It was a politic recognition of western rural support for the revolutionary cause. When Jefferson sought to supplant the Anglican Christian establishment with a secular republican variation, the dissenters fought it as another effort to impose hierarchical "community" standards on the individual. In independent Virginia, authority rested not on royal prerogative or patriarch but on written law, and the commonwealth was not a community ruled by the gentry but a fractured and polarized provincial society where tidewater gentlemen still dueled and backcountry evangelicals roused illiterate farmers at camp meetings. Western lands again beckoned speculative Virginians, and common folk joined ambitious entrepreneurs in the quest for riches. But their common ambition no longer molded Virginia society. The "metaphor of money," present from the earliest settlements in the Chesapeake, challenged the "metaphor of patriarchy" as never before.[5]

The Social Question

Revolutionary virtue had not perished because the people lost faith. It had withered before a more compelling vision of a better life for ordinary people, one that had tangible rewards and greater utility in defining individual identity. There was no denying the material benefits of an expanding economy or the prospect for advancement in a country presumably blessed with abundance. A decade before the American Revolution erupted, John Adams had declared, "I always consider the settlement of America as the opening of a grand scheme and design in Providence for the illumination of the ignorant and the emancipation of the slavish part of mankind all over the earth."[6]

A decade after the revolution, Adams was bemoaning their unrelieved impoverishment. But he never doubted that a powerful historic process was at work. In his controversial essay on the social legacy of the revolutionary experience, J. Franklin Jameson described its character thus: "The stream of revolution, once started, could not be confined within narrow banks, but spread abroad upon the land. Many economic desires, many social aspirations were set free by the political struggle, many aspects of colonial society profoundly altered by the forces thus let loose. The relations of social classes to each other, the institution of slavery, the system of land-holding, the course of business, the forms and spirit of intellectual and religious life, all felt the transforming hand of revolution."[7]

Jameson's assessment of social realities makes too little of the persistence of poverty, and his argument for the social leveling accomplished by landholding—for example, the abolition of primogeniture and entail, confiscation of loyalist estates, and, most important, the distribution of public lands in the western country—obscures the limited effects of measures that proved more symbolic than real. Compared with the misery of Europe's common sort, of course, there seemed to be little doubt about Crèvecoeur's description of the social improvement Americans enjoyed. Benjamin Franklin had toured the Scottish highlands in the 1770s and 1780s and had seen wretched tenants living in the midst of opulence. Jefferson noted the despair of common Europeans in his continental trip of 1785 and contrasted their condition with the happier one of ordinary Virginians.

Europeans visiting the United States in the following years, however, wrote of hovels from which emerged the impoverished and undernourished of the new republic. The more generous public land laws of the United States, the abolition of entail and primogeniture, and the seeming obsession of Americans to sustain freehold property should have mitigated these conditions. "Instead of the lands being equally divided, immense estates are held by a few individuals," observed a traveler in rural Virginia in the 1790s, "whilst the generality of the people are but in a state of mediocrity."[8]

Doubtless, the seventy European visitors who wrote of social conditions in the country exaggerated the poverty, but they did not have to exaggerate when they wrote about the splendid homes of federalist America. On the eve of the French Revolution—his social conservatism already entrenched—Adams described a hypothetical nation where one-tenth held property and the remainder owned very little. He predicted that majority rule would bring ruin to the propertied in the name of liberty. The United States was presumably no exception to this statistical conjecture, because Adams made no mention of it. Thirty years later, comparing the United States and Europe, he noted that a majority of Americans had no property but confidently predicted they would not join in a revolution because of it.

Revolutionary British America lacked a pervasive sense of class consciousness, but it was a class society as measured by the ability of those from below to move up in the social order. Although the revolution had little effect on this upward social mobility, it held out opportunities for horizontal mobility—especially in a great internal immigration from east to west when new lands were opened. (The Northwest Ordinances of 1784 and 1787 validated this process in the territories, but the movement of peoples occurred within the states as well.) The society was less democratic in the cities and in the commercial agricultural regions, where a commercial and propertied elite coexisted with an expanding lower class. It looked more democratic in the West, where farms were small and wealth was more equitably distributed. But even in the robust West the inequities of a revolutionary age persisted. The West *looked* more democratic because struggling farmers picked up and moved west, where prospects seemed better. They joined younger men starting out. The combination of two social groups—one indebted and nonconformist, the second restless and more radical—lent a vitality and an earnestness to frontier life. They were no match, however, for the opportunists and speculators who accompanied them.[9]

Such nuances helped to sustain arguments that postrevolutionary society was more egalitarian, depending on where one lived or how one viewed social roles. As the value of labor rose in the estimation of society, the parallel measure of manual work apparently diminished. Artisans had become more assertive during the American Revolution, but they did not move very far up the ladder. Statistically, the United States remained a society of disparities in wealth. Income and wealth were as inequitably distributed in the United States in 1800 as in British America in 1776—this despite the confiscation of loyalist estates, the elimination of primogeniture and entail, and the opening up of the West to settlement. True, the departure of loyalists had meant the dispersal of 2,200 estates, mitigating social inequity based on landholding, but inheritance practices were little affected by the end of primogeniture and entail. More significant, the poverty of the East persisted as one moved farther west, where speculators took advantage of the postwar disruption to acquire western land from economically distressed veterans. The assumption of state debt by the federal government benefited those who had purchased certificates for one-tenth of their face value, creating a moneyed class that owned $32 million in federal debt. Property in slaves exacerbated wealth inequity in the slave states.[10]

The inequities in wealth that had characterized prerevolutionary British America remained. In the egalitarian atmosphere of the revolutionary age, their persistence had often exacerbated social tensions, but they had not always heightened popular demands for a general social leveling. In the revolutionary lexicon, liberty had assumed a greater urgency than equality, but the war had accelerated demands for social change, not only from opportunistic "middling sorts" but from the "lesser sorts" as well. The United States, the discontented were now saying, "was to be a revolutionary society precisely because it would not have the permanent classes of privileged rich and dependent poor that Americans associated with the 'old' societies of mercantilist Europe."[11]

What such beliefs conveyed more closely approximated the social milieu Alexis de Tocqueville described a half-century later, a society whose democratic roots took hold in the revolution but did not mature until much later. This was the social revolution promised but left unfulfilled, in part because those who railed against the social leveling inspired by the war and the dangers of mobocracy were determined to stifle it and, more important, because they ultimately found ways to dissipate its strength. Circumstances necessitated a redefinition of *revolution*. As the *Pennsylvania Gazette* observed on the meaning of the Constitutional Convention: "The year 1776 is celebrated (says a correspondent) for a revolution in favor of *Liberty*. The year 1787, it is expected, will be celebrated with equal joy, for a revolution in favor of *Government*."[12]

A New Political Culture?

The first task of those who wanted to limit the political impact of the revolution was to divide the rapidly growing electorate that emerged with the creation of the states during the war. Elites managed to preserve the old property or freehold qualifications for voting but could not prevent radically changing beliefs that the vote should mean something more than ownership of property. Such a notion was emblematic of the egalitarian spirit of the revolution and the heightened aspirations for social advancement, yet property counted a great deal in postrevolutionary culture for those aspiring to a political career. Certainly, the proportion of wealthy and propertied in the legislatures dropped considerably, and that of yeomen and farmers (particularly in the North) increased. Habits of deference to those with established power and influence still mattered. Indeed, the democratic promise of the revolution, visible in the wartime committees and the new faces in local politics, distracted from the opportunities offered to elites. "In large portions of the United States," Robert Wiebe argues, "the Revolution actually strengthened gentry rule by channeling popular ferment toward the British and the American Tories, seeming to purge society of its worst aristocratic sins, and exalting the patriot gentry as protectors of a purified republic."[13]

Virginians continued their colonial habits of trooping into town on election day, carousing and drinking the whiskey provided by candidates for office, most of them gentry from "long-tailed families" who had the common touch with the "vulgar herd." By a perverse but understandable logic, the lack of a secret ballot and the solicitation of a vote with a day of festivity may have advanced democracy and the meaning of a person's vote more than do modern practices. Voters personally knew candidates, what they stood for, and what benefits they could provide for a vote. No matter that the reality was a republic where opportunists and speculators threatened to prevail. The revolutionary faith of a society of independent freeholders still held, even as property lost its proprietary role in shaping one's identity and became another commodity. This was the parallel challenge of the revolutionary heirs: to persuade ordinary people that ownership of property carried with it an achievable prestige identified with material possession and, even in a society of inequities in wealth and property, not only held out the prospect of social betterment but set one a significant notch or two above the dispossessed, who did not profit from their labor by acquiring property. "Dominion is founded on property," Ezra Stiles declared, citing James Harrington's *Oceana,* and "a free tenure of lands, and equable [not equitable] distribution of property enters into the foundation of a happy state."[14]

In this putative social transformation, Americans redefined the purpose of politics by altering the social dynamics within government. The benefits were many, but perhaps the most crucial, writes Gordon Wood, was the fortuitous discovery of a political truth: "The stability of government no longer relied, as it had for centuries, upon its embodiment of the basic social forces of the state . . . [but] upon the prevention of the various social interests from incorporating themselves too firmly in the government."[15]

A vision romantic and belied by political realities, perhaps, but it served to remind Americans that there was no turning back to the classical politics and its unquestioned assumptions of the organic society and its hierarchical structure. No longer should Americans have to rely so completely on inherited social institutions—family, church, estate, or ruling classes—for guidance in fashioning the new society. In theory, the only distinctions that mattered were those of talent or virtue. In practice, Tocqueville wrote almost a half-century later, Americans displayed another distinctive trait—a "passion for wealth [which] is . . . not stigmatized in America and provided that it does not pass the boundaries which the need for public order assigns it, men hold in honor."[16]

Abandoning the monarchical society required a new definition of society, not an integrated unity of social ranks but a society of individuals, often hostile and competitive, who believed they were both equal and unequal. This was convoluted thought to a European aristocracy shaken by the social explosiveness of the French Revolution, which prompted Joel Barlow to offer his thoughts on what the American experience had taught. Advising the "privileged orders" of Europe, Barlow wrote: "[Americans] feel that nature has made them equal in respect to their rights; or rather that nature has given to them a common and equal right to liberty, to property, and to safety; to justice, government, laws, religion, and freedom. They all see that nature has made them very unequal in respect to their original powers, capacities, and talents. They become united in claiming and in preserving the equality, which nature has assigned to them; and in availing themselves of the benefits, which are designed, and may be derived from the inequality, which nature has also established."[17]

"This Lust for Slavery"

Regardless of the inequalities to which Barlow alluded in his response to the privileged orders of Europe, the shift from a society of ranks to one of individuals prompted reconsideration of the most serious flaw in the young republic—slavery. Historically, Americans had looked upon the "peculiar institution" as the lowest form of human servitude, but the revolution and the postwar redefinition of the worth of labor prompted them to perceive it as anomalous or to find more scientific means to justify its retention in a republican society. Early in the colonial debate over liberty and freedom, several patriot Whigs (most notably James Otis) had spoken eloquently about the incompatibility of slavery and freedom. Blacks fought for their freedom in the revolution; black petitioners forcefully argued a natural and God-given entitlement to liberty from bondage. Religious groups often supported their cause. In Pennsylvania, they organized the Society for the Abolition of Slavery, which ultimately counted such prominent Federalists as John Jay and Alexander Hamilton among its supporters. Massachusetts ended slavery by court order in 1783. White legislators in Maryland and Virginia (inspired, perhaps, as much by economic motives as a belief in the republican social contract) passed laws encouraging manumission. Those not moved by religious persuasion responded to environmentalist arguments, which held the Lockean view that all men had natural rights (including the right to freedom). Once liberated from the shackles of his environment, the slave would enter society as an equal member.[18]

The revolution may have inspired Americans to reevaluate the place of slavery in a republican society, but the liberating experience did not prompt them to erase the color line. Certainly in the South but also where legislatures abolished slavery, uncertainties over the assimilation of freed blacks into society reinforced other instincts. Even in the West Indies, where miscegenation had blurred racial categories, British Americans drew a color line. In the natural order, sex, age, and race placed people on different social planes, and of these three, color was an ascribed characteristic about which whites remained unyielding. To liberate a slave was to release a man or a woman from bondage. A freed slave, even if a mulatto or a quadroon, wore forever the badge of color. And in the hierarchical social order that persisted in the United States, the freed person would occupy a place above the slave, of course, but below the poorest whites.[19]

In short, the environmentalist dream of a withering away of slavery dissipated in the fears of whites that people of color could never be assimilated into white society. Whites had been English and had become Americans to vindicate their English rights. Blacks may have been English subjects, but whites did not believe they instinctively thought like Britons. Jefferson addressed the issue in his *Notes on Virginia,* but racial inequity was too deeply entrenched in Virginia to permit egalitarian sentiments—whether rooted in scientific rationalism, environmentalism, or religious faith—to persuade whites to think so differently from their forebears. Most Virginia planters eventually came to regret manumission, pressed the legislature for laws prohibiting private manumissions, and assailed religious leaders who preached equality for freed blacks. By 1806 Virginia law required freed blacks to depart the state. The color line was bent but not broken. In the southern churches, freed blacks often found themselves discriminated against or banned altogether. In the South, whites looked suspiciously on black organizations, believing that freed blacks were conspiring to bring down the institution of slavery.[20]

Antislavery beliefs strengthened during the revolutionary epoch, certainly; so, too, did antislave sentiments. The United States was a multiracial society at independence, but few whites gave serious consideration to the cultural dynamics at work. David Ramsay, writing on population in the opening chapter of a contemporary book on South Carolina, ranged across the ethnic landscape, surveying Germans, New Englanders, Scots, Irish, Swiss, and Dutch, but wrote little about the contributions of Africans. In the coastal regions of the state, particularly, miscegenation may have been a social reality, but most North Americans were uncomfortable with any suggestion that the "new man" was anything more than what Crèvecoeur said he was—a European. The federal naturalization law of 1790 applied to whites.

Given the universality of revolutionary rhetoric, presumably the American creed of equality applied to all. In truth, the achievement of that dream would have required a revolution in thought far more radical than John Adams believed had occurred. It would have necessitated a transformation in white beliefs about race and the future of a society proudly declaring itself free as it denied universal rights to peoples of color. "Afraid of the diversity within themselves," writes Ronald Takaki, "[white Americans] feared cultural and racial diversity in the society around them."[21]

In the crafting of the Constitution, however, the circumstance of slavery dictated another agenda, as delegates to the Philadelphia convention in the summer of 1787 soon discovered. One of the great debates at the convention involved an often bitter dispute between a majority willing to accept representation calculated in proportion to the numbers of white and "other free citizens and inhabitants" and three fifths of "other persons" and a minority desiring an equal representation in Congress for each state. As they became deadlocked over this issue, James Madison suggested that what really divided them was not size "but . . . their having or not having slaves."[22]

Madison readily accepted the proposal for two branches of Congress, a lower house in which the three-fifths rule would obtain and an upper house in which each state would have two representatives. Eventually, the great compromise stood. In the ratification battles fought in the various states, legislators condemned the tremendous advantage the South obtained in the proposed federal government. Antifederalists protested that the Constitution sanctioned "drenching the bowels of Africa in gore, for the sake of enslaving its free-born innocent inhabitants." Nonslave states now stood obligated to defend slave states against slave rebellion. Others feared unknown future entanglements and somberly predicted that "this lust for slavery [was] portentous of much evil in America, for the cry of innocent blood, . . . that undoubtedly reached to the Heavens, to which that cry is always directed, and will draw down upon them vengeance adequate to the enormity of the crime."[23]

The Patterns of Disorder

American leaders had neither created the revolutionary state nor tolerated the militarization of society. They confronted the classical dilemma of victors who have inspired a people to join a movement and then discovered that the followers are no longer marching to the same drumbeat. In classical republicanism they possessed a coherent theory to explain the menace of executive power and its corrupting influence; in revolutionary pamphlets they crafted the ideology to mobilize a people. But they had neither a coherent philosophy nor a useful social theory to address the powerful and uncertain forces dormant in British America and unloosened by the revolution.

The most visible and immediate threat was the disorder plaguing postrevolutionary society, a condition prompting some of the revolutionary generation (among them Alexander Hamilton) to advocate an internal police force in the form of a professional army and militias. However persuasive the arguments for such a course during the postwar uncertainties, the experience of the prerevolutionary years had taught that armed troops could not impose order. The experience of war had confirmed its corollary, that the community fighting in a localized conflict must maintain its own discipline. There was no doubting the immediacy of the political crisis in the 1780s or the persuasiveness of those who believed the revolutionary credo of liberty stood imperiled by the disorder. But beneath those apprehensions lay deeper fears about the implications of *forced* order. Loyalists could leave the country or accept the new republican order, but only one in nine chose the former course. Most joined the inner migration of loyalists and patriots who simply moved to another town or to the frontier.[24]

In the years immediately after the toppling of royal authority and the attaining of independence, of course, the urgency with which persons sought to improve their material lot out of frenzied self-interest could be explained as validation of Crèvecoeur's assessment of what happened to Europeans when they arrived in the New World. "The rich stay in Europe, it is only the middling and the poor that emigrate," he wrote. "A European . . . suddenly alters his scale; . . . he no sooner breathes our air than he forms schemes, and embarks in designs he never would have thought of in his own country. . . . Thus Europeans become Americans."[25]

On the frontier, Crèvecoeur's "new man" might be the opportunistic schemer but more often was the survivor (see map 2). Life there was beyond polite description for eastern visitors. One characterized the "whole society . . . about as wicked as fallen human beings can be on this side of utter perdition. Female seduction was frequent, quarreling and fighting customary—drunkenness almost universal, and therefore scarcely a matter of reproach." People were friendly but lived like "abandoned wretches . . . , like so many pigs

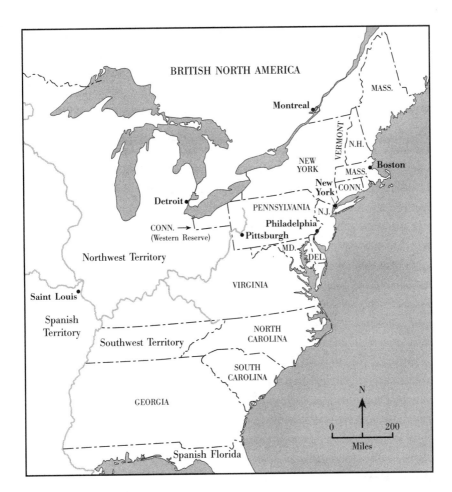

2. The United States, 1789.

in a sty." The postwar population surge did not relieve their condition. In western Pennsylvania, where a rebellion against federal excise taxes on liquor erupted in 1794, the population almost doubled in the decade after the revolution, and the numbers of landless jumped from one-third to one-half in some towns. By the mid-1790s, when the defiance brought an invading federal army bent on restoring order, the wealthiest 10 percent owned one-third of the land. Most of the profiteers (among them President George Washington) were outsiders. Put bluntly, writes the chronicler of the Whiskey Rebellion, "Nothing like the mythical classless frontier society ever existed in the western country."[26]

The occurrence of disorders on the frontier and elsewhere was less frightening than fears of what this portended. Reconciling the revolutionary spirit with a society of liberty *and* order was less troubling to "old" than to "young" revolutionaries. The former had made war not against tradition but against monarchy. Disorder robbed the young of their future. A sense of crisis prevailed among those who ruminated over the country's political condition in the 1780s, a sentiment irretrievably linked to the social disturbances of the era and perceptions that a new tyranny now menaced the confederation. For some, its locale was the state legislatures, most of which, wrote David Ramsay, were "elective despotisms" composed of men "committing blunders from ignorance."[27]

Critics fumed that state governments were helpless before popular agitation, much of which occurred outside legal recourse for resolution of grievances. Yet, "the very weakness of the constituted authorities . . . [and] the very democratic character of legislative politics in the 1780's . . . prevented the eruption of more serious violence during the Confederation period."[28] Little matter that the democracy so feared from below had failed to dominate any state government save Georgia's and Pennsylvania's or that the states were performing well in reducing the public debt. The gravamen for those urging a strengthening of the confederation seemed to be the danger to republic government, now threatened by the people themselves in their mobbing, flouting of the law, and intimidating their representatives.[29]

What also disturbed the delegates who gathered at Philadelphia to fashion the final document of the revolution was the success with which and especially the manner in which state legislatures had addressed a bewildering variety of postwar popular demands ranging from the disposition of land to the volatile question of the public debt. In the process, coalitions had pushed legislation in a spirit that appeared more a response to the urgency of popular demands than a circumspect attentiveness to constitutional restrictions or a veneration for constitutional liberties. Jefferson bemoaned this state of affairs in his *Notes on Virginia:* "The concentrating of the power of government in the same hands" defined "despotic government. . . . 173 despots would surely be as oppressive as one. . . . An elective despotism was not the government we fought for."[30]

In several states, these battles moved beyond the legislatures and resurrected memories of hostile crowds and armed farmers raging against the tyranny of government. One of the most visibly threatening was the rebellion in Massachusetts in 1786 led by Daniel Shays, a revolutionary veteran and a member of the state's new generation of debtors. The immediate goals of the insurgents were debt relief and a cessation of farm mortgage foreclosures. As in the prerevolutionary crisis over taxation, the debate over whether to levy taxes to pay for a debt soon deteriorated into a confrontation between those who exercised authority and those now defying it. The insurgents found sympathizers among landowners, who bore the heaviest burden in the state's frantic effort to pay off the revolutionary war debt with higher assessments, and disaffected artisans in Boston.[31]

State authorities now had a psychological weapon to wield against those who defied laws passed by a representative assembly and executed under a written constitution. Shays and his followers had threatened the constitution, announced General Benjamin Lincoln, who commanded the regular troops who snuffed out the rebellion, but the event frightened the nationalists and reaffirmed the contentions of those who argued that liberty and republicanism were now imperiled. As James Madison pointed out, these were not confrontations between "the Class with, and the class without property" but between large and small propertyholders, lenders and borrowers—people who disagreed on financial questions but who shared social values. In the fracturing of the young republic, their violent protest signaled that the social bonds of patriots had weakened.[32]

A few years later, as Britain and Spain were locked in a diplomatic dispute over British settlements on Nootka Sound on modern Vancouver Island, both governments encouraged separatist movements on the northwestern and southeastern frontiers, respectively. When a body of commissioners from Georgia carrying papers for intended settlements descended on Natchez, then under tentative Spanish control, Spanish officials expelled them. In retaliation, Georgians complained, the Spanish unleashed Indian assaults on land speculators and fur traders at Muscle Shoals and Chickasaw Bluffs. One of the frontier leaders roared defiantly against the "incrochen tyrents," warning his colleagues that the Spanish would soon control the best lands in North America. Spanish resistance prompted the frontiersmen to alter their tactics. Some plotted the liberation of the Floridas and Louisiana; others, such as John Sevier and George Rogers Clark, intrigued with and against the Spaniards. Most of the frontier plotters operated beyond the effective control of either the Spanish or the U.S. government, and for more than a decade after the revolution, rumors of plots and counterplots reverberated among frontier peoples.[33]

The entire affair galvanized particularistic frontier settlements, where defiance of central authority fired people infuriated with the passivity and indifference of remote state governments. From their founding, such frontier settlements as Transylvania in Kentucky or in western North Carolina (both set up by speculators and settlers in defiance of their respective state governments) had sustained themselves. From 1783 until 1786, they convened, petitioned, and protested to individual state governments. For the next two years, the western question dominated politics and sharpened sectional divisions. A Virginian speaking at the state ratifying convention in 1788 spoke for expansionists when he said, "I look upon this as a contest for empire. . . . This contest of the Mississippi involves this great national contest; that is, whether one part of the continent shall govern the other."[34]

His remarks were a reminder of what had happened in the three western counties of North Carolina, which had broken away and created the state of Franklin, then unsuccessfully applied for admission to the confederation. The region had deteriorated into civil war. The state had been able to reassert its authority, but the pioneers' bitterness and feelings of betrayal remained. The frenzy with which the expansionists promoted statehood worried social conservatives, who expressed concern about the "epidemic . . . spirit of making new states." "If every district so disposed may for themselves decide that they are not within the claim of the thirteen states," declared a New Hampshire assemblyman, "we may soon have ten hundred states, all free and independent."[35]

The number was preposterously inflated, but the apprehension over what was happening in the West was real. Spanish diplomacy became more conciliatory toward westerners. The governor at New Orleans announced that immigrants would be welcomed into Spanish territory, provided generous land grants, and accorded all benefits of Spanish subjects. In a dramatic departure from historic policy, he granted religious toleration to non-Catholics. Unruly and ungovernable frontiersmen made over into compliant subjects—the plan was daring but doomed. When Jefferson got wind of the policy of "settling the Goths at the gates of Rome," he scribbled, "I wish[ed] a hundred thousand of our inhabitants would accept the invitation. It will be the means of delivering to us peaceably what may otherwise cost us a war."[36]

Only the most cynical of the postrevolutionary elites in North America expressed thoughts as somber as those of Simón Bolívar in 1830 when he wrote of factions and social strife and the ungovernability of Spanish America's independent states. But those who gathered at Philadelphia certainly shared the kind of frustration Bolívar later expressed. In its first decade, the United States had been consumed by localist democracy whose advocates were not so much political theorists or ideologues as persons who demonstrated their politics through deeds. "The localists lived their ideals: they constituted a political culture and sought to create political and economic institutions compatible with that culture."[37]

That the Founders' solution for reconstituting the political order was not that of the factious Creoles who dismembered the Spanish empire and carved its scattered pieces into so many little fiefdoms warrants closer attention. One factor, certainly, was the comparatively more promising economic prospects for the United States in the early years of the republic. Another, presumably more critical, was the sharply differing political experience North Americans instinctively identify in Latin American political culture. A third reason lay in the increase in opportunities for horizontal if not vertical mobility offered by the opening of western lands for settlement and the parallel comment that the early republic may have suffered from poverty but its poor were not mired in misery.[38]

The most persuasive explanation may have been Madison's adroit connection between the Articles of Confederation and the internal commotions and uncertainties in his memorandum "Vices of the Political System of the United States." Under the Articles, the states had ignored congressional requests, encroached on federal matters, and even violated foreign treaties, but their greatest culpability lay in not providing adequately for congressional assistance to quell "internal violence." "In developing the evils which viciate the political system of the U.S." he noted, "it is proper to include those which are found within the States individually, since the former class have an indirect influence on the general malady and must not be overlooked in forming a compleat remedy."[39]

Nowhere were the stakes higher than in the western country. American negotiators came away from the peace negotiations believing they had secured the inner domain of North America in a great diplomatic coup, but within a few years U.S. sovereignty over the region and throughout the new nation was at bay. In actuality, the western country was still up for grabs, as it had been at mid-century, before the French and Indian War. Romantics spoke about a revolution triumphant to the Mississippi, but Spanish interlopers, French and British traders, and the great Algonquian confederacy could not be subdued save by conquest. Whatever gains George Rogers Clark had made among the Indians during the western campaigns of the revolution vanished before the invasion of land-hungry and Indian-hating whites. Clark was unable to drive the British from the region. Along the Ohio, murderous whites and vengeful young Indians—both seemingly beyond the control of any higher authority—

had fashioned social organizations remarkably similar in their capacity for sustaining conflict. That the Congress was understandably concerned about the future of the western country was evident in the crafting of the Northwest Ordinances of 1784 and especially the redrafting of that law in the act of 1787, which presumed that the mixed population of the western territory—Indians, blacks, French-Canadians, and Anglo-Americans, among others—required close supervision and a period of tutelage in republican institutions before they could participate fully in the political life of the nation. Those Anglo-Americans migrating to the frontier, of course, believed they carried all their rights with them.[40]

From the end of the American Revolution until the mid-1790s, southern and Great Lakes Indians drew on their experiences in the imperial wars of the eighteenth century and the conflicts that followed to fashion a pan-Indian alliance. Legend has it that they were counseled by Alexander McGillivray, a Creek-European, and Joseph Brant, a Mohawk who moved among whites, but in truth they developed their own strategies for confronting the invading whites. Some had customarily dealt with Europeans and wished to preserve British trade; others derived their organizational strength from a militant religious nativism. They stood in the way of the white advance. In 1782 Henry Brackcnridgc of Pittsburgh expressed a common white sentiment when he wrote: "I am so far from thinking the Indians have a right to the soil, that not having made better use of it for many hundred years, I conceive they have forfeited all pretence to claim, and ought to be driven from it."[41]

Before that task could be undertaken, however, the power of government had to be reaffirmed.

The Power of Government

The conjuncture of such frightening events galvanized the disciples of the wartime nationalists and one-time enthusiasts of revolutionary state politics, who now "shared in the impression that the great American experiment was going wrong," to reclaim what they feared was rapidly slipping from their grasp.[42]

They did so by grasping an opportunity—codified in Article 1, Section 10 of the Constitution—to strip the states of the "powers that had wreaked such havoc in postrevolutionary politics: the power to coin money, to emit bills of credit, to make anything but gold and silver coin legal tender, to pass laws impairing the obligation of contracts, or to lay any import or export duties."[43] A national government of states with enumerated powers replaced a confederated government of states, but at both levels government's intrusive reach, particularly into the economic marketplace, was sharply curtailed. Majoritarian democracy, which a generation of progressive historians identified as victim in the constitutional consensus, fell before "elitist democracy." Classical republican philosophy weakened before the acknowledgment that self-interest better suited the character of individual North Americans in pursuit of gain.[44]

Unlike English revolutionaries of 1688, who had restored ancient liberties, American revolutionaries of 1776 spoke of traditional liberties but embraced modernity in their political thought. This difference, Michael P. Zuckert argues, perhaps best explains their behavior in the postrevolutionary era. The Constitution validated the decade-long struggle of the nationalists, which had commenced in the often vitriolic debates over revolutionary finance and deepened with the gentry's shame over European disdain for the young country's venture in self-government. Federalist critics of the confederation of state governments had their own definition of *justice,* which for them constituted a substantive measure by which government must be judged. State legislatures violated the principle when they passed unjust laws that intruded into private contracts or printed paper money.[45]

In the sometimes fierce exchanges in the state legislatures opponents of the Constitution invoked revolutionary rhetoric, but the votes that counted were those of the gentry. In Virginia and New York, where public sentiment against ratification of the Constitution ran strong, the gentry were able to intimidate the legislative naysayers. Others very quickly learned the art of the political compromise that effectively relinquishes little. James Madison promoted the Bill of Rights not out of conviction but as a means of calming public anxieties and persuading antifederalists that the amendments constituted a fundamental compromise. In truth, the antifederalists deserved the accolade of the Founders, since "they did not fail to *see* the opportunity for American nationhood the Federalists seized so gloriously, but they could not join in grasping it."[46]

In the course of things, once-vigorous opponents of a stronger national government acknowledged that weakness at the top was a prelude to disaster. Jeffersonian Republicans, ideological heirs to the antifederalists, acquiesced in the Constitution in order to gain access to the national political arena. Lance Banning explains their motive and how it affected the first great political debate: "Paradoxically, then, it was the appearance of a deeply felt opposition to the policies of our first administration which assured the quick acceptance of the Constitution that had been committed to its care." As much as the empowered federalists, "the opposition had to have an unchallengeable constitution on which it could rely."[47]

As Madison had once feared, there was no ridding national politics of interest groups even as others spoke of an autonomous government unshackled from their machinations. Frankly, there was another disturbing issue here. In the revolutionary elections and in those in the 1780s, the tendency had been a reversal of the late colonial practice of high incumbency. Arresting this trend was a Federalist goal, yet, as Madison himself admitted, there was little way of predicting that the "better sorts" who served in the national government might not also weary of the demands of office. As things turned out, the first Congress did have a high proportion of propertied and influential men who had disparaged the democratization of state politics.[48]

In the Constitution and the symbolic influence it conveyed they were able to reaffirm their place in the persevering hierarchical society. Ordinary citizens required guidance, those who looked for a better life, the space and opportunity the West would provide. There, not only the laborer and the speculator but the nation staked its claim to identity and success. Before the revolution, the western question had sharply divided colonials; the war and its democratic passions had brought social incquities and demands from below for greater participation in government. During the war the expansionists had managed to undermine the political base of the antiexpansionists. Franklin knew the importance of the interior domain when he pressed hard for the Mississippi as the boundary in the peace negotiations; George Washington encapsulated its political meaning when he spoke of a "rising empire."[49]

The Whiskey Rebellion

In the West, the federal government exercised legal but not effective dominion over a vast patrimony where settler and speculator demanded law and order. In these remote and often fractious places of tremendous natural endowment, the United States would be able to realize the "empire of reason." There, communities became territories and territories, states. The historic evil that befell republics—expansion into alien places and rule over discordant and alien peoples, thus requiring imperial dominion—could be avoided.

The reality of the western country was particularistic societies where universalist principles were localized in fact, where the inequities of the East were replicated in frontier towns, where opportunists often did as well as the industrious, and where antislavery laws coexisted with a virulent and persistent racism. Frontiers have their own social dynamic, and the western country displayed the ambiguities that yet frustrate governments in dealing with peoples on the fringe. Whites dispossessed Indians but fought among themselves. Whites became Indianized. The West had its promoters and visionaries, who championed development and change, and its localists, who resisted innovation. A national government that dispensed lands to settler and speculator, and to its soldier-citizens, and that set aside public lands for the support of education, was also a government that could use its power in a repressive manner. The West had to be conquered before it could be developed.[50]

President Washington's calculated use of force was a defining moment in his presidency, as critical as his response to the European war between France and Great Britain that erupted in 1793, a reaction to events in Europe and on the North Atlantic. Fundamental principles of neutral rights were at stake. In his response, the president's purpose was undeniably political. The Farewell Address, remembered for its warnings about "entangling alliances," probably ensured the election of Vice-President John Adams as his successor. In any event, a military response would have been risky. Nor would it have resolved the fundamental issues.

The putative threat to national security in the western country was a different matter. Washington's decision to use force against the Whiskey rebels of western Pennsylvania involved no direct threat to federal power or national honor. The president chose a military confrontation for other purposes. Here was a battle that could be won, in a place where a military response could affirm the legitimacy of government and at the same time the legitimacy of the use of power. Western Pennsylvanians refused to pay an excise tax on corn liquor. Any federal officer who dared try to collect the tax risked life and limb. But the implications of such defiance went far beyond western Pennsylvania. Washington recognized what was at stake when he wrote, "The western states stand as it were on a pivot; the touch of a feather would almost incline them any way."[51] Washington and Hamilton resolved to make an example of the western Pennsylvanians.

The first task, however, was another campaign against the Indians. Unlike the disastrous forays of 1790 and 1791, that of 1794 under General Anthony Wayne got under way in a more purposeful and professional manner, demonstrating Washington's predilection for drill and maneuvers before commitment to battle. Wayne drilled his troops relentlessly for more than a year before venturing deep into Indian country in the Ohio valley. The preparation bore fruit in the summer of 1794, when Wayne's army won a stunning victory in the Battle of Fallen Timbers. In the following year, the United States negotiated a treaty with the British (the Jay Treaty) providing for formal British relinquishment of the northwest forts and another with the Indians (the Treaty of Greenville) abating the Indian threat in the Ohio country.

None of this mitigated the president's determination to set an example for those who defied legal authority on the frontier. Some of the rebellious westerners tried to secure British support in a secret meeting with the British minister, George Hammand. But Hammond and Hamilton had already established an informal understanding about improving Anglo-American relations, and Hammond rebuffed the westerners. Farther south, Kentuckians were in arms over navigation rights on the Mississippi River. Rumors of a separate state in Creek country founded by Georgians circulated. Whiskey rebels were not alone in their defiance of federal authority, but they were, indisputably, more vulnerable. Moreover, they did not respond to peaceful overtures. "Forbearance," the president wrote Hamilton, "seems to have had no other effect than to increase the disorder."[52]

The Whiskey Rebellion was an armed uprising in western Pennsylvania that began in mid-July 1794 when fifty armed men descended on the house of John Neville, the federal excise tax collector for western Pennsylvania, to demand his resignation and the surrender of his records on domestically distilled liquors. Neville refused and in the affray a man was killed. The following day between four hundred and eight hundred locals returned; there was more shooting, and others were killed. In the following weeks seven thousand western Pennsylvanians trooped into Pittsburgh, site of a federal arsenal. Other violent confrontations erupted in Hagerstown, Maryland; Carlisle, Pennsylvania; and the Virginia and Kentucky backcountry. In a reprise of the political agitation surrounding the Stamp Act crisis of 1765, Friends of Liberty associations sprang up, their leaders assailing Washington, Hamilton, and the central government for the arbitrary imposition of an "internal" tax in phrases their forebears had employed to denounce George III and Parliament. Washington resolved to make the Whiskey rebels pay for their defiance. He nationalized 12,950 militiamen from New Jersey, Pennsylvania, Maryland, and Virginia and took personal command of this "Watermelon Army." Visibly stung by the denunciations of his autocratic style emanating from the democratic societies, Washington informed Henry Lee, who volunteered to command a force to suppress the rebellion, that he believed "the insurrection as the first *formidable* fruit of the Democratic Societies" and "if these Societies were not counteracted . . . they would shake the government to its foundation."[53]

Newspapers carried on a war of words among the fractious revolutionary heirs and the disinherited. The Friends of Liberty, for whom the Whiskey rebels were more a political convenience than they were ideological allies, railed against the Federalist tyranny and championed the revolutionary cry of freedom for ordinary people. Friends of Order related horror stories from France and referred contemptuously to the "sans culottes" of Pittsburgh and the republican ideologues who justified their lawless behavior. News that Washington intended to send an invading army into the interior precipitated acrimonious debates in eastern cities, superficially along class lines, as middle- and upper-middle-class residents warned about threats to property and order. The Watermelon Army mobilized to put down the disorders in western Kentucky may have been led by the socially prominent and genteel, but among its ordinary soldiers and militia were recent immigrants, poor conscripts, and substitutes who enlisted to earn bounties. Washington was inspired by this "army of the constitution," volunteers who understood "the true principles of government and liberty . . . [and stood as] ready to maintain the authority of the laws against licentious invasions, as they were to defend their rights against usurpation."[54]

The United States fought its first serious internal war with gentlemen on both sides of the ideological battle commanding armies of the dispossessed against the dispossessed. Undeniably, one legacy of the Whiskey Rebellion was the affirmation of central authority and the reaffirmation of its inland "rising empire." A more consequential one was the party politics that drew their rancor and strength from the factionalism engendered in the Federalist decade. Washington had won a Pyrrhic victory, however. Localism not only survived but flourished. In the aftermath, the president renewed his attacks on the democratic societies. Allowed to continue, he wrote, "they will destroy the government of this country."[55]

Indeed, the concern over national security and order diverted Hamilton from his economic program and calls into question his reputation as the Founders' "leading champion of economic growth." Indisputably, Hamilton's renowned reports on manufactures, public credit, and a national bank constituted a major contribution to early economic planning, "but economic development was far from foremost among Hamilton's objectives. He sought above all the stability and staying power of the national government."[56]

Madison and especially Jefferson expressed surprise at such priorities. Their reaction was another indicator of the divisions now firmly and, presumably, irrevocably set between two generations of revolutionaries, between those who spoke of order and those who retained their faith in liberty. As political alignments had yet to assume precise party affiliation, ideological distinctions and groupings yet served as a means to carry out political goals.[57]

Until a generation of American revolutionaries proved the contrary, philosophers had generally agreed that a republic could not survive as an empire—Rome was often cited as example—because those who transformed a republic into an empire would inevitably find a reason to subvert domestic liberties in order to maintain it. Madison in the *Federalist Papers* came to a different conclusion: "Extend the sphere . . . and you make it less probable that a majority of the whole will have a common motive to invade the rights of other citizens."[58]

If a society's most ambitious and opportunistic members dispersed over a larger realm, this argument held, there would be less likelihood of conflict. Dispersing the population had yet another pragmatic benefit. In the revolutionary age, immigration slowed, and although U.S. society was relatively homogeneous, divisions over ethnic and religious issues persisted. At the constitutional convention, the debate over representation in Congress (by state or by population) went beyond the large state-small state conflict; it also involved antagonism between those states where slavery persisted and those where it had been abolished. Economic interests predominated in these constitutional quarrels, but the character of the debate (and the later efforts by the Federalists in 1798 to make it more difficult for immigrants to become citizens) revealed that political leaders were also concerned about a pluralistic society, where individuals identified with ethnic or religious groups.[59]

John Adams articulated their fears. Years later, he tried to explain the dangers of unrestrained liberty to Jefferson: "You certainly never felt the Terrorism excited by [Edmund] Genet [the French minister, whom Washington refused to receive], in 1793, when ten thousand People in the Streets of Philadelphia, day after day, threatened to drag Washington out of his House, and effect a Revolution in the Government, or compell it to declare War in favour of the French Revolution, and against England."[60]

Contemporaries sometimes misunderstood Adams's ruminations about the young republic's condition and its prospects as an indication of latent monarchist beliefs. Jefferson was not unmindful of the dangers. He expressed similar alarm in 1799 about the admission of vessels from revolutionary Saint

Domingue into U.S. ports. But his understanding of the social metaphors and customs so vital to the survival of the Virginia gentility in a world of small farmers proved more useful than Adams's horror stories about liberty run amok. In a republic, public leaders must be persons of merit and stature and character; they must not comport themselves in the manner and style of the privileged. The revolutionary yearning for liberty was a cry of the past and thus of history, but history is a process: the revolution was not yet complete.[61]

Liberty need not be a prelude to disorder or anarchy, Jefferson recognized. Liberty could be as readily enlisted as order in a national cause. Washington had spoken of a "rising empire" in the West and had invoked order to subdue it, but Jefferson realized that empire by using power even as he spoke of the "realm of liberty."

Part 2 The Revolution from Below

Forced to fight the internal and external enemies of the French Republic, I
made war with courage, honor, and loyalty. I never swerved from the rules
of justice toward my greatest enemies; I have tried . . . to soften the horrors
of war, to spare men's blood. . . . Often, after a victory, I welcomed as
brothers those who the preceding day were under the colors of the enemy.
By forgetting their errors and faults I wanted to make the cause of liberty
legitimate and sacred to even its ardent enemies.
François-Dominique Toussaint-Louverture (1801)

Nous c'est nanchon la guè! Ou pas tendé canon' m tiré?
We are a nation of war! Don't you hear my cannon firing?
Haitian proverb

If this combustion [Haitian revolt] can be introduced among us under any
veil whatever, we have to fear it.
Thomas Jefferson (1799)

We purchase coffee from her [Haiti], and pay her for it; but we interchange
no consuls or ministers. . . . And why? Because the peace of eleven states
will not permit the fruits of a successful negro insurrection to be exhibited
among them. . . . It will not permit the fact to be seen, and told, that for the
murder of their masters and mistresses, they are to find friends among the
white people of these United States.
Senator Thomas Hart Benton (1825)

4

The Caribbean on the Eve of the Haitian Revolution

Two contradictory realities about slavery complicate our efforts to understand the revolutionary age in the Americas. The first was the confluence of universalist values that resonated from the ideological, philosophical, legal, and religious currents of the age. Just as the American Revolution undermined the rational basis for monarchy, the transformations in Protestantism and Western thought challenged once seemingly unshakable views about slavery and especially about its victims. If denial of natural rights and liberties justified rebellion for the Christian slaveholder, what of the slave? Curiously, the problems of maintaining and controlling a large captive labor population offered less persuasive evidence for those who looked to the abolition of slavery than the belief that slavery was an impediment to human destiny. In the 1760s and 1770s, in both Europe and the Americas, an antislavery ideology emerged that drew its strength from intellectual and religious currents and the prospects for improved living standards of ordinary people. Enlightenment thinkers, often torn between their convictions about individual autonomy and their desire for a rational social order with its gradations of rank, were increasingly persuaded that slavery was the least suitable institution for the creation of the progressive society.[1]

Guillaume Thomas François Raynal (the French priest dismissed from his parish for his radical views and principal author of the multivolume *Histoire des Deux Indes*) expressed the befuddlement of a generation in his assessment of slavery in the Americas. Human progress, self-interest, and the pursuit of wealth, he believed, had accompanied human degradation. Raynal conceded the intimate link between slave labor, the cultivation of lands, and British supremacy in the imperial wars with France and Spain. "But without this labor, these lands, acquired at such high costs, would remain uncultivated." The productivity of the Americas and slavery were intertwined, he conceded, but his convictions about slavery remained unchanged. "Well then, let them lie fallow, if it means that to make these lands productive, man must be reduced to brutishness, whether he be the man who buys, or he who sells, or he who is sold."[2]

There was a second reality, especially disturbing to those who believed that revolution in human thought and certainly in deed would inevitably doom slavery. In the Americas slavery had grown stronger, the slave more degraded. Slavery had posed a legal and moral problem in European thought from the age of Aristotle. Slavery rarely preoccupied those who discussed the institution in the New World until the eighteenth century. Productive economies required a labor force. Supplying and maintaining that labor force demanded increasingly violent mechanisms. The industrial revolution of the age inspired the opportunistic slaveholder as well as the republican ideologue who vowed to bring down monarchical government.[3]

By 1776, the New World contained 2.5 million slaves, laboring in workshops, mines, mills, households, and fields. They provided the labor force for the most profitable cargo in transatlantic trade—sugar, cotton, coffee, and cacao from the Caribbean; tobacco, rice, and indigo from North America; gold and sugar from the Spanish kingdoms of the mainland. Over 350 years the great maritime nations had brought ten million Africans to the New World in an involuntary human migration central to the economic development of the New World (see table 1).[4]

Where African slavery was ill-suited for agricultural labor, as in colonial New England, the trade nonetheless stimulated shipbuilding and banking and provided a lucrative career for enterprising merchants. A triangular trade— textiles, firearms, and rum to Africa, slaves to the West Indies, and sugar to Europe and the ports of North America—had made fortunes for men of commerce in Britain and France and sustained a thriving illicit trade in Boston. From its profits, the English built canals, railroads, factories. With independence and a more diversified economy, the United States depended on cotton

Table 1   Slave Population of the Americas, 1770

	Slaves	*Total Population*
British America	878,000	2,600,000
North America	450,000	2,100,000
Caribbean	428,000	500,000
Portuguese Brazil	700,000	2,000,000
French West Indies	379,000	430,000
Spanish America	290,000	12,144,000
Spanish Caribbean	50,000	144,000
Spanish Mainland	240,000	12,000,000
Dutch Caribbean	75,000	90,000
Danish Caribbean	18,000	25,000

Source: Adapted from Blackburn, *Overthrow of Colonial Slavery,* 5

picked by slave labor, its chief export to English textile mills. From 1700 the vigorous expansion of trade in these commodities and the enormous wealth they generated brought the European powers into often destructive wars for trade. The trafficking in African slaves accompanied this growth, creating presumably inseparable and ineradicable bonds between slavery, empire, and the modernization of the Atlantic world in the eighteenth century.[5]

Race and Color in Plantation Societies

The American Revolution reached southward into the Caribbean, affecting its political, economic, and social rhythms in several ways. For one thing, the American struggle for independence was a world war in which the Caribbean served as a theatre (principally in engagements on the high seas) and, more important, as a source of supply for the revolutionary cause. With commercial treaties or secret arrangements with Britain's European rivals, U.S. shippers gained access to Caribbean ports and laid the foundation for a more vigorous economic policy in the aftermath of the war. Finally, the American Revolution provided the Caribbean with a political ideology that struck directly at empire and, by implication, at the social and economic institutions of empire.[6]

But the legacy of this transference of revolutionary ideology was different than in North America. In the Caribbean, the pattern of European empire took a form strikingly divergent from that of the Atlantic seaboard. Before the

American Revolution, two prototypical kinds of colonies prevailed in the New World. The first were settlement colonies (with largely European populations and social characteristics), which predominated on the mainland. The second, the exploitation colony (some of which began as settlement colonies), satisfied the economic and social priorities of the plantation rather than the social priorities of transplanted European communities. Exploitation colonies appeared on the mainland, and pockets of settler communities existed in the Caribbean islands dominated by plantations. By the mid-eighteenth century, the economic interdependence of these colonies had created presumably strong and lasting ties. After 1763, when mainland British Americans began agitating over metropolitan commercial restraints, they sensed sympathy on the part of the West Indians. Raising the flag of rebellion against empire, the patriots were persuaded that the grumbling English planters in the Caribbean would rally to their cause.

In reality, the superficial economic and political compatibility between mainland British America and the West Indies belied their fundamental differences. British North America was a congeries of fractious and often disputatious colonies, but revolutionary ideology and a sense of common cause had reinforced the faith in community and the capability to replace one master with a government of their own making. West Indians, by contrast, had settlements but, when measured by European standards and experience, no unifying sense of community. More vulnerable and more dependent than the mainland colonists, disaffected planters in the British West Indies had yet another fear. They were a white minority in a black and colored world. If Englishmen in the West Indies rallied to the cause of liberty, they would have to arm their slaves. Reacting angrily to their timid response to the Stamp Act, John Adams roared, "But can no punishment be devised for Barbados and Port Royal in Jamaica? For their base desertion of the cause of liberty? . . . Their mean, timid resignation to slavery? . . . They deserve to be made slaves to their own Negroes. But they live under the scorching sun, which melts them, dissipates their spirits and relaxes their nerves. Yet their Negroes seem to have more of the spirit of liberty."[7]

Adams may have sensed the distortions that economic realities and racial dynamics gave to revolutionary ideology in the British West Indies, a society where those at the top felt themselves as trapped as the masses beneath them. The plantation system had taken a firm hold in the French and British Caribbean. Plantation economies produced staples for export. By the mid-eighteenth century, the Caribbean plantations' labor force came primarily from Africa. The system generated enormous wealth. But political control resided in the metropole. Such general characteristics could be found in plantations from the Mason-Dixon line to the Brazilian northeast. What made Caribbean and not British American mainland plantations the model for the plantation complex of the eighteenth century was the dynamic of one staple (sugar), the comparatively large number of slaves on a typical plantation (fifty or more), the use of gang labor, and the large proportion of slaves (75 to 90%) in the population. Unlike British North America and certainly the United States, most free persons were either black or colored, and growth in the slave population came principally from imports, not from natural increase in population.[8]

Slavery existed throughout the hemisphere, but the numbers of slaves in the Caribbean had a profound psychological effect on West Indies slaveholders, who willingly took up the political cause against monarchy. But Caribbean slaveholders uniformly rejected the social changes they perceived in even the mildest proposals for amelioration of slavery even as they acknowledged its brutality. Barbadian planters, for example, were as outraged as Adams and his patriot contemporaries by metropolitan colonial measures. They suffered doubly from what they considered intemperate abolitionist attacks. Yet, as Jack Greene points out, "their resentment was mitigated by an acute awareness of their dependence upon the metropolis for protection against their own slaves."[9]

In the early years of plantation agriculture, planters had tended to use indentured white, not African, labor, but they were inevitably frustrated by the difficulties of retaining white workers. For one thing, white servants possessed limited rights, recognized by law and included in their contract. When they had served their labor-time, they could aspire to a plot of land and become small farmers. By the early eighteenth century, British mercantilists were persuaded that white laborers in the West Indies created opportunities for rival manufacturing in the islands and thus fomented separatist thought. Moreover, the supply of white labor was inadequate. Whites could escape. From a purely economic standpoint, particularly where shipping costs were concerned, the enslavement of European vagrants, indentures, convicts, or war captives would have been more advantageous than the costly enterprise of importing Africans into the West Indies. But such a choice was inconceivable, even in an age when European states often placed severe restrictions on liberty or took the life of the individual, for Europeans' collective social consciousness now rejected the enslavement of other Europeans.[10]

With the decline of Dutch West Indian plantations, the French became the rivals of the British in Caribbean sugar plantation colonies. In the early days of settlement (as was the case with the British), the intention of the French was to populate France's West Indian possessions (principally Guadeloupe and Martinique) with white settlers. The first colonists were subsistence farmers who had an economic equality. When sugar was extensively developed in the 1650s, its impact profoundly changed French Caribbean society. In the twenty-five years after 1644, the number of sugar plantations on Guadeloupe rose from one to more than one hundred. By 1789, the French West Indian plantation complex (now including Saint Domingue, acquired in 1697) numbered fifteen hundred estates.[11]

Enjoying the support of the French government, the first generation of French sugar planters in the West Indies rapidly displaced the white farmers from their small holdings. Most of these dispossessed small landholders left the islands. Those who remained formed the new poor of the towns or went into foothills or unclaimed areas to survive on small plots. As in the British islands, planters imported white indentures (*engagés*), who were paid better than wage laborers in France. The practice died away in the eighteenth century as African slaves replaced them. By then, the social patterns reflected both economic and racial dynamics. Whites divided into *grands blancs* ("big whites") and *petit blancs* ("little whites"), but whatever class divisions developed from these categories were marginal when compared with another social reality. French West Indian society divided by race—black, white, and colored—and by caste—slaves, free persons of color, and whites.[12]

Sugar required large tracts and a captive labor force. The reason had less to do with notions of white debility in the tropics than with demands of the crop and the parallel social and economic structure of exploiters and exploited. When the sugar revolution hit Barbados, the planters used indentured whites, then mixed indentured and slave labor in the fields. In time, however, Africans replaced whites in unskilled tasks and then in the skilled labor market. In such circumstances, small farmers could not survive. Sugar drove them under. Barbados in 1645 had twice as many whites as slaves. Twenty years later, it had 745 plantation owners and more than 80,000 African slaves. Planters preferred white laborers but were unable (or unwilling) to provide them with plots of land once their indentures were over. Those white laborers who remained were ill-treated; their contemporaries fled to other islands in the dwindling hope of acquiring a small farm. Poor whites migrated from Barbados to Nevis or Guiana or Trinidad or even the Carolinas. "Everywhere" writes Eric

Williams, "they were pursued and dispossessed by the same inexorable economic force—sugar."[13]

Though it lagged behind that of the British and the French West Indies, Cuban plantation sugar began to develop rapidly after the British occupation of 1762. In Cuba, the British invaders found a small but aggressive insular oligarchy composed of planters who looked to sugar to get rich. Cuba's sugar planters, unlike those in the British and French islands, operated virtually without government approval or support. Responding to the growing market for sugar, Cuba's Creoles took advantage of the British intrusion and ambitiously expanded production, obtaining large numbers of slaves through British traders. The island possessed all the attributes needed for sugar production—a fertile soil with proximity to seaports, forests to supply lumber to build and fire the boilers, cattle to feed slaves and to haul goods, and skilled labor to fabricate tools. In the three decades after the British seizure of Havana, wrote Manuel Moreno Fraginals in his epic study of Cuban sugar, "all the factors braking sugar development were eliminated and the island was transformed into the top world producer. Sugarmill towers broke into our fields and became part of the scenery."[14]

Before the end of the seventeenth century, then, West Indian islands were becoming stratified plantation communities, the social demarcations determined not only by wealth but also by color. For the ruling whites, racial identity and power were synonymous. On the basis of landed wealth and political influence, the Caribbean social hierarchy appeared to replicate that of Europe on the eve of revolution. In Europe, however, social status depended as much on family status as on wealth; in the Caribbean, wealth and racial identity assumed a critical role in determining status. African slavery and the plantation system formed a region in which white indentures and black slaves labored collectively in the fields and skilled whites in the towns lived as precariously as country laborers. The pace of social stratification varied from island to island, of course, but by the mid-eighteenth century white immigration had fallen sharply and the numbers of Africans and colored had risen dramatically. Poorer whites who could not compete for land joined small landholders, petty shopkeepers, artisans, servants, and bankrupted planters in an outmigration.[15]

The whites who remained enjoyed the social distinction of a "leveling up": they benefited from the absenteeism of planters and now served as managers or owners of black laborers. The dominance of this small white elite—planters who remained on the islands, lawyers, merchants, clergymen—extended into every economic and political activity on the islands. Mobility for a more numerous group of poorer whites—clerks, small traders, and overseers, for example—improved somewhat, especially when these possessed the minimum property qualifications for voting. Racial affiliation bound these whites to a social hierarchy determined to retain plantation slavery and to prevent any erosion of their power by the broadening of opportunities for free persons of color—former slaves who had purchased their freedom or had been manumitted. The latter often found themselves not only stigmatized but denied access to public office or privileges such as jury service or public relief. Legally free and thus entitled under British law and tradition to the fundamental rights enjoyed by whites, the free person of color could not cast off the inferiority ascribed to black slaves.[16]

British settlements in the West Indies became plantation societies—sugar factories largely owned by absentee landlords or ruled by resident white slaveholders who constituted England's overseas "shabby aristocrats," pretentious frontier nabobs who imagined riches in sugar and a comfortable life for themselves in England. In the meantime, they lived precariously, burdened with debt and fearful of the numbers of blacks, colored, and poor whites among them. In such a world, maintenance of the labor force and preservation of the social order required discipline. Slaves had to be reminded of their task. That slave labor was considered too critical to the livelihood of planters (who had no recourse to white indentures) to justify physical abuse except as a last resort was largely a myth. Here and there, an English lord may have extended an uncommon philanthropy, but the permanently enslaved endured a much harder life than the white indentures. As one slave declared, "The Devil was in the English-man, that he makes everything work; he makes the Negro work, the Ass work, the Wood work, the Water work, and the Winde work."[17]

As the eighteenth-century plantation sugar economy tightened its hold on the West Indies, proslavery ideology assumed a spiritual purpose: explaining why it was necessary in *British* dominions for this kind of society to persevere. Understanding this transformation helps to explain why the antislavery movement in Europe and the New World, which appeared to have broad appeal in the age of the American Revolution, confronted such challenges. True, the abolitionists, especially those in Great Britain, became more persuasive and more influential in the years following the American Revolution, but so did British Caribbean slaveholders, for whom slavery was less a question of morality than one of power. European values, whether informed by pity or by prudence, deteriorated into callousness and indifference.[18]

Sugar plantations required a labor force, which, the planters averred, had to be constantly replenished by the slave trade. Planters preferred males to females and were inattentive to the physical well-being of their charges. Such attitudes befuddled economic rationalists in London but made sense to the West Indian slaveholders. A healthy and vigorous black population threatened a *slave* labor force and the preservation of a structured social order of white over black. In railing against abolition as a deprivation of property rights, Caribbean planters were no different from slaveholders in mainland British America. The overwhelming numbers of blacks in their midst sharply intensified their thinking about slavery. In 1760, for example, nowhere in continental British America (save the low-country areas of South Carolina and Georgia) did blacks outnumber whites. But in the West Indies, the racial imbalances were overwhelming and, to the whites, frightening. In war their situation was especially perilous, as the West Indians pressed London for naval protection against French invasion, saying that the numbers of white militiamen suitable for colonial defense were inadequate. Few dared to arm their African slaves. The governor of Antigua blamed the problem on the expansion of plantation agriculture and the depletion of small farmers. Efforts to encourage Scots and Palatines to immigrate were fruitless, as were fines levied on white planters for their failure to retain white servants. Indeed, when whites served as militiamen, they often proved unreliable or, more unsettling, resentful of being called "to defend the . . . wealthy . . . at the expence of their lives."[19]

Slaves fled to avoid the brutality of labor on sugar plantations, to keep from starving, to keep from being worked to death, or (as the legendary runaway Esteban Montejo in late-nineteenth-century Cuba) to gain liberty. Newcomers escaped into the countryside. Creole Africans went into the cities. Their reasons for flight were similar—a remorseless and oppressive labor throughout the year. In July and August came holing; then came the planting and manuring of the cane before dry weather in November and December; afterwards, perhaps a few days of rest at Christmas before harvesting began early in the new year. During harvesting, time was essential, for sugar cane that is not quickly processed turns sour. Thus, milling and boiling went on throughout the day and into the night, with a stoppage only on Sundays and with slaves working in 16- and 18-hour shifts. After the harvesting and processing came grass-picking in the pastures or in gullies to provide feed for the cattle, which provided the offal for the summer manuring.[20]

Such accounts might have provoked sympathy and even calls for action among London's coterie of eighteenth-century abolitionists, but in the Caribbean, universal values resonated to local beliefs. These were slaves, and slaves were property. That reality permeated British West Indian society and allowed those who ruled it to shape colonial laws accordingly. A Bermudian act of 1730, for example, acknowledged that English law prescribed loss of life and estate for the murder of a slave but then noted: "But here in his Majesties Colonies and plantations in America the Cases and Circumstances of things are wonderfully altered."[21] Horror stories about the severity of the slave regimen circulated in England, but the planters had their own interest groups to divert attention. Indeed, the economic uncertainties faced by the sugar planters sometimes generated an unexpected sympathy for them in Parliament. Not a few were absentee landlords, ensconced in England. They joined with slavers to protect their common interests. When in 1750 Horace Walpole decried "the British Senate, that temple of liberty, and bulwark of Protestant Christianity, . . . pondering methods to make more effectual that horrid traffic of selling negroes," members of Parliament (among them Edmund Burke) rallied to the planters' defense.[22]

In a similar acknowledgment of economic reality, the church accepted slavery but urged otherwise reluctant West Indian planters (who declared that propagation of the Gospel among their slaves made them more obstreperous) to provide instruction in Christianity. When the planters objected, the Society for the Propagation of the Gospel acquiesced and forbade the teaching of Christian tenets to its Barbadian slaves. In Bristol (a slaver's town), church bells tolled to celebrate the defeat of a parliamentary bill (proposed by William Wilberforce, one of the early proponents of abolitionism) ending the slave trade. Anglican clerics spoke approvingly of the slave trader John Newton, who asked for church blessing before setting out on a slave-hunting expedition to Guinea. Newton officiated over twice-daily worship services aboard ship and declared a day of fasting and prayer for the crew. Occasionally, Enlightenment rationalists—Adam Smith, for example, who declared that slavery was inefficient and expensive—joined the chorus of moral outcries, but they seemed unpersuasive. Most Britons identified the well-being of empire with the slave trade. As one slaver put it, "In a word, from this trade proceed benefits, far outweighing all, either real or pretended mischiefs and inconveniences."[23]

As an abolition movement strengthened, however, the proslavery camp required its own ideologues. Among them were two Jamaican planters and chroniclers, Edward Long and Bryan Edwards, who managed to square their

Whig values of liberty and the denunciation of executive power with defenses of slavery. Social as much as economic considerations permeated their arguments. Slaves, wrote Long, came from barbarism and threatened the social order of the island. British concepts of freedom had little relevance in the Afro-Caribbean world. In Jamaica, socially pretentious sugar planters, land-rich and capital-poor, lived fearfully amidst lower-class whites ("redlegs"), mulattoes and free colored, and African slaves. For more than fifty years after 1739, they waged an intermittent war against maroon societies (communities of escaped slaves) or defended the island against external attack.[24]

Condemning the Jamaican slaveholders' tolerance of miscegenation, Long nonetheless praised them as benevolent and attentive to their slaves. Edwards, who wrote as the slave revolt on Saint Domingue raged, was more dispassionate. Inevitably, as Jamaicans grew more alarmed over the prospect of slave rebellion, he retreated into slavery's defense: "In countries where slavery is established, the leading principle on which the government is supported is fear; or a sense of that absolute coercive necessity, which leaving no choice of action, supersedes all questions of right."[25]

He voiced the West Indian planters' inner fears about the world the slaveholders had made. Resentful of the rising chorus of abolitionist criticism yet determined to preserve the social order, they were as much exiles as the enslaved masses. Danger lurked everywhere—in the visible and violent form of natural disaster, disease, invasion, or slave insurrection. In more subtle but seemingly no less threatening ways, the slave system was imperiled by European perceptions of human corruption and social degradation throughout slave society and by white males' sexual liaisons with slave women.

Believing themselves misunderstood by their compatriots in the mother country, British West Indian slaveholders nonetheless dreamed of returning to their homeland. No matter how sumptuous or refined their lives could be in the West Indies, there remained always the longing for a baronial estate in the English countryside. Long estimated that two-thirds of the planters' children packed off to England for an education never came back to the islands. In part, this outmigration of talent could be explained by the prevalence of a system of primogeniture, whereby the youngest had no incentive to return, or the better prospects offered in the metropolis. The legacy of the islands was a society bereft of a sustaining Creole elite, where the "most successful left and the least successful stayed." Even the absentees who had the means to flaunt their wealth back in England often failed to buy their way into polite society and became social misfits. Those who had sprung from the upper classes and gone off to the islands to make their fortune eased their way back into English upper-class life, of course, "but many more West Indian nabobs faced envy, ridicule, and social ostracism."[26]

Such an experience may have happened more often to Jamaicans than to the white residents of British possessions in the eastern Caribbean. Jamaica did not become British until 1655, when a Cromwellian invading force, having failed in its assault against Santo Domingo, seized the island from a beleaguered Spanish garrison. The sugar revolution did not take hold in Jamaica until the third decade of the eighteenth century, but in the next forty years the plantation system developed rapidly. By 1775, Jamaica had 50 percent of the British West Indies's population, and its productivity contributed an equal proportion to the metropolitan wealth derived from the empire's Caribbean domains.

But Jamaica was a fragmented, untamed society. Its size and its dense forests enabled runaways and maroons to maintain separate and defiant communities until the end of the century. The island retained its "frontier" cultural image. Its ruling white elite, obsessed with wealth and status, created one of the harshest slave regimes in the Caribbean and made little room in the social order for skilled whites, who might otherwise have become (as elsewhere in the British West Indies) its defenders. Jamaica on the eve of the Haitian revolution was the embodiment of social degradation and evil.[27]

The Perils from Within

The most dynamic slave plantation society in the late eighteenth century lay in the French West Indies. There prospered an economic domain where bureaucrat, merchant, and colonist presided over the most advanced methods in coffee cultivation, in the development of new varieties of cane for sugar production, and in the construction of impressive irrigation systems. Slave plantations relied on slave trade bounties and remission of duties on colonial reexports. France's richest plantation colonies—Guadeloupe, Martinique, and Saint Domingue—possessed a slave population that grew from 379,000 in 1770 to 650,000 two decades later and whose labors yielded annually more than 217 million *livres* (9 million English pounds) in exports by 1789. In that year, the export economy of the British West Indies (with a land area approximately half that of the French islands and a labor force of 480,000 slaves) realized five million pounds. Through the *exclusif*, 50 percent of the profits from colonial production went to France's mercantile and metropolitan houses. Bordeaux and Nantes owed their prosperity to commerce with French colonies.

The French West Indies were not only prosperous but well prepared to maintain the security of a large and vital slave labor force. If necessary, colonial administrators could organize and arm virtually all free males—whites and *affranchis*—between the ages of sixteen and sixty into militias to supplement the small garrisons of regulars and naval forces. French Guiana (with only 10,000 slaves) and Saint Lucia and Trinidad (acquired in the British defeat in the American Revolution) were considerably less prosperous, and Louisiana had passed into Spanish possession, but the wealth of Guadeloupe, Martinique, and Saint Domingue inspired French imperialists to believe that the dream of a reconstituted French empire in the New World could become a reality in their lifetime.

At the same time, paradoxically, monarchical France's support of the British North American revolutionaries and the achievements that came with it contributed greatly during the 1780s to rising criticism of social privilege and of the heavy costs of governance within France. Pressed, the beneficiaries of the colonial system frantically maneuvered to protect their interests. When the monarchy sought to reform colonial regulations, it was denounced for undermining the nation's prosperity, which depended on colonial wealth. In the Indies, planters spoke disparagingly of a metropolitan regime no longer capable of a rational response to their needs—relaxing the exclusif, which benefited their expanding commerce, but coupling this reform with more stringent regulations of finances and treatment of slaves—and looked to Britain and the United States for models of enlightened administration of plantation economies. In Paris, their emissaries eagerly joined political clubs, where participants talked about enlightened policies, not inherited privilege. In the islands, they complained endlessly of corrupt and meddling officials.[28]

The more visible threat to planter prosperity, then, appeared to come from without. In actuality, it lay deceptively within the slave regime. As these transatlantic debates raged between colony and metropole, French West Indian planters were inattentive to the subtle differences explaining the security of the slave regime in Virginia, which they took as their model, and their own system. Virginia's planter aristocracy built its economic foundation on slavery, but its social underpinning was a populous and deferential mass of poor whites, who could be armed and mobilized in its defense. British North America and the United States had slave revolts and maroon societies, slave conspiracies and intrigues, but whatever threat plantation slavery confronted seemed minimal when compared with what could be mobilized to suppress it. In a curious but understandable way, leaders in Virginia and elsewhere in the southern United States could afford to be less cautious in their professions about liberty and progress. The social base of their power was more secure.

For one thing, slave resistance and the means by which Caribbean slaveholders could deal with it were different. From the beginning of the European conquests, slaves had fled servitude and become maroons. The first runaway was an African-American slave brought to Hispaniola in 1502 who escaped into the mountainous interior to live with Indians. Flight, or *marronage,* became a reality wherever plantation societies grew—from the southeastern United States to Mexico, Peru, Brazil, and everywhere in the Caribbean. Though the names varied—*palenques, quilombos, mocambos, cumbes, ladeiros,* or *mambises*—maroons demonstrated that African slaves, despite their cultural or linguistic differences, were capable of creating communities in the midst of plantation societies. Some were small and vanished quickly but others persisted, grew large, and defied efforts to subdue them. In several societies—Brazil, New Granada, Cuba, Ecuador, Hispaniola, Jamaica, Mexico, and Suriname—whites unable to subdue powerful maroon communities in turn had to make peace with them, offering freedom and recognition of territorial integrity as a price for peace.[29]

Though treated no better than slaves in the British or the Spanish West Indies, Saint Domingue's Africans were less rebellious, a curiosity variously attributed to the colony's strict military government or the possibility of escape into the mountains. Compared with slaves elsewhere in the Caribbean, Saint Domingue's were more effective in their resistance—fleeing into the hills and there establishing isolated communities, with their own leaders, and barricading themselves against invaders; deserting in large numbers, especially in wartime; exchanging information so as to facilitate the theft of food; and suicide. The most serious revolt in the eighteenth century was the conspiracy of Mackandal, who rejected Christianity for African magic, united isolated maroon bands, and terrorized plantations. The French captured him in 1758 and burned him at the stake. Planters grew suspicious of any assemblages of slaves, even if the intent was to Christianize and thus, as the argument ran, pacify rebellious Africans.[30]

The prevalence of maroon societies complicated the operation of slave plantation economies, but almost nowhere did the maroons contribute significantly to bringing down the institution. Only the Haitians accomplished that goal, and they were able to do so in part because of the links between marronage and slave revolution in French Saint Domingue. Maroons in Saint Domingue were less numerous than elsewhere and, it should be added, seemingly less formidable than in Jamaica. They ill fit the designation of "restora-tionist" societies. The maroon society led by Mackandal in the 1750s is often cited as prototypically restorationist, since Mackandal possessed the essential attributes of a messiah ruling an isolated community of runaways. In actual-ity, Mackandal did not operate outside the plantation system. He invoked African traditions and religion in the hope of destroying the plantations. Among his followers were house and field slaves.[31]

In the first two decades of the eighteenth century, planters faced continual threats from maroons whose leaders motivated their followers with cries of freedom, African identity, and land. In the aftermath of the Mackandal con-spiracy, when coffee planters expanded into hills where maroons lived, the displaced maroons became more aggressive in fashioning ties with plantation slaves. There were now fewer maroon redoubts to which these slaves could flee, of course, but the "spirit of maroonage as a revolt trickled down into the consciousness of the plantation slave."[32]

Although marronage existed in the British West Indies, where slave regimes even harsher than those in the French West Indies prevailed, noth-ing comparable to the slave uprising on French Saint Domingue in 1791 oc-curred in the British Caribbean. An important consideration in explaining the Saint Domingue revolt, then, may lie, not in the severity of its slave regime, but in French thinking about what was necessary to preserve slavery. For the British, retention of slavery required ever more stringent measures to limit the possibilities of freedom. To the French, however, maintenance of a stable labor force required some reassurance of freedom. As one French official ex-plained in the 1770s, "Only the hope of liberty can sustain or animate the fi-delity of the slaves in a state of degradation and poverty and attach them to their masters, or to white blood, which amounts to the same thing."[33] He could not have imagined that the hope of liberty would unleash a violent uprising.

5

The Slave Rebellion

The North American war of independence provided an ideology and a model of republican governance. The Latin American struggle against empire, which commenced a generation after the American Revolution had ended, liberated a continent. Both inspired the replacement of colonialism with new states and dreams of building nations. Yet neither struggle achieved what the Haitians brought about in twelve years: a nation that had destroyed colonialism, ended slavery, and proclaimed racial equality. The consequences were both inspiring and frightening. Haitian revolutionaries waged guerrilla warfare against one of Europe's mightiest powers. In the course of a devastating war they not only destroyed the Caribbean's most productive economy but eliminated its ruling class—in an era of expansion of the plantation economy and an increasing dependence on slave labor from the Chesapeake to Brazil.[1]

In its origin, character, and bewildering course, the revolution from below in French Saint Domingue defies facile explanation. A triumphant slave revolt occurred in a colony that had experienced comparatively little organized resistance to the slave regime. In the earliest stages of the movement, from 1791 to 1793, its leaders were ambiguous about slavery. Toussaint-Louverture rarely spoke in ideological terms and himself sold slaves. Those Africans who in 1791 rose up on the Plaine du Nord did so in the name of king and church,

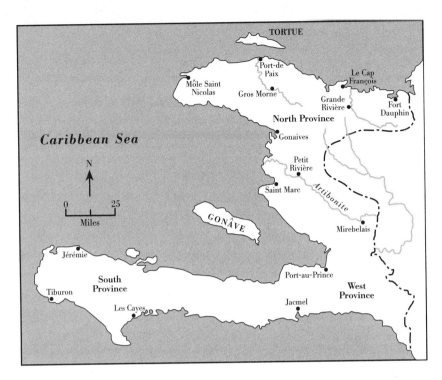

3. Saint Domingue, 1789. South Province lay to the west of West Province.

not because of the Declaration of the Rights of Man or the promises of revolutionary France (see map 3). In the British and French military intrusion that followed, some of the rebellious slaves followed their leaders and served in royalist armies dispatched by governments intent on preserving the institution of slavery. Others continued the struggle principally to repel the foreign invader. Only in the final tumultuous year did the expulsion of the white intruders and the end of the plantation slave economy in Saint Domingue become inseparable goals.[2]

The Slave Regime of Saint Domingue
Were the slaves of French Saint Domingue subject to more severe treatment than slaves in the British West Indies? If so, did their condition provide a catalyst for rebellion? French planters fell under the seventeenth-century *code noir*, which obligated them to provide both physical and spiritual care for their slaves. British Barbados and French Saint Domingue exhibited a similarity in social structure—a tiny white elite atop a larger layer of small shopkeepers, poor freedmen, and a massive slave base. In living style and cultural prefer-

ences, English and French planters displayed strikingly similar characteristics: "a peculiar compound of imitation and adaptation, civilized tastes and colonial crudities, elegance and extravagance, formality and licentiousness." But the code noir (1685) and the contemporaneous Barbadian slave code (1660) created very different legacies in race relations.[3]

Slaves were brutally treated under both regimes, though the death rate in the French islands seems to have been higher. Hilliard d'Auberteuil reckoned that more than 500,000 of the 800,000 slaves brought to Saint Domingue in the century after 1680 perished, agreeing with Père Labat, the seventeenth-century observer, that one-third died during their first few years in the colony. Gabriel Debien, surveying plantation records and official correspondence for eighteenth-century Saint Domingue, concluded that mortality rates between the third and eighth year of importation reached 50 percent. The causes of this excessive mortality were explained not so much by the brutal treatment of slaves as by other conditions, both psychological and physical: despondency, overwork, disease, and nutritional deficiency. The slave trade discouraged any improvement. "In such a system," concludes a student of the French sugar business, "the death of an individual slave was significant only for its economic consequences."[4]

Typologies of slave resistance and rebellion are numerous. Virtually every generalization must be qualified when assessing the origins of the Saint Domingue revolution. Brutal conditions, large numbers of Africans, divisions indicating weakness among ruling elements, and slave frustration—all are identifiable as critical elements in prerevolutionary Saint Domingue. Yet, assessed without taking into consideration the external ideological and political forces pressing on the colony, they do not satisfactorily explain the origins, course, and conclusion of the Haitian Revolution. Saint Domingue's slave regime may have been as harsh as those of the British or Dutch West Indies, but its slaves were less organized and less rebellious. The cause of Saint Domingue's slave rebellion was not so much in the repressiveness of its slave system but in the chaotic social, economic, and political dynamics reverberating in the colony during the 1770s and 1780s.[5]

A disturbing reality for those who ruled in the West Indies was the growing reliance on free colored and even African slaves for the defense of the plantation system. From the earliest days, free coloreds and slaves were used in military activities and as police in the European colonies in the West Indies. By the mid-seventeenth century, colonial governments were regularly employing Indians and African slaves in defense of the islands. As white immigrants became scarcer with the expanding plantation system, the use of Africans and free coloreds in the militia became more crucial. A British soldier posted to the West Indies was considered to be under a virtual death sentence. The legacy for the British islands was the Africanization of the military and, more subtly, the expansion of African slavery into domestic service, trade, huckstering, and fishing. As poorer whites were pushed out, slaves and free coloreds moved up a notch or two in the social order.[6]

Slaves were generally considered unreliable and untrustworthy as soldiers. A French description of their behavior during the siege of Martinique during the Seven Years' War refers to them as lazy and inspired only by the opportunity to escape the drudgery of plantation work or to wear a uniform. If promised freedom as a reward for military service, however, they proved better soldiers. Even so, where few free coloreds were available, it was necessary to use slaves in wartime, though in the British islands, authorities were careful to place them in companies with white militiamen. The problem of reliability was apparently less serious in the French islands, where the prospect of manumission after military service was more certain, and the status of free coloreds there improved dramatically. In the seventeenth century, a French observer wrote of the Africans of Saint Domingue: "They are valiant and hardy in the face of danger, and, during all the desperate encounters which our colonists of Saint Christopher Island have had from time to time with the English, they have been no less redoubtable to this nation than their masters."[7]

Over the years, Saint Domingue's slaves and free coloreds had developed a familiarity with arms. Plantation owners released trusted Africans for military and police duties. As their numbers grew, so did apprehension about slaves in possession of weapons in a colony where they greatly outnumbered whites and free coloreds. By 1762, free coloreds and whites served in colonial defense, but planters resisted creating separate military units of slaves. After the war with Britain, they formed regiments to pursue runaways who had escaped to the Spanish portion of the island, where labor conditions were considerably less severe. After the French entered the American Revolution in 1778, a British fleet assaulted Martinique, where the French mobilized 850 free coloreds and 2,000 Africans in the island's defense. Records listed the free coloreds as militiamen; the Africans probably were servants to the troops. The following year the French dispatched an expedition against Savannah under Count Charles Hector d'Estaing that included more than five hundred free Africans and mulattoes from the French West Indies, among them Henri Christophe.[8]

Race, Color, and Social Status

As the economic productivity of Saint Domingue advanced, generating a wealth uncommon in the British and the Spanish Caribbean, the more tolerant racial and social ambience of the colony in the early eighteenth century diminished. Grands blancs and petits blancs became increasingly alienated, largely because the latter sensed declining opportunities for advancement in an economy where property ownership translated into social status. In the competitive atmosphere the petits blancs rapidly became a marginal labor force, as the grands blancs preferred affranchis—free coloreds and free blacks—to fill many of the skilled jobs in the expanding plantation economy. Elsewhere in the Caribbean, the status of artisan was ordinarily the highest social achievement of the free coloreds, but in Saint Domingue the free coloreds included French-educated planters, tradesmen, artisans, and small landholders. Affranchis and even slaves spoke derisively of the "little whites" as *faux blancs* or *blanchets*. Free coloreds were an intermediary caste, but their rapid advancement occasionally alarmed even the grands blancs. Some became plantation owners in the coffee-growing areas of the mountainous West and South Provinces. The social implications of their rapidly acquired wealth, wrote a colonial official in the 1750s, were ominous: "These men are beginning to fill the colony and it is the greatest perversion to see them, their numbers increasing among the whites. . . . These coloreds . . . imitate the style of the whites and try to wipe out all memory of their original state."[9]

Restrictions against the free coloreds followed in the next decade: in 1764, prohibitions against the practice of medicine and pharmacology; in the following year, against employment as court clerks, bailiffs, and notaries. By 1788, free coloreds were obliged to file for a permit to conduct any trade save farming. They could not legally enter France and were denied the right of assembly, refused noble status, and effectively barred from the regular military. Whites called on the free coloreds to apprehend runaways and police the slaves. The collective rage of the free coloreds found expression in a 1790 pamphlet: "[We are] a class of men born French, but degraded by cruel and vile prejudices and laws."[10]

With its forty thousand whites, thirty thousand free coloreds, and five hundred thousand African slaves, the colony possessed the tiered social structure ordinarily found in sugar plantation economies, and its rulers just as determinedly used the social controls of other West Indian slave societies. The greater prosperity of Saint Domingue, however, and apprehensions about the potential for social convulsion, did not unify the colony's slaveholders. Tensions that cut across racial and class lines made for greater ambivalence about social identity. Among the whites, for example, coffee planters stood against sugar planters on some questions but united with them against lawyers and merchants. More infuriating, all found common cause in their denunciation of the rowdy petits blancs—the shopkeepers, clerks, street peddlers, itinerant seamen—many of them drawn to the colony with the prospect of cashing in on its bounty.

Nor did there appear to be a unifying social bond among the colony's half-million African slaves, the largest group in the Caribbean plantation economies. What made Saint Domingue's slave community different was not the proportion of slaves to free coloreds or whites but the rapidly escalating number of new arrivals from Africa (thirty thousand annually from 1785 to 1790); not the unity engendered by common bondage (perhaps two dozen linguistic groups were represented on a typical plantation of two hundred slaves) but the reality that young African men in their twenties dominated. In the lowlands, one-half of the slaves were Creoles (born into slavery in the New World), who professed Christianity, grew their own food, and, if they acquired a limited use of French, occasionally rose to become an artisan or a domestic. A vague social kinship based on the experience of slavery found expression in songs, meetings at market, and the growth of vodun (voodoo), which provided a unifying cult for Bantu, West African, and Christianized Creoles.

In the 1780s, however, other matters preoccupied the whites. Indeed, the most troubled and dissentious elements in the colony were not the slaves but a vocal minority of white planters (who had benefited by France's commercial ties with the American revolutionaries and disliked the return of restrictions) and the free coloreds (some of whom had actually served in a regiment sent to Georgia). Among the latter were men who came back to Saint Domingue determined to alter the caste system; they appealed to the government, but French officials were disinclined to do anything that might disturb the colony's social structure. Nonetheless, as in England, antislavery groups coalesced, here to form the Amis des Noirs to protest conditions on the plantations. In the late 1780s, when the government announced modest reforms, furious planters spoke openly of independence.[11]

The Free Colored Revolt

French officials had been hearing such rhetoric for a generation. What made it more frightening now was the rapidly changing politics of the colony as authorities cracked down on the "patriarchs of the colonial family" who were demanding representation in the States-General. News of the July 1789 Paris revolution prompted an outburst of joyous enthusiasm that quickly turned ugly. Bands of petits blancs donned red cockades and celebrated by rioting. Others quickly formed patriotic societies or organized to take over from intimidated French officials. In the north the grands blancs created their own Assembly of the North and raised an army to safeguard their interests. When a rival general assembly in the south—dominated by smaller planters envious of the grands blancs and contemptuous of the white rowdies beneath them—declared for independence, the large merchants and lawyers who held sway in the Assembly of the North just as swiftly aligned themselves with French authorities in denouncing that act. The collapsing royalist bureaucracy had little recourse except to appeal to the free coloreds. "It has become more necessary than ever not to give them any cause for offence," the governor instructed district commandants, "to encourage them and to treat them as friends and *whites.*"[12]

Divided over means, these white factions were in general agreement over such goals as colonial autonomy and liberalization of commerce. They were united in their determination to preserve the social order, the plantation economy, and the institution of slavery. Montesquieu touched a humanitarian nerve when he wrote that "sugar would taste much sweeter if the cane did not require the work of slaves." All the same, the reality, white planters believed, was that slaves transformed into free laborers would not work for pay but would "return to their lazy and improvident habits."[13]

The French Revolution and its egalitarian promises—nobly expressed in the Declaration of the Rights of Man and the oratory of the Amis des Noirs in France, who were calling for abolition of the slave trade—threatened Saint Domingue's white planters. Presumably, the ideological promise of equality reached deep into French West Indian society. Americans had drawn a color line and incorporated it into revolutionary ideology; they had exalted liberty and property rights. French Revolutionary professions of equality lacked the important qualifications Americans used to exclude peoples denied full membership in the revolutionary family—qualifications based on color or gender or property. More important, the racial demography of U.S. society made such distinctions much easier. Thomas Jefferson could write in fulsome praise about equality and liberty because white elites in Virginia had a mass of poor whites shielding them from the black slaves at the bottom.

Saint Domingue's circumstances after 1789 were infuriatingly more chaotic and complex. The situation taxed the most humane and creative impulses of French revolutionary leaders. In the early days of the French Revolution, several in the Constituent Assembly (notably the Comte de Mirabeau) brought up the issue of racial equality and slavery. But even as Thomas Clarkson, the famous British abolitionist, arrived in Paris anticipating a decisive vote against the French slave trade, the white planters were forming their own pressure group, the Club Massiac. By the spring of 1790, the antislave trade cause in France had lost whatever immediacy it had possessed the previous summer. The Constituent Assembly affirmed the traditional practices and property rights of the colonies. Criticism of the status quo in the colonies was unpatriotic, incitement of unrest there, a crime.[14]

The immediate problem for the whites, whose representatives in France demanded that the colonies be accepted as equals, lay not with putative organizers of slave rebellion but with the free coloreds. These individuals who had chafed under social and legal discrimination for years, had won the Amis des Noirs to their cause, and now they sensed an opportunity to gain social equality. Their economic role in the colony since mid-century, especially as rural coffee planters, had been impressive. Yet as they prospered, the social resentments of the poor whites increased. The free coloreds were careful to reassure the grands blancs about slavery, though some hinted at its eventual abolition. Most of the whites remained unpersuaded, and in Saint Domingue the few who dared to identify with the free coloreds were harassed and beaten.

In France, the dilemmas of the free coloreds became more obvious as some moved aggressively toward accepting the *universality* of the Declaration of the Rights of Man and then applied it according to the *particularism* of the French West Indies—a statement of equality for all nonwhites (which included the free blacks) and the manumission of mulatto but not African slaves. Inclusion of the nonwhites denied French colonial racial pretensions; manumission confirmed them. Free blacks joined with free coloreds in France in the spirit of the declaration, but white allies in the Amis des Noirs generally spoke of *European*, not African, roots in their discourses on the free coloreds. In response, some free blacks exalted their African heritage. As race and slavery became entangled issues, whites and free coloreds became estranged. When news of the lynching of free coloreds in Martinique and Saint Domingue filtered into the debates, the Constituent Assembly became more hesitant about alienating colonial whites.[15]

Frustrated, the free coloreds grew bolder as prospective leaders returned from France. One, Vincent Ogé (whose brother had died in a fight between free coloreds and government militiamen on the Artibonite Plain in the spring of 1790), arrived in Saint Domingue in October. He denounced the French governor for refusing to proclaim the decree of March 1790, which had not specifically mentioned the free coloreds but had given the vote to "all persons" aged twenty-five who satisfied residential and property qualifications. When news of this ambiguous proposal reached Saint Domingue's revolutionary whites, encamped at Saint Marc, they scorned it: mulattoes were not "persons" and if "persons" included "men" then the decree must apply to slaves, which was unthinkable. Ogé denied accusations that he was inciting the slaves or that he believed the decree applied to any save the free coloreds.[16]

Thus commenced the free colored revolt. Ogé raised an army of three hundred free coloreds in the north and demanded an end to racial discrimination. Though he recruited no slaves, the white planters reacted with terror. When the impetuous Ogé attacked Le Cap, planters suppressed the free colored revolt with uncommon severity and subjected Ogé and his cohorts to a two-month trial. The penalty was confession of their deeds and a grisly public execution. In the public square (on the side opposite to that reserved for execution of whites) their arms and legs were broken and they were strapped to wagon wheels, feet up, to die. Then they were decapitated. News of Ogé's martyrdom reached Paris, and Robespierre electrified the assembly by proclaiming that France would abandon the colonies "if the price is to be your [the slaveholders'] happiness, your glory, your liberty. . . . We will sacrifice to the colonial deputies neither the nation nor the colonies nor the whole of humanity."[17]

These were spirited and inspiring sentiments, but it was clear to astute observers that the deputies had little stomach for confronting the colonial question, which meant dealing with slavery itself. The assembly's sole concession was a decree stating that a free colored legitimately born to free parents enjoyed rights equal to those of whites. Among Saint Domingue's whites, the assembly's decree provoked outcries and talk of violent resistance. Fearful, Governor Mauduit refused to promulgate the assembly's decree, but the whites were not pacified. Aided by rebellious soldiers, outraged free coloreds killed Mauduit by hacking off his head. (A mulatta who held his feet during the grisly decapitation was rewarded with the directorship of the Port-au-Prince hospital.) When the news reached France, the Constituent Assembly begrudgingly conceded equality to the free coloreds against the advice of Joseph Barnave, a Saint Domingue planter and a member of the Club Massiac, who roared: "You do not know the island! If you yourselves had lived there for a while, you would see things differently."[18]

The Slave Rebellion of 1791

It was too late to pacify the free coloreds. By August 1791 they were gathering in the south and the west, preparing for civil war with the whites. Neither side anticipated the slave insurrection that erupted on the plain near Le Cap. The Caribbean Creole Moreau de Saint-Méry proved the most perceptive about the explosiveness of the situation when he observed that extending the "Rights of Man" to the free coloreds meant something more ominous: "For if once the slaves suspect that there is a power other than their masters which holds the final disposition of their fates; if they once see the mulattoes have invoked this power and by its aid have become our equals—then France must renounce all hope of preserving her colonies."[19]

The whites on Saint Domingue had seemed casually indifferent to the impact of revolutionary rhetoric on the slaves. By the time news of the July 1789 uprising of the "white slaves" reached the West Indies, there had been outbursts on Guadeloupe and Martinique and gatherings at Fort Dauphin in Saint Domingue. Scattered violent protests were quickly and violently crushed. Curiously, as a contemporary noted, the whites were so preoccupied with stamping out the efforts of free coloreds for equality that they were inattentive to the psychological impact that their bloody retaliations—murder, hanging, and torture—were having on the slaves. Some of the whites were members of the Circle of Philadelphia, an occult Masonic group that reverberated with talk of a future society that would have no rank and complete equality. The Philadelphians were revolutionary leaders at Cap Français in the heady days before the black rebellion of 1791. One wrote later, "We took the intoxicating cup of novelty without realizing that it contained poison that would tear up our own intestines."[20] (See map 3.)

As yet the slaves had only local leaders, but theirs was no irrational outburst of mindless violence. In early 1791, as rival bands of small whites and big whites vied for the support of two regiments of fresh troops from revolutionary France, the slave Jean-Jacques Dessalines was forty years old and dutifully serving his master. Henri Christophe worked at a hotel, listening to bizarre stories about a revolutionary decree that declared all men free and equal. François-Dominique Toussaint Brèda (who two years later would take the name of Louverture, "the one who opened the way") was in his hut reading Raynal: "A courageous chief only is wanted."[21]

Toussaint was not ready to assume that role. The leader of the uprising on August 21 near Le Cap was Boukman Dutty—born in Jamaica, a high priest, the first in a profusion of revolutionary captains. As headman on a plantation,

Boukman was alert to the internecine political battles among the free coloreds and whites. At Bois-Caiman on August 14 Boukman and a woman had led a vodun ceremony at which Boukman challenged: "Throw away the thoughts of the Whitegod who thirsts for our tears, listen to freedom that speaks to our hearts."[22]

The intent was to rid the colony of slavery *and* of whites. Modern scholars occasionally describe the August 1791 uprising as violent recourse to obtain rights presumably granted by the French monarch but denied by whites to the free coloreds. The universal principles expressed in the Declaration of the Rights of Man, then, meant less than those embodied in a monarchical society of king and church. To the slaves, the tricolor cockade sported by those who mouthed French revolutionary slogans symbolized freedom for the whites, not for the Africans. In their campaign of destructive fury, some donned the white (or royalist) cockade. C. L. R. James described their fury: "The slaves destroyed tirelessly. . . . They were seeking their salvation in the most obvious way, the destruction of what they knew was the cause of their sufferings; and if they destroyed much it was because they had suffered much. They knew that as long as these plantations stood their lot would be to labour on them until they dropped. The only thing was to destroy them. . . . 'Vengeance, vengeance' was their cry, and one of them carried a white child on a pike as a standard." The report of a special committee established by the colonial assembly determined that in the beginning the leaders had not intended to burn the plantations or kill whites. At the Noé plantation, however, slaves joining up had taken the opportunity to exact revenge for ill treatment. They killed the manager and a white refiner, then torched the house and fields.[23]

A seemingly unorganized and horrifying slave rebellion had supplanted the free colored revolt. Twelve thousand slaves from two hundred plantations, and maroons armed with machetes, burned cane fields and plantations. They spread across the plain and into the mountains, gathering followers. Whites fled. Soldiers marched out from Cap Français to engage the insurrectionaries, but the slaves eluded them. The assembly in the north sent a desperate plea to the governor of Jamaica for fifteen thousand rifles. Within a week of the uprising, the official in charge of defense dispatched appeals to the governors of Spanish Santo Domingo and Jamaica and to the U.S. Congress in the "name of humanity and their respective interests [for] prompt and fraternal aid."[24]

The calculated savagery of the earliest days of the rebellion knew no color line. Within a month, slaves had destroyed a thousand plantations and killed hundreds of people. They strapped white planters to racks and cut them in half, raped their daughters and wives, and decapitated their children, impaling their heads on pikes. Women stuffed the severed genitals into the mouths of former masters and rapists as they bled to death. In reprisal, whites killed indiscriminately, imitating the rebellious slave practice of staking decapitated heads or hoisting tortured victims on crosses. In Cap Français, they hanged slaves in the streets and in the public square, joyously raising the British flag out of gratitude for the assistance—which included, among other things, slave-hunting dogs—they had received.[25]

But the frenzied retaliation merely served to increase the ranks of the guerrillas. They lacked ideology but not purpose, even in the uncertain early years, when whites refused to believe that the slaves had acted without the provocation of disgruntled free coloreds, the Amis des Noirs, or even royalist counterrevolutionaries. As the successive leaders of the revolt faltered, the rebellious slaves insisted on continuation of the struggle. In the tumultuous early weeks of the insurrection, slaves deserted plantations and became maroons, fugitives, and deserters. Desperate whites advocated making peace with free coloreds in South and West Provinces in order to field an army to contain the uprising, but the understanding collapsed with a renewed civil war — white and colored planters against radicals in the cities in West Province, free coloreds versus whites in South Province, free coloreds and slaves against whites in the north. By the end of the year, the leaders of each side were arming slaves.[26]

Confronted with a rebellion from below, the French determined to forge an alliance between whites and free coloreds. In the spring of 1792, the government gave the two groups an opportunity to make common cause when it recognized free persons as citizens. To Saint Domingue's warring factions, the decree was a reminder that color might divide, but the common status of propertyholder united. Two radical civil commissioners, Légér Félicité Sonthonax and Etienne Polverel, descended on the colony with six thousand troops to enforce the decree. Their zeal roused the whites to new outbursts against the pretensions of the coloreds. When Sonthonax and Polverel heard of the overthrow of the monarchy, they deported the governor, replaced white colonial officials with free coloreds, and imprisoned or deported others considered seditious to the revolutionary order. In the fall of 1792 their forces retook the northern plain, and in early 1793 they compelled thousands of slaves to surrender.[27]

Sonthonax was a patriot of the French Revolution, but he nonetheless understood the portent of the slave rebellion on Saint Domingue. The rights of man, he believed, could not exist in a land of slavery. "Get the Convention to do something for the slaves," he confided to a friend in France. "The poor slaves are fighting for a king they would detest if the representatives of the nation dared remember that the slaves of the New World are fighting for the same cause as the French armies." These were powerful sentiments, but Sonthonax soon betrayed them as he consolidated his hold on the colony. His constituency was Saint Domingue's free coloreds, who at different times had fought *for* and *against* the slaves. They rallied to hear his speeches. Whites grumbled about the loss of their stature in the new social order and the empty promises to preserve their slave labor force.[28]

In more settled international conditions, Sonthonax's policy of maintaining Saint Domingue's precarious social structure through alliance with the free coloreds might have succeeded; but the impact of French revolutionary rhetoric and the outbreak of a European war dramatically altered the context of the French colonial question. In Saint Domingue race, color, and caste had become so intertwined as to give the colony a distinctiveness apart from other European colonies. In the past, movement from one class to another—for example, a manumitted black slave from a plantation taking up residence in town—had mitigated some of the social disabilities of color and caste, but the internal war between the whites and the free coloreds had sharpened the social divisions between white and nonwhite, slave and nonslave. In 1793 the French Revolution expanded beyond national borders, distracting attention from the social divisions within France and strengthening national consciousness. In French Saint Domingue social fissures were only deepened.

The social dynamics of this confusion were explainable, given the course of events in the preceding years. Free coloreds and even some free blacks (both of whom owned slaves) had been able to exploit French revolutionary ideology and move up in the social hierarchy. They had a social interest in a prosperous colony, but their demands for political participation had infuriated the petits blancs. Jonathan Brown, one of several nineteenth-century chroniclers of Haiti, castigated the petits blancs for their outrageous behavior when free blacks pressed for concessions, especially the right to vote in parish elections. "The great proprietors who still held their power and influence in the north," wrote Brown, "were prompted to mildness even in the eyes of open insubordination, by their growing jealousy of the petits blancs."[29]

A few months after the victories over the slaves in the north, revolutionary France went to war against Holland, Britain, and Spain. For more than two years, the Spanish portion of Hispaniola was enemy territory, thus providing the isolated and retreating insurrectionists a sanctuary. Three of the rebellion's leaders—Toussaint among them—joined the Spanish military, and the guerrilla war promptly revived. In the meantime, a rival governor, less amenable to free colored demands, arrived in the colony, and Sonthonax threw his energies into undermining him. Free coloreds rallied to Sonthonax and the republic, but the new governor responded by landing two thousand men at Cap Français on the afternoon of June 20. The fighting raged throughout the night.

Faced with apparent defeat, Sonthonax sent word to the black insurrectionists gathered on the Plaine du Nord that any who joined his ranks would be freed. This freedom was conditional, and it applied only to the north, but the slaves apparently took the promise as absolute. Early the following day, they attacked the beleaguered town. "From the summit of the mountains down the road to the plain," remembered a terrified white, "came immense hordes of Africans. They arrived with torches and knives and plunged into the city. From all sides flames were lifted as in a whirlwind and spread everywhere." Ten thousand persons, most of them whites, perished. The captain of a U.S. ship in the harbor described houses crumbling from artillery fire and panicked whites jumping into the water, swimming desperately toward ships of the French fleet.[30]

The commitment to free slaves depended on their willingness to fight in French companies and to commit themselves to agricultural labor on the plantations. Sonthonax tried to withdraw his pledge to the blacks, but relented when confronted with a combined Spanish and black army invading from the east. In late August he again announced the abolition of slavery, but practical considerations required black labor on the plantations. Under his southern commander, André Rigaud, free coloreds had waged a war of extermination against white planters. Obviously, Saint Domingue's economy could survive without the planters but not without the labor force. Liberty meant not freedom from work but an obligation. "In France," he told them, "everyone is free, but all work for their living—at St. Domingo, subject to the same laws, you shall follow the same example; return to work or to your former owners."[31]

The Revolt Finds a Leader

Hearing accounts of the torching of Le Cap and the frenzied escape of terrified whites, few North Americans attributed the colony's descent into civil war to whites and free coloreds. They had begun the violence, but the gruesome accounts of Le Cap's destruction made their actions appear more purposeful. In truth, none of the leaders of the black revolution had articulated a revolutionary agenda; the slaves themselves had petitioned church and monarchy to address their condition. They had sensed their situation required a political solution, but they were uncertain about tactics. They were not so naive as to believe (as had ordinary British Americans in 1776) that revolution had occurred in their hearts and minds and was therefore fulfilled. But they lacked a leader. The French king, whose name the slaves had often invoked in their war cries, had been executed in January 1793. "For the moment," wrote James, "the blacks did not know where their true interests lay."[32]

Understandably, they responded when the Spanish recognized their equality by offering guns to shoot other whites. Toussaint himself readily accepted a Spanish commission, though he alertly insisted that the Spanish recognize him as an independent leader. He explained his actions several years later. Abandoned by people of color in 1792, the blacks had had little choice save to accept the offer that had come from the Spanish Crown a year later, when France and Spain were at war. Until 1794 republican France had remained silent on the matter of "natural rights" for Saint Domingue's blacks. They had thus been "forced . . . , in spite of themselves, to throw themselves into the arms of a protective power that offered the only benefit for which they would fight."[33]

Toussaint fought against the republic, then astounded his Spanish commander by proposing freedom for all the colony's slaves as the most expedient policy. When the Spanish governor refused, Toussaint promptly made a similar offer to Laveaux, the French commander. Rebuffed by the whites as a "fanatical African," Toussaint demonstrated his perception of the slave cause in a proclamation of August 1793: "Brothers and friends. I am Toussaint Louverture, my name is perhaps known to you. I have undertaken vengeance. I want Liberty and Equality to reign in San Domingo. I work to bring them into existence."[34]

By what moral or political authority did he presume to lead a revolution not yet formed or to discard the name Brèda (the estate outside Cap Français where he had labored as coachman and manager of livestock) for the more exalted name of "the opening"? He was relatively old, had suffered few of the hardships common to ordinary plantation slaves, and was no longer a slave. He was a Christian in command of a guerrilla army of young Africans, a former slave who moved easily among the slaveholding free coloreds and whites, and a former slaveowner as well. None of these presumed liabilities seem to have diminished his stature among those he commanded. In the complex social milieu of prerevolutionary Saint Domingue, Africans, free coloreds, and whites held in high esteem anyone would could survive in a black, colored, or white society. Toussaint possessed a skill admired among Haitians—the ability to manipulate and outfox the foreigner.[35]

In 1793 Toussaint understood that civil war among whites and free coloreds had shaken but not destroyed Saint Domingue's slave economy. The explosive course of events had alerted the British to the perils—and the opportunities—posed by the slave rebellion and had persuaded the British prime minister, William Pitt the Younger, that Britain must quell this insurgency lest it threaten slavery in the British West Indies. Jamaica alone had three hundred thousand slaves. From its ports the planters had dispatched supplies to Saint Domingue, and, when French planters and slaves had hastily departed the French colony to seek refuge in the British West Indies, British officials had discouraged them. Attacking Saint Domingue also revived lingering sentiments within the British ministry for absorbing the French West Indies. White planters of the French colony would doubtless welcome them as liberators, knowing a British military presence guaranteed their security.[36]

The patterns of response were neither uniform nor easily predictable. On French Martinique, white planters hastily put down an incipient slave rebellion by inviting the British to shield them. Events took a different course on neighboring Guadeloupe, where British occupiers were driven off in 1793 by a superior French force under the command of a radical French commissioner, Victor Hugues, who liberated the slaves in the name of the French Revolution. Hugues was mercilessly vindictive against white planters. Those not driven away were executed. In the ensuing years he invaded Grenada, Saint Vincent, and Saint Lucia. By decade's end, when he became governor of French Guiana, metropole politics had changed dramatically, and Hugues accommodated its conservative agenda by restoring slavery.[37]

Fearful southern political leaders in the United States were apprehensive about the consequences of admitting fleeing West Indian whites and their slaves. The governor of North Carolina issued a proclamation urging citizens to prevent the entry of such individuals into the state. Others were opportunistic. For the Cuban slaveholders who had suffered from official inattentiveness to their pleas, the prospects of developing a plantation system and crushing their French rivals prompted one wealthy Creole planter, Francisco de Arango y Parreño, to write of "the solid advantages we can draw from the very jaws of misfortune" and "the golden moment to expand agriculture."[38]

The British Occupation

In Europe, France and Britain were enemies; but "beyond the line" in the Caribbean, Saint Domingue's violent outburst had necessarily altered political loyalties. Unable to rely on French troops for protection, white planters in the French colonies readily assented to treaties permitting British occupation of Guadeloupe and Martinique in February 1793 and of Saint Domingue in August. Amid the gloating about an easy campaign were occasional muted warnings of potential disaster, but Pitt dismissed them as exaggerations of the slaves' capacity to resist a powerful invading force. The town Jérémie fell on September 20 without a fight, to an army of mostly white planters, Môle Saint Nicolas, the Antillean Gibraltar, three days later. In both battles the whites collaborated with the invaders. Afterward, the British advance slowed, but by March 1794 the invaders numbered five thousand regulars, twice the number Sonthonax had to defend the colony.

Desperate, Sonthonax had already begun arming blacks to preserve the republic and then reversed the earlier decrees on plantation labor. Slaves who had fought in the civil wars were offered freedom if they took up arms in the defense of the regime. By now such words were meaningless. The General Emancipation of August 1793 had meant not freedom but transformation of the black from slave to serf, a forced labor system that increasingly made blacks more conscious of their collective strength. For most, then, the offer from Sonthonax was an opportunity to acquire weapons and sell their services to the Spanish army of fourteen thousand advancing from the east. In Port-au-Prince Sonthonax organized a stubborn defense for several months; then, confronted with an assault of two thousand British troops, he abandoned the city on June 1.

Saint Domingue now had two occupying armies—British and Spanish—both committed to the preservation of the plantation economy and the slave labor force required to sustain it. Combined, the two armies possessed a seemingly overwhelming advantage in confronting a resurgent slave rebellion. Five years of civil and racial conflict among blacks, mulattoes, petits blancs, and grands blancs had profoundly shaken the colonial social structure. Free coloreds had resorted to arming blacks in the defense of social equality with whites; the commissioners dispatched by the French Republic championed their cause, then, threatened by invasion, they abruptly took their property in order to save the regime. Preoccupied with the social crisis at the top, they were unmindful of the social revolution occurring below. Those who only a few years before had been virtually powerless now began to sense their collective strength. As whites abandoned plantations, the slaves stopped working the cane fields and took to subsistence agriculture on small plots. Losses of manpower from yellow fever, malaria, and dysentery—the effects of which were complicated by heavy drinking—compelled British commanders to begin organizing black military units by offering freedom as an inducement to join. Blacks soon outnumbered whites in the occupation army, and Saint Domingue was again plunged into a war pitting blacks against blacks.

Yet another confusing episode in the war was offering contradictory evidence to those who argued that from 1791 the intent of the blacks was to rid the colony of slavery and to banish the whites. Undeniably, by the end of the decade, these became the goals. But the process by which abolition and banishment of the whites were transformed into unqualified demands by Saint Domingue's black liberators was much more complicated. The rebellion began not as a struggle for African freedom but as a conflict between whites and free coloreds over social equality. In the beginning the blacks were observers, then participants, sometimes at the behest of whites or free coloreds but always with a different agenda. Their leaders, certainly Toussaint, displayed a remarkable ability to maneuver or to alter allegiances as the fortunes of war dictated. Toussaint served the Spanish, whose presence reinforced slavery, the plantation economy, and white rule. In May 1794 (after Sonthonax had returned to France to obtain validation of his decree), when Toussaint learned that the national convention had abolished slavery in Saint Domingue, he abruptly abandoned the Spanish and declared for the republic, offering his services as military commander. He turned against the Spanish with fury, forcing them to retreat eastward and inspiring Rigaud in the South to rouse the blacks against the British. The Haitian revolution had found its leader and its cause. For ten years an army of black soldiers, poorly armed and poorly provisioned, waged guerrilla war against an alliance of foreign armies and white planters.

To foreigners, this was no heroic struggle but a racial war of often undeniable brutality. Often forgotten are the early phases. Whites and free coloreds had initiated the carnage. In their assaults against mulattoes in 1791, wrote James, "the whites committed frightful atrocities. . . . They killed a pregnant woman, cut the boy out and threw it into the flames. They burnt them alive, they inoculated them with smallpox. Naturally, the Mulattoes retaliated in kind."[39] Although slaves did resort to such barbarism, the example of white duplicity remained. Both the British and the Spanish encouraged slaves to surrender and then massacred them or sent them into slavery. The Spanish moved into the north and sent word to exiled French planters in the United States to return. When they arrived at Fort Dauphin, the Spanish commander urged blacks under his command to slaughter them. Eight hundred whites died.[40]

Any realistic hope of reviving the slave plantation regime in the north was now out of the question. Spanish troops raided the estates, seizing slaves and equipment and sending them to Cuba. In 1795 France compelled Spain to withdraw from the anti-French coalition and cede the eastern portion of Hispaniola. The entire island was now French territory, but the political situation in the western third was no clearer than before. Toussaint controlled land from the mountains of the North Province along the edge of the Artibonite Plain to the port of Gonaives, which permitted him to limit access to West Province. Elsewhere the colony fell under the control of others—a mulatto force in the north, the remnants of white French forces in Port de Paix, the British and their planter allies in the West (which lay directly south of North Province), and the mulatto André Rigaud in most of South Province (the peninsula extending to Jérémie).

By now the British commanders had lost much of their earlier enthusiasm for waging an offensive campaign, but they dared not withdraw and expose their own slave colonies to assault. In 1796 reinforcements arrived. Most lacked any immunity to tropical diseases. Confined to Haiti's diseased-ravaged ports, they succumbed with frightening rapidity. The British were able to maintain plantation agriculture in their zone of occupation, but they could not sustain an offensive campaign against the implacable Toussaint. When Sonthonax returned from France with nine hundred soldiers, began arming slaves, and then compelled them to serve in his republican army, they resisted. Such tactics provoked Rigaud in South Province, who abruptly declared against the French and unleashed his soldiers in a slaughter of white planters. Elsewhere in the Caribbean, the news was similarly dispiriting for the British. Unable to stamp out the guerrilla "brigands" on Saint Lucia, British commanders agreed to repatriate them to French domain and integrate former slaves into the West Indies battalion. But the damage to the sugar plantations from the loss of labor was substantial.[41]

Early in the following year came dispiriting news from France. Robespierre fell from power, and the disaffected planters found a champion in Francois Barbé-Marbois, who had served as intendant in Saint Domingue and who spoke enthusiastically about the restoration of the plantation regime and its slave labor force. In February came yet another challenge for Toussaint. A new British commander, Lt. Gen. John Simcoe, arrived in Haiti to assume command of a thirty-thousand-man army. Almost immediately, that army was thrown into a defensive posture by the combined attacks of Rigaud and Toussaint. The British lost Mirebalais in West Province but staved off a guerrilla assault on Jérémie and Port-au-Prince. In late May, Simcoe went on the offensive. His haggard and sun-stricken troops took the interior town of Mirebalais without a fight, but the guerrillas torched the city before leaving. Toussaint gave Simcoe no time to savor the victory. He reversed the march of his army and struck toward Saint Marc on the coast. Simcoe had a choice: he could fight a debilitating guerrilla war in the interior or take his forces back to a defensive position on the coast.

Such was the military strategy of Toussaint the general. His political maneuvering in these days was Machiavellian. Despite his misgivings, when he heard of the drift toward conservatism in France, he did not assume that the battle for abolition was lost. On the contrary, as Sonthonax's credibility diminished, Toussaint secretly worked against him. He curried the favor of the French by sending his sons, Isaac and Placide, to study in France. The cause he led was the cause of France: "To restore men to the liberty which He [God] gave them, and which other men would have deprived them."[42]

Toussaint's leadership of the slave rebellion now appeared secure. He had brought the news of the abolition of slavery by the French Assembly. He enforced the decree by force, seizing abandoned plantations and granting ownership to the slaves as partners of the French republic. Yet he protected whites from black reprisals if they were willing to share revenues and to pay an average tax of twenty percent. In June, when Sonthonax was relieved of his post and ordered to return to France, Toussaint enforced the order—probably to demonstrate his fidelity to the motherland. Perhaps he hoped to persuade French officials that the colony would remain French only if they listened to him.[43]

6

The Haitian Revolution

The collapsing of the British force in Saint Domingue embarrassed the British government and galvanized the opposition. In the House of Commons there were denunciations of the costly West Indian campaign — ten million pounds and perhaps one hundred thousand casualties. Toussaint did not relinquish his advantage. In February 1798, with the mulatto army of Rigaud in South Province mobilized against Jérémie, Toussaint's forces marched on Mirebalais, which was defended by a phalanx of forts. For twenty days, his black commanders, Moyse and Dessalines, threw their black guerrillas against the two British-held forts. When they fell, the way to Port-au-Prince lay open. In South Province, the insurgents failed to capture Jérémie but managed to sever land communications between the two cities. When the new British commander, General Thomas Maitland, arrived in March, the British cause was hopeless. Years of rotten food, alcoholism, disease, and the endless guerrilla war had devastated troop morale. In West Province, where the British presence had helped to maintain plantation agriculture, the planters began to leave.[1]

In a makeshift truce with Toussaint, the British agreed to withdraw from Port-au-Prince, Saint Marc, Arcahaye, and Croix-des-Bouquets, abandoning their military facilities to the Haitians. Toussaint pledged to safeguard the lives and property (except slaves, of course) of those who remained. Maitland demanded a commitment that the black revolution would be confined to Hispaniola. Toussaint resolved that the British must get out altogether, but another complication developed when the Haitians found themselves unwilling participants in the undeclared naval war between France and the United States.[2]

In the meantime a new French agent, the Count of Hédouville, landed at Santo Domingo and hinted of a bizarre plan whereby Toussaint and his black insurgents would be dispatched to attack Jamaica and, possibly, the United States. Haitians had carried on a small but significant commerce with U.S. traders, though from the beginning southern politicians had denounced the rebellion as a threat to southern slavery. With Toussaint and his black liberators committed to a foreign campaign, Rigaud's power on Saint Domingue would grow. Toussaint got wind of the plan, as did Maitland. In the weeks that followed, the British general schemed with both Toussaint and the French agent. Maitland's maneuvering was a ploy to protect Jamaica from the revolution and to undermine the French in the Caribbean. In a secret treaty, the British promised to leave Haiti in return for Toussaint's pledge never to invade Jamaica. Haitian trade with the British and the United States would not be affected.

Persuaded that they were able to control Toussaint, the British plied the Haitian leader with gestures and gifts. They returned ten thousand captured slaves to Haiti. They offered to make Toussaint king of the island. But his cunning had not noticeably weakened his lingering sentiments for France and the revolutionary promise: "Don't forget," he responded to his British benefactors, "that I represent France and that the Revolution shall always continue to be a bond for us with the mother country."[3]

The War of the Knives

With the British departure, Toussaint had only one rival, Rigaud. Two of the early heroes of the slave rebellion had already departed. Toussaint's intention was to isolate Rigaud, his onetime ally but now his rival in a struggle for power among black and mulatto chieftains known in Haitian history as The War of the Knives. The civil war was as much racial as economic, between affranchis, overwhelmingly mulatto, and former slaves, overwhelmingly black. If the mulattoes emerged triumphant, they would establish the political and economic agenda, to the detriment of the freed slaves and even the black elite. In a society where economic interests might overcome ideological divisions, a bourgeois alliance in such circumstances would have been a realistic option. But in Saint Domingue, race and class divided rebellious elites in ways that appeared illogical anywhere else. Rigaud did not hate blacks; Toussaint did not despise mulattoes. Both required a loyal constituency. "Each of them needed the united force of a party, sustained by the force of commonly shared attitudes, in a society where the parties were confounded with the classes and the classes with color."[4]

The first step for Toussaint was a sequence of agreements with the United States and British governments. To the first he conceded the right of armed vessels to enter Saint Domingue's ports and simultaneously denied such visitations to French warships. With both he signed commercial treaties and pledged not to propagandize the slave insurrection among either Jamaican or North American slaves. Rigaud's South Province did not benefit from the trade concession, however. This signaled the onset of a bitter exchange of charges and countercharges, which a French emissary, Philippe Roume, tried to settle. When Rigaud withdrew in a huff, Toussaint persuaded Roume to declare Rigaud a rebel. In mid-1799, Saint Domingue collapsed in another racial civil war. Both Rigaud and Toussaint wanted power, but each sought different methods of getting it. "Rigaud would deluge the country with blood . . . and slaughter indiscriminately whites, blacks, and even the leading chiefs of his own colour," wrote the newly appointed U.S. consul, Edward Stevens, dispatched by a government anxious to promote the colony's independence. "Toussaint, on the contrary, is desirous of being confirmed in his authority by the united efforts of all the inhabitants. . . . Were his power uncontrolled he would exercise it in protecting commerce, encouraging agriculture, and establishing useful regulations for the internal government of the colony."[5]

When Rigaud's mulattoes commenced the War of the Knives, they indiscriminately killed whites and blacks. Before Toussaint could take the offensive, Rigaud ordered the mulattoes of West and North Provinces to make war, so infuriating Toussaint that he dispatched Dessalines and Henri Christophe to check Rigaud's advance. Toussaint led his own troops into the fray in the North, swearing revenge against his former comrade. A ship's captain described his behavior in a letter to the Charleston *City Gazette*, which reprinted stories of Saint Domingue's fall into civil war: "Toussaint gave the word that not one mulatto should be suffered to reside within his territory," wrote the American correspondent. "Everyone of that description that could be found was either shot or drowned." In Port-au-Prince conspirators were seized and executed by cannon fire or taken offshore, jabbed with bayonets, and tossed into the bay. Mulattoes threatened Le Cap but failed in their attack, and Toussaint ordered fifty mulatto civil and military officials executed. When his army retook Môle Saint Nicolas, the numbers executed rose to five hundred mulattoes. For the attack on South Province, Toussaint massed a black army of fifty-five thousand. On the sea, U.S. warships ferried black troops to the fighting and laid down a bombardment of mulatto emplacements.[6]

The War of the Knives might have ended in late 1799 had it not been for the furious defense of Jacmel by Alexandre Pétion, the mulatto commander. On the verge of humiliating defeat, Rigaud got a reprieve from France. The Directory had fallen. In its place stood Napoleon Bonaparte, who named Toussaint commander-in-chief of Saint Domingue but with the admonition that he must not make war on any except the British and must end the blood feud with Rigaud. Toussaint placed little trust in Napoleon's words—there were too many rumors about the restoration of slavery and the empire—but he was not ready to declare for independence. What he needed was control over the entire island. Only such power would persuade the French to permit him to rule the colony as he believed it must be governed. Dutifully he sent agents to Rigaud, offering peace and pardons for his rebellious behavior. Rigaud was defiant. Toussaint renewed the war, and Rigaud took flight to France.

Toussaint's Saint Domingue

With Rigaud's departure, the War of the Knives ended, but the racial conflict persevered. To break the mulattos, Toussaint gave the governance of South Province to Dessalines, who commenced a bloody retaliation in which as many as ten thousand mulattos may have perished. In early 1801, Toussaint invaded the eastern part of Hispaniola and triumphantly entered Santo Domingo on January 26. With the entire colony under his control, he returned to Port-au-Prince and, with blacks dominating, persuaded the Central Assembly to adopt a constitution making him governor-general for life with the right to name his successor. Catholicism became the state religion, and males from fourteen to fifty-five were required to join the militia. Slavery was abolished, thus vindicating a ten-year struggle, but the plantation economy, though severely damaged, remained. To stave off economic collapse, Toussaint revived plantation agriculture and hastily ordered the importation of black workers to provide an agricultural labor force.[7]

For the time being, his power within Saint Domingue was complete. But the colony suffered the devastation brought on by a decade of continual war. Perhaps one-third of the population had died. In towns ravaged by burning and shelling, the desperate often nailed a few boards across the remaining beams to form a makeshift shelter. In the countryside, plantations lay abandoned, the fields untilled and the country houses deserted. Suspicious of white and mulatto politics, Sonthonax had tried to maintain the plantation economy by relying on the voluntary labor of blacks and permitting a system of *fermage*, the seizure of renting of abandoned farmland. The state collected half the profits, and planters were encouraged to work alongside their black laborers. The French commissioner had also been an avid promoter of a literacy campaign among the slaves. But the relatively altruistic approach had not brought about a revival of the economy.[8]

Sonthonax had challenged Toussaint's judgments and policies and had suffered expulsion. They disagreed on the wisdom of a political union of blacks and mulattoes to forestall a French threat to restore slavery. With Sonthonax out of the way, Toussaint was able to introduce his own plan. An export economy could not survive without a stable labor force, and if the blacks refused to labor in the fields they must be coerced. "In order to secure our liberties, which are indispensable to our happiness," he declared in the labor decree, "every individual must be usefully employed, so as to contribute to the public good, and the general tranquillity."[9]

So desperate was the need for labor that the constitution of 1801 permitted reintroduction of the slave trade. Toussaint did not share Sonthonax's suspicion of the white planters and began inviting them to return. They had expertise needed for the economic recovery. In the new Saint Domingue, however, their behavior would be governed by laws and economic good sense. They must be family men who encouraged marriage and legitimacy among their workers. Only in this fashion would a stable and just social order evolve. There would be no use of the whip, and the planters would work in the fields with the blacks and share the profits. In the Department of the South, wrote U.S. emissary Edward Stevens, Toussaint's regime wrought impressive changes: "The cultivators . . . have been recalled to their respective plantations, the various civil administrations re-organized and the most effective measures adopted for the future peace and good order of the department."[10]

Whites were politely grateful and accepting. They had no other choice, though on the plantations they sometimes drove their captive laborers with the slave-driver ferocity of earlier years. Learning that the former manager of the Brèda estate, where Toussaint had been enslaved, was languishing in the United States, Saint Domingue's new ruler invited him to return and supervise work on the estate. Toussaint told him: "Be just and unbending, make the blacks work hard, so as to add by the prosperity of your small interests to the general prosperity of the administration of the first of the blacks, the General-in-Chief of St. Domingue."[11]

There was no color line, yet color still mattered. Some of the whites, particularly the women, fawned over the black consul, sending him amorous letters and locks of hair. At grand public receptions he dressed simply yet, in the fashion of a European monarch, insisted on deference. He sometimes reproached people of color in these gatherings, urging them to dress and behave like Europeans. He never trusted whites. They behaved obsequiously but dreamed of the restoration of *their* Saint Domingue. In Toussaint's domain, whites held authority only in local government, never as French officials. He brought thirty thousand guns from the U.S. arms merchants and with them he armed black laborers. "Here is your liberty," he shouted to them in his impromptu reviews. Privately, he talked of raising an army and liberating Africa. He wrote plaintive letters to Napoleon and Josephine, begging for the return of his sons. Josephine responded, asking about the condition of her plantation, which lay in ruins after the British occupation. Toussaint had it restored at government expense and began sending the profits to her. Such ambiguous behavior reassured neither the whites nor his black followers.[12]

There was no declaration of independence. Saint Domingue, as far as Toussaint understood and the new constitution apparently confirmed, was a French dominion. His black generals were befuddled by his actions, but he had no realistic alternative. His once-reliable understanding with the British and U.S. governments had just as suddenly collapsed. The British lost their enthusiasm for a free Saint Domingue in a Caribbean of slave colonies and in 1801 negotiated a momentary peace with France. In October 1800, the United States and France formally ended the undeclared naval war that had commenced two years before and had justified the commercial agreement and military assistance given to Toussaint. As the strategic imperatives for maintaining a connection with revolutionary Saint Domingue weakened, the early apprehensions about slave convulsions in the Caribbean revived.

Toussaint's prospects for survival were already diminishing within Saint Domingue. In the exercise of power and, especially, in his understandably ruthless measures in restoring the plantation economy, Toussaint had divided the country. Himself a liberated slave, he knew the slaves' "desperate longing . . . for freedom, dignity, and self respect," yet his conviction that slaves were undisciplined, ignorant, and possessed of a "self-destructive rage" persuaded him that they required "firm direction from above."[13]

Miraculously, the restored economy remained productive, and the plan might have worked had Toussaint been able to quell the rapacious appetite of his generals for power and money. The military should have helped to police the system; instead, the black generals pillaged it. They acquired plantations and amassed fortunes—Henri Christophe, $250,000; Dessalines, thirty plantations. A secret French report of December 1800 described a ravaged society where the liberators became the persecutors. Toussaint was "hypocritical, sly, playing the religious devotee, orders crimes and protects the abuses and dilapidations of his creatures. . . . Dessalines, a ferocious and barbarous Congo, swears he will drink the blood of whites. . . . Throughout the North [there is] . . . terror and desolation. The towns are deserted and men are fleeing a country in which they can no longer exist."[14]

Saint Domingue was now a military state where the blacks had black, mulatto, and even white masters, preparing them through hard work for the inevitable French invasion and, in the meantime, shamelessly exploiting them. Former slaves may have admired and even idolized Toussaint, but they were understandably ambivalent about his social policy. They had little access to land in a militarized society where compulsory agricultural labor existed. They resisted Toussaint's rural decrees. Freedom had little meaning without a small plot and the opportunity to cultivate it. In October 1801, alienated rural workers in the North channeled their fury against the plantation regime in an uprising in which some three hundred, most of them whites, died. The putative leader of the rebellion was Toussaint's nephew, Moise, who despised his uncle's accommodation with the white planters. Toussaint put the revolt down with his customary severity — the conspirators, including the now-supplicating nephew, were executed. Toussaint now believed that perhaps Napoleon, who had never acknowledged his letters with a response, would realize that the old regime could never be restored in the colony. At the same time, Toussaint himself failed to grasp that his agenda for creating a modern economy without slavery but with a forced plantation labor system was a fundamental denial of the slaves' own unarticulated definition of freedom.[15]

The impact of revolutionary Saint Domingue on other slave societies, the strategic importance of the island during the Franco-American "quasi-war" from 1798 until October 1800, and the intentions of Toussaint regarding independence were already critical issues in Europe and especially in the United States. In late 1798, the U.S. emissary in Saint Domingue, Edward Stevens, had sent Secretary of State Timothy Pickering a report extolling Toussaint's capabilities in governing the island and his moderation in dealing with his enemies. Stevens recommended approval of Toussaint's offer of a special commercial relationship with the United States. Early in the following year, the U.S. Congress debated the matter. The measure roused old fears about slave rebellion. As the U.S. Congress considered the proposal to expand trade with Toussaint, Thomas Jefferson ruefully confessed to James Madison: "We may expect therefore black crews, and supercargoes and missionaries thence into the Southern states. . . . If this combustion can be introduced among us under any veil whatever, we have to fear it."[16]

With these somber words, Jefferson expressed a generation's fears. The issue went beyond the obvious economic advantage of such a trade, said Albert Gallatin, echoing Jefferson's warnings about the international dangers of the slave rebellion. If the intention of Toussaint were Saint Domingue's independence, then the British must oppose it. So, too, should the United States, Gallatin continued: "Suppose that island, with its present population, under present circumstances, should become an independent State. . . . If they [Haitians] were left to govern themselves, they might become more troublesome to us [and] might become dangerous neighbors to the Southern States, and an asylum for renegades from those parts."[17]

Napoleon the First Consul was already calculating what to do with Toussaint. In France, the invasion force—twenty thousand men, mostly Swiss and Polish conscripts—readied for embarkation to the West Indies. As far as Napoleon was concerned, Toussaint had demonstrated his infidelity with the invasion of western Hispaniola and his denial of Santo Domingo's harbor to French ships. Measured against this defiance, his supplicating letters to Napoleon or his acts of generosity to the white planters meant little. The final proof was the constitution of 1801, which had made Toussaint virtual dictator of the island. What was France if it could not rule over its West Indian domain? Napoleon had overthrown the Directory in 1799; he had not rejected its plan for the recovery of its once-bountiful Saint Domingue. In the artistry of his deception, he was Toussaint's superior. In January 1800, Napoleon declared that Saint Domingue's blacks would remain free and would enjoy equality of rights with French citizens, named Toussaint commander-in-chief of the Army of Saint Domingue, and, in March 1801, appointed him captain-general of the colony, third in command after the minister of marine and Napoleon.

Toussaint had anticipated French thinking about Saint Domingue, but he had presumed that Napoleon dared not risk the lives of the white planters with an invasion. His miscalculation lay in not recognizing that the white planters were less fearful of another civil war than apprehensive about the future of a sugar economy dependent on a free labor force. But Napoleon, too, miscalculated. Twenty thousand white troops, admirably trained for rapid deployment and capable of foraging, could terrorize an enemy on a European battlefield, but the kind of war Napoleon faced in Saint Domingue was different. For a successful campaign in the West Indies, he needed twice, perhaps three times as many troops. The British experience in the tropics should have instructed him about the high casualties suffered by even the experienced army in such places. He magnified the problem of the expedition's commander (his brother-in-law, General Charles Victor Emmanuel Leclerc) by insisting that the occupation require no more than six weeks. Black guerrillas, Napoleon believed, were no match for seasoned French troops—on any battlefield. On arriving, Leclerc was to promise the blacks whatever was necessary to permit a peaceful occupation of the country. (The First Consul sent Toussaint's sons with Leclerc, carrying a letter pledging freedom for blacks to their father.) When his soldiers had taken their positions, Leclerc was to demand the surrender of the blacks. If they refused, his troops were to hunt them down. Their leaders were to be bribed, cajoled, intimidated, and harassed until they gave up the fight. Then the blacks were to be disarmed and Saint Domingue restored to its French white planter class. That meant the restoration of slavery.

Even as Toussaint reprimanded his fractious black generals—most of whom were understandably suspicious of his clever maneuvering—Napoleon was reconsidering his earlier accommodating policy toward the black consul in Saint Domingue. In late August, prospects for an eastern empire dwindled with a French defeat in Egypt. A month later came the treaty ending the undeclared naval war with the United States, the Peace of Amiens with Great Britain, and the Louisiana cession from Spain. Dramatically, the economic and strategic imperatives for the recovery of Saint Domingue coalesced. Neither the British nor the U.S. government, Napoleon was assured, would interfere. Saint Domingue would be the centerpiece of a restored French Empire encompassing the Floridas, Louisiana, French Guiana, and the French West Indies.[18]

The French Invasion

Toussaint got news of the Peace of Amiens in early December 1801, as he was undertaking a bloody purge of two thousand enemies for their participation in the Moise rebellion. Clearly, he now realized, Napoleon had not needed his warnings, so he quickly began stockpiling supplies in the interior and moving his own troops along the coast. When the fleet arrived at Le Cap, Leclerc sent word to the regional commander, Henri Christophe, demanding a surrender.

Christophe ordered Le Cap's population out of the city and put it to the torch. When Leclerc's troops landed, they marched by charred ruins. It was a portent of what lay ahead, but the French were inspired by the predicted ease of this conquest.[19]

By mid-February, most of South Province, Jérémie, and Port-au-Prince had fallen to the conquerors. Only then did Leclerc pause before embarking on what he now realized would be a costly interior campaign. Leclerc had the fierce General Donatien Rochambeau to wage racial war, but Toussaint relied on Dessalines, whose armies swept over South and West Provinces in an incendiary and bloody frenzy. "One cannot form an idea of those cannibals," wrote one observer to a New York newspaper; "they not only murder the white race, without consideration of age or sex, but they also direct their barbarity on some . . . who show . . . interest for the fate of the whites."[20]

Perhaps now was the moment to negotiate, and Napoleon had time for another ruse. He dispatched Isaac and Placide to Toussaint bearing Napoleon's only letter to the black consul. The letter reeked of French insincerity, and Toussaint realized that Leclerc needed more time to get the second contingent of troops ashore. When Toussaint persuaded one of his sons to declare for the rebellion, Leclerc declared him a rebel and renewed the offensive, directing one force to defend Port-au-Prince and the bulk of his troops against Toussaint's headquarters at Gonaives in North Province. The French again found themselves in a guerrilla war. To the south of Port-au-Prince, Dessalines's soldiers laid waste to plantations and left piles of murdered whites to greet the French. "The heaped up bodies still had their last attitudes: they were bent over, their hands outstretched and beseeching; the ice of death had not effaced the looks on their faces."[21]

From the beginning, Haitians established the character of the war. In an assault of one rebel fort, the French lost 425 men. Leclerc set down an artillery siege, vowing to bomb the defenders into submission. But the blacks defiantly raised a red flag, the signal that there would be no quarter. When the shelling quietened, the French heard the black defenders singing French revolutionary patriotic songs. For the first time, French soldiers began to doubt their purpose in Saint Domingue. "Our soldiers looked at each other questionably; they seemed to say: 'Are you our barbaric enemies? Are now we the only soldiers of the Republic? Have we become servile political instruments?'"[22]

Dessalines's tactics, especially the killing of whites, prompted the French to retaliate by murdering their black prisoners. (In one shooting, wrote C. L. R. James, six hundred blacks died.) In these circumstances, there could be no turning back. Dessalines had dared to give a cry that even Toussaint had feared to utter—independence. Two months of war had cost Toussaint heavily—the defection of one general depleted his troops by 50 percent—but Leclerc, too, had suffered casualties—seven thousand of them. His tactics were alienating the mulattoes. His commanders complained of shortages of water bottles, clothing, and medical supplies.

As Leclerc began to despair over the prospects of a prolonged war, there was a dramatic, and largely unanticipated, reversal of fortune. Henri Christophe, apparently at Toussaint's urging, offered to surrender if the French promised blacks their freedom. Leclerc readily agreed, and his fifteen hundred regulars joined the French army. In early May, Toussaint accepted the same conditions. He rode into the French camp at Le Cap and was greeted enthusiastically by the populace. Dessalines, who had sworn never to yield, surrendered. Neither Toussaint nor Dessalines saw it as a defeat; their decision was a calculation.[23]

Already, yellow fever was decimating French ranks, and Leclerc himself was rapidly failing. As the oppressive summer came on, the death rate would doubtless increase. Now was the time to negotiate, giving Leclerc time to pause and reflect on what lay ahead if French troops remained on the island. By mid-summer 1802, ten thousand French troops had succumbed. Attendants had little to give them save four oranges a day. Their bodies raged with fever and they choked on the black vomit. Leclerc lost 65 percent of his staff.[24]

In desperation, he turned more and more to his recruited black generals—Dessalines and Christophe—to engage the black marauders in the countryside. Sensing his former adversary's perilous situation, Toussaint worried about who would rule if the French suddenly departed. Just as he had outwitted and then crushed his rivals in the War of the Knives, Toussaint now began plotting to keep Dessalines or Christophe from replacing him. But they were already scheming with Leclerc to betray the black liberator. In a precisely executed ruse, the French commander persuaded Toussaint to enter his camp, put him under arrest, and sent him to France in July 1802. He was sent to the Fort de Joux in the Alps, where Joan of Arc had been imprisoned. He died from mistreatment and malnutrition the following April, persuaded to the end that he was loyal to the egalitarian ideals of the French Revolution.

Leclerc had assumed that Toussaint's departure would end the resistance and that he would be able to carry out Napoleon's order to disarm the black population. But the effect of Toussaint's loss and especially of the disarmament measure was to revive the revolution. It was a prelude, the blacks believed, to the restoration of slavery. Supplied by North American smugglers, blacks began rearming and joining the brigands harassing French troops. What the revolt now required was another leader. Leclerc and the whites unwittingly supplied that person: fifty percent of the French army was composed of black troops, and *their* commander was Jean Jacques Dessalines.

Through the summer of 1802, the combined French-black armies of Rochambeau and Dessalines laid waste to the Haitian countryside. Saint Domingue collapsed into another race war, with whites and blacks committing atrocities that surpassed even the bloodletting of the early years of the rebellion. A Spanish official, queried about the numbers of rebellious and pacific blacks, responded in a secret report: "One does not speak of rebellious blacks and peaceful blacks. With the exception of the few who are in the domestic service of the whites or make up the two companies in the Cul-de-Sac, . . . all the rest, including women and boys, are stubborn rebels."[25]

There was a reason for the escalation of violence. In August, the Haitians confirmed that Napoleon had already approved measures for restoration of the slave trade and slavery in the French West Indies. This would mean the return of white planters. Blacks and mulattoes now had a unifying cause, and the French terror visited on them only served to make them fight as mercilessly as their persecutors. The most determined resistance came from those mulattoes who had taken advantage of the whites' flight from the colony to seize their land. With Toussaint's surrender, whites had returned to reclaim their properties.[26]

Though most of the black colonial troops remained loyal, Leclerc sensed that he could not depend on them now that word of Napoleon's restoration of slavery had rejuvenated the guerrilla cause. He recommended a drastic solution: "It is necessary," he wrote Napoleon, "to exterminate all the mountain people, men and women, sparing only children under twelve; half of the blacks on the plains should be destroyed and not a single mulatto wearing epaulettes should be left in the colony."[27] A year earlier, James Stephen, a British political leader, had prophesied that Napoleon's plans for Saint Domingue would alienate black chieftains and their soldiers. The revival of slavery, Napoleon had solemnly declared, applied only to Martinique and other French territories where it had not been abolished, but the Haitians learned that the French had reintroduced slavery to Guadeloupe. Leclerc was correctly persuaded that such a move was reviving the black revolt and undermining his command.[28]

Pétion, Christophe, and Dessalines abandoned the French command. Of the group, Dessalines was the wiliest. He retained his French links until it was obvious the French were too weak to stifle the rebellion. Leclerc referred to him as "the butcher of the blacks. Through him I carry out my foulest directives."[29] But Dessalines was manifestly shrewder than the French general imagined. By treachery and manipulation, he consolidated his power among the gaggle of black leaders. When they met in late November 1802 at the Arcahaye Conference to declare for independence and raise the red and blue banner, Dessalines was their chosen leader. Leclerc was already dead from the black vomit.

The rebellion entered its final, deadliest phase. Leclerc had resolved to disarm the blacks and had turned to brutality and torture as a last resort. His successor, Rochambeau, vowed to exterminate them. Blacks infected with the disease of liberty could never be enslaved, he told his lieutenants. Thousands were ferried into the harbor, bayoneted, and pushed into the sea. Rochambeau ordered the hold of one vessel (*The Stifler*) to be made into a crude gas chamber. The black rebels retaliated. When Port-au-Prince's whites built a gallows in the marketplace, blacks constructed their own on a nearby hilltop. Rochambeau was not discouraged. Despite a winter in which his troops perished from the fever or other maladies, the strength of his army in April 1803 was equal to that of Leclerc's first expedition. Most of the island's coastal cities were in French hands. Rochambeau decided to press the war of extermination with a new weapon—killer hunting dogs brought from Cuba, trained to stalk, kill, and then devour their human prey.[30]

The summer of 1803 might have witnessed even further setbacks for the Haitians had not a dramatic change in the international situation directly benefited the revolution. In May, the Peace of Amiens, which had permitted Napoleon to wage the war against the Haitians without British interference, ended. Within a month, Britain and France were again fighting in the West Indies. In July, British ships blockaded Saint Domingue's ports, cutting off the food supply. One of Rochambeau's generals wrote of famine in the towns.[31]

From their mountain fastnesses, the rebels swept down on the French. They burned plantations and killed whites unable or unwilling to get out of their way. One fleeing white, Peter Chazotte, described the devastated countryside near Jérémie: "I beheld the most awful and desolating spectacle; no less than ten square leagues of country illuminated by volcanoes. I stood gazing in despair for two hours."[32]

Losing the war, the retiring French used their power to extort the white planters. As troops morale disintegrated, Rochambeau and his officers sported in lavish banquets and orgies. In October, the French evacuated Port-au-Prince. When the blacks arrived, fewer than one hundred whites remained. Toussaint would have spared them for the new Haiti; Pétion wanted to send them into exile. But Dessalines remembered them as persecutors. The whites had begun this war; their atrocities were no less severe than any committed by the blacks. He ordered eighty-two of them executed immediately and would have had every white killed had he not suddenly departed for Le Cap. Pétion, left in command, put the whites to hard labor clearing rubble from the town.[33]

Rochambeau took refuge at Le Cap. In the fall, hemmed in by a black army and a British blockade, he made a ten-day truce with Dessalines and arranged with the British for safe transport of his men to Jamaica. In late November, the white planters and their families clustered in Le Cap sailed for Cuba, where sugar was entering a grand and prosperous era. Dessalines immediately proclaimed independence. When his generals met at Gonaives a short time later, they named him governor-general for life over Haiti. On January 1, 1804, Haiti joined the United States as the second independent state of the New World.

The Second Independent State of the New World

A dozen years of war and civil strife had devastated the country, but the Haitians had rid themselves of slavery, and in the final two years of the struggle blacks and mulattoes (some of them former slaveholders) had found a common enemy, the whites. In the aftermath of victory, the old political hatreds soon resurfaced, and for twenty years Haiti's prospects appeared to shift with the fortunes of four leaders.

The first was Dessalines, who declared himself emperor and in menacing words spoke of liberating the slaves on French Martinique. In the new Haiti, the constitution decreed, racial distinctions legally disappeared—everyone, including the Polish and German legionnaires dispatched by the French, was black. No foreigner could own property in Haiti. To reassure Haiti's trading partners (especially the United States) Dessalines pledged that the black liberation would be confined to the island, but within the country he could be unrelenting. Politely queried about the severity of his policy toward former French colonists and the impact it was having on Haitian trade, he said, "Such a man does not know the whites. Hang a white man below one of the pans in the scales of the customs house, and put a sack of coffee in the other pan; the other whites will buy the coffee without paying attention to the body of their fellow white."[34]

As had Toussaint, he looked east to the Spanish portion of the island, where for three centuries ranching had sustained the economy and most agriculture was subsistence farming. Toussaint had planned to transform eastern Santo Domingo's cattle ranches into the French-style plantations that prevailed in the West and had dispatched his brother, Paul, to bring the Spanish ranchers to heel. Leclerc's invasion and the attempted restoration of slavery frustrated his project. The Spanish preferred white French domination and worked actively with the French. In February 1805 Dessalines decided to invade when he learned that the French commander had approved Spanish slave raiding across the mountainous frontier. Two Haitian armies crossed the frontier, one into the North and the second via a southern route toward the city of Santo Domingo. The southern army of twenty-one thousand laid down a fierce siege in early March, but the combined French and Spanish defenses held. In their retreat, the Haitians sacked the interior towns of Monte Plata, Cotui, and La Vega, killed the inhabitants of Moca and Santiago, and wasted fields, cities, and churches. In Moca, "only two people survived, thanks to corpses having been piled up on those still living in the church where the principal massacre took place."[35]

Dessalines was obsessed with erasing the color line in Haiti, but the economic reality of private property resting almost exclusively with the colored grated on his sensibilities. He wanted to eliminate social distinctions based on color and economic distinctions based on property. The difficulty of accomplishing both rent asunder the alliance of mulatto (the "old liberated," some of whom claimed property from their fleeing white fathers) and black (the "new liberated"). Legal distinctions between these groups had technically ended in 1794 with abolition. The constitutional declaration that all Haitians were black and that no white foreigner could own property in the republic expressed admirable social goals, but these did little to confront the reality that at independence most of the mulattoes were propertied and most of the former slaves were landless. "The sons of the colonists," Dessalines warned, "have taken advantage of my poor blacks. Be on your guard, negroes and mulattoes, we have all fought against the whites; the properties which we have conquered by the spilling of our blood belong to us all; I intend that they be divided with equity."[36]

As emperor, he presumably had the authority to bring the proposal to reality. Carrying out such a radical plan, however, required a government with a social base among rural blacks and a military capable of enforcing the plan. And, more than anything, Dessalines's politics aroused latent hostilities among mulattoes who resented the dramatic rise of a propertied black aristocracy. In such circumstances, any effort to ignore the social reality of racial divisions within Haiti was foolhardy. He could try to appease blacks with dispensations of confiscated land; he could try to placate mulattoes with lofty reassurances that black and mulatto were united in struggle against a common *white* enemy. But he could not reconcile black and mulatto, nor could he survive without his generals, most of whom had become large property holders. The generals were largely insensitive to his professions of egalitarianism and were amenable to making their own arrangements with the disaffected. The "old liberated" now fashioned a momentary alliance with some of Dessalines's ambitious officers. An insurrection erupted in South Province, a mulatto stronghold. The generals gave it their tacit blessing. In October 1806 the emperor was assassinated outside Port-au-Prince.[37]

His death brought on fourteen years of civil war, begun when Henri Christophe, who had served under both Toussaint and Dessalines, presumed to continue imperial rule. The mulatto factions, headed by Pétion, managed to put forward a draft constitution limiting executive power. Christophe mobilized a force to march on Port-au-Prince, but Pétion's mulatto allies were able to hold out. Haiti again appeared to divide along lines of class and race— Christophe, the pretentious black aristocrat in his kingdom in the North, Pétion, who professed republicanism, in the republic of the South and the West. Despite undeniable differences in land policy and governing principles, the two Haitis were little more than the domains of rival elites.

Foreign observers who, contemptuous of Haiti's prospects for survival, prophesied that such bitter feuds would doom national unity were mistaken. Despite the economic uncertainties wrought by a long and destructive war, Haitians had achieved much. They had effectively ended Napoleon's ambitions for a revived French Empire in the New World. More than this, Saint Domingue's revolt of free coloreds and the subsequent black revolution had overturned a *white* government, ended slavery within the colony, and with independence challenged European colonialism and slavery elsewhere. Certainly, the division between free colored and black had persisted until the very last years of the revolution, when Leclerc's invasion had compelled these groups to unite under the banner of independence and racial unity. Of the revolutions of the New World, the Haitian accomplished the most radical transformation of the social structure and thus offered, wrote a Latin American historian, an undeniable expression of the "intrinsic revolutionary sentiment."[38]

The black state projected a dual image to the world: to the abolitionists and black freedmen, more evidence of slavery's inevitable demise; to those who believed economic development and a hierarchical society depended on slavery, a menace. These contradictory assumptions about the place of Haiti in the Americas explained much about the sometimes greatly differing accounts of visitors. Some were bewildered by the survival of monarchical and imperial forms in a country that professed to be a republic yet survived on bayonet rule. Others were impressed with the abilities of Haiti's leaders to demonstrate to a white world that the black was capable of self-government. Thus, the British consul Charles MacKenzie (writing in the 1820s, as the issue of abolition in the British West Indies raged in London) wrote of Dessalines as a "base and treacherous murder[er] of the unfortunate white French inhabitants" who gained control of the land and "attached the laborers to the soil." In contrast, a resident of Christophe's northern "kingdom," William Harvey, remembered polite Haitian officers (many of them former slaves) and penned a flattering portrait of Christophe's government.[39]

Conditions in the countryside reinforced this duality, as the agricultural policies of the early years appeared to shift between those designed to maintain the plantation economy without slavery, which dictated a wage-labor system, and efforts to provide those who had fought against slavery land of their own, which required division of the estates into smaller plots. In the continual uncertainty imposed by these two contradictory urges, Haitians again found themselves fighting old battles. For the most part, those who held land were mulattoes; those who had labored on it as slaves were black. The first had a vested economic interest in maintaining plantation agriculture; the second had a just social claim to a plot of their own. In trying to reconcile them, the state was often tempted to manipulate one group at the expense of the other, and vice versa. When Dessalines threatened mulatto interests with his plan for dividing the land among those who fought for it, he paid for it with his life.[40]

Both Christophe and Pétion began dividing the land, but the manner of its distribution and the size of its holdings dramatically changed the character of Haitian agriculture and with it the rural social structure. Christophe waited until his last years in power to distribute land, but Pétion commenced to parcel out large plots to his high-ranking mulatto officers and smaller ones to blacks. One result was the creation of a rural peasantry of small landholders. In both cases, the intent was to bring about self-sufficiency in foodstuffs, which meant a shift away from the colonial policy of agricultural productivity designed exclusively for export and the accompanying dependence. In the long run, these changes acquired for Haiti a distinction unique among the larger islands in the Caribbean, a rural population composed largely of landholders of small plots. The impact of land distribution, wrote one sympathetic observer, "created a consciousness of national existence."[41]

But the immediate effect of striving to maintain agricultural productivity both for export and for consumption meant that former slaves divided their time between working for someone else (usually under circumstances painfully reminiscent of slavery) and tilling their own plots. Though slavery no longer existed, a social process found in colonial French Saint Domingue remained: men were drawn into the military, and women managed food production. During the war of independence, women had played an important role in the struggle; some had joined in the fighting. In later years visitors to Haiti often noted the numbers of women in agricultural labor. In time, lower-class women moved into town and went into business as coffee speculators and merchandisers. By the mid-nineteenth century, their numbers in Port-au-Prince gave them a political power no Haitian president could afford to ignore.[42]

Pétion died in 1818; Christophe committed suicide two years later. Pétion's successor, Jean Pierre Boyer, reunited Christophe's North with South and West Provinces. In 1822, he reversed Dessalines's and Pétion's hesitant policy in a proclamation of Haitian rule over the Spanish portion of the island. Alerted to a movement in the United States to send emancipated slaves to Africa, he began promoting immigration of American blacks to Haiti. "Those who come," he declared, "being children of Africa, shall be Haytians as soon as they put their feet on the soil of Hayti."[43]

The Haitian Symbol

Haiti was thus an alternative for the manumitted blacks suspicious of white encouragement of migration to Liberia. Freed blacks could migrate voluntarily to Haiti. By the mid-1820s U.S. newspapers were printing offers from the Haitian government agreeing to pay transportation costs to emigrants and providing them with communal landholdings (fifteen hectares for each group of twelve) and assistance in acquiring title to land. Those who came as farmers and agricultural workers were especially encouraged, but the plan provided aid for those who were tradesmen. Despite problems with reimbursement, immigrants continued to arrive, their numbers surpassing the numbers who went to Liberia. Yet the plan did not provide Haiti with an agricultural labor force. The North American blacks who came preferred the opportunities associated with life in the city, not the drudgery and harshness of rural life. Antebellum U.S. blacks shared with whites a belief that wealth and property led to social improvement. Haiti as symbol of black defiance and achievement, however, retained a special place in their estimation.

By then, the Haitian state, divided territorially between rival former revolutionary leaders, had been consolidated under the rule of Jean Pierre Boyer and (after 1822) extended over the Spanish-speaking eastern portion of the island. A distinctive Haitian national revolutionary literature, written largely from the perspective of the mulatto elite, began to appear, kept alive by the oral tradition and passed down to later generations.

In the United States, especially during the first half of the nineteenth century, independent Haiti served both politicians and poets—the first as frightening symbol of race war and slave insurrection, the second as metaphor for natural catastrophes. The "lesson" of Haiti was alien to Western ideals of progress and humanity. Proslavery forces cited Haiti as a pariah state in the Caribbean. Its existence prompted U.S. leaders to chart a conservative policy for the region during the Spanish-American wars of independence and helps to explain U.S. policy toward Cuba throughout the nineteenth century. Antislavery leaders exploited the Haitian example as warning of the inevitable fire that would ravage the nation if slavery remained. Their opponents responded with stories of racial extermination and "mongrelization." Neither was the truth about Haiti. Both could not be true, but both were believed. What was forgotten was the image of Haiti as a "primary symbol for those blacks who were striving to counter the argument that free blacks were incapable of sustaining civilization outside the confines of slavery."[44]

Haitians had brought down a colonial master in a long and frighteningly violent struggle. After more than a decade of political tumult and uncertainty, they had managed to survive in a hostile world. Their enemies and detractors were ensconced in power throughout the Caribbean, in North and South America, and in Europe. For almost two decades, it seemed, their views had remained firm and unyielding, despite evidence of Haiti's efforts to integrate the country into the Atlantic economy and to conduct normal diplomatic relations with other governments. Secretary of State John Quincy Adams, responding in 1822 to an appeal from the Haitian government of Jean Pierre Boyer (who had unified the country) for recognition and for an end to discriminatory trade measures, conceded that "if there is a difference of color between the sons of the United States and those of the Haitian Republic, there is amongst them similarity in sentiment and will power."[45]

President James Monroe deemed that the principle of self-determination did not apply because "the establishment of a Government of people of color in the island . . . evinces distinctly the idea of a separate interest and a distrust of other nations."[46] He excluded Haiti from the symbolic protection of the Monroe Doctrine. "Curiously," writes Brenda Plummer in her authoritative yet sensitive history of U.S.-Haitian relations, "the doctrine coincided with the Haitians' own policy prescriptions." Unprotected and fearful of their vulnerability, they occupied the eastern portion of Hispaniola so as to "preclude the possibility of foreign infiltration." In this defensive endeavor, however, they were seen as "uncivilized aggressors and usurpers, bent on destroying [the Dominicans'] language, religion, culture, and tenuous claim to membership in the white race."[47]

Alert to likely French and British recognition and to the growth of Haitian-United States trade, Secretary of State Henry Clay suggested that recognition now made sense. It was a feeble proposal, however, and Clay soon deferred to domestic political opposition. Congressional diatribes against Haitian participation in the Congress of Panama and sarcastic comments about the role of men of color in the new Latin American governments demonstrated Haiti's international reputation. Even as Simón Bolívar urged his contemporaries to oppose Haiti's participation in the Panama conference, South Carolina senator Robert Y. Hayne denigrated Latin American leaders as "men of color . . . [who] are looking to Hayti . . . with feelings of the strongest confraternity. . . ." His colleague, the robust Thomas Hart Benton of Missouri, added: "I would not go to Panama to *'determine the rights of Hayti and the Africans'* in the United States."[48]

Slave discontent and revolt everywhere in the New World, but especially in the Caribbean, was routinely said to have a Haitian connection or inspiration. The charge was exaggerated but nonetheless believed. Passed on to blacks through oral tradition and invoked by black leaders in hortatory passages, stories about the uprising of enslaved against master found their way into the revolts of the era—from the Gabriel Prosser slave plot in Virginia in 1800 to the Bahia revolt in Brazil thirty-five years later. After the 1816 slave revolt in Barbados, a white Barbadian denounced the abolitionist William Wilberforce for his putative advocacy of slave rebellion throughout the Caribbean and, particularly, for his toasting of Henri Christophe. Haitian soldiers, Barbadian planters swore, were arriving on the island to rouse the slaves. (In actuality, Christophe manifested little apparent interest in the uprising, declaring, "Since the first Declaration of our Independence, the maxim of the government which preceded mine, as well as my own, has been not to interfere with the internal affairs of our neighbours.")[49] A captured black rebel from the Denmark Vesey slave conspiracy in Charleston in 1822 related that Vesey read to him "all the passages in the newspapers that related to St. Domingo, and apparently every pamphlet he could lay his hands on that had any connection with slavery." Others in the rebellion told of letters dispatched to Haiti for aid and of promises "that St. Domingo and Africa would come over and cut up the white people if we only made the motion here first."[50]

Haiti was symbolic for both friend and foe. In the 1820s free blacks in the northern United States celebrated Haitian Independence Day. British abolitionists looked to the social regeneration and cultural forms occuring there as examples of black capabilities and used these in their pleading for abolition in the British West Indies. Perhaps more significant, when the debate over abolition in the British West Indies revived in the mid-1820s, the Haitian "experiment" became less a model for what would happen in the British colonies than an example of what could occur if Parliament did not abolish slavery. When their critics resurrected graphic tales of the violence associated with the Haitian revolution, abolitionists responded that the white planters had brought this carnage on themselves. Nothing so devastating could take place in British dominions, particularly if West Indian planters learned from the example of Haiti, which had made significant strides in education and acceptance of Christian practices under Christophe and Boyer.[51]

On the eve of emancipation, predictably, both sides in this debate sponsored studies on Haiti that came to opposite conclusions about the Haitian model. Its demographics were impressive; emancipation had wrought strong growth rates, which strengthened the emancipationist cause. Its export economy was more robust that skeptics had speculated in 1804, given the devastation of the sugar plantations, the international barriers, and the oft-made prediction that Africans would not work in a wage-labor economy. But the Haitian economic record was mixed. Christophe had revived the plantation economy in the North and kept the rural population at work—with impressive results.

In South and West Provinces, however, where Pétion and his mulatto generals had established a republic, the state began selling land to individuals. Pétion parceled out acreage to the military to retain its loyalty in the event of an invasion by his northern adversary. The effect on the export economy was devastating. Owners of small plots readily commenced subsistence farming. Few wished to labor for someone else. When Boyer reunited the country, the difference between the two economies was striking: Christophe's abandoned treasury was full. Boyer resolved to follow Pétion's, not Christophe's, policies and ordered the division of plantation lands into plots for distribution to officers and ordinary soldiers. In the invasion of the eastern portion of the island in 1822, Boyer imposed a similar regime on the Dominicans—whose rural traditions were communal landholding for cattle-raising and timber—by decreeing the end of slavery and the granting of individual tracts to ex-slaves. Problems over entitlement forced some Dominicans to wait to receive title; others, desperate for protection against their former masters, joined the Haitian army.[52]

At bottom, the economic record of Haiti was a secondary consideration. It had not revered to "barbarism and savagery." It had not become a black replica of the yeoman republic idealized in the United States, of course. Its republican traditions were French, not British or North American; and its liberalism was muted by the limitations of authoritarianism and state control over market forces. Its "idiom of revolutionary consciousness had been historical and cultural rather than 'the mirror of production.' The oppositions which had struck most deeply at capitalist domination and imperialism had been those formed outside the bourgeois hegemony."[53]

To the outsider, Haiti was a contradiction: a sophisticated and pretentious mulatto bourgeoisie and foreign community in the cities living cheek by jowl with illiterate peasants; militarism to assure the preservation of social order amid fierce republican traditions and defiance; political order attributed to European influences; and revolutionary outbursts generally identified with black incapability. What critics decried as chaotic and meaningless violence, however, assumed predictable patterns in a society where a sovereign people retained the right to take back power from an irresponsible government. Violence was a "constitutional proceeding," observed James Theodore Holly, a black American missionary and longtime resident of Haiti, for the supreme law of the country stipulated that "the Sovereignty of the nation resides in the *collectivity of all the Haitian people*, and the safeguard of the constitution is confined to their *patriotism*. Hence, when the representatives betray their trust, the people by such a revolutionary movement take back from them the power that had been confided to those deputies."[54]

A pariah among the slave societies of the New World, in Europe and in the Americas, Haiti's triumph inspired the enslaved and those who fought slavery. It was a refuge, an independent black state in a sea of slavery, accepting as citizens Africans and Amerindians. "If prosperous and secure, Haiti represented both a moral and a political check on slavery everywhere. If feeble and anarchic, it encouraged the forces of degradation and destruction."[55] Distribution of land to soldiers and peasants may have weakened the agricultural export sector and raised doubts about the willingness of emancipated slaves to hire out as free laborers, but these were social and political, not economic, choices of Haitian leaders.

At stake was national survival. Haitians had driven the French out in 1804. Until the end of the Napoleonic wars, the country remained relatively secure from another invasion. But in the European peace settlement of 1814, restored monarch Louis XVIII retained permission to regain France's Caribbean possessions. A secret article singled out Haiti as a French colony. Haitian reaction was directed not only against France but against all intruders (identifiable by color and foreign origin) and thus reinforced the regime's understandable preoccupation with national security rather than economic development. Haitian nationalism "was a unique expression of nationalism for the period since it was directed not only against France but against all white men. It was . . . racist in nature but was not defined primarily as a black ideology."[56]

Haiti exhibited both the modernizing influences identified with Atlantic economies and, simultaneously, its own distinctive contributions to civil society and the political process. At one level, the nation-state, crafted in the authoritarian manner by Christophe and the republican spirit by Pétion, brought Haiti closer to the model of the Atlantic metropolitan powers. These manifestations of adaptability did not significantly lessen their suspicion and hostility toward the black republic. For its survival the nation state undertook severe measures of national security, as the occupation of the Spanish portion of the island demonstrated. Ultimately, Haiti had to draw on the powerful human resources of the nation, the people. Civil society derived its strength and purpose from its African and anticolonial roots. Here the ideology was a once-white brotherhood now absorbed within the revolutionary tradition, Freemasonry, which permitted Haitians a civil religion other than Catholicism or voodoo and cut across lines of class and color. In peasant agriculture and preserved Afro-Caribbean traditions, then, ordinary Haitians preserved the revolution from below *and* the nation.[57]

The economic irrationality associated with this subsistence agriculture— a belief in land as the domain of gods and personal security—signaled the onset of economic decline, rural impoverishment, and militarism. It meant that unlike France, "the Haitian state did not have to tread easy in the face of a powerful and dangerous bourgeoisie . . . [nor] to advance . . . the cause of capitalist development."[58] In this sacrifice, which was considerable, Haitians recognized what the passionate attachment of the peasant to the land could mean for preservation of the nation. "At the first cannon shot, the cities are destroyed and the nation is on its feet," Dessalines warned prospective invaders.[59]

Part 3   The Revolution Denied

The prosperity of the whites [in colonial Mexico] is intimately connected with that of the copper-colored race, and . . . there can be no durable prosperity for the two Americas till this unfortunate race, humiliated but not degraded by long oppression, shall participate in all the advantages resulting from the progress of civilization and the improvement of social order.

Alexander von Humboldt (c. 1801)

Americans! We must break the bonds of ignominy that have shackled us for so long. To do so we must unite. If we do not fight among ourselves, the war will be won and our rights guaranteed.

Miguel Hidalgo y Costilla (1810)

It is . . . borne out by the maxims of politics and derived from the examples of history that any free government which commits the folly of maintaining slavery is repaid with rebellion and sometimes with collapse, as in Haiti. . . . Is there a more fitting or proper means by which to win freedom than to fight for it? Is it fair that only free men should die for the liberation of the slaves? Is it not proper that the slaves should acquire their rights on the battlefield and that their dangerous numbers should be lessened by a process both just and effective?

Simón Bolívar (1820)

7

Iberoamerica on the Eve of Revolution

France lost most of its New World empire in 1763 but gained at least partial revenge by its sustenance of the American Revolution. For Spain (also a participant in the American cause in the Gulf campaign), the peace settlement left a more troublesome legacy. It acquired formerly French domain west of the Mississippi River and the Isle of Orleans and transferred the Floridas to Britain in order to recover Havana. But this empire required more authoritative governance because it was changing too rapidly and, paradoxically, too slowly for both rulers and subjects. Confronted with a parallel challenge, the British had elected to redefine empire; the Spanish elected to reconstruct it.[1]

Though the choice required fundamental changes in policy as well as thinking about the purpose of empire, the "Spanish way" of modernizing the king's domain momentarily heartened a generation of Spanish liberals. Charles III assumed the throne in 1759 and surrounded himself with young, ambitious men—among them the Conde de Floridablanca (Joseph Moñino) and Pedro Rodríquez de Campomanes—who put into practice the governing principles laid down by the Benedictine monk Benito Jerónimo Feijóo, who had readily accepted rationalism and the Enlightenment without rejecting traditional Roman Catholicism. The inspired bureaucrats commenced in Spain with agricultural reforms and limitations on the role of the Church in the universities. When the Jesuits resisted, they were banished from Spanish universities and, soon afterward, from Charles's kingdoms in the New World. Compared with the accommodating habits of earlier Spanish monarchs, such policies seemed less reformist than purposely confrontational. Their intent was to augment the power of the Bourbon state and raise the revenues necessary to manage the fragmented domain of the Spanish king. Minister of the Indies José de Gálvez, persuaded that the old tradition of permitting viceroys to intercede between authorities in the home country and Creoles, Indians, and the burgeoning numbers of mixed-race peoples had diminished the Crown's authority, put the issue succinctly when he wrote that the Creoles were "too bound by ties of family and faction in the New World to provide disinterested and impartial government."[2]

Like their British counterparts, Spanish imperial modernizers employed the logic and phraseology of eighteenth-century rationalist thinkers. They spoke of dominion instead of kingdom and pointed to the debilitating features of a Spanish America dominated by a privileged elite that stood in the way of economic progress and social justice. Articulated by José del Campillo in the 1730s, the new design for empire provided for inspections (*visitas*), administrative changes, and new economic strategies. The Spanish state had to alter deeply ingrained notions of identity among the children of the conquerors, who belonged to the aristocratic society of conquest, not commerce, and who spoke of familial, not community, loyalties. Charles III's domains in the Americas were also places where an antireformist elite held sway, creating a "situation that resulted in great wealth for the few at the expense of the Indians [and] misdirected lower classes."[3]

Virtually no privileged group escaped the reformers' scrutiny. In 1765 came decrees that struck directly at the dominance of merchants in Seville and Cádiz in imperial commerce and permitted nine other Spanish ports to trade with Cuba, Santo Domingo, Trinidad, and Margarita. Gálvez went to Cuba and then on to Mexico as *visitador* with instructions to improve colonial administration, raise additional revenues, and revive the moribund Mexican economy. In six years, he rebuilt and in the process streamlined Mexico's financial and political structure. He revived mining, improved customhouse efficiency, and increased the amounts raised as tribute from Indians. The effect in the colony was to undermine older, more privileged groups—the clergy, the guilds, and, of course, the Creole elites—and to benefit those in the government bureaucracy and the military and the more competitive entrepreneurs.[4]

Spanish reformers confronted two fundamental problems in their plans for reformation of the empire. The first was the enormous expanse of dominion that had to be defended against European interlopers, particularly the British; the vast area made military defense imperative and in turn made that dependent on new revenues. Carrying out these new policies without alienating Spanish-American elites required political as much as administrative skills. Regulations could not be enforced without relying on local officials—unless, of course, the Spanish were willing to administer *and* police the empire with European Spaniards. The second obstacle, related to the first, was inherent in the Spanish (and, to a lesser extent, in the Portuguese) Empire. Spanish officials were introducing vast administrative changes at a time of economic uncertainty and sweeping social change, brought on by growing tensions between European (peninsulars) and American Spaniards (Creoles) and, especially, the weakening of a stratified society amid the blurring of social ranks based on color or heritage. And they were undertaking these changes when Creoles harbored doubts about their place within the empire and their rightful heritage as the children of the conquerors.

In other words, the "rationalization of empire," intended to achieve unity, in actuality contributed to its breakdown. The Ordinance of Intendants, designed to bring efficiency to a moribund and corrupt administrative system, not only failed to bring about anticipated results but "had a disruptive effect on existing Spanish institutions" (especially in the Rio de la Plata) "and tended to break the unity of colonial government at a critical period."[5]

The Perils of Reform

These imperial reforms, designed to raise money and strengthen the bonds of empire, came in an era of Spanish (and Portuguese) political and economic decline. In an unintended way, they merely drew attention to debilities of an imperial system driven by political and religious considerations, which required continual interference and made inevitable the widespread evasion of the law. The application of the Crown's wishes often depended, then, on the whim of the enforcing official across the oceans or on what circumstances dictated. Some Creole dissidents began to look on the British occupation of Havana in 1762 as a model of imperial purpose. A priest in Puebla was turned in to the Inquisition for declaring: "We would be better off with the English than with the *gachupines.*"[6]

Another effect was that the *practical* limitation on regal power meant that colonial habits and forces took on a life of their own and were impervious to manipulation or meaningful change from above. Efforts to enforce new rules—however commonsensical—were often ineffectual. Jorge Juan and Antonio de Ulloa write: "It is common for all citizens in this deeply embedded system to receive an order and reply by saying they will obey it, but cannot carry it out because of some qualification concerning the law. If the order comes directly from the king, they give it special distinction by kissing it, placing it above their heads, and adding later in the proper tone of voice: 'I obey it but do not execute it because I have some reservation about it.'"[7]

Peninsular-Creole relations involved a dialogue of social elites, despite visible Creole resentment over real and imagined discrimination. Creole preoccupation with intrusive Bourbon reformers may have diverted attention from more ominous and potentially more dangerous events, the hundreds of minor revolts from all sectors of society—mestizos, castas, Indians, blacks, peoples of mixed races. These violent outbursts grew more frequent after 1750. Occasionally, their origin lay in specific grievances involving the workload on a plantation or in Indian protest against more aggressive tax collectors or resistance to assimilation. Indeed, as John Coatsworth points out, "the most complex rural rebellions were those involving diverse strata of the rural population, each with its own needs and goals."[8]

Sometimes, rebellions spread throughout a region and involved several disparate social groups. Indians resisted the secularization of society, particularly when authorities intruded into community religious rites or clergy began charging for burials, marriages, or confession. Non-Indian poor in colonial Mexico fared little better in the agricultural crises of the late eighteenth century. Competing with Indians and mestizos who migrated from the countryside, they joined the growing army of urban destitutes whose miserable lot Alexander von Humboldt described in his classic account of late colonial Mexico. Mestizos railed against restrictions imposed by the Caracas Company (which enjoyed a special commercial status in Venezuela) and against increased customs duties in Ecuador. Mulattoes and mestizos joined vagabonds in local violence on ranches, in the fields, and in the mines.[9]

Revolts grew not only more frequent but more destructive. In the Mexican *Bajío* (Mexico's granary, the agricultural region west and northwest of Mexico City), racial and ethnic hatreds against white overseers exploded into a regional uprising against foreign interlopers. Creole elites, initially responsive to these outbursts, dramatically altered their views when it became apparent that only the state stood between them and the menacing forces from below. In Mexico, "elites depended on the authorities to assure the domestic tranquility and to stifle even the very beginnings of a class war. Thus any breakdown of law and order reinforced the loyalty of elites to Spain—as long as Spain could be identified as protector."[10]

The most serious uprising of the era was the 1780–1783 Túpac Amaru rebellion in Peru, where abuses by *corregidores* (local officials who collected Indian tribute and regulated Indian labor) and conservative landowners drew the attention of a suspicious visitador. Expectations that the reforms would prove ineffectual triggered the revolt, which spread beyond the provinces where the greatest abuses occurred and ultimately involved mestizos, Creoles, and Spaniards. The implications of this uprising for the Peruvian and Spanish-American revolutionary experience are profound. Surprised by the violence of a rebellion that cut across racial and class lines, Creoles recognized that in order to protect themselves, they had to support a cacique to command the movement. In this fashion, they "hoped to avoid being surprised" by an Indian uprising and reserved effective control of any such movement to themselves.[11]

What explained such defiance? A partial answer, doubtless, lay in that instinctive hostility of the backlander toward conformity, particularly if the demand is made by a government that has benefited from his adventurousness. Such frontier particularism was common in the Portuguese, Spanish, French, and British Empires, and the hostility of frontier peoples to the intrusive authority of government continued to thrive in Brazil and in the United States, especially, for many years after independence. Indeed, in both countries the frontier spirit of individualism became a part of national mythology. What is important here is to place this outburst of defiance in the historical context of the hemispheric imperial debate in the era after 1763—the Portuguese, Spanish, and especially British efforts to alter or, at least, to redefine the political and economic role of colonies in the national agenda, a reassessment that occurred in an era of accelerating social and economic change.[12]

After the 1762 British occupation of Havana, Spanish administrators became more acutely conscious of the slow transformation of Spanish-American societies from the economic dependence of the sixteenth century into more self-sufficient entities. The economic growth of the eighteenth century, necessitated in large measure by shortages and inequities in the tightly controlled metropolitan commercial network, had brought about an intercolonial trade. In the process, Creoles came to play a more important role in the economic and social life of the empire, especially in the mining sector and in the plantation economies. As mining declined, the Spanish treasury suffered, but the Creoles often shifted their attention to other endeavors. Mexico and Peru, the richest colonies, became more self-sufficient, particularly in agriculture and livestock, and even in manufactured goods.[13]

As did his British counterpart, Charles III understood the implications of such economic self-sufficiency, certainly for imperial revenues, but also for the credibility of imperial rule: "The security of the Americas must be measured by the extent of their dependence on the metropolis," he realized, "and this dependence is founded on their need of consumer goods. The day they can supply all their needs themselves, their dependence will be voluntary."[14]

The Bourbon economic reforms undertaken after 1762—new forms of taxation, the French-inspired intendancy system, the disentailment of estates and church property, and expansion of overseas trade—momentarily revived a nation whose economic and political strength had suffered a severe battering in the transatlantic imperial wars. But these changes struck directly at the Creoles. In 1778, the year before Spain formally became a belligerent in the American Revolution, the Crown announced *comercio libre*, literally "free trade" but in actuality a form of neomercantilism, since the directive opened up trade only *within* Spain's empire. Spanish America benefited very little from changes that were mistitled "reforms." Underdeveloped by comparison with the British and North American economies, the region had little comparative advantage: its now unprotected markets were flooded with goods, and the shortfall in its exports to pay for them had to be made up with the export of bullion. In the Rio de la Plata, the interior textile and wine industries suffered from higher taxes and imports. In Mexico, the most populated and advanced colony, nascent industries were jeopardized. A generation of dominating Spanish merchants descended on Venezuela when the Caracas Company (which monopolized the export-import market from the 1730s to the 1780s) lost its contract, infuriating Venezuelan Creole *hacendados* who anticipated greater access to international markets for their cacao, hides, cotton, tobacco, and indigo.[15]

The Social Tensions of a Multiracial Society

In many respects, then, Spanish-American Creoles appeared to share with their North American contemporaries the understandable frustrations that accompanied threatening economic changes. In British as well as Spanish America, the conviction that relatively autonomous and self-sufficient outposts had come of age and did not warrant such highhanded measures from the metropole found wide reception. There existed a parallel resentment among Spanish-American Creoles over the inattentiveness of the Spanish bureaucracy to the social status and inherited privileges of these descendants of the *conquistadores,* who had contracted a mythical but, as far as the Creoles were concerned, a nonetheless binding social compact with the Crown. Such tangible threats heightened the Creoles' doubts about their place in societies undergoing the social stresses accompanying immigration from the motherland and demographic changes within the empire, especially the dramatic increase of mestizos, blacks, and mulattoes. In Nueva Granada, Indians, slaves, mestizos, mulattoes, and the castas doubted their misery would be alleviated if power fell into the hands of Creole patricians.[16]

In their sense of alienation in the new empire crafted from afar, Creoles were as frustrated as their counterparts in British North America after the Seven Years' War, but they were more hesitant in their defiance of royal authority. Almost a decade before the revolutionary struggle commenced, Humboldt described their *consciencia de sí* as a proud boast: "I am not a Spaniard, I am an American."[17] Their challenge also conveyed something not widely evident among rebellious Whigs in British America—a strong and occasionally embittered rejection of identity with Bourbon Spain, its values, its traditions, and its heritage. And, more than their British-American counterparts, they were confronted with a dual challenge to their inherited dominance from the union of Indian and caste and the visible numbers of nonwhites who were prospering.[18]

Creoles appeared to lack the conviction that a reasoned dialogue with metropolitan Spaniards would make a difference in altering policy or that their collective grievances could serve as the unifying force of a revolutionary ideology. Within the Creole society that emerged in Iberoamerica in the eighteenth century, divisions among old Creoles (those who traced their place in the social order to inheritance and privilege) and so-called new Creoles (the Spaniards who migrated to the New World and married into traditional Creole society), though not as sharply defined as the more visible peninsular-Creole antagonism, were as critical in explaining the coming of revolution as the often disputatious exchanges between British Americans in the early 1770s.

The most discontented Creoles represented a generation whose social and political values had taken form in an earlier age but who now felt compelled to redefine their relation with the Spanish Crown. Some changed with the onslaught of ideas and economic decrees from the Old World; others resisted. Creole sentiments often depended on concessions necessarily yielded by a faraway Crown unable to enforce its will in New World kingdoms. José de Gálvez recognized the gravamen of the matter in 1779, the year Spain formally committed its forces to the British North American revolutionaries: "Even if the kind of Spain possessed all the treasuries, the armies, and the storehouses in Europe, it would be an impossible task to . . . send the number of troops needed to defend the localities exposed to invasion." The Spanish established a militia system (much larger in its design than what actually emerged) commanded by officers from the established families of the Spanish kingdoms and incorporated battalions based on occupation or ethnicity. Creole elites thus assumed the task of defending Spanish America. Gálvez made explicit the social purpose of this plan: Creoles must be persuaded that "the defense of the king's rights was linked to that of their own properties, the security of their families, their homeland, and their happiness."[19]

Such concessions did not always reinforce loyalty to the Crown. Rather, the privileges granted often strengthened the resolve of both rural and urban elites to enhance their social status or reminded them of the privileged world of the conquerors. Creoles fashioned their self-identity from an artful fusion of the memory of the conquest and its inherited social privileges with the belief that their experience in the New World entitled them to retain what had been passed down to them. In these circumstances, they heartened to the sometimes passionate oratory and writing of the age—much of it emanating from the American and the French Revolutions—more than to the putatively less threatening measures imposed on them by a Spanish or a Portuguese imperial bureaucracy. As embittered as British-American Whig patriots over their political condition, they were less disposed to rebellion because their resentments over past treatment were less unsettling than their apprehension of what lay ahead if the society of estates and privilege gave way to that of "economic man," where one's social status depended largely on skills and the ability to take advantage of opportunity. Creoles saw the profound political and economic changes wrought by a transformation in the thought of British Americans about their place in the British Empire. They failed to grasp a parallel but subsumed change in their thinking about social identity: the unexpected revolution in British America, where the weakened corporatist society of privilege and estates gave way to the "new American," who was persuaded that social status depended on material possessions and achievement.[20]

John Adams, who had spoken of the "revolution in the hearts and minds of the people," would have scoffed at the suggestion that Iberoamerican elites in the era before independence experienced a similar transformation of thought. An unexpected revolution in the United States had to do with the liberation of the individual in matters of conscience in a hierarchical society. The new sci-

ence of American politics removed from governance the burden of reconciling the competing and divisive interests of social groups. What this signaled
for the British-American colonial families (some of whom held strong convictions about their *social* rights and privileges) was accommodation to a
changed political order or exile. This appeared far more revolutionary than
the social price the Creole elites were having to pay under the administrative
reforms emanating from the Spanish and the Portuguese Crowns in the late
eighteenth century.

In actuality, Spanish-American Creole elites stood to lose much more because the social structure was not only more complex but more sensitive to
economic change and administrative decision-making. Iberoamerica replicated the social structure of Spain and of Portugal. Political influence and economic benefit derived from a kinship system and familial power. In the early
eighteenth century, the notable families—descendants of sixteenth-century
conquistadors and favored immigrants—still held sway in Portuguese and
Spanish America. Basque merchants coming to the New World used their kinship ties in Spain to enhance their commercial endeavors. Under the changes
of eighteenth-century modernization, however, the kinship system—protected in the economic sphere from competition—began to weaken as the
transatlantic economy expanded and Bourbon monarchs expanded the authority of the state at the expense of the old families. The children of the conquistadors remembered an earlier conquest, that of their forebears, who had
conquered, claimed their rights, and resisted an intrusive state and the New
Laws of the sixteenth century. By the end of the eighteenth century, stories of
those challenges and commitments formed a new mythology, which encouraged separatist thinking.[21]

Some adjusted to these changes, permitting bureaucrats and merchants to
intrude into their world. This was the quiet revolution, whereby newcomers
married into the old families and created a new familial power base. They
brought not only new ways of looking at things but also desperately needed
capital for the economic expansion that attended eighteenth-century reforms.
These modernizers became Creolized in a generation, accepted Enlightenment thought, and, with the understanding that Enlightenment notions of liberation did not apply to the castas (a point of view similar to that held by British-
American patriot Whigs), were advocating liberal reforms *within* the empire
in the early nineteenth century.

Others, however, lost too much under the bureaucratic, economic, and intellectual onslaught from metropolitan reformism. Monarchs limited ecclesi-

astical privileges, and secular officials assumed control of positions the Hapsburgs had relegated to the church. In order to finance its wars, the Spanish state imposed *consolidación* on the Mexican and the Central American church, which with increased taxation deprived the old families of a source of capital and imposed a social cost as well, as the church had to curtail its charitable activities. The pensions of the notable families diminished in the early eighteenth century, the antiquated tax structure (heavily dependent on mining and Indian tribute) was overhauled, and by century's end those notable families involved in commodities (cattle, grains, wools, and so on) found themselves slapped with higher taxes in trade. In such fluid societal conditions, the newcomers, particularly if they came from respectable families or fashioned new kinship systems through intermarriage, stood to gain in wealth and influence.

In Portugal, similar reforms initiated by the Marquis of Pombal were less damaging to Brazil's rural aristocracy, principally because they resulted in no significant loss of influence or office. More so than its Spanish counterpart, the Portuguese-American bureaucracy was bonded to Brazilian elite society through kinship, Brazilians benefited from the administrative changes, and the Brazilian plantation aristocracy retained an affection for the ruling Braganza house, which survived the sometimes irritating obtrusiveness of the bureaucracy. Pombal himself set the standard when he instructed the new governor and captain-general of Mato Grosso: "Do not alter anything with force or violence . . . ; act with great prudence and moderation, a method which achieves more than power."[22]

In any event, the notables determined to cling to inherited privilege shared a demographic reality with their compatriots who called for administrative and economic reform: they were a minority in a world of Indians, blacks, mestizos, and mulattoes. Some of the Creoles, of course, recognized that economic liberation required at least a degree of social reformation. Few of them were prepared to accept the reality of a world where the castas might have as much opportunity as the Creoles. Within the limited social arena of peninsular-Creole society, the relative advantage or disadvantage in social mobility based on familial connection or influence was more discernible than the subtle impact Bourbon reforms had on social identity among Indians or mestizos. Nonetheless, Creoles had reason to be apprehensive, even as they encouraged Indian and mestizo unrest in order to frustrate Bourbon administration.

Just as the Creoles were adjusting to new ideas about social identity and privilege, so, too, were those beneath them, but the response was different. What this portended for the demands by these groups was everywhere an uncertainty, particularly as Indian, mestizo, mulatto, and black began to assume different *economic* functions. Social mobility as defined by race was one thing, by economic function, quite another. Throughout Iberoamerica, the expanding and diversifying economy changed social relations. The migration of mestizos into Indian communities as tenants and the outmigration of Indians into mestizo towns, the unappreciated role of blacks and mulattoes as artisans and vendors (particularly in Argentina), and the growing numbers of tenants in Brazil were but a few of these changes. Traditional descriptions of social status—"pure blood" or "master and man" or "landowner"—no longer served to guarantee one's place in the social order. Wealth and property had not displaced the subjective criteria for determining social status (as had occurred in the United States); their use, however, had redefined those criteria. Spanish policies blurred social distinctions based on race; instinctively fearful Creoles clung to racial categories to justify their social positions.[23]

More frightening was the social mobility that Spanish administrative changes inspired among the great masses at the bottom of the pyramidal social structure. Indians were subjugated, bound by debt peonage and tribute to servitude. Between them and the white elites, Spanish officials identified a variegated class of mixed-race people—mestizos and mulattoes, or *pardos*—who constituted the castas, a social spectrum where racial, social, and economic distinctions were often finely drawn. Their growing numbers and the opportunities offered the pardos to purchase a certificate of legal whiteness (*cédula de gracias al sacar*) unsettled the Creoles (most of whom had some Indian parentage) because such policies sharpened the antagonism between Spaniard and Creole as they blurred social divisions between whites and the castas.

Reforms, in other words, constituted a subtle form of social policy that hit directly at Creoles and roused them to denunciation and subtle acts of defiance. In the Rio de la Plata, the Creoles forbade slaves and even free coloreds from wearing anything but coarse laborer's garments. In New Granada, where Spanish courts were overwhelmed for petitions for the certificates of whiteness, Creoles jealously guarded their inherited privileges as the people of color, benefiting from the Crown's directives, inched upward in the social hierarchy. Creole aristocrats of Venezuela, many of them slaveholders, fiercely opposed the granting of certificates of whiteness to the pardos as "subversion of social order [leading to] a system of anarchy [and] the ruin and loss of the states of America, whose people have to live here and suffer the dismal consequences of this policy."[24]

Elsewhere, the dynamic of color and class had sharpened social divisions. The traveler John Mawe, visiting the Rio de la Plata during the British invasion of 1807, described Buenos Aires as a stratified society of Europeans, Creoles, mestizos, Indians, "brown mixtures of Africans and Europeans," and "mulattos of various degrees." Struck by the sharp division in living conditions between Europeans and Creoles on the one side and the mass of the population on the other, Mawe speculated about the probable legacy of miscegenation: "All these races intermix without restraint," he observed, "so that it is difficult to define the minor gradations, or to assign limits to the ever-multiplying varieties. . . . This may be regarded as a momentary evil; but may it not be conducive, in the long run, to the good of society by concentrating the interests of the various classes?"[25]

Mawe was attentive to the subtle changes in one's social identity as one moved from the countryside to the city. In Brazil, he identified the "middling classes," by which he meant subsistence farmers, families with fifty slaves or even one or two slaves, and a rural free population. Later studies show that nonslaveholding farms made up from 40 to 70 percent of Brazil's population. But there is little compelling evidence that their social identity depended more on their relation to a market economy than on the mores of Brazil's master-slave plantation society. Those in power clung to a social vision predicated on social stability and legal inequality. Like their Spanish-American contemporaries, Brazilian Creoles sensed an economic threat from the eighteenth-century administrative changes emanating from Pombal's reforms. Despite seemingly irreconcilable differences with the metropole, they believed their political and social choices were limited and clung to the Braganza court (which moved to Rio de Janeiro in 1807).[26]

Social dynamics thus did much to explain the conflicting impulses among Creoles on the eve of the wars of independence. Inevitably, the social tensions engendered in late colonial Spanish America by the burgeoning numbers of castes and the intrusion of peninsulars heightened Creole political animosities. More important, Tulio Halperín-Donghi observes in his seminal history of Latin America, "the triumph of the peninsulars did not depend on any of the traditionally recognized justifications for social and racial ranking in Spanish America; similarly, it made less tenable the marginalization of the mestizos by the white Creoles."[27]

Theirs was the dual image of revolution that characterized the age—the restoration of old privileges and freedoms within the traditional order or, conversely, the creation of a new authority that nonetheless preserved the social order. Always, there was the question of what the socially abused would do. Manuel Abad y Queipo graphically described the potential convulsions Mexican Creoles feared from the masses beneath them when he wrote about "the conflict of interests and the hostility which invariably prevails between those who have nothing and those who have everything, between vassals and lords. To some extent these conditions are prevalent all over the world. But in America it is worse, for there are no gradations between classes, no mean; they are all either rich or poor, noble or vile."[28]

Aware of undeniable disparities, he failed to perceive a contradiction that had befuddled those who had made revolution in British America and then grown frustrated in the society that emerged from revolution—a person *employed* as an artisan or a laborer would occupy not a caste, which sharply restricted social mobility, but a class, which permitted it. In these circumstances, the social distinctions of an earlier age withered before the uncertainties brought by change and the equally disturbing prospect that the state may no longer serve to reinforce older social values and traditions or to control pressures from below. In an empire that was "both too traditional and too modern," change either came glacially or rapidly. The survival of the empire depended on the precarious loyalty of its political elites and the authority the colonial order was capable of commanding in its own defense, but the Spanish king's Creole subjects had no intention of relinquishing the benefits of their inheritance. Theirs was a conditional loyalty.[29]

Origins of the Latin American Revolutions

Creole discontent, as volatile as that of British North America on the eve of the American Revolution, found expression in comparable ways—in tracts denouncing arbitrary rule and in political agitation in the cities—yet there was no comparable dramatic prelude, no series of Spanish decisions that mobilized an entire population as had British pressures on Boston. Creoles articulated their grievances with a similar intellectual fury; some, at least, recognized social disabilities that only a revolutionary political agenda could address. They hesitated because they could not reconcile their apprehensions about revolution and independence. British-American elites debated similar questions, but they did not generate parallel fears of the explosiveness contained in Spanish-American society or of the precariousness of their position.

And the character and purpose of metropole policy were not so clear-cut as to justify a resort to violent resistance. For those who follow a linear analysis of the breakdown of the Spanish empire, the impact and legacy of the Bourbon reforms and Creole-peninsular antipathies can yield contradictory conclusions. On the one hand, the measures taken by the Spanish (and to a lesser extent the Portuguese) Crowns in their New World possessions reversed (or certainly threatened) many of the gains Creoles had made. In a curious but understandable way, however, these policies advanced Creole interests and status. In the *cabildos* (the nearest equivalent to local government in the Spanish Empire), Creole participation was strengthened at the expense of imperial bureaucrats. In Mexico, the forming of a Creole militia and the granting of special privileges (*fueros*) to its officers "weakened the prestige and authority of civilian administration and . . . enhanced the sense of creole identity," write R. A. Humphreys and John Lynch, and "thus created conditions which helped to precipitate the collapse of the imperial regime they were intended to prolong."[30]

Despite these limited gains, Creoles nurtured deep resentments over their perceived unworthiness. Responding to a report that characterized them as "submissive" and unsuitable for important offices, a brilliant Creole lawyer in Mexico City, Antonio Joaquín de Rivadavia, lashed out: "This is a war we have suffered since the discovery of America. . . . We have been depicted as suspicious creatures, full of our own opinions, resentful of reproof, and—the ultimate insult — it has been alleged that Mexico is apparently moribund."[31]

In their secret report on conditions in Peru in the 1740s, Jorge Juan and Antonio de Ulloa had alerted the Crown of Creole-peninsular antagonism, muted before the eighteenth century, and its debilitating social scars. "Their mutual antipathy," they wrote, "reaches such an extreme that in some ways it exceeds the unbridled fury of two nations, completely at odds, who vituperate and insult each other. . . . Throughout Peru a general sickness afflicts those cities and towns containing both factions." Juan and Ulloa attributed the social malaise to "excessive vanity, presumption, and pride which pervade the Creoles; and, second, the miserably wretched conditions of the Europeans who arrive in the Indies from Spain." The arriving European worked hard, rose in society, and validated his newfound status by marrying into an established family. Jealous Creoles became even more obsessed with glorifying *their* social status and denigrating the lineage of others, with such vehement determination that "they themselves blurt out each other's imperfections . . . [and detail] all the deficiencies, stigmas, and flaws which denigrate the pure lineage of the others. . . .; Thus, in a very short time everyone knows the background of every family, even if he has not looked into it very carefully."[32]

The social implications of these reforms were even more unsettling. Gálvez reversed the old policy of segregating Indians and urged them to acculturate by speaking Spanish and dressing like Europeans. The goal was national unity, a departure from the traditional view of the "king in his many kingdoms," who parceled out land, Indian labor, and other benefits to the heirs of the conquerors and the church. There were disquieting reports of the colonial reaction to imperial reforms in British North America. But Floridablanca was persuaded that the opportunities bestowed by the reforms—advancement for the mercantile classes, greater social mobility, and material prosperity—more than compensated for the risk of raising expectations among those who would not benefit. "Greed and interest," he declared, "are the main incentives for all human toil, and they should only be checked in public matters when they are prejudicial to other persons or the state."[33]

Rationalism, self-interest, and reform—these were alien concepts in the Spanish Empire until the eighteenth century, and the Creoles looked on the new administrative directives with uncertainty and unease. They did not manifest their opposition in the frenzied and determined manner of British Americans, however. Bourbon policies had differing results throughout the regions of the empire, depending on the ability of local administrators to adjust—in other words, to comport themselves as *politicians,* not functionaries—and on the intangible bonds linking the American Spaniard to the Crown. The strength of such ties could be deceptive, as Colin MacLachlan has demonstrated, for they revealed the dependence of the Crown on strong-willed emissaries to preserve the hierarchical administrative structure.[34]

Creoles instinctively perceived both opportunity and threat in the Bourbon alteration of empire. Very quickly, they began to call upon the Crown to acknowledge their inherited rights as the children of the conquerors. They were lords of the land, they had brought Christianity to the Indian, they had built the empire's great cities. They had founded great families, some with private armies. In northern Mexico, Gálvez himself had called on a *hacendado* to crush a local rebellion. Over the years, they had grown accustomed to deference, in the local councils (*cabildos*) or in the more important royal courts (*audiencias*), when they appeared to ask for redress of grievances.

Though their specific grievances against the intruding royal government often differed from those cited by their contemporaries in British North America, Portuguese and Spanish Creoles nonetheless were kindred spirits. The impact of Pombal's policies appeared to be less provocative to Brazilians, although they roused angry denunciations in Minas Gerais. Francisco de Miranda, one of the precursors of Spanish-American independence, visited the

United States in the year after the winning of independence. "Good God," he wrote, "What a contrast to the Spanish system!" A few years later, Thomas Jefferson, then serving as minister to France, received a letter from a Brazilian: "Nature made us inhabitants of the same continent and in consequence in some degree patriots."[35]

Spanish-American Creole and Portuguese-Brazilian *mazombo* were almost uniformly suspicious of imperial motives, ultimately concluding that the beneficiaries of the new policies would be the arriving *peninsulares*, often their replacements in the administrative bureaucracy. Not only their pride but their purses felt the blow. Liberalization of trade within the empire, presumably an impetus to further demands from the Spanish-American commercial bourgeoisie and offered as one explanation for rising discontent, was in reality a threat. "The reason is not hard to discover," writes Claudio Véliz: "the merchant class were not interested in . . . facilitating thereby the way for a competition that could prove ruinous to their interests."[36]

Historians have begun to look more closely at the financial crisis of empire and the effects of metropole taxation policies on Creoles and Indians. Opposition to Spanish financial measures certainly roused the Creoles, aggravating their economic grievances against the mother country, but these alone were insufficient to make them rebellious. There is little doubt but that the *intent* of Spanish economic policy was the "destruction of colonial industry which might compete with that of the metropolis."[37] The impact of free trade most noticeably registered its impact in the years after the American Revolution, when Spanish exports to Spanish America rose dramatically. Even with this surge in economic activity, Spanish agricultural producers responded more enthusiastically than industrialists to the expanded overseas markets, one indication that the policy did not achieve its purpose. "A clearer [Creole] grievance," observes John Fisher, "was that the very success of free trade encouraged the migration to America of large numbers of peninsular Spaniards, whose privileged positions in both the bureaucracy and commerce, coupled with their dynamism, enabled them to profit at the expense of creole producers and displaced local merchants."[38]

Spanish and Portuguese Creoles following the ideological war between London and its upstart colonials in North America from 1763 to 1776 heartened to its intellectual vitality. They looked on the imperial debate under way in the British Empire as instructive in its prospect for resolution of conflict between colony and metropole. But they often mistook the level of discourse (which they rightly judged *the* great political debate of the age) for a lively discussion of the New World's political *future* when, in actuality, it represented a sometimes fearful, often revealing exchange over the British imperial past and, especially, over a parallel question of social status within that empire. Aware of the noticeable British surge of pride at war's end and a parallel determination to address the colonial question, the admiring Creoles nonetheless failed to perceive British anxieties and fears at work in this great imperial debate.[39]

Creoles read Newton, Locke, Rousseau, Voltaire, Diderot, Montesquieu, and Adam Smith, but it was not the liberating rhetoric of Enlightenment thought driving some of them on a collision course with Spaniards—many of whom were reading the same forbidden tracts—but the reality that they must find a way to enhance opportunity but not jeopardize their property rights. Their reluctance to commence a war of independence certainly conveyed uncertainty, but they were willing to take risks. Mindful of their diminished stature among a generation of Spanish liberals, they looked increasingly for succor to London and to kindred spirits in the young United States. They responded to North American daring, bravado, and especially the intensity with which a generation of revolutionaries voiced their cause.[40]

At the same time, discontented Creoles were disturbed by the somber appraisals of their capacity for self-governance emanating from a few of their putative foreign admirers. Fray Servando Teresa de Mier, one of the Mexican revolutionary pamphleteers, who visited Napoleonic France and resided in Philadelphia in the heady days of Jefferson's presidency, heartened to Abbé de Pradt's stirring refrains about independence as a natural process. For Spanish America, however, de Pradt recommended not republican governance but monarchy. In his fury, Mier turned to Thomas Paine. Mier's *Memoria político-instructiva* echoed the North Americans' fiery words about the evils of monarchy: "In the long term, liberty and a king are incompatible. . . .—What is the history of kings, as a great bishop has said, but the martyrology of nations?"[41]

Creoles readily identified with the defiant North Americans and their protest. Bourbon economic policy, aimed at raising revenue, inspired outbursts in Spanish America as parallel measures from London did in British America. Commerce and presumably shared grievances against metropolitan controls strengthened the ties. Spanish aid to the American Revolution—in loans, in indirect military support in the form of Spanish assaults against British Florida, and in the opening of Caribbean ports to American shipping—strengthened Creole determination to advance the cause of economic autonomy. Too late, perhaps, the Spanish realized that their clandestine promotion of U.S. independence contributed to weakening their controls over their own New World Kingdoms. The American Revolution was a subversive force. As early as 1768 a French agent had warned: "I believe not only that this country will emancipate itself from the Crown of England, but that in the course of time it will invade all the dominions that the European powers possess in America, on the main land as well as in the islands."[42]

Spain could not modernize the empire because it was too dependent on Spanish America for sustaining the homeland. Bourbon reforms called for alteration of empire in an age when Spain itself required restructuring of an economy and a society where the vital productive sectors had diminished as highly visible consuming sectors (such as the bureaucracy and the church) had grown. For Spaniards the Atlantic "kingdoms of the Indies" were a drain and a curse. Creoles noted the debility of the motherland and often quoted a damning passage from Montesquieu: "The Indies and Spain are two powers under the same master; but the Indies is the principal one, and Spain nothing but an accessory."[43]

But counterpoised in every inspiration from North America about the justness of the Creole cause were reminders of their own inexperience and, more unsettling, of the prospect that those from below might not follow them. Creoles initially heartened to the appeal from Túpac Amaru, leader of the short-lived Peruvian rebellion, to unite against common economic grievances imposed by from afar. Their enthusiasm diminished considerably when Túpac Amaru declared his social policy: total war against Europeans, abolition of slavery, and reconsideration of property laws. His followers stormed into towns, killing whites indiscriminately. Creoles now joined Spanish forces in suppressing the rebellion, using colored troops from the coastal region. The sadistic cruelty of the campaign was as much the result of Creole revenge as Spanish determination to quash the movement. Nothing so frightening had occurred in British North America.[44]

These internal uprisings had their provenance generally in the social costs of economic growth brought on, at least in part, by the disproportionate economic burdens shifted to the poor. In their character and their goals, some resemble the "primitive rebellions" that dwelt on local grievances or were restorationist. Despite these qualifications, one can find in these local rebellions the stirrings of nationalism and independence. A modern generation of marxist scholars argue that they were not rebellions but revolutions whose collective power was directed "at overturning the social and economic structures that exploited the many for the benefit of the few." For a short time, at least, the rebellions managed to bind thousands of peoples from different places along the ethnic and racial spectrum—poor whites, slaves, free persons of color, and Indians—and thus raise the specter of class warfare.[45]

Creole elites often divided sharply over myriad issues, but the prospect of rousing unknown and frightening forces from below caused them to pause. As long as Spain could protect them from this menace, Creoles were hesitant about pressing their demands. But their loyalty was qualified; their Americanism had grown. The sum of anxieties and protest over grievances had generated a sense of patriotism. Among a large number of Creole disaffected, doubtless, professions of nationalist sentiments and desire for liberty rang hollow, but there was an intangible emotional dynamic at work in preindependence Spanish America, what Rafael Altimira called "the formation within the bosom of colonial society of consciousness of its national personality."[46]

What the alienated Creoles required was the inspiration to act.

8

The Feared Revolution

An event—the 1807 French invasion of Spain and the arbitrary removal of King Ferdinand VII—not an ideology triggered the rebellion in the Spanish monarch's transatlantic kingdoms of seventeen million people and four viceroyalties that stretched from California to the tempestuous straits of Magellan and from the tropical lowlands of the Orinoco basin across the forbidding Andes to the Pacific Ocean (See map 4). The reaction to Ferdinand's overthrow in Spain and Spanish America was one of defiance and rebellion. Yet the apparent universality of sentiment against the French usurpation of the Spanish throne and the declarations of support for the deposed Spanish king offered little reassurance to the Creoles that they commanded a unified people.[1]

From the beginning of the violence, the revolution was riddled with contradiction and ambiguity. Spanish resistance to French rule commenced almost immediately, led by a central junta in Sevilla that elevated Spanish "colonies" (which were, in fact, "kingdoms") to the status of the provinces of Spain and thus entitled them to representation in the Cortes of Cádiz of 1812. Spain and Spanish America were one nation, but Spanish America was not entitled to equal representation. To the Creoles, this was peninsular imperialism in the guise of constitutionalism, but to metropolitan Spaniards the "pacification of America" was a unifying issue. Men who disagreed passionately over popular sovereignty and self-determination in Spain were often in agreement on the retention of Spanish America. Interpretation of motives was a different matter. Reformers who applauded the constitutions of 1812 and 1820 alertly sensed that the white Creoles were risking war not for independence but for a new relationship with the Spanish Crown. Absolutists advanced the obverse of this argument: the collapse of royal authority that followed the French invasion and Ferdinand's forced abdication prompted the rebellion.[2]

Throughout Spanish America but especially in those regions where social tensions complicated the political situation, reaction to what was happening in Spain from 1808 varied. Even where Spanish colonial officials acted independently, drawing on their dwindling resources to maintain their authority over the *cabildos,* Napoleon's action provided the opportunity the Creoles had long awaited. It was the catalyst for the children of those Bourbon families who had migrated to Buenos Aires or Cuba, fought for acceptance, and fashioned a modern secular ideology to replace the traditional social catechism of the children of the conquerors.[3]

Miranda, the Precursor

The task, then, was to convince those Creoles doubtful of the necessity for action. Certainly, the moment of greatest opportunity was also the moment of greatest danger, but the most outspoken of the revolutionary precursors, the Venezuelan Francisco de Miranda, could point to the success of American revolutionary leaders in mobilizing a people for war but preserving their place in society. Disaffected Creoles had a choice of revolutionary models, Miranda informed Pedro Gual, one of the perpetrators of a 1797 conspiracy in Venezuela: "Two great examples lie before our eyes, the American and the French revolutions. Let us discreetly imitate the first; let us carefully avoid the disastrous effects of the second."[4]

As did other revolutionary precursors, Miranda invoked a cultural nationalism—a reminder of ancient Indian empires and the ageless resentments about mistreatment by the modern Spanish state—to inspire a generation increasingly alienated from the motherland. Though an international presence and, presumably, a person of influence among powerful North Americans and Europeans, Miranda doubtless confounded his confidants with his plotting. William Pitt the Younger, one of his putative benefactors, understood the political and especially the commercial advantage to Great Britain of an independent Spanish America, but the British prime minister must have been befuddled by Miranda's plan of government—a Creole "Inca" emperor presiding over a government with an upper chamber of appointed notables and a lower chamber of elected citizen legislators, whose moral behavior would be carefully monitored by two censors.[5]

Miranda was more comfortable in Europe or the United States, where universalist credos often found warm reception among political leaders who had little to fear from the masses beneath them. But Venezuela was a particularist society whose elites inhabited a more precarious world. Aversion to independence was an instinctive response of a dominating landed aristocracy in a colonial export economy (60 percent cacao) dependent on a slave labor force. By the turn of the century, when Venezuela's population approached nine hundred thousand, whites constituted 20 percent (of whom only 1.3 percent were peninsular Spaniards); slaves, 10 percent; Indians, 18 percent; and free blacks and pardos, 45 percent. Most of the population lived in the coastal valleys and the interior *llanos*. The concentration and mix of such disparate social and ethnic groups contributed to the colony's potentially explosive social tensions, especially in the province of Caracas, where most of the land and slaves had fallen into the grip of 658 families (1.5 percent of the population). Their reach spread from the Caracas valley in three directions; they controlled the militia, held the choice seats in the ruling *cabildos*, and received preferential status at the university. They lived splendidly and they did not want their lives to change. They chafed under Spanish pressures but were restrained from raising the flag of rebellion by something stronger than objection to Crown policy. They were fearful of losing their slaves and, just as frightening, of starting a rebellion in which large numbers of free blacks, pardos, and even the poor whites—none of whom shared their social view—would inevitably take part. What they wanted was "independence without war and liberty with a slave and subservient population."[6]

Liberation had been the credo of Haiti's rebellious slaves, and the attendant racial war and destruction of property Venezuelan Creoles feared could occur in their own land constituted too great a risk, whatever the economic benefits. Yet if they failed to act, the course of imperial reform would ultimately weaken their position. The upward mobility of the pardos, inspired by the sale of certificates of whiteness, especially alarmed the Creoles, who protested the enrollment of pardos at the university or their appointment to the militia. Such indulgence was ruinous, "an insult to the old, distinguished and honoured families."[7]

What prompted them to pause was their experience of short-lived but frightening agitation by the wretched in their midst. In 1794, as stories of the Haitian slave revolt had swept the colony, the slaveholders had successfully campaigned against a new Spanish law designed to improve the condition of slaves. The following year the colony had been convulsed by an uprising of slaves led by free colored leaders who espoused French revolutionary rhetoric. Before the military could suppress the revolt, the slaves had ransacked plantations and killed landowners. Two years later, when the conspiracy at La Guaira and its cries of liberty and equality had shaken the colony, Creoles had readily assisted the Spanish in stifling what they perceived as dangerous to their social position.[8]

A few years later, Miranda returned to a United States now led by aged revolutionaries who spoke of liberty in spatial, not ideological, terms. Jefferson was president, warily charting U.S. policy toward a Spanish Empire already collapsing on its northern Florida frontier. Former vice president Aaron Burr was hatching a bizarre plot to liberate Florida, Texas, and Mexico. Miranda instinctively heartened to these impulses and in 1807, with the timely assistance of a few prominent New Yorkers, secretly organized an expedition for the liberation of Venezuela. Among the crew were one hundred North Americans, lured with promises of gold and silver to fight in a cause they only vaguely understood.[9]

Venezuela's powerful Creole planters and merchants *did* understand. They were less concerned about Miranda's philippics against an "oppressive unfeeling government" than what his rebellion portended for them. Though they grumbled about Spanish policies and the inconveniences occasioned by the war, they enthusiastically donated money and men toward the defeat of a man they called an "abominable monster." A parallel reality to these incipient, radical Creole ideas was embodied in Miranda's actions. Certainly he was alert to the interest of certain European powers in the prospect of bringing down Spanish rule in the Americas, but there were profound limitations for the success of what were essentially urban movements involving small cadres in places where the population was mostly rural.[10]

The Porteño Revolt

Where urban sentiments could be focused on a common danger, of course, the Creole agenda was more promising. In Buenos Aires, Creoles drew on their deserved reputation as the city's defenders against British invasions in 1806 and 1807. Animosity between Creole and Spaniard had deepened in the late colonial period, as elsewhere in Spanish America, but in Buenos Aires the lower classes, who had difficulty finding work and often lived at subsistence levels, displayed an uncommon hostility to the prevailing order. Their numbers, which made up approximately one-third of the population, consisted of imported slaves, freedmen, and those of mixed parentage. Their presence accentuated Creole and Spanish apprehension about the dynamics of the social structure. Indeed, race and caste were perhaps the only things on which Creole and Spaniard could agree.

The British invasion presented the Creoles with an unavoidable challenge to organize this mass of unpropertied and alienated. As the Spanish viceroy and the wealthy fled into the interior, they organized the mobs of blacks and mulattoes into a militia to protect the city and their property. In the second invasion, which embarked from British-held Montevideo, the *porteños* captured a nine-thousand-man force and compelled its humiliated commander to abandon Montevideo. Creoles swelled with pride. "They appeared to awaken as from a dream," wrote the contemporary observer Henry Brackenridge, "or rather to be aroused into life, from a state of lethargy or stupor."[11]

The vulnerability of the city persuaded porteño Creoles that they must act rather than remain disgruntled but passive spectators of the political dynamics of their environment. In 1809, when a group of Buenos Aires peninsulars plotting to seize power fell to quarreling among themselves, the Creole dominated militia of 3000 and not the depleted Spanish garrison of 371 served as the only reliable guardian of public order. Creoles tended to divide along social lines—the propertied favoring the military and traditional social values, those from the artisan or professional ranks expressing more radical views—but they generally agreed that the city's future lay in commercial liberalization. This put them into conflict not only with Spanish monopolists who opposed granting concessions to foreigners but also with agricultural interests in the interior as well. On the eve of the May 1810 declaration of independence, the disparate political groups in Buenos Aires—proindependence Creoles who preferred constitutional monarchy over republican government and socially conservative, anti-Creole Spaniards opposed to independence but committed to the creation of a republic—had fashioned a coalition of necessity. Acting alone, neither had the means to sustain their cause. Ideological enemies, they shared a reliance on the militia to carry out their will. Their dependence on essentially pragmatic military leaders was a disturbing portent for Argentine politics.[12]

In Buenos Aires, the revolution assumed the form of plots and intrigue as rival factions mobilized to assume direction of the revolutionary agenda. In

May 1810, when they learned of the French overthrow of Seville's junta, Creoles pressed for a *cabildo abierto* (an open town council, generally dominated by property owners, clerics, and officials) and organized armed bands. By the time they had gathered to debate a course of action, a few outspoken naysayers were calling for support of the Spanish viceroy in the name of the deposed king. But the Creoles, sensing they held the military balance, invoked the name of the people and insisted on a patriot junta. Theirs was not a call for representative government, however, but the revolution of a minority who uttered a hollow pledge of fidelity to King Ferdinand and ruled through a junta, ruthlessly persecuting those who dared to defy them. They put down resistance in Córdoba, expelled and sometimes executed Spaniards, and created a Committee on Public Safety to terrorize those who opposed them.[13]

Within the radical inner circles, the revolutionary ardor inspired fantastic schemes ultimately linked to the junta's international pretensions. Alert to the diplomatic problem of declaring independence while currying the favor of the British government, then a Spanish ally, Mariano Moreno proposed a bizarre plan calling for a revolutionary insurgency in the Banda Oriental and southern Brazil: "Plan of Operations which the Provisional Government of the United Provinces of the Rio de la Plata should Pursue to Consolidate the Great Work of Our Liberty and Independence." He was explicit in his description of the plan's social purpose: "The foundations of a new republic have never been cemented unless rigor and punishment were mingled with the blood of all citizens who might obstruct progress. . . . If a revolution is not directed aright, if intrigue, ambition and egotism smother the spirit of patriotism, . . . then the emancipation of a nation will produce all sorts of excesses, and will cause the upheaval of the social order."[14]

Such was the price of liberty. Its intimate connection to the rights of property holders found expression in 1812 when the revolutionary junta publicly explained to Buenos Aires's slaves that "your longed-for liberty cannot be decreed right away, as humanity and reason would wish; because unfortunately it stands in opposition to the sacred right of individual liberty [of slaveholders in their property rights]."[15] The immediate legacy of such division was uncertainty among those who had instilled a military discipline into the ranks but could not sustain it in the campaigns into the interior, where the popularity of the cause diminished. Manuel Belgrano, marching from Santa Fe to Salta in 1812, wrote morosely of desertions and the "total indifference" and even "mortal hatred" among those encountered.[16]

There was a more disturbing factor for those who were mindful of the social changes accompanying revolution: the voicing of ever more strident egalitarian credos as blacks, mulattoes, and unemployed joined the military ranks. In the interior, where landed families prevailed and social attitudes were more conservative, the reach of the revolutionary regime for new recruits caused more concern. One legacy was an army recruited from among the castes and slaves donated to the cause as a sign of commitment. In the early years at least, the revolutionary government spared the economically active male population from military service. But the absorption of the lower classes into the military did not strengthen the movement for democracy. On the contrary, "the distance between soldiers and officers grew noticeably with the increasingly authoritarian discipline."[17]

The professionalization of the military reinforced among recruits colonial notions of deference and loyalty to their Creole officers. In the beginning of the crisis, the mobilized castes had served as a link between the social elites and the popular sectors of society. In the course of the revolution, they became the means by which the elites exercised control over those sectors. In other regions, however, the numbers of castes and Indians and the concomitant fears of their strengths among Creoles altered the dynamics of the social revolution Buenos Aires had commenced. In Upper Peru, where royalist suppression of the initial conspiracy had been particularly severe, Creoles initially welcomed the Army of the North from Buenos Aires as a liberating force. But uncertainty about disturbance of the social equilibrium in a province where caste lines were sharply drawn—apprehensions accentuated by the demands for arms from the lower classes in La Paz—created tensions among local Creoles and the newcomers. Royalist counterrevolutionaries exploited such fears, mobilized their forces, and in June 1811 inflicted a devastating defeat on the Army of the North.

The pro-Indian policy was part of the strategy of the Buenos Aires revolutionary junta to end the age-old state of Indian servitude and, more immediately, to expand the Army of the North. A thousand men composed the Army of the North when it set out for Upper Peru; by the time it arrived, it had grown to nine thousand. Yet there was a realization, even among some in Buenos Aires's revolutionary cadres, that Indian emancipation, however useful as a means of raising an army of liberation, was as threatening to Creole patriots' privileges as to Spaniards'. Such Creole fears were especially prevalent in the Andean massifs where Indians greatly outnumbered whites. In such interior provinces as Tucumán the revolutionary emissaries were more circumspect in assuring that the domination of the *gente decente* over the castes prevailed.

Incorporating Indians (who constituted a minority in Tucumán) into the revolutionary army did not disturb the social structure.[18]

Within two years of the May 1810 revolution, a conservative band displaced the radicals, instigated its own reign of terror, and just as suddenly fell from power. Its successor was the revolutionary legislative assembly, dominated by the imperious liberal Bernardino Rivadavia, who spoke grandly of educational reform, broad civil rights, and opposition to the slave trade but who exercised power arbitrarily. When his enemies attempted a military coup, he suppressed them as mercilessly as any Spanish governor. In the aftermath came the dissolution of the provincial juntas and the "oligarchy of the intellectuals." For a year, Rivadavia and his coterie appeared secure. Then, in October 1812, they became the victims of yet another coup.

This time, however, the perpetrators included significant newcomers to the cause, émigrés (the most notable was José de San Martin) with military experience who rallied Rivadavia's enemies with cries of constitution, democracy, and independence and called the provincial revolutionaries back to the cause. The victors soon proved as incapable of bringing unity to the movement as their predecessors. Delegates to a constituent assembly denied admission to representatives of José Gervasio Artigas's Banda Oriental. Artigas admired the United States and was outspoken in his advocacy of independence. In the fall of 1813, Spanish troops arrived in Montevideo. Two months later, the revolutionary army commanded by Manuel Belgrano, who had played a critical role in the porteño revolution, suffered a humiliating defeat to royalists in Upper Peru. Had the arriving Spanish officials been more alert to the despair among La Plata's Creoles and offered a conciliatory proposal, they might have restored royalist authority. They were adamant about restoring the colonial status of the city. In Buenos Aires, the hardliners now had persuasive evidence of Spanish intentions. The only recourse was independence.

Throughout these troublesome years Buenos Aires's revolutionary leaders tried to persuade the social sectors of the city that despite their sometimes fratricidal behavior they had inherited the mantle of legitimacy from the Spanish Crown. In their determination to prevent a restoration of the old order they resorted to intimidation, persecution, and execution of plotters against the revolutionary order. One result was a loss of confidence in them, particularly among Buenos Aires's powerful merchants and what remained of the upper classes. There was no organized opposition but there was cautious detachment—a reserve born of the realization that those whose wealth and prestige depended on commerce and the governmental bureaucracy could not afford to disdain the revolutionary order. The city's social elites took public oaths of support to the revolution. In the process they fashioned bonds of solidarity based not on ideological commitment but on mutual self-interest. Such manifestations of adherence to the cause could not substitute for what had collapsed in the revolution's wake: "an entire context of institutions, of collective beliefs, of values, which the Revolution destroyed. . . . As a replacement for the complex system of loyalties inherent in that system [the revolution] offered only loyalty itself."[19]

Elsewhere in the Southern Cone, the revolution meant defiance not only of Spain but of Buenos Aires. Montevideo in the Banda Oriental had benefited much more from *comercio libre* than had Buenos Aires, and its reaction to the precipitating events in Spain had been very different. Montevideo's merchants clearly believed they could profit better under an enlightened Spanish regime. The dramatic surge of the independence movement and the determination of the Spanish to pacify the countryside in the Rio de la Plata prompted Artigas (who had organized a band of smuggling gauchos on the Brazilian frontier) to lead a resistance. Artigas had a following among intellectuals, clergymen, and lawyers in Montevideo, but his social base lay among the estancieros who stood to lose their land if they could not prove legitimate ownership. Artigas pacified the countryside with help from Buenos Aires.

But in 1811 his plans went awry when he began negotiating with the Portuguese. Their intent was to capitalize on the breakdown of the Spanish Empire and dominate all the Banda Oriental. It was a grave miscalculation, since his revolutionary allies in Buenos Aires preferred Spanish to Portuguese control of the province. Artigas declared withdrawal was preferable to abject surrender, a declaration of provincial sovereignty. He led four thousand soldiers and four thousand civilians into triumphant retreat. The act of defiance made Artigas a hero. He persisted in resisting the centralism of the porteño revolutionaries, even as they aided his return to the Banda Oriental. Outraged, they declared him an outlaw. In occupying Montevideo, however, the Buenos Aires revolutionaries found it difficult to impose a centralist regime on a people with federalist sentiments and reconciled themselves to having Artigas in power. He returned to a devastated province in 1815.[20]

The second center of resistance to porteño radicalism lay in Paraguay. When the Buenos Aires Creoles proclaimed the May revolution, the cabildo abierto in Asunción decided to straddle the issue by professing obedience to the Regency in Spain and friendship to Buenos Aires but without recognizing its authority. Offended, the Buenos Aires junta dispatched an expedition into the province. Outraged Paraguayans mobilized five thousand in resistance. But there was no opportunity for Asunción's royalists to seize control. Power in the province lay with those who commanded loyalty in the countryside. A junta deposed the intendant and defined Paraguay's revolutionary course. As in the Banda Oriental, one person—Dr. José Gaspar Rodriguez de Francia—crafted Paraguayan revolution and articulated nationalist sentiment. In the process he created a power base in the countryside among small farmers, estancieros, and peasants. His was a political skill at social control and manipulation through deception.[21]

Venezuela—Creole Revolt, Pardo Revolt

In Buenos Aires, revolutionary Creoles divided largely on their attachment to the political agenda of the cities' intellectual or military factions; in the interior provinces (Tucumán, Córdoba, and the Andes provinces) and the Littoral provinces (Santa Fé, Entre Rios, and Corrientes), on the longstanding resentment of country landowners and traders toward Buenos Aires. For both, events in Spain during the critical years of 1808–1810 merely confirmed their separatist convictions. In Venezuela and Mexico, by contrast, the Creoles had deeper concerns about the impact of revolutionary turbulence on the social order. Theirs was a more precarious social condition.

As the economy weakened from the European wars and the pardos grew more encouraged by a beneficent Crown, Venezuela's Creoles recognized that they had to take political action. Hearing of the French invasion of Spain, they asked for a meeting of the cabildo to decide the fate of the colony. Naturally, the Spanish rebuffed them and noised it among the pardos and poor whites that their position would be worsened if the Creoles had their way. This worked well enough until the spring of 1810, as news of the Seville junta's collapse prompted cabildos throughout the empire to take action. When Spanish authorities refused to go along, the Creoles formed their own junta.

United by class interest, they divided on a course of action. In the beginning the moderates, who dominated, promptly rejected any notion of admitting Miranda on the grounds that he was an atheist with dangerous social views, but in other respects they proved liberal—abolishing export duties and the *alcabala* (sales tax) on certain consumer goods and providing for town elections. In any event, their influence over events within the city and especially among juntas in the province noticeably diminished. In late November 1810 the U.S. commercial agent in La Guaira reported a conspiracy of Spaniards against the junta and another, "equally dangerous . . . with the design of seizing and usurping the Executive power, of massacreing all the Europeans, & lastly of freeing the negroes, and placing the mulattoes & them on an equal footing with the rest of the whites."[22]

The military expedition dispatched by the Caracas moderates to quash this uprising probably represented their last attempt to maintain command of the incipient rebellion. By the spring of 1811, a more radical element based in the Patriotic Society, which favored independence, dominated. But the fragmentation that characterized the rebellion in Venezuela had already taken form. Once suspect to the Creoles, Miranda now entered Venezuela with their blessing. He and Bolívar fashioned the Patriotic Society into a political forum where the Creole elite were able to express *their* conception of independence: "a *cercle de pensée* with aspirations of political control of the movement, and it effectively pushed the congress . . . to declare on 5 July 1811 the independence of the Republic of Venezuela."[23]

Its social agenda contrasted sharply with that of the national congress, where the pardos had found a hearing. Bolívar himself called upon the congress to heed the leadership provided by the society. The constitution of the first republic reflected the Creoles' view of how a republic should be ordered: privileges and legal discriminations were swept aside but in their stead was the inequity of a franchise based on property. The slave trade perished; slavery did not. Indeed, the Creoles promptly supported measures for a national guard to capture runaway slaves and to police agricultural labor. Blacks and pardos recognized that the Creole revolution promised little and began organizing their "insurrection of a different type," as royalist officials noted.

The most serious occurred in Coro. Beleaguered Spanish commanders were quick to respond, sending agents and priests into the coastal areas to encourage the growing divisiveness between Creole and black. Bolívar, not yet the convert to abolition, vilified the blacks and their free colored allies (who randomly killed whites and destroyed property) as an "inhuman and atrocious people, feeding on the blood and property of the patriots, committing . . . the most horrible assassinations, robberies, violence and destruction."[24]

Despite such condemnations, the uprising persuaded many Creoles, most of whom were opposed to abolition, to hesitate in their support of independence. The pardo insurrectionists of Venezuela were not genuine royalists, fighting for king and church against the Creole perfidy. In the Venezuelan llanos and countryside, the pardos were "neither royalists nor upholders of order and religion. . . . These men embraced the royalist cause as a pretext for avenging class hatreds [and] in order to gain the social liberty they desired."

Most Venezuelan Creoles, mindful of distorted but frightening stories about the calamity that had befallen Haiti's slave society when leaders had extended political liberties to the oppressed, instinctively understood this. "They spoke frankly that political equality symbolized an opportunity for the castas, who would seize on the concession to advance their goal of social equality."[25]

Royalists capitalized on Creole apprehensiveness, recruited pardos to their cause, and waged a merciless counterrevolution. The Creole cause received a further setback in March 1812 when an earthquake devastated Venezuela from the interior to the coast. In Caracas, Bolívar himself rescued people from crumbled houses as unsympathetic clergy told benumbed townspeople that the earthquake was God's retribution for the impertinence of independence! The first republic now began to collapse from within, and rebellious Caracas began to lose its tenuous hold over patriot juntas in the provinces. In the llanos, the fearsome guerrilla chieftain José Tomás Boves threw his support to the royalists, and Spanish troops easily dispelled Creole forces from western Venezuela. In their predicament, Creoles elevated the aged Miranda to commander-in-chief and gave him sweeping powers, but the fire of revolutionary zeal no longer burned within him, and, as the Spanish pressed on Caracas, he began negotiating a peace settlement. If the royalists would safeguard patriot lives and property, Miranda would surrender and leave the colony. He was en route to exile when an outraged Bolívar arrested him and turned him over to the Spaniards.[26]

By the end of the year Bolívar himself had fled to Cartagena, where he explained to the New Granadans that Venezuela's "most grievous error" was the "system of tolerance" in the first republic. Regrettably, Bolívar warned, in an ominous prophecy of the "war to the death" that he would inflict on his native land, Venezuela's revolutionary junta had "based its policy on poorly understood principles of humanity, which do not authorize governments to use force in order to liberate peoples who are ignorant of the value of their rights."[27]

The Richest Kingdom of the Crown

Buenos Aires, neglected and on the periphery of empire, made the Creoles' choice of independence a logical option, despite their often rancorous disputes over tactics. Dynamics of race and social identity complicated the revolutionary strategy in Venezuela and perhaps made inevitable the war to the death that followed the demise of the first republic. In New Spain (Mexico), Napoleon's invasion of Spain prompted the provincial viceroy to call for unity among Creoles and Spaniards and to accommodate Creole autonomists by appointing them to office and encouraging discussion of public issues. His efforts were not enough to assuage them. As their sense of the diminished authority of Spain deepened, their latent Creole resentment of peninsular domination increased and they became more outspoken.

Mexico was the richest kingdom in the Spanish Empire in the New World, a corporatist social order where status based on privilege and inheritance—a subjective calculation of one's "place" in society—did not readily fit into modern social classifications. Upper classes included those who owned estancias, haciendas, and mines and those in the highest echelons of the bureaucracy and the church; the middle class, merchants, professionals, managers of rural property, and lesser bureaucrats; and the lower classes, small shopkeepers, vagrants, and the jobless. Beneath them were colonial Mexico's indigenous peoples (three-fifths of the population), who lived on the haciendas or labored in the mines and possessed no property or goods but who had hopes of a better life. A "considerable part" of these "miserables" lived in small towns and survived by fishing, hunting, or subsistence farming. The castas (a fifth of the population) lived in similarly precarious circumstances.[28]

Evidence of social modernization was already appearing in Mexico, but the society lacked for any institution that encouraged even modest notions of upward mobility. At the top of the social hierarchy the animosity between Creole and *gachupíne* (as peninsulars were called) had divided New Spain into two seemingly irreconcilable factions. Peninsulars deprecated the Creoles as untrustworthy, frivolous, and lazy; Creoles responded with damning slurs that concealed Creole jealousy of anyone who had "pure blood." Despite these fissures, the hierarchical social structure remained largely intact, principally because those in each sector jealously guarded their privileges and, in mystical faith, looked to the king to settle matters. On the surface, colonial Mexico exhibited the characteristics of José Ortega y Gasset's "invertebrate society" of peoples with differing values and aspirations—"Indians, castes, nobles, soldiers, priests, merchants, and lawyers but there were no citizens."[29]

In actuality, New Spain underwent change from the earliest years of the conquest. The creation of privileged estates and the formation of castes had been an evolutionary rather than a dynamic process until the quarter-century before the 1810 revolt, a period of impressive but uneven economic growth. Commerce and mining offered a more rapid ascent in the economic strata of colonial Mexico, but these avenues did not alter the patterns of investing in land, nor did the acquisition of wealth as a merchant or a mine owner diminish the belief that enduring social status depended on land ownership. What galled many of the Creoles was the knowledge that much of the new wealth in commerce, especially in the capital and in most important provincial cities, accrued to recent immigrants, who exploited their newfound wealth to rise in the social hierarchy as descendants of old Creole families were falling. Achievement, not inheritance, marked the peninsulars, relatively few in number, as a distinctive social elite—European Spaniards whose "arrogance sprang from the conviction of . . . superiority to the colored masses about [them], an attitude . . . confirmed by . . . command of the chief avenues leading to financial success. . . . The upper-class American Spaniard was born a gentleman and demonstrated his superior status by conspicuous consumption."[30]

Over the years, then, even Indians and castes, with luck and enterprise, acquired limited social mobility, but the social dynamics of an economy undergoing transformation could easily be misinterpreted. At the turn of the century, Alexander von Humboldt despaired of the social injustice and inegalitarianism in Mexico City and contrasted social opportunities for the lower classes with those for their contemporaries in Philadelphia. But such a discerning observer may have failed to note the amelioration of conditions for the dispossessed or the unfavorable conditions for popular uprisings in the cities, where a more heterogeneous society offered better prospects for mobility than the countryside. Most important, a repressive state apparatus stood ready to crack down on popular uprisings. By any measure, Mexico City on the eve of revolution was less vulnerable to urban violence than Paris in 1789.[31]

The Hidalgo Revolt

Such changes were slow to alter the ingrained social values of the hierarchical society and posed little realistic threat to Creole or peninsular, but Creole resentment over perceived loss of status nonetheless heightened in the early years of the nineteenth century. In 1808, when news of events in Spain shook the colonial bureaucracy, peninsulars were fearful of anything that hinted of independence. In September they removed the viceroy, threw radical Creoles into jail, and installed a viceroy of their own liking. They formed militias, drawing their recruits from among the workers of Spanish merchants. This preemptory counterrevolution reached into the countryside and revived old antagonisms. Creoles who wanted to share power were again reminded of their secondary status in the kingdom.

Amid an economic downturn exacerbated by an agricultural crisis in 1809, when production fell and prices rose sharply, embittered Creoles vowed to oust the Spaniards. On this occasion, however, outbursts of popular agitation commenced in Guanajuato and in the Bajío, where the economic crisis had dramatically reduced employment among miners, worsened the condition of Indian labor, and reversed the once ambitious prospects of a small Creole professional class.

Miguel Hidalgo y Costilla, one of the growing numbers of frustrated Creoles, had so infuriated ecclesiastical authorities with his denunciations of Mexican social injustices that they had compelled him to resign his academic position in Valladolid. He took up the lowlier role of parish priest in the village of Dolores. As the social crisis deepened in the Bajío, he began using his parish as a gathering place for discussions about the political situation. Hidalgo moved easily and comfortably among Creoles, mestizos, mulattoes, free blacks, and Indians (he spoke several Indian dialects). But, unlike most Creoles, he was sympathetic to the suffering of the Indians and the castes. A convert to the Creole conspiracies that swept the region in 1809–1810, Hidalgo became leader of the Querétaro cabal. Indians and castes had little comprehension of Creole ideology but instinctively understood the symbolism of the Spanish monarch as their "father." One of the Creoles, Ignacio Allende, who argued for their inclusion, explained, "As the Indians were indifferent to the word liberty, it was necessary to make them believe the insurrection was being accomplished only in order to help King Ferdinand."[32]

But the new viceroy uncovered the plot and crushed it. Hidalgo resolved to act, however. On September 16, 1810, as people arrived for Sunday Mass, he declared the *grito de Dolores,* less a call for national independence (though, ultimately, it became identified as the initial demand for independence) than a passioned appeal for an end to the injustices suffered by Indians and castes. Certainly, his listeners sensed what he was calling for and flocked to the standard. Within a month, sixty thousand, many armed with nothing more than bows and arrows, had gathered in his army. In the mining town of Guanajuato (which fell to the insurrectionists in late September), miners, unskilled workers, and convicts joined them. Their cry was now "independence and liberty," and Hidalgo invoked the Virgen of Guadalupe, Indian and Spanish in her symbolism. "Once [he] had taken the banner of Guadalupe . . . and placed it at the head of his forces, the dissident priest became transformed into a revolutionary-prophet in the leadership of a Marian crusade, the chosen person to whom the Mother of God communicated."[33]

Neither the Creoles nor even Hidalgo, who obviously sensed the bitterness among the Indians and castes, correctly gauged the passions they were unleashing. This was a popular movement, Hidalgo believed, justified in its assaults on Europeans and their property and in its abolition of the burdensome Indian tribute, but the character of the insurrection that ensued revealed no singularity of purpose nor unity in a common cause. Hidalgo provided leadership and articulated grievances for a movement that drew its strength from local, not national, social dynamics. Its eruption into a regional insurrection that shook the most populous cities of Mexico could be explained as much by the disunity and quarreling among elites, which provided opportunity to act, as by vengeful retaliation from the lower orders for their undeniable misery.

The conspiracy had originated among urban Creoles and the frustrated "provincial bourgeoisie" in Valladolid and Querétaro. Hidalgo had shifted its appeal to the dispossessed and alienated in the Bajío, where economic conditions and a surplus of labor enabled estate owners to exploit their rural dependents. Rebel leaders drew their recruits from among dispossessed tenants, muleteers, unemployed miners, bandits, the lower clergy, and artisans. Where economic dislocations had permitted estate owners to impose lower wages or drive tenants from their lands, the rebellion found recruits; where property owners could not afford to alienate those beneath them, as in the villages of the central highlands, it failed.[34]

Hidalgo proclaimed the "liberty and independence of the Mexican nation" and promised to consider Spaniards not as "enemies but only as obstacles to the success of our enterprise." In the battle for Guanajuato, however, the destructive potential and racial animosities of the rebellion terrified both peninsular and Creole elites. The Spanish administrator of Guanajuato, anticipating a rebel assault on the city, moved the town's militia, the Spaniards, and their wealth into the *alhóndiga*, the granary. This left Guanajuato's impoverished and lower classes virtually defenseless and made the town a more inviting target. Against the Spaniards in the alhóndiga "who do not decide to become our prisoners," Hidalgo warned, "I shall use every force and strategem to destroy them without any thought of quarter."[35]

His army struck Guanajuato with uncontrolled savagery. The attackers massacred and mutilated the granary's defenders (some of whom were Creoles) and destroyed the mines. People watching the battle from the nearby hills soon joined Hidalgo's troops in the looting of stores and houses. "Guanajuato presented the saddest picture of disorder, ruin and desolation," wrote

Lucas Alamán. "The plaza and streets were scattered with broken furniture, discarded goods taken from the stores, and liquor bottles tossed aside by drunken attackers who committed all kinds of excesses."[36]

After Guanajuato the army marched on Valladolid (now Morelia), which surrendered without a fight a month after the revolutionary cry of Dolores. But the character of the revolt had already taken a different form. In the countryside, landowners in the path of Hidalgo's marauding wave provided food to spare themselves, cities readily surrendered, and Creoles adopted a circumspect neutrality. They maintained nominal loyalty to the government, but they failed to take the field against the insurgency. Correctly sensing the social threat from below that accompanied class and race war, they spoke less about autonomy and conspiracy. Home rule, not an egalitarian social order, was their goal. Violence against authority by rural people was not uncommon in Mexican history. What made the Hidalgo revolt as frightening to Creole as to Spaniard was the number of participants and the broad appeal of the movement. As the army marched it grew "prodigiously," wrote a contemporary, conveying a frightening impression of tremendous strength.[37]

The response of city dwellers to Hidalgo's movement, however, was noticeably less enthusiastic. In October 1810 Hidalgo turned his army of eighty thousand toward Mexico City and confronted a Spanish army of twenty-five hundred. On October 30 the two armies waged a fierce battle. When darkness came, the royalists, though surrounded, managed to break through and escape into the valley of Mexico. Hidalgo lost half his men to desertion. The next day, preparing for an assault on the city, he dispatched runners to the Indian villages in the valley, calling for recruits. But the Indians, many of whom feared the loss of communal lands, did not respond favorably to his call for assistance, and, indeed, condemned Indians who followed Hidalgo as traitors. Hidalgo called on the viceroy to surrender. When he refused, Hidalgo had the choice of unleashing an army he could no longer control on the city or retreating before Spanish reinforcements arrived. Hidalgo chose to withdraw to Querétaro, where he established his command. He now had an army of forty thousand, ill-disciplined but almost six times the number of an advancing Spanish army. In a manifesto he denounced the Spaniards for presuming to represent the true faith and warned Americans "not to be seduced by our enemies: they are not Catholics but political opportunists; their God is money."[38]

More exhortations followed, but Hidalgo must have sensed that the Creoles had abandoned his cause. In mid-January 1811 he led his army out of Guadalajara to engage his Spanish foe. Within six hours, the Spaniards routed the rebels. In retreat, his officers removed Hidalgo from effective command. For a few months they managed to sustain what was now an insurgency, but it was clear that Indians and castas were no longer rallying to the cause. "No longer animated by grand, unifying idea and not seeing their goals achieved," wrote Villoro, "they retained only the destructive impulses of the enraged, without precise plan or objective, refusing to be submissive to anything or anybody."[39]

In March, a royalist force captured Hidalgo and three other commanders at the town of Nuestra Señora de Guadalupe de Baján. They were chained, taken to Chihuahua, condemned, and executed. Their severed heads were placed in parrot cages mounted in the granary at Guanajuato. There they remained until 1821.

Morelos, the Successor

The frustrated insurgents found another leader, José María Morelos, a priest who led a band of guerrillas in the south. Morelos had studied with Hidalgo in Valladolid. He shared Hidalgo's frustration with the Mexican small merchants and tradesmen and sensed the social injustices of the age, but he had little use for the random violence committed by Indians in the Hidalgo revolt. Anarchy was ineffective as a means of achieving national unity, he solemnly recognized. His army was small, disciplined, and committed to war against royalist forces, not against whites, too often the victims of Hidalgo's troops, nor against "the rich simply because they are rich, must less against rich criollos."[40]

This seemed a curious position for a priest born of a mestizo father and a Creole mother (who had died in the *tierra caliente* of Michoacán), a former mule driver who had suffered more than Hidalgo. Morelos raised an army and in November 1812 took Oaxaca, a rich province. Hidalgo had marched on Mexico City with eighty thousand undisciplined men; Morelos commanded three thousand trained soldiers. He used the Indians as support. They took booty and spoils, but Morelos tried to placate the Creoles with tax reform and a political agenda offering an alternative to the royalist regime, set forth in 1813 at the Congress of Chilpantcingo. This was shortly followed by a declaration of independence and an impassioned appeal to Creoles and suspicious castas. Only the hated gachupines had no place in the new society. With such lofty sentiments he sought to reconcile the nationalism of the Creoles with the demands from below for social justice. Indian tribute and slavery were abolished, but the revolutionary cry was religion and *patria*. In the patria there were no Indians, no mulattoes, no castas. All but Europeans were Americans.[41]

Still, the Creoles remained unconvinced. They were hesitant about the social agenda, though Morelos made clear that Mexico's political freedom must precede social reform. In *Sentiments of a Nation,* Morelos expressed traditional Scholastic thought when he wrote that sovereignty resided in the people, who relinquished it to their governors, and that laws apply to all save privileged bodies. He espoused social equality and economic opportunity but believed in private property. In 1812, a secret club within the revolutionary organization, the Society of Guadalupe, called for the seizure of haciendas and their division into smaller tracts among the poor, but there is no proof Morelos approved the plan.[42]

As his military prospects dwindled in the face of royalist victories, however, Morelos's declarations became more threatening. Proclaiming the elimination of castas and Indians as social designations was unsettling to the Creoles, but exhortations about the right of Indians and campesinos to own the lands they worked struck directly at the Creoles's place in the social order. Their fears appeared confirmed when they read the *Medidas Políticas,* an incendiary document attributed to Morelos but emanating from the Guadalupes, that called for seizure of property from the wealthy—cleric, Spaniard, or American.[43]

Such rhetoric heartened the new viceroy, momentarily frustrated by the Spanish liberal constitution of 1812—a document drawn up by delegates to the Spanish *Cortes,* which had been called by the junta governing in the name of Ferdinand. Twenty-one Mexicans had participated in its sessions, and they had proudly announced that the constitution prescribed representative government for Mexico. But in the following year the viceroy instituted a brutal campaign against the guerrilla chieftain. In late 1813, he drove Morelos from Valladolid and pursued his fleeing insurgent army (and the rump congress accompanying it) into the countryside. Divided and on the run, the congress issued a new constitution in October 1814 that, among other things, weakened Morelos's power.[44]

Most of the Creoles had already abandoned the insurgency. Some joined the royalist forces that hounded the retreating insurgents throughout central Mexico in 1815. Morelos was finally captured as he waged a diversionary campaign designed to give the fleeing congress an opportunity to escape. As with Hidalgo, he was first defrocked, then tried before civil authorities. A royalist judge condemned this champion of the "true faith," as he described his cause, as a heretic and a traitor. Such a condemnation, one of the inquisitors informed the viceroy, "would be very useful and fitting to the honor and glory of God, serve the king and the state, and perhaps offer the most effective means of extinguishing the rebellion and . . . reproaching the rebels for their errors [in following Morelos]."[45] He was shot on December 22, 1815.

The Social Question

The civil war within the American Revolution had been a feud of "neighbor against neighbor," cutting across social demarcations, of white Tory against white patriot, of elites versus elites. As in Spanish America, blacks fought on both sides, but revolutionary British American patriots had not confronted the Society of Castes, the mass of Indians, mestizos, mulattoes, and blacks whose outbursts and insurgencies had antedated and in many ways anticipated the rebellion the Creoles had proclaimed. Once the fighting had commenced, these newcomers had shown much of the ambivalence the Creoles themselves displayed. Both royalist and patriot exploited the castas, drafting them into armies with promises of freedom or heightening expectations of social advancement. In Peru and Upper Peru (now Bolivia), the majority of royalist soldiers were Indian. In the central highlands of Peru, patriot insurgent leaders "had a great deal more in common with the colonial elite than with the peasants, Indians, and poor *mestizos*" of the region, which explains why they fought on both sides or exploited the confusion to ransack haciendas for cattle.[46]

Despite these apprehensions, the initial phase of the Spanish-American revolutionary movements had instilled an egalitarian spirit in society and a corresponding Creole ambivalence about the legal status of Indian, mulatto, and mestizo. Even in Venezuela, the first constitution prohibited further importation of slaves, made Indians equal with citizens, and specifically condemned older laws that denoted civil degradation. In the Liberal Assembly at Cádiz, which produced the short-lived 1812 constitution, Spanish-American delegates, in a tactical maneuver designed to gain greater representation in the proposed common parliament, successfully fought a peninsular move to exclude Indians from citizenship. In the end, they agreed that the basis for representation would include those natives of Spanish dominion but they did not annul the "certificates of whiteness." This meant, for example, that Africans whose parents were legally married and freed, who served the nation, and who had a profession or trade could receive citizenship. Another decree allowed pardos to attend the universities and become priests.

These were minimal concessions to a generation of outcasts who had little faith in Creole professions of an enlightened social order and sensed opportunity in the anarchic conditions of the rebellion's early years. In Venezuela and New Granada, particularly, the civil wars plaguing the *patria boba*, the "foolish fatherland" born in the patriot enthusiasm of 1810, offered grim reminders about the fragility of nationhood to those who made revolution without a broad social base. In New Granada, wealthy Creole patriots had rousted demoralized royalists and created provisional juntas. Within a few months, the populace divided between centralists led by the charismatic Antonio Nariño at Santa Fe de Bogotá, and federalists at Tunja, who found their ideologue in Camilo Torres.[47]

Ordinary people had little comprehension of this revolution from above and the principles its creators had espoused in the constitution of 1811. The revolution had been the work of elites determined to safeguard old privileges. Nariño, who assumed the civilian executive power of Cundinamarca and with the blessing of the electoral college became dictator, was alert to the dangers of political fragmentation and division among the elite in the determination to eschew modest changes in governance. In prophetic words that haunted the elites of postrevolutionary Latin America, he warned: "If we don't change our ways, we'll go to our execution and ruin, buried under these fine unworkable constitutions. . . . Our greatest present evil is partisanship and division."[48]

Centralists were victorious in 1812 and 1813. By early 1814, Nariño's forces had triumphed from Bogotá south to Popayán, but, as patriots swooped into regions where hacendados felt themselves threatened by counterrevolution from above and turbulence from below, their appeal noticeably diminished. Granadine elites were equally fearful of Nariño's expeditionary bands and the success of royalists in rousing blacks and pardos. The Frenchman Gaspar Mollien, traveling the cordillera between Cartagena on the Caribbean coast and Pasto on the Ecuadorian frontier, wrote of encountering few whites and many coloreds. Social and racial conflict in the Cauca Valley, which paralleled this route, sprang from deep-seated tensions among local elites dependent on slave labor to exploit resources, In Popayán, where whites made up less than one-fourth the population, slaveowners were alarmed by Nariño's appeal to slaves in the western cordillera for his war against southern royalists. The tactic, he persuasively argued, was necessary to counter royalist recruitment of slaves for the counterrevolution.

With the exception of a qualified manumission decree in Antioquía, little came of these measures, and, following Nariño's defeat and capture in Pasto in May 1814, the cause of patriot liberation of slaves diminished. But the equivocation of the popular classes about the revolution did not deter New

Granada's Creoles. On the contrary, the apprehensions and frustrations of the southern campaign persuaded them that only a declaration of independence (July 13, 1814) would institutionalize the new political and social order. In his assessment of the social questions plaguing the republic and the measures required to address them, Nariño anticipated Bolívar's celebrated transformation of conscience by several years. "No one better understood," wrote Indalecio Liévano, "the sorrows that awaited the republic if it fell into the hands of an oligarchy that threw up obstacles in its desperate quest to fulfill for all granadinos the benefits of nationhood."[49]

In the "Memorial of Grievances" (the "Creole Testament"), Camilo Torres had condemned the artificial distinction between Creole and peninsular as political and social absurdity and predicted the fall of Spanish rule if it persevered. In assuming power, however, Creole elites had preserved the invidious social distinctions between themselves and the people they presumed to lead. In the political and social convulsions of these years Torres had failed to perceive what Nariño intuitively sensed: nationalism assumed a spiritual definition among people who harbored a fleeting hope that they might be governed by men sympathetic to their plight, who bore the same complexion, and who would help them overcome the burdens of their miserable lives.[50]

"War to the Death"

For the Creoles of Venezuela, the fears of social discord had run deep from the beginning, and royalists had been able to bring down the first republic. Savoring victory, they refused to accommodate the chastened Creoles and commenced a war of repression. When Bolívar (who had fled into New Granada after the fall of the first Venezuelan republic in 1812) returned as liberator of Venezuela in 1813, he condemned Spaniards for their atrocities and made clear that the struggle in Venezuela was a just war. Those Spaniards who joined his struggle would be forgiven. They were Americans. Those who rejected his amnesty would be killed.[51]

Condemning his defiant Spanish enemies for a counterrevolution of undeniable savagery, Bolívar launched his "war to the death," a campaign of destructive fury through cities and towns where his men shot almost every European they found. In such grim circumstances the second republic was born. Bolívar marched into Caracas in early January 1814 and spoke triumphantly before the assembly, which had granted him extraordinary power. In eloquent phrases he assured them he would not abuse that power, that he could never be the oppressor of the Venezuelan people.[52]

Patriot victories in both east and west offered assurances of the second republic's future. The "nation" of which he wrote, however, resided on a social base as narrow as that of the first republic. Blacks, mulattoes, freedmen, mestizos—most of whom had earlier identified with the royalist cause—found little in Bolívar's words to mitigate their hostility toward Creoles. The rebellion in Venezuela was as much Creole against Creole as Creole against Spaniard. Bolívar himself admitted the reality of civil war when he sadly recounted "that our conquerors are our brothers and our brothers triumph only over us."[53]

Parallel to the conflict between Creole and Creole was a more destructive and ominous violence. In the llanos, the black royalist officer José Tomás Boves, who commanded more than ten thousand vengeful troops, renewed his war against the whites, combatants and civilians. Jailed in Calabozo as a Spanish traitor by the republicans in 1810, Boves had gained his freedom when Spanish officials concluded that the revolution offered little to the plainsmen. Their intent was to incite a racial war from below against the white *mantuanos*. In Boves they found a willing leader of the pardo revolt. Bolívar had vowed to make war against Europeans; Boves pledged to kill the whites and take their land. The plainsmen waged racial war. In Calabozo Boves ordered eighty-seven whites executed; in the Aragua town church, more than four hundred; and in Barcelona, it was widely reported, almost a thousand. Bolívar explained the legitimacy of the independence struggle in words a Creole hacendado or even a Virginia planter readily comprehended, but Boves instinctively understood the social code of his ferocious black soldiers. His troops were former slaves, assassins, convicts; they were undisciplined guerrillas; and the only human quality they respected was courage.[54]

Bolívar denounced the pillaging but confirmed Creole fears when he reluctantly permitted landowners to dispatch patrols to capture fugitives and enslave them. He was fighting a war on two fronts: one against the Spanish army and, as events soon demonstrated, another against the equally formidable llaneros of Boves from the south. For a few months in early 1814, the lingering hatreds between Creole and peninsular in Venezuela appeared to lessen before this sobering reality. But Boves adhered to no arrangement between the despised whites. His colored soldiers devastated a patriot army at La Puerta on February 3. A week later, Boves's lieutenant, Francisco Rosete (a Canarian shopkeeper), led a contingent of liberated plantation slaves against the town of Ocumare. There the conquerors raped the women and killed three hundred, then severed noses, ears, breasts, and penises from corpses and triumphantly nailed them to doors. When Bolívar heard of Ocumare's fate, he ordered the execution of Spaniards in La Guaira and Caracas prisons. More than a thousand were slain by shooting or by decapitation with machetes.[55]

The Spanish soon renewed their war against the second republic. In early May, the Spaniards massed on the borders of Caracas province with the most formidable and best equipped army yet mobilized in the counterrevolution. Bolívar resolved to meet them before they penetrated further. On the savannas of Carabobo, the patriots won a tremendous victory on May 28. Bolívar returned to Caracas. Within two weeks he was marching again toward Carabobo to battle Boves's llaneros. When Boves's army met Bolívar patriots in mid-June, the wretches of the plains prevailed. They took no prisoners and killed a thousand of the enemy. A month later, Boves triumphantly entered Caracas, inaugurating a reign of terror that diminished only when his guerrillas scurried out of the city to engage the patriots. Bolívar explained the defeat to a crowd of stupefied Creoles when he blamed Creoles, not Spaniards, for the civil war. One of his royalist adversaries had a similar premonition about the socioracial conflict that loomed in Venezuela. The pardos would kill the white Creoles, he predicted, then turn on white Europeans. Neither British nor American commanders in the American Revolution would have had reason for such a sobering assessment.[56]

Boves died in battle in December 1814, but his colored plainsmen had brought down the second republic and resurrected old fears among Creoles and Spaniards. The character and especially the motivation of the llaneros have continued to intrigue both North American and Venezuelan historians. There was a frightening but undeniable social democracy in these fierce invaders from the Venezuelan outback. In his military and civilian appointments, Boves paid no attention to color. Pardos with no opportunity to occupy important posts under Spaniard or Creole became high-ranking officers and occupied important positions in local government. In Caracas, men who had been servile laborers or even slaves governed. Boves inverted the social pyramid. He dispatched vagrants and beggars to work on the haciendas. He made sure that provisions for the city were promptly delivered. The despised social structure and hacienda economy could not be eradicated by decree but through evolutionary change.[57]

Always, there was uncertainty about what Boves would do. In this respect, Spaniard and Creole were in agreement about the pardos. Ethnicity was only a partial explanation for their suspicions, however, Llaneros were from an alien world: they lived differently; they fought differently; they looked at *every-*

thing differently. Waging guerrilla war in the countryside, Boves could be brutally sadistic and cruel, even by the harsh standards of revolutionary Venezuela; as the campaign progressed, he sometimes comported himself more in the fashion of a royalist officer. Without legal authority he created tribunals and made appointments, yet no Spanish official dared raise the issue with Boves. His notions of command and warfare befitted the countryside. He organized squadrons of men from the same region to foster comradeship. He demanded respect for local populations and removed from battle those who abused people in the presence of their children, yet in unleashing his mass army on the cities he encouraged savage behavior. He fought a guerrilla war where officer and ordinary soldier endured similar hardships and spoke of common goals.[58]

As fearful as it was to contemplate, this was the kind of war Bolívar must wage in order to triumph.

9

The Price of Victory

In mid-February 1815, a powerful Spanish armada with eleven thousand soldiers (the largest ever sent by Spain to the Americas) sailed from Cádiz under the command of Pablo Morillo. This was the counterrevolution the royalists had been hoping for—the restoration of Ferdinand VII's legitimacy in his kingdoms. Everywhere, the rebellion against Spanish rule was in disarray. Patriot ranks were fractured and bitterly divided, especially in Venezuela, where Morillo's army invaded. In April, Morillo took Margarita; in May, he marched into Caracas. That summer he launched a drive westward, and by October 1816 New Granada's revolutionary chieftains were in retreat. Across the ocean, Spanish conservatives spoke optimistically about the reconquest of Buenos Aires.

Among the Creoles traumatized by the popular uprising in New Granada and especially in Venezuela, the initial response to Morillo's arrival was reassuring. Had Morillo imitated his royalist compatriots in Mexico and made his peace with the Creoles, he might have quenched the revolutionary fire in northern South America. In establishing a revolutionary order, Creoles had often exacted a fearful price from royalist sympathizers. In fratricidal New Granada, where the independence movement had drawn its strength not from ideological consensus but from separatist sentiments inherent in the old geographical division of the country, the population initially welcomed Morillo's army. In victory the Spanish were swept along by the class and racial animosities that had engulfed Venezuela. They commenced by rounding up Creole leaders—federalist and centralist—and submitting them to prompt trials and punishment. Some were banished, others, heavily fined, conscripted into the royalist military, forced to work, or imprisoned. The Spanish executed five hundred of the Creole patriot elite.[1]

But the counterrevolution did not revive the old order. In some respects, the conquering Spanish royalist army proved unable to provide anticipated support for those who had suffered and fought to restore it. And international circumstances after 1815, especially the British decision to permit arms shipments to Spanish-American insurgents, benefited the rebel cause. The fundamental obstacle to Spanish-American royalist plans stemmed from an unambiguous legacy of the experience of revolutionaries and counterrevolutionaries during the first five years of war: "Neither could gain a decisive victory without mobilizing the lower classes, and no victory so gained could be without social consequences."[2] (See map 4.)

Creole response to the social unrest from below had set the standard for the Venezuelan battlefield. Once unleashed, there seemed to be no end to the violence, no mitigation of its savagery. Boves himself had fallen victim to its opportunism when he marched into Caracas in 1814, seizing booty and property and dividing the spoils not with his impoverished llaneros but with royalists and foreign businessmen. When Morillo took Caracas and listened to stories of a ravaged countryside where unburied bodies lay in disgusting heaps, he pledged forgiveness. Statistics about the Venezuelan carnage of these years are unreliable, of course, but in 1815 a journalist estimated that 134,000 (not counting the 13,000 dead from the 1812 earthquake) had perished in the warfare commencing in April 1810. Half of them were whites.

Yielding to the demands of vindictive royalists, Morillo seized rebel property (including seven of Bolívar's haciendas) in confiscations that struck two-thirds of Venezuela's Creole families. Its economy devastated, reconquered Venezuela was as much liability as asset under royalist domination. More critically, the pardo armies unleashed by the royalists against Creole patriots now posed a social dilemma. A "war of colors" had begun, according to one Spanish official; the pardos would remain "natural enemies of society" until the Crown liberated them from their inferior legal status. The experience of war had conditioned even loyal pardos to expect much more. Morillo was attentive to such arguments, but the social condition of Venezuela in 1815 could not

4. Latin America, 1830.

readily be ameliorated only by addressing the subordinated place of the pardos in society. What mattered as much was *where* and *how* these people had always lived. In the cities, perhaps, an authoritative presence of royal authority coupled with a sincere determination to rectify grievances of the dispossessed would have advanced the reconquest. In the countryside, scattered pardos behaved as "savage tribes," wrote Morillo; they "form bands of thieves, accept and harbor deserters, and commit every kind of excess and disorder."[3]

Boves had made commitments to the pardos; Morillo, though sympathetic, was in no position to fulfill them. In the process it was Bolívar, not Morillo, who realized that a harsh counterrevolutionary regime would ultimately defeat Spain's purpose. Boves's death and Morillo's entry into the Venezuelan cauldron may have benefited the drive toward independence by stifling the caste war and providing Creole patriots with an opportunity to draw on the democratic spirit of the llaneros and, especially, their hatred of whites. In Buenos Aires, patriot elites fired with the liberal sentiments that had taken root in the cities never relinquished their control of the independence movement. In Venezuela, however, the dynamics of the war assumed very different patterns. Before Bolívar could hope to triumph, he had to fashion an alliance with country chieftains—authoritarian men who thought in military, not political, terms. The struggle had reached a dramatic turning point, Bolívar shrewdly noted: "The death of Boves is a great loss for the Spaniards because they will probably not find another chieftain with his qualities."[4]

The experience of Venezuela's popular insurrection had also changed Bolívar's thinking about slavery. In Kingston (where he had taken refuge after six months of fighting in New Granada), he issued in September 1815 the famous Jamaica letter, a long and passionate attack on Spanish misrule. From Jamaica he went to Haiti, where Alexandre Pétion provided assistance (seven ships, six thousand men with arms and ammunition, a printing press, and several Haitian advisors, *los franceses*) in return for a pledge that the liberation of Venezuela would include the liberation of slaves. In December of the following year Bolívar launched his campaign in the Guianan lowlands.[5]

The revolution now had a singular purpose—to liberate the continent—and to that cause Bolívar vowed to enlist Creole, pardo, and slave. Incorporation of the pardos in the cause, unthinkable a few years earlier, now seemed a realistic choice. A Spanish report acknowledged that the pardos stood to benefit more from the revolution than from the restoration of colonialism. The reason had less to do with any transformation of Creole thinking about the social rights of pardos than the circumstance of war. In rejecting the 1812 constitution, Ferdinand VII had removed many of the benefits provided to the pardos. In 1815, a royalist general perceived the dangers in this and recommended a reconsideration. "Venezuela has returned to the domination of the King," he wrote, "thanks to the efforts of the inhabitants themselves and the armies under the Royal banner were composed almost entirely of Pardos and people belonging to the other castes." In the process the pardos had advanced in the social order. "The darkest Pardo became accustomed to giving orders to whites and to treating them on at least equal terms. . . . In the case of these people no other means remains than to take them from their inferior class."[6]

Ferdinand was not persuaded, however, and the people of color the Creoles both feared and despised began joining the patriot causes. Emancipation for the slaves was a different matter. Bolívar freed his own slaves and in two decrees of mid-1816—perhaps the most perilous year of the revolutionary cause—declared that those who fought would gain their freedom, but his Creole compatriots refused to follow his example. In truth, slaves had little wish to take on the white man's war, but they did not participate (as in 1812–1814) in a separatist campaign of war against whites. Through gradual and often subtly complicated changes in revolutionary tactics, Bolívar managed to enlist pardos and slaves in the patriot cause.

Royalist forces still contained pardo militias and perhaps two thousand slaves and former slaves fighting under Spanish command, but Morillo's unsuccessful appeals to the Crown to lift discriminatory decrees coupled with the increasing patriot commitment to social equality benefited the rebel cause. Some patriot leaders who delighted in the confiscation of royalist slaves into their ranks were reluctant to seize Creole property for the same purpose, but then, who among them could argue that in a time of general conscription of men and property a slave should be exempted? One means of recruitment was to permit owners to provide a slave for their own obligatory service or require a levy of 10 or 20 percent of an owner's slave work force (with a promise of compensation) for the revolutionary cause. Those who served were promised their freedom. Few of them were returned to bondage. The issue of abolition came up again at the Congress of Angostura (February 1819), where Bolívar pleaded with the Creoles to abandon slavery and, as before, found them sullen and resistant when he spoke of the "dark mantle of barbarous and profane slavery."[7]

The Heritage of Revolutionaries

In the American Revolution, slaves had won their freedom by fighting, and the war had accelerated the cause of abolition in the northern states. But for Bolívar there were few reassuring similarities in the U.S. experience. Massachusetts abolitionist and Virginia slaveholder may have railed at one another about the compatibility of liberty and slavery, but they united in a singular cause. Political, not social, issues were central to the revolutionary agenda.

This comparatively fortuitous circumstance was born not of ideological commitment but of social circumstance: as the war entered its most perilous days, the Continental Army had unsettlingly larger numbers of social marginals, to be sure, but these were mostly *white* males. When he ventured into Massachusetts to take command of the revolutionary army, Washington expressed his dismay about the "strangeness" of the troops he now commanded, but he ultimately learned to relate to them if not fraterize with them as equals.

Bolívar's choices were more perilous. He had to mobilize an army of predominantly *colored* social outcasts. In the llanos, or upper valleys, of the Orinoco and Apure Rivers his troops were pardos and former slaves who had no sympathy for slaveowners' property rights, royalist or patriot. When he decreed the abolition of slavery in Guayana and Apure, the slaveholders there were too weak and few in number to challenge his abolitionist measures. Creoles *were* heartened by his occasional somber warnings about *pardocracia* and the parallel fears about the rule of castas over whites. Suspecting a coup among the pardo officers to bring down the Creole officer corps. Bolívar retaliated against its putative leader, General Manuel Piar, a mulatto who had commanded the liberators of Guayana. Piar had steadfastly refused to acknowledge Bolívar as supreme commander. For his defiance, Piar was tried by military tribunal and shot in October 1817.[8]

Bolívar's troops held Guiana; patriot commands in Cumaná, Maturín, and Barcelona harassed Morillo's troops. Their officers were of unquestioned loyalty, but to assure a patriot victory in Venezuela Bolívar sought another convert, José Antonio Páez, Boves's successor, who had mobilized an army of llaneros in the Apure valley. On the last day of 1817, Bolívar departed Angostura, marching his three thousand men almost three hundred miles to Apure plains. There he promised the suspicious Páez that his followers would be rewarded with public lands for their services to the revolution. Páez committed his llaneros to the struggle, but they did not leave the Apure, nor did they abandon their practice of making war for booty. Páez's followers marched under the same black flags and fought with the same furiosity but served the patriot cause because *white* royalists ruled in Caracas and treated them in a disdainful and imperious manner. Bolívar behaved unlike most Spanish or Creole officers. Among the plainsmen, the Liberator was "folksy, strong, bold, capable of anything; . . . live[d] like the toughest soldiers, without fear of beast, heat, cold, wind, or the enemy; and [was] at the head of his troops fighting with the same courage."[9]

Would the pardos acquiesce in Creole rule when the conflict ended? Bolí-var's Angostura address of 1819, delivered at a critical moment in the course of the war, provides a summation of the political and social dilemmas confronting the Creoles. Conscious of their place in history in the waging of a long struggle for liberty and alert to the example of republican governance in the United States, they were tormented by fears of the kind of society emerging from the war they were fighting. And they confronted independence and republican governance with few certainties. "We are not Europeans, we are not Indians," he told the Angostura delegates. "We are but a mixed species of aborigines and Spaniards. . . . We are disputing with the natives for titles of ownership, and at the same time we are struggling to maintain ourselves in the country that gave us birth against the opposition of the invaders."[10]

To a generation of North American observers already skeptical of the capacity of Spanish Americans to establish a southern model of the United States, Bolívar's words conveyed a sinister intent. Perhaps unaware of the social and political convulsions that had accompanied the war for independence in British North America and, indeed, persisted for a generation, he expressed admiration for the federal constitution of the United States but believed it inappropriate for Venezuela. North Americans were a unique and fortunate people. Clearly, Venezuela's fundamental laws had to take into account such diverse factors as climate, resources, and traditions of the people before extending those liberties North Americans had incorporated into their constitution. Venezuela merited a "government preeminently popular, preeminently just, preeminently moral; one that will suppress anarchy, oppression, and guilt—a government that will usher in the reign of innocence, humanity, and peace; a government wherein the rule of inexorable law will signify the triumph of equality and freedom."[11]

A noble summation. A year later, Bolívar wrote General Francisco de Paula Santander, explaining the necessity of a proclamation emancipating the slaves in Cauca and their conscription into the patriot army. Slaves were needed for the army. Fighting was a "fitting and proper" obligation for those who wanted freedom. To maintain slavery in a free government was folly, for it would lead to rebellion or worse, as had occurred in Haiti. This was less a question of principle than of political necessity: "Is it fair that only free men should die for the liberation of the slaves? Is it not proper that the slaves should acquire their rights on the battlefield and that their dangerous numbers should be lessened by a process both just and effective?" There was another, more fundamental, issue: "In Venezuela we have seen the free population die and the slave survive. I know not whether or not this is prudent, but I do know that, unless we employ the slaves . . . , they will outlive us again."[12]

In truth, the victory had not yet been achieved in Venezuela. On the Apure, where foreign legionnaires had arrived to join the patriot cause, Páez's llaneros had fought fiercely but had not triumphed, as Bolívar had earlier anticipated. Now was the time to strike at New Granada, where royalist troops had grown weary and desertions had increased. In August 1818, Bolívar had dispatched Santander to Casanare, a sparsely settled and poor province. There, Bolívar intended to amass his invasion force against royalist troops scattered from Cartagena to Quito. Despite continual harassment from rebel contingents, they were a formidable opponent. And to depart a yet unsecured Venezuela meant still another risk. By transferring the war from one battlefield to another, Bolívar intended to compel Morillo to make a choice: he could fight in New Granada, which meant removing his army from Venezuela; or he could remain in Venezuela, fighting a series of skirmishes with Páez's llaneros, and lose New Granada.[13]

This was typically Bolívarian strategy—high risk but great rewards. Shortly after the Angostura conference he left with his army for the Apure, fighting several battles with Morillo. In May 1819 he gathered his lieutenants in a war council in a cabin, and, as they sat on cattle skulls, laid out his strategy for the liberation of New Granada. Later that month, he departed for Casanare to join with Santander for the heroic march across the Arauca and the rain-drenched Casanare plains, where the combined armies of twenty-one hundred men waded waist-deep in water and then ascended into the Andes. At thirteen thousand feet the toll on the men from exposure and the debilitating effects of altitude and animals were devastating. A fourth of the British legion perished on this march. Without Bolívar, they would not have pressed on. In the villages on the way down, the patriots replenished their losses by conscripting locals, often at gunpoint. Such practices revolted many of the foreigners, but without these new troops, the victories that followed, culminating in the triumph at Boyacá on August 7, would not have been achieved.[14]

Three days later, Bolívar entered Bogotá. Deserting Spanish troops were now joining his army. In the Cauca valley, popular forces—most of them bandits and runaways—rose against the remnants of Sámano's royalist troops; some took refuge in still-royalist Pasto. In the fall, leaving Santander in command of New Granada, Bolívar set out for Venezuela, and in December the congress at Angostura incorporated several of his political views into the constitution and declared the union of Venezuela and New Granada. Morillo still held Caracas, but Bolívar had the advantage. Spanish troops wore uniforms they had brought three years previously. Many were barefoot. They lived little better than patriot foot soldiers. Diseased and immobilized, they festered in poorly equipped hospitals or houses, subsisting on unsalted beef. Local administrators, Morillo discovered, now profited from the war by guarding civilian merchandise.[15]

The nightmare Morillo had feared three years before had become reality: defeat came not on the battlefield but in the deterioration of morale. Early in 1820, the royalist commander got discouraging news from Spain. In Cádiz, a dispirited group of Spanish officers led by Major Rafael de Riego, angry over the prospect of leading an expeditionary force to Spanish America, revolted. They compelled the king to restore the constitution of 1812. Morillo had little choice but to declare for the constitution and call for negotiations with his enemy Bolívar. When they met Morillo was dumbfounded. His adversary, who had fought so persistently and so valiantly, was a little man dressed in a frock coat who rode into camp on a mule. The six-month armistice that followed, without Spanish recognition of Venezuelan independence, of course, ended the "war to the death" and served to acknowledge Colombia's de facto autonomy. Morillo shortly left for Spain. His task of waging war to preserve an empire had ended; Bolívar's dilemma of creating something to replace it was just beginning. The task of pacification of a continent now lay with the Creoles.[16]

Bolívar's frustration was understandable. A war to the death had required an army of committed and disciplined troops. Slaves would demand freedom as the price of their service and pardo or slave would demand a stake in the postrevolutionary order. As an enlightened Creole and an astute commander, Bolívar had grasped a truth about those from below who fight to preserve the interests of those from above: self-preservation and self-interest may be risked in the cause of liberation, but those who serve the victorious cause will impose their own demands.

This became manifestly obvious when a renegade Spanish commander broke the truce and renewed the war in Venezuela. To defeat him, Bolívar had to rely on Páez's llaneros. After the victory at Carabobo (June 24, 1821), he entered Caracas, named a compliant colleague as president, and departed for Bogotá. But the real power in Venezuela was Páez, who was surrounded by a coterie of military officers demanding rewards for their services. This was yet another challenge to Bolívar's authority. He was president of Colombia and had acquired both military and civilian power despite his profession that in a republic these must be separate. When he offered to resign the presidency in order to confront the defiant Venezuelans, Colombia's congress rejected his offer. He was thus left with the task of pacifying the Venezuelan caudillos with generous grants of land. In a decree of July 1821 he divided the territorial bounty in Venezuela among Francisco Bermúdez, Santiago Mariño, and Páez by the expedient of establishing regional jurisdictions under the command of each. Páez enjoyed the advantage, however; he controlled the region around Caracas and the country's best and most dedicated soldiers.[17]

Within a few years Páez was *the* Venezuelan caudillo. With his base of support he challenged civilian liberals in Bogotá and by the end of the decade severed Venezuela from the political artifice Bolívar fashioned in the federation of Gran Colombia. In the lower assembly of the government in Bogotá a dedicated coterie condemned the military *fuero* and called for a denial of the vote to soldiers in the 1825 elections. But they were still needed, as General O'Leary recognized: "The government was still sustained through the influence and power of the caudillos who had made independence. Institutions by themselves had no force at all; the people were a machine which had ceased to function, being too ignorant to take action; what is known as a public spirit did not exist."[18]

Bolívar accommodated the Venezuelan caudillos with reluctance, persuading himself that the civilian governments taking form in the liberation of a continent would ultimately prevail. Discord had accompanied the creation of free nations, he had written in Jamaican exile in 1815, a year of despair for the revolutionary cause. On that occasion he had attributed the debility to the precariousness of the situation. His words hinted at a deeper problem, for Bolívar and his contemporaries faced the twin challenges of waging a long and arduous campaign for independence, which they achieved in heroic fashion, and creating nation-states with no usable Iberian or North American reference.[19]

The Course of Revolution in the Rio de la Plata

In the southern theatre of the continental war, San Martín had experienced a similar frustration. Ensconced in the Argentine interior, he had witnessed the ruinous consequences of the initial revolutionary strategy in the aftermath of Ferdinand VII's return to the throne and the onset of counterrevolution in Venezuela, Chile, and Upper Peru, where a royalist army repelled an invasion of the Army of the North and appeared ready to strike at Tucumán in the Argentine interior. Spain, he firmly believed, must be expelled from Peru. The route through Upper Peru now closed, San Martín decided on a flanking strike through Chile, where royalists had stifled the initial Chilean movement for home rule. He put together a new force—the Army of the Andes, made up of mestizos, pardos, and blacks—and disciplined it into a fighting force. In 1817, accompanied by Bernardo O'Higgins, the exiled Chilean patriot, San Martín led the Army of the Andes into Chile. It turned back the royalists, and O'Higgins installed a revolutionary government.

Such a military strategy required organization and leadership, but its ultimate success did not resolve the sociocial questions that had imperiled Bolívar's plans for liberating the north. Buenos Aires had presumed to lead the Río de la Plata in a united revolutionary front and had unleashed war throughout the region. But virtually everywhere the result had been to inspire provincial opportunists, such as Artigas in the Banda Oriental and Dr. Francia in Paraguay, to fashion their own revolutionary agenda. Buenos Aires's revolutionary directorate had employed the Army of the North as a social and political instrument of its power, a reminder that the revolution was more than a movement for home rule; it was a break with the past. Increasingly, however, the revolutionary cause became more dependent on local chieftains and family elites for donations of men and money or on local officials—men who in the colonial era occupied positions of secondary importance in the Spanish administrative hierarchy—whose cooperation was now vital.[20]

Buenos Aires brought the revolution to the countryside, but it was not able to extend the authority of central power into the interior. The legacy of this for the postindependence years was a cadre of provincial and rural authorities whose solidity and loyalty to the landed families proved stronger than that of their superiors. In the capital, revolutionary leaders were acutely sensitive to sharing power with subordinates but displayed a seeming indifference to similar pretensions by lowly subordinates in the interior. Part of the explanation, or course, was their apprehension of unruly gatherings of people in the cities and what their numbers portended for those who ruled, but porteño reliance on these people to supply men and material for the war was a necessity. To follow another course would have required vast resources to replace them with officials of unquestioned loyalty.[21]

As the political authority of the civilian revolutionary leaders weakened, the revolutionary dynamic in the countryside followed a social pattern dictated by local conditions and behavior. The revolutionary junta in Buenos Aires had recognized the role of black soldiers in the Upper Peruvian campaign and declared them equal to whites and Indians. This position did not necessarily contradict the statutory requirements for citizenship, which imposed socioeconomic restrictions and further subjected Afro-Argentines to proving that they were freeborn children of freeborn parents. When the revolution moved to the interior, the junta reminded the inhabitants of the commitment, but in Córdoba officials stripped black officers of their command. Nonetheless, black soldiers continued to serve in the ranks as a means of obtaining their freedom. San Martín's Army of the Andes numbered 50 percent former slaves recruited in Buenos Aires and the Argentine interior; they fought in Chile and, later, in Peru and Ecuador.[22]

War not only encouraged opportunists to mold new power bases but accustomed rural people, especially the elites, to acceptance of violence, brutality, and looting as unavoidable aspects of political life. Those who led campaigns encouraged such thinking. Military officers gloried in the virtues of ferocity. Little wonder, then, that in the campaigns in the Banda Oriental inhabitants attributed rapine and pillaging more to government troops than to Artigas's band of scofflaws and outcasts. In such an ambience it is easy to see why Artigas and Dr. Francia have become model social revolutionaries to a modern generation of historians. In Uruguay, where pillaging and crisscrossing of the terrain by rival armies had devastated the rural economy, Artigas announced in 1815 a provisional regulation that the properties of royalists would be distributed among Indians, free blacks, and poor Creoles. Devoid of capital, the rural Uruguayan cattle economy, Artigas believed, could be rejuvenated with an infusion of labor on small holdings where a man with a hut and two corrals (and cattle sequestered from seized royalist properties) would be able to survive.[23]

Though it was clear he intended the measure as an expedient to revive the rural economy and applied it only to abandoned lands, its revolutionary implications for altering the social structure disturbed the estanciero class. Bartolomé Mitre described Artigas as a renegade and a vandal. After the Argentine declaration of independence at the Congress of Tucumán in 1816, which established the United Provinces, the Argentine revolutionary junta tried to obtain a settlement with Artigas, but, as one chronicler wrote, "to speak of reconciliation with Artigas was to speak to the desert, [because] his obduracy could neither be softened by compassion, nor his pride humbled by dangers."[24]

The experiment was short-lived, collapsing under the Portuguese invasion of 1816 and Artigas's failure to transform its beneficiaries into a reliable social base of support. What followed was a lamentable return to the old habits of pillaging and rapine. Artigas enlisted the support of the revolutionary cabildo in Montevideo, composed of men who shared his commitment to the revival of the rural economy and the need for a labor force if not the redistribution of land to the dispossessed. The experience offered yet another example of the shift of political power from an urban to a rural base and a parallel dissolution of order in the countryside. During the Portuguese occupancy Uruguayan landowners fared better; indeed, the Portuguese tried to encourage sentiments for annexation of the Banda Oriental to Brazil through decrees calling for the development of the province and apologizing for the damage caused by the invading army. Yet it was clear, wrote the U.S. consul in Montevideo in 1821, as the population again confronted Argentine pressures, that the experience of the preceding years had culminated in a widespread "dread [of] the total annihilation of all order and an end of all tranquility."[25]

In Paraguay, Dr. Francia skillfully crafted what dependency theorists regard as an alternative development model and a social revolution. Denying both Spanish and Creole elites an opportunity to dominate the Paraguayan economy, they contend, he protected the independent nation from the debilitating economic condition afflicting many of the new republics. Francia's power base went beyond the urban social elites, undeniably, but Paraguay experienced no social revolution of consequence, save of course for those measures designed to enhance his power. His dictatorial methods restructured Paraguayan society at the top—merchants and opposing Creole property-holders suffered—but retained slavery and the Indian draft so as to guarantee a rural labor force for his rural allies. The rhetoric was often egalitarian, but the style was very much in the tradition of a Bourbon provincial administrator. Colonial Paraguay was a patrimonial state; so was Dr. Francia's Paraguay.[26]

Chile: The Frustrated Revolution

Revolution meant war in the countryside fought by armies with large numbers of castas led by Creole liberators who articulated the hopes of the dispossessed even as they sacrificed their lives to preserve a hierarchy that benefited the few. This was an oft-repeated charge among those who cite Latin America as the failed revolution, but the reality was more complex. The liberation of Chile from Spanish rule may serve as example. Chile's proclamation of home rule was the work of a traditional landowning social aristocracy. Two hundred Creole (and some European Spanish) families, most of whom had some Indian heritage but were not mestizos, dominated the great haciendas of the central valley, relying on a subservient and impoverished mestizo labor force. "Illiteracy, vagabondage, crime and drunkenness were widespread, and social evils such as these were denounced in vivid detail by the more enlightened Chilean thinkers."[27]

This oligarchy of Creole families (the most powerful was the Larraín clan) commenced the Chilean Revolution, and from the beginning they had little intention of jeopardizing their interests by emulating the egalitarian platform of their Buenos Aires compatriots. In 1814 the patriots who had installed the *Patria Vieja* (Old Fatherland) suffered defeat at the battle of Rancagua and in Chile. They were less secure than before, and Spanish repression galvanized the Chilean Creoles to revive the struggle. For three years they endured a savagely repressive counterrevolution from Spanish governors, one of whom, Francisco Casimiro Marcó del Pont, vowed not to "leave the Chileans tears with which to weep."[28]

A spirited Chilean guerrilla resistance was the response. In 1816, with the declaration of independence by the United Provinces at Tucumán and the appointment of Juan Martín de Pueyrredón as Supreme Dictator, San Martín and Bernardo O'Higgins raised their Army of the Andes for the assault on Chile. San Martín, who had plans to push northward against Peru, suggested that O'Higgins assume executive power in Chile. In early 1817, the Army of the Andes departed from its training site in Mendoza, crossed the mountains, and at the battle of Chacabuco (February 12, 1817) triumphed over the royalist army. Chile's assembly named San Martín as executive but he promptly stepped aside for O'Higgins.

When he returned to Chile as conqueror and ruler, O'Higgins pledged order and liberty, which pleased the Creole rural aristocracy, and a plan for the amelioration of the Araucanians, Chile's indigenous peoples. The government he installed was thus dictatorial and paternalistic, in the Bourbon neomercantilist tradition. Absolute power was vital if the happy society were to be realized. The 1818 constitution echoed radical sentiment for protection of the poor by the state, either through public assistance or through providing them with employment. This called for stern leadership, but O'Higgins was a modest man, a sometime reader of eighteenth-century Enlightenment thought, who possessed courage and determination but appeared to waver at critical moments. A Chilean confided to a British sojourner: "There is too much wax, and too little steel in his composition; however, there are few better, and many worse men than Don Bernardo."[29]

O'Higgins confiscated royalist property, abolished titles of nobility, and condemned entailment, but he was no laissez-faire liberal. The state, he declared, must intervene not only in the economic but in the social order to enhance opportunity for both upper and lower classes. This was not social revolution. O'Higgins wanted only to end the society of privilege, not to create the egalitarian society. He cultivated prominent Chilean notables, none of whom identified with his reformist policies. Friends warned him of the power of the aristocrats and advised him to crush them; he did strike, albeit unsuccessfully, at the *mayorazgo* (entailed state), the putative legal foundation of the economic and social power of the aristocracy. He antagonized church interests and irritated commercial interests by using his office for personal gain. In the end, he failed for want of a rural social base, and from 1820 until his departure three years later his experience in Chile was a litany of frustration and defeat. As in Argentina, the provinces successfully defied the capital, and O'Higgins chose exile rather than subject Chile to civil war. This was perhaps his greatest contribution to Chile, though his choice did not prevent the country from collapsing into civil discord in the 1820s.[30]

Mexico: Independence by Agreement Among Elites

Bolívar had invoked the cry of the continental struggle, American against European, but the resolution of that struggle depended on the circumstance of place and on the relationship between Spaniard and Creole and then between Creole and casta. With the onset of the "War to the Death" any lingering notion he retained about restoring the social compact vanished.

The struggle in Mexico had taken a different form. With the execution of Morelos, the countryside deteriorated into local conflicts with royalist armies in pursuit of guerrilla bands. Except for a momentary scare in 1817, when Francisco Javier Mina, a disgruntled Spanish liberal, called for restoration of the 1812 constitution and led an invasion, the Mexican theatre during these years resembled less a battleground in the campaign for independence than a war in the shadows, where isolated bands of guerrillas raided cattle ranches or struck at villages. Spanish officers and administrators confidently predicted the restoration of royal authority in the richest of Spain's New World kingdoms.

The expected collapse of the insurgency, however, was illusory. Mexico's rebels had acclimated themselves to guerrilla warfare, similar to that the Spanish partisans had waged against the French invader. They purposely broke into small units, taking advantage of the vast terrain the pursuing Spanish soldiers had to traverse. They attacked, withdrew, then hit in another place. When a confident viceroy offered amnesty, they resumed peaceful lives, awaiting another opportunity to strike. In Veracruz, their control of roads enabled them to block shipments from the port; they collected taxes from terrified merchants and travelers. In the mountains of Guanajuato, they amassed a force sufficient to swoop down on the regions surrounding Guadalajara and Valladolid (now Morelia). By 1818, a Spanish official acknowledged, Creole and peninsular had acquiesced in the permanency of the insurgency. In some areas, he reported, there was trading between merchants in royalist towns and guerrillas in the mountains. Royalist officers who insisted the country was pacified because cities were under Spanish control were naive.[31]

After a decade Mexico's Creoles seemed no closer to restoring the "social contract" with the Spanish Crown than on the eve of struggle. Further, they were yet riven by passionate quarrels over the revolution and the social disruptiveness accompanying it. "This was not a war between nations . . . nor a heroic struggle of a people for liberty . . . ," wrote Lucas Alamán, "[but] a rising of the proletarian class against property and civilization. . . . The triumph of the insurrection would have been the worst calamity to have befallen the country."[32] He wrote these words years later, but memories of the savagery at Guanajuato in the first month of the Hidalgo revolt burned within him. One hundred thousand Mexicans had perished in this war. Had he forgotten the "clamor for justice," when Mexicans asked to be treated as "enslaved citizens rightfully demanding their freedom" and not as "bandits," or the political struggle identified with Hidalgo and especially with Morelos and the constitution of Apatzingán, which had called for an independent republic?[33]

That liberal goal had largely collapsed by 1815 with the restoration of absolutist rule in Spain. Mexico's Creole elites had to find means other than an insurgency to achieve their goals. On the eve of what appeared to be a victory over the insurgents, Mexico's royalists received the disquieting news of the Riego revolt in Spain and the restoration of the 1812 constitution. Among the conservative Creoles, the clerical hierarchy, and the military, the prospects for the kingdom under an invigorated Spanish liberalism were similarly unsettling. In the following months, they conspired to create an independent Mexican Empire. Creoles who had earlier joined with royalists in their rejection of Hidalgo's and Morelos's social revolution found in Agustín de Iturbide's *Plan de Iguala* a means of achieving their goals. The plan provided for independence and equality of citizens, thus satisfying such guerrilla chieftains as Vicente Guerrero. Creoles and even some royalists (both of whom felt betrayed by the reformist and anticlerical laws emanating from the Spanish

Cortes) rallied to Iturbide's Army of the Three Guarantees—an independent monarchy, the supremacy of Roman Catholicism, and the equality of Creoles and Spaniards.[34]

Virtually nothing in Iguala paralleled Bolivarian revolutionary ideology. The experience of eleven years of war had not significantly altered Mexican Creoles' social priorities. Iguala offered an opportunity to achieve what they had been conspiring to bring about when Hidalgo's revolt had erupted in 1810. Spanish merchants looked favorably on a Creole government that would re-open trade; Creole miners and landowners, who had suffered in the guerrilla wars, found an opportunity to rebuild through peace; the alienated castes who had rallied to Hidalgo joined what was a popular movement to make Iturbide emperor—the protective, venerated leader. The Creole who had condemned Hidalgo and his successor as men who "desolated the country [and] . . . sacrificed millions of citizens" now proudly declared: "Without bloodshed, without incendiaries, without murders, without robberies, in short, without tears and without lamentations, my country became free."[35]

Mexico had preserved the social order because its liberation had not depended on an invading patriot army. On the surface, this appeared to be the unambiguous revolution: independence by the agreement of whites and the acquiescence of the castes. A deeper assessment of the settlement prompted more sobering judgments. For the autonomists, the conspirators of 1808 whose plans had gone awry with the Hidalgo rebellion, the victory of Iguala was only a momentary triumph. Iturbide's empire, which stretched from the forty-second parallel in the north into Central America, survived only two years. Unified in their opposition to Spanish rule, Mexico's first generation of political leaders quarreled incessantly. Despite the promise of independence, the generation that applauded the peace settlement confronted a future of civil war and discord.[36]

Peru: The War Within the Revolution

Peru, the last bastion of Spanish rule, was the ambiguous revolution. Already in sharp economic decline in the final decade of the eighteenth century, royalist Peru retained its hold on Creoles' loyalties even as their compatriots elsewhere were expressing their resentment of peninsular arrogance and perceived an opportunity to do something about it. Their reasoning had less to do with access to office (Peru's Creoles suffered proportionately in this regard) than with their instinctive fear that the kingdom's racial and ethnic makeup—only 140,000 whites in a society of more than one million Indians and castes—

bound Creole and Spaniard in a social bond no ideological force could sever. Experience had taught them a lesson: from the mid-eighteenth century until 1821, when San Martín prematurely declared Peruvian independence, Indians protested regularly against the multiple servitudes heaped on by the colonial system and its rulers.[37]

Thus, when revolution came to Peru, Indians had little reason to believe it would mitigate their condition. An exception was the movement in La Paz in Upper Peru, where in the summer of 1809 a revolutionary junta included Indian delegates, granting them the same rights as Creoles and mestizos and committing the movement to address their grievances. The cause soon collapsed under a fierce Spanish counterinsurgency. Three years later, Peruvian Creoles determined to wrest reforms from an uncompromising Spanish viceroy raised a rebel expeditionary force of Indians and mestizos and marched on La Paz, Puno, and Arequipa. In La Paz, undisciplined Indians slaughtered the Spanish garrison, then joined in attacking Spaniards and pillaging their property.

In the aftermath, Spanish repression was swift. For three years, the Spanish systematically and effectively destroyed the momentary unity of Creole, mestizo, and Indian. By 1815, the counterrevolution appeared secure. Creole rebels had no agenda incorporating Indian grievances. They were virtually in accord with royalists in their contempt for the masses and their fear of Indian rebellion. Even from afar, prospects for the patriot cause looked bleak. In his Jamaican letter of 1815, Bolívar had scribbled an ominous prediction: "Peru . . . without doubt suffers the greatest subjection and is obliged to make the most sacrifices for the royal cause; . . . the fact remains that it is not tranquil, nor it is capable of restraining the torrent that threatens most of its provinces."[38]

Afterwards, the unity of royalists and Creoles on the social question gradually diminished. In 1820, when the Riego mutiny compelled Ferdinand VII to restore the 1812 constitution, the viceroy's position weakened further, but this did not prompt Peru's Creoles to raise the revolutionary banner. In Chile, however, the revolutionary triumph under San Martín and O'Higgins had invigorated the determination of the southern liberator to strike north. Chile's patriots had built a navy (with a British admiral, the mercenary Lord Cochrane, in command), obtaining ships and crews in Great Britain and the United States. They had liberated Valdivia, the Spanish port, driven Spanish commerce from the South Pacific, and imposed a blockade of the Peruvian coast. Cochrane wanted to strike directly at Callao and Lima, ridding Peru of royalist control. San Martín was more cautious. Peru, he believed, had to be liberated by Peruvians, supported by his army. To adopt another strategy was to run the risk of plunging Peru into the bloodshed and anarchy that had befallen the Rio de la Plata in 1820.[39]

Given the dissensions within their own ranks and their fascination with San Martín's political professions, Peruvian royalists were at first inclined to negotiate. When talks finally occurred, however, they rejected outright independence. Confronting a blockade and a threatening public, the viceroy evacuated Lima, allowing San Martín to call a cabildo abierto of Peru's Creole elites, who declared for independence and named him supreme civil and military governor. This was a political act designed to address the anticipated social disorder in the wake of the viceroy's abrupt departure. An English chronicler, Basil Hall, described their fears: Creoles believed "that the slave population of the city meant to take advantage of the abscence of the [royalist] troops, to rise in a body and massacre the whites." Peru's Creoles lived fearfully amid a multitude of castas. "It was not only of the slaves and of the mob that people were afraid," wrote Hall, "but with more reason of the multitude of armed Indians surrounding the city, who, although under the orders of San Martín's officers, were savage and undisciplined troops."[40]

Empowered by the Creoles, San Martín alternately pleased and infuriated them by expelling Spaniards (confiscating their property), decreeing the freedom of children born of slaves after 1821, and abolishing the hated Indian tribute. In the mountainous interior, however, his authority meant little. There, Spanish troops and montoneros (guerrillas often led by Creoles and mestizos) waged a civil war of plunder and vengeance. Among the montoneros were populists whose cause was the community, Indians with scores to settle, and small bands of vagrants and bandits. The montoneros of central Peru, unlike those of Upper Peru, played an important role in the revolution in their harassment of Spanish forces. They were effective guerrillas, but they displayed no collective purpose to the continental revolution. Their hatreds, commitments, and suspicions were regional.[41]

San Martín's position weakened under the rivalries among Chileans, Argentines, and Peruvians, his habit of rewarding discontented Creoles with commands, and resentment over idle soldiers encamped outside Lima instead of fighting in the sierra. Frustrated, San Martín headed north to Guayaquil to meet with Bolívar, who had liberated Quito with his victory at Pichincha. His intention was to bring Ecuador under Peruvian command, to get aid for the Peruvian campaign, and to win over Bolívar to his plan for a constitutional monarchy in the liberated states. The liberator of the north consented to none of these, and an angry but chastened San Martín returned to Lima, persuaded that this ambitious and boastful Venezuelan possessed the wherewithal to liberate Peru. A month after the Guayaquil meeting, his influence sharply reduced among the Peruvian elite, San Martín left for Chile.[42]

The country fell into anarchy, the Spanish controlling the south and rival patriots warring over the north. In their desperation, the Creoles had little choice except to call on Bolívar and his army. The liberator of the north triumphantly entered Lima in September 1823, where he was named supreme military and political commander and presented with what his aide-de-camp Daniel O'Leary properly described as a "corpse"—four divided patriot armies (Peruvian, Argentine, Chilean, and Colombian), a royalist army, two presidents, a dictator, and a congress. In the north, a disgruntled ex-president hostile to his presence began talks with the Spanish and was overthrown by his own troops. This sign of commitment to the patriot cause from below heartened Bolívar. Despairing over Peru's condition, he was nonetheless persuaded that the international situation favored the cause of independence if the patriots could hold out. British policy sought an independent America, he had written his most devoted commander, the Venezuelan Antonio José de Sucre, four months before his entry into Lima: "England . . . desires to form an alliance with all the free peoples of America and Europe . . . in order to place herself at the head of those peoples and rule the world."[43]

The place he called a "chamber of horrors" must be tamed. To this end he railed against the traditional hierarchy for its fealty to the colonial regime and, when its representatives hesitantly committed to the revolution and chose their own political leaders, intimidated them into acquiescing in his demands. In early 1824, a compliant congress named him dictator, a title he considered repugnant to his political principles but necessary in a society where the populace (regardless of one's place in the social hierarchy) remained indifferent to any cause except that of self-interest. Bolívar strengthened the patriot army with new recruits from Colombia and renewed the war of liberation, paying for it by seizing royalist property, squeezing funds from the church, and imposing taxes. As Bolívar brought an enforced unity to patriot ranks, royalist determination to persist withered, particularly after Ferdinand VII (restored to complete power in October 1823 by a French army) ended Spain's liberal experiment. With Sucre's aid, Bolívar assembled a nine-thousand-man army, led it into the rugged highlands, and in August 1824 won a stupendous victory at Junín in a clash of cavalry in which no one fired a shot. The victorious army came down from the mountains for the decisive confrontation with royalist troops at Ayacucho in December, the determining (though not final) battle for independence. Sucre, not Bolívar, was in command. "Upon your efforts," he told his soldiers, "depends the fate of South America."[44]

Had they failed, a royalist Indian force was prepared to sweep down on them as they fled. Other minor skirmishes followed, but Ayacucho doomed any hope of a Spanish counterrevolution. The inevitability of Spanish-American independence, which the British were prepared to guarantee with their navy and which President James Monroe had acknowledged in his December 1823 message to the U.S. Congress, was a reality the Spanish were unable to prevent. Ayacucho, Bolívar wrote a few weeks later, brought "domestic peace," but there must be a "guarantee for our existence." The social conservatism that consumed him in later years had already begun to quench the inner fire: "I foresee civil war and disorder breaking out in all directions and spreading from country to country. I see my native gods consumed by domestic fire." The only recourse was to imitate the European powers at the close of the Napoleonic wars and create a federation, "a temple of sanctuary from criminal trends."[45]

National Consolidation

The new states appeared to be a generation away from experiencing the benefits of a creative and progressive liberal state. From Mexico to Argentina, reports of U.S. agents or travelers were filled with tales of plunder, anarchy, disorder. A U.S. emissary to Buenos Aires in 1832 solemnly reported, "There is here neither law or liberty—no sense of national honor or national justice or national dignity."[46]

The judgments of other prominent Americans were more cautious. Political retardation had less to do with choices Latin American leaders made than with what their revolutionary experience had meant to them and, perhaps more important, what they now confronted. Generalizations are particularly hazardous, for the diversity of new republics, despite their shared language and institutional inheritance, had tremendous implications in the formative years of independence. Spanish America on the eve of rebellion, unlike British North America in the 1770s, was not a political arena where ideologies debated inalienable rights and orators expounded on the power of colonial assemblies but rather a patrimonial state, linked in a precise and comprehensible way to the Crown. Their titular head forcibly removed from his seat of authority, his Creole subjects were thrown into disarray and confusion. Their first commitment as revolutionaries was an expression of political loyalty to the deposed monarch and opposition to the usurper.

On other questions, most notably the unexpected and violent outburst of the *castas,* such as the Hidalgo and Morelos Revolts, or the prospects of slave rebellion, which occurred in Venezuela, the Creoles were less conscious of the political than of the unanticipated social consequences of the revolutionary turmoil. They were again confounded by the social issues that had been altered in unexpected ways by the long years of struggle. Had they planned one revolution but unleashed another? In the beginning of the wars, Creole patriots had successfully articulated a political grievance against the metropolitan state and, as circumstances required, made some concessions to win the support of the castas. In the process, they fashioned a broad coalition of disparate and potentially divisive political elements. With independence, such a fragile coalition could not easily survive.[47]

War had altered the relationship between whites and castas but had not significantly disturbed the hierarchical character of society. With some qualification, certainly in the amount of devastation caused by a decade and a half of war and in the ethnic makeup of the revolutionary armies, the North American revolutionary experience was not so dissimilar. But its leaders, though contentious and often ideological, had not swayed from their task of creating viable government. They attributed the dismal Latin American record in post-revolutionary statecraft to racial makeup, authoritarian character, social environment, and inherited alienation from Western democratic traditions. John Randolph, the Virginia firebrand who railed against Henry Clay's professions of pan-American unity in Congress, summed up the conventional wisdom: "You cannot make liberty out of Spanish matter."[48]

North American revolutionary ideology, economic development, and U.S. continental expansionism reinforced public belief in a nationalistic political culture in the United States, but Spanish-American liberators had another agenda. Monroe's 1823 message to Congress, crafted by John Quincy Adams, had subsumed the contradictory issues of Anglo-American cooperation and hemispheric unity in a unilateral policy. As Adams recognized, the importance of the document may have had less to do with preventing a French-supported Spanish reconquest than with advancing Adam's reputation in the political arena and assisting those who presided over the nation-state to appropriate nationalist sentiments by defining the foreign policy of a democracy. In such circumstances, there could be no crusade on behalf of democracy in Latin America. "Liberty and independence are magic words in this country, and objects which we think ourselves bound to wish to all distant communities of men, who may appear to be struggling for them," wrote the editor of the *National Gazette*, alluding to the public faith in universal credos, "without consulting their disposition and capacity to put them to good use."[49]

Universals best served those who governed in a particularist society already persuaded of its own exceptionalism, articulated in the credos of achievement but ultimately rooted in its sociocultural mythology. "As to an American system," Adams pronounced, "we have it; we constitute the whole of it; there is no community of interests or of principles between North and South America."[50]

By 1830, the United States had not only created an American polity with its own ideology but had embarked on the heady task of nurturing a distinctive republican culture. Troubled but not diverted by the persistence of tradition or the contradictions of national unity or purpose endemic to particularist societies of place, U.S. leaders crafted a liberal nation-state, designed to serve the interests of the few, and learned the political art of sharing power while pretending they were servants of the people. They created necessary and instructive fictions, which, once accepted, provided individuals with a sense of belonging to a nation with an identity and a purpose.[51]

The new Latin American republics had yet to unshackle themselves from a debilitating past, many North Americans believed, in an age when North Americans were mythologizing their national history. Troubled by the contradictions of their own historical record, particularly the persistence of inequalities and the growing numbers of dispossessed, the contrast with what they saw in the new republics to the south was reassuring. The American Revolution, Ralph Waldo Emerson firmly held, had enabled a people to enjoy the blessings of progress, but revolutions that served the "interest of feudalism" inevitably led to "barbarism."[52]

Other observers, more sympathetic than Emerson, recognized the seemingly insurmountable difficulties of governance in places devastated by war and among peoples of bewildering racial and ethnic variety. A British naval officer touring Colombia during the mid-1820s perceptively noted that the Creole elite possessed the intellectual capability to lead but warned, "To harmonize the constitutions and governments with the feelings, the habits, and the prejudices of the mixed and different races of the population, will indeed be a task of no ordinary difficulty." He added, prophetically, "There is, perhaps, no greater mistake, that in order to be free, a nation has only to will it."[53]

Part 4   The Revolutionary Legacy

We have no concern with South America; we have no sympathy, we can have
no well founded political sympathy with them. We are sprung from different
stocks, we speak different languages, we have been brought up in different
social and moral schools, we have been governed by different codes of law,
we profess radically different codes of religion.
Edward Everett (1821)

I hope . . . [for] a cordial fraternization among all the American nations, and
. . . their coalescing in an American system of policy, totally independent of,
and unconnected with that of Europe. . . . The surplus of population in
Europe and want of room render war, in their opinion, necessary to keep
down their excess numbers. Here, room is abundant, population scanty, and
peace the necessary state for producing men to whom the redundant soil is
offering the means of life and happiness. The principles of society, then,
there and here, are radically different.
Thomas Jefferson (c. 1823)

America is ungovernable. Those who serve the revolution plough the sea.
Simón Bolívar (1830)

In my opinion the main evil of the present democratic institutions of the
United States does not arise . . . from their weakness, but from their
overpowering strength; and I am not so much alarmed at the excessive
liberty which reigns in that country as at the very inadequate securities
which exist against tyranny.
Alexis de Tocqueville (1835)

IO

Tocqueville's America

In May 1831, two French aristocrats commenced a ten-month study of the prison system of the United States. The initial result of their sojourn was an 1833 publication on U.S. penitentiaries, but the most memorable contribution of this visit was a two-volume work entitled *Democracy in America,* a social portrait of the young republic written by the only member of this duo Americans remember, Alexis de Tocqueville.[1] Jacksonian America, he wrote, was an egalitarian society, where (except for minorities) people might be rich or poor, but according to *American* standards, which meant that opportunities existed in abundance to be born poor but to die rich. In society as in politics, majoritarian wishes and impulses not only prevailed but dictated the rhythms of national life. Contemporary foreign visitors and Americans validated his judgments. Michel Chevalier, who came to the United States two years after Tocqueville departed, described a country of few paupers and a people generally comfortable with their condition. Even Mrs. Francis Trollope, whose disdain for public habits punctuated her account of American life, departed with the conviction that people in the United States did not suffer from want of life's necessities. Everywhere one looked, there were examples of rags-to-riches biographies, which included, appropriately, President Andrew Jackson.[2]

Such was the judgment of an astute observer who appeared to be validating American "exceptionalism," the belief that North Americans, in contrast to the revolutionaries of Saint Domingue and Spanish America, had demonstrated that the authority of law and democratic society were capable of coexisting. In its half-century of existence, the United States had experienced social and political disorder and the persistence of impoverishment and, most damning, had expanded slavery's domain, but it had escaped dictatorship or militarism. As Tocqueville contemplated the society that had taken form in the young republic—from the pervasive democratic habits of daily life in the more settled East to the often raucous town politics of the trans-Appalachian West—he warned of the "tyranny of the majority," but he conveyed few doubts about America's future.[3]

This was unsurprising, given the persuasive festiveness and celebration of Young America in years when Latin America appeared to be plunging into the long despair of the postcolonial era. North Americans had shorn themselves of imperial rule, created the republic of liberty, and, just as quickly, set out to disprove the philosophers by creating an empire of liberty in the West. They described the Haitian revolution as a threat to slavery as an institution and, in more sweeping denunciations, as a menace to civilization. They applauded Latin American revolutionaries for repudiating monarchy, doubted their capacity to emulate the United States' example, and damned their leaders when they proved unable to fashion lasting political institutions. They had taken the measure of the revolutionary age in the New World and found the Haitian and Spanish struggles wanting in virtually every respect. In 1825, as Bolívar drifted between optimism and despair over the revolutionary legacy, a Boston banker and poet exalted: "The achievement of American independence was not merely the separation of a few obscure colonies from their parent realm; it was the practical annunciation to created man that he was created free."[4]

The Exceptional Revolution

The political culture that took form in the United States after independence appeared to justify Tocqueville's encomia for its unique capability not to resolve but to mitigate persistent social and class antagonisms. What happened was the displacement of a conservative elite by better organized opportunists who not only wanted to share power but, more important, were determined to reshape the nation's political institutions and values. In the process occurred one of several sea changes in the political culture. The United States shed the European character of its politics. City folk and farmers did not exchange places except in American mythology. Rather, the more settled cosmopolitans of the seaboard now had to recognize the political clout of small-town people and farmers whose newfound prosperity and, more important, whose importance as producers of national wealth were undeniable. Jefferson's triumph meant not only the defeat of those conservatives who had persevered in the 1780s and ruled in the 1790s but, more fundamentally, signaled a victory of republican ideology, "so enduring that no politician would again think of defending the old order of an elite leadership and passive citizenry."[5]

In Latin America, as in Europe, the difference in meaning between the "better sort" and "meaner sort" conveyed a belief that the social status of these persons was unchangeable. In the United States, however, these words denoted those who subscribed to the imperative of self-improvement and those who, through want of determination or moral character, had opportunities but refused to better themselves. Such an interpretation required a myth of a yeoman republic to take hold of the national imagination—a republic sustained by faith in the unifying power of a common language and in a democratic society expressed in fervent patriot celebration, the broadening of the suffrage, and a people who believed they were exceptional. "It is difficult to describe the rapacity with which the American rushes forward to secure the immense booty which fortune proffers to him," Tocqueville wrote. "He is goaded onward by a passion more intense than love of life. Before him lies a boundless continent, and he urges onward as if time pressed, and he was afraid of finding no room for his exertions."[6]

In defining their distinctiveness, Americans looked as much to their recent past, necessarily sanitized in its retelling, as to the seemingly boundless opportunities that lay in their future. Jefferson may have been privately troubled about the fusion of contradictory dynamics—the classical and the modern, philosophy and progress, agrarianism and capitalism, localism and nationalism—but he never revealed uncertainties in his public posturing or in his use of power. People yearned for a nostalgic celebration of the revolutionary "golden age." Although only four signers of the Declaration of Independence were still living in the early 1820s, the passion for what Edward Everett called "our heroic age" swept even isolated communities. Every Fourth of July, aging and decrepit revolutionary veterans, most of them ill-treated by a cause they had served, were trundled out as town icons. Inevitably, with the perceptions of class divisions and, especially, the heightened social expectations of artisans and even ordinary laborers, Independence Day acquired a new meaning for those wishing to dramatize their demands. One toast to independence invoked labor's cause: "The Working men—the legitimate children of '76; their sires left them the legacy of freedom and equality. They are now of age, and are laboring to guarantee the principles of the Revolution."[7]

Very little in the Latin-American cultural heritage and revolutionary experience, most North Americans were persuaded, had prepared its peoples for the republic of choice, where individuals possessed freedom of conscience and determined their social identity. Rectification of old grievances may have been the choice of the country's "Lessor Denominators" as a proper way to celebrate the revolutionary heritage. It was not the prevailing sentiment, however, in a society where individuals calculated, weighed, computed, and viewed life as a gamble usually worth the risk. Such was possible in a society Tocqueville described as modern, where large-scale organization posed no inevitable barrier to *individual* social mobility. Unlike Europe's aristocratic society with its hierarchies, the democratic society of America was devoid of permanent classes or immobilized groups of people bound together by economic function or ascribed social status. What one did for a living may have given an indication of one's prospects for material improvement, but it did not determine thought, religion, habits, behavior, or character. Democracy was too powerful a social force, opportunity, too widespread to preserve artificial distinctions in social status. The singular mark of status was money, the reward of "virtue" and "intelligence," which prompted the contemporary social commentator Francis Bowen to declare that wealth was "the only distinction that is recognized among us."[8]

Modern society, as Tocqueville recognized, retained large-scale units that dwarfed the individual—for example, the plantation or the large estate—but the democratic urgency of the age dictated the triumph of the small property-holder, the individual. In this vision, other types of modern institutions—plantation agriculture, industry, the military, or the administrative elites already making their appearance—were threats to a democratic society. Tocqueville was reluctant to concede that such organizations possessed not only powerful economic or political functions but social roles as well and, as such, possessed a symbiotic relationship to "democratization, or that these hierarchies constituted particular examples of a single social fact as providential as democratization—the division of labor."[9]

The Inegalitarian Society

A fluidity of society that persuaded Tocqueville of a general equality of opportunity proved a deceptive measure of an egalitarian society, however. The

United States lacked (in Tocqueville's era and today) a precise class system, but it did possess (and yet displays) a multiplicity of class structures that varied among communities and depended on such variables as location, comparative economic development, or size. In such a society, wealth can be inequitably or equitably distributed and status high or low. Tocqueville recognized inequities of wealth, of course, but he was routinely distracted by the existence of so many men on the make. James Fenimore Cooper, one contemporary not persuaded by the distinguished French visitor's conclusions, pointed out that equalities of opportunity provided "in a social sense the very means of producing the inequality of condition that actually exists. By possessing the same rights to exercise their respective faculties the active and frugal become more wealthy than the idle and dissolute."[10]

As the sharp ideological divisions of the first quarter-century of U.S. independence weakened in a political climate perhaps inaccurately called the Era of Good Feelings, a new generation of political aspirants began to take advantage of the changes wrought in the creation of new states and the expansion of the electorate. Until the 1820s (the presidential election of 1824 generally stands as the epochal divider between two ages of politics) gentry elites had managed to maintain a firm grip on political power with little more than dutiful acknowledgment of the "people's will." Following a faulty logic that new voters would be grateful and keep them in office, they acquiesced in proposals for white manhood suffrage in the original states (except South Carolina and Rhode Island) and encouraged it in the new states in order to attract settlers. Before they realized what was happening, they were suddenly confronted with a massive electorate more inclined to respond to a leader who could rouse their emotions or appeal to what members of the old order disdainfully called the "mobocracy."[11]

In the spirit of a putatively egalitarian age, political ideology, once a great debate between learned men over the nature of government, had as much to do with character, personality, and the ability to attract a following. Jackson was the symbol of the age. When he left office in 1837, turning over the presidency to the country's first "party politician," Martin Van Buren, even Whig opponents who had railed against Jackson's tyrannical use of power and blatant appeal to the masses had begun to imitate his political style in electioneering. They knew well enough that the most dramatic expansion in the electorate had occurred among white males of modest means and that the surest means of keeping government out of the hands of the vaunted common man lay in creating political machines for control at the local level and political parties at the state and national level dominated by men of means. "There never was a period in the history of our country," wrote a westerner, "in which its public men have sought popularity, power, and office with so much avidity . . . [and] display a dissoluteness altogether incompatible with the genius of a sober-minded people."[12]

Continental Empire

The impact of a widening suffrage and the response to the spirit of an egalitarian age permitted political architects of an "inland empire," which disproportionately benefited the few, to persuade the public that national expansion was for the people, not the developers. No one leader of the age better symbolizes this contradiction and its meaning for the legacy of the American Revolution than Thomas Jefferson. Rightly praised as the philosopher of American libertarian values and the democratic vision, he was also the inheritor of the revolutionary imperial design that had begun to take shape during the French and Indian War, when ambitious speculators looked to trans-Appalachian territory for development. Before the American Revolution, the dispute over expansion was largely a debate between rival social elites. During the war, small farmers and artisans gained new influence, and the antiexpansionist upper crust left the country. In the 1780s, the debate again raged between coastal and urban affluent and poor farmers from the interior, but it took a form unlike that of the prerevolutionary age. The way to deal with the democratic menace, the framers of the Constitution resolved, lay in erecting institutions to check the excesses of popular government and to prevent the rise of a multitude of unpropertied in the cities.[13]

Jefferson warred with the Federalists over the first, but as president he avidly promoted the second, the creation of a continental empire. More precisely, the Jeffersonian vision was of two empires. The first required the acquisition of new domain, Louisiana from France and Florida from Spain by purchase (and often duplicitous means); the second required aggressive promotion of U.S. commercial interests, especially in Latin America, even if such efforts required violation of espoused Jeffersonian principles. Thus, to placate southern slaveholders and the French government, Jefferson acquiesced in French pressure to cut off a growing trade with Toussaint-Louverture's Saint Domingue in 1801. A year later, when he realized the implications of French Caribbean strategy for his continental goals, he shifted in his tactics.[14]

Nothing was more crucial to U.S. survival, he ultimately concluded, than the goal of directing population and economic development to the western country. Jefferson was indisputably a territorial expansionist, but he professed a stronger commitment to the empire of liberty and its implications of self-determination. Acquisition of contiguous territory constituted a means to an end. Never a strong believer in the "doctrine of Montesquieu," which held that republics persevered only when their territorial bounds are comparatively small, he casually rejected the prophetic warnings that the union would be imperiled as the nation's boundaries extended further south and west. In the summer of 1803, responding to those who argued that Louisiana's acquisition could eventuate in the rise of new confederacies, he wrote: "The future inhabitants of the Atlantic and Mississippi states will be our sons. . . . We think we see their happiness in their union and we wish it. . . . God bless them both, and keep them in union, if it be for their good, but separate them, if it be better."[15]

The reach of central authority into the periphery was limited, even for a vigorously expansionist government. Though the determination with which Adams pursued annexation of the Floridas replicated Jefferson's earlier absorption with acquisition of New Orleans and thus conveyed the purposeful goals of securing national strategic goals and unity in the guise of creating an "empire of liberty," the U.S. government sometimes advanced its own interests by accommodating local or regional agendas and traditions. Louisianians were the country's first territorial people not residing in the original United States. They doggedly held on to French and Spanish civil law because it preserved valued features of family law and did not deny rights of citizenship to free persons of color even as they welcomed the common-law feature of jury trial in criminal cases. In 1805, less than two years after the Louisiana cession, the U.S. Congress brought the newly acquired territory under the general provisions of the Northwest Ordinance but tolerated the continued use of local laws.[16]

As the sections of the country increasingly divided over Jefferson's and Madison's policies regarding neutral rights on the high seas and the parallel issue of Anglo-Spanish intrigue in the western country, an acrimonious debate over Louisiana's future erupted in the disputatious Eleventh Congress, when Josiah Quincy of Massachusetts argued that statehood constituted a "great usurpation" fashioned by "the slave vote" for the purpose of enhancing southern political power with the addition of "the mixed, though . . . respectable race of Anglo-Hispano-Gallo Americans who bask on the sands at the mouth of the Mississippi." In this exchange, Federalist New Englanders may have been more articulate, but their opponents proved more resourceful. Louisiana was admitted to the Union in 1812 (even though its population had *less* than the required number of free persons as defined in the U.S. Constitution). Its admission altered the meaning of empire for Americans because the new state contained significant numbers of foreigners (among them, French planters who had fled Haiti) who had not elected to become Americans.[17]

Already North American leaders had identified Caribbean security and development with that of the U.S. South, even as they viewed Spanish Florida as a more pressing objective for U.S. expansionists, a situation requiring a circumspect policy toward Spain and its alienated New World dominions. From the Spanish perspective, hopes for retaining the northern provinces diminished rapidly after 1808, even as remote cabildos took pledges of loyalty to the deposed Ferdinand VII. The situation in West Florida was symptomatic of the chaos within the region. In West Florida, Anglo-American residents, responding to U.S. pressures, overwhelmed the weak Spanish garrison in Baton Rouge in September 1810, declared the independence of the republic of West Florida, and called for annexation to the United States. President James Madison promptly dispatched U.S. troops into the region, laying claim to the territory between the Mississippi and Perdido Rivers as a part of the Louisiana Purchase. As the United States and Great Britain plunged into war in the summer of 1812, Georgia-based filibusters invaded East Florida in 1812, though Spanish resistance and congressional opposition compelled Madison to back down.

In the following year, Andrew Jackson led his marauding Tennessean militiamen into West Florida and another U.S. force under General James Wilkinson seized Mobile, which Washington refused to return after the peace settlement of Christmas 1814. In the spring of 1818, Jackson struck again, providing Secretary of State John Quincy Adams with unarguable evidence that Spain could not retain the Floridas. The diplomatic cession of the province came the following year with the signing of the Transcontinental Treaty. Farther west, the Mexican insurgent Bernardo Gutiérrez de Lara commanded a band of Mexican insurgents and Anglo-American filibusters in an invasion of Texas. His Republic Army of the North captured San Antonio and declared Texan independence. In their counterattack, Spanish loyalists retook the province in a campaign of devastation and pillage. By 1821, as Mexican and Spanish elites fashioned a peace treaty consummating Mexican independence, Texas, in the words of its last Spanish governor, lay in "chaos and misery."[18]

Migration played a significant role in the shaping of continental empire. On the eve of the War of 1812, one-sixth of the population lived in the West, replicating, it was said, the pattern of settlement and community spirit of seaboard states. The myth of the West had already gripped the public imagination. In 1813 Americans read *The Adventures of Daniel Boone,* an epic tale of a man who had ventured ever westward. Ultimately, enterprisers now endowed with the "angelic spirit" caught up with Boone and he moved on, cursing the plunderers who despoiled the pastoral West in search of wealth. Speculators and despoilers of "civilization in the wilderness," however, were not the singular problem in the west. More fundamentally, the impressive growth in western population did not translate into impressive economic gain for the country. Many lived at near-subsistence levels; others produced enough for their own consumption and a small surplus to use for trading. Some drifted, unemployed or underemployed. A New York congressman lamented in 1810 the "great evil . . . under which the inhabitants of the western country labor, . . . [a situation that] arises from the want of a market."[19]

Before the end of the decade, however, another great internal migration got under way, exceeding not only in size but in social and political impact that of the century's first decade. This was the democratic landscape Tocqueville traversed, spirited and raucous particularistic settlements with their singular notions of what mattered and did not matter and where a man defined himself. South of the Ohio River, of course, the patina of refinement crafted by the plantation aristocracy made for subregional contrasts. "Servitude in any form is an evil," wrote an English commentator, "but the structure of civilized society is raised upon it."[20]

Wealth on the frontier divided people along social fault lines just as it did back east, and settlers displayed the most spirited acquisitiveness in their pursuit of the acknowledged source of wealth: land. Though public land was sold in equitable fashion and in the democratic spirit of the era, the belief that land was a natural right of every citizen inspired untold fraud and chicanery. Officials expressed shock at the casualness with which the beneficiaries of this federal largesse displayed such contempt for the law. Their disorderly behavior followed predictable patterns, given the circumstances of western settlement. The western country was a peculiar democracy—government was both oligarchic and tolerant. Lacking sufficient federal support, territorial governors were either unable or unwilling to manage development or guarantee individual rights. An imperial system that should have been a failure achieved the goals of empire. What explained this apparent paradox was the character of U.S. continental expansionism. Most of the immigrants were native-born, white, and Protestant. They demanded governance under the familiar political institutions and practices of the East even as they segregated, expelled, or even killed those who were different. Public officials at every level of government stood culpable, by either indifference or complicity.[21]

Denied to Indians and black persons though proclaimed as one of the several universal principles differentiating the United States from the new Latin American republics, self-determination provided ideological justification for creation of an inland empire in the name of freedom. The drive to subdue a continent (expressed as the nation's manifest destiny) inevitably diminished the appeal of the empire of liberty—the United States as exemplar of freedom rather than crusader. Neighboring governments that at first encouraged immigration of Anglo-Americans—the Spanish in Florida and, later, the Mexican in Texas—came to regret it and too late tried to stem the flow. Bolívar spoke of a United States menacing the entire hemisphere in the name of liberty. Luis de Onís, who negotiated Florida's cession, wrote that "Americans . . . believe that their dominion is destined to extend, now to the Isthmus of Panama, and hereafter over all the regions of the New World. . . . They consider themselves superior to the rest of mankind."[22]

The Texas rebellion against Mexican rule in 1835, inspired by the relentless pressure from Presidents John Quincy Adams and Andrew Jackson to purchase the province, appeared to validate Bolívar's prophecy, but the making of rebellious Texas was a more complicated process. The first Anglo immigrants into Texas had established virtually autonomous communities, though their leaders had established relatively harmonious relations with Mexicans. Texas's immigrant population grew from 2,000 in 1827 to 4,200 in 1830 (the year Mexican restrictions were passed) and 5,600 a year later. When the rebellion commenced in 1835, the number of American immigrants stood at 30,000. Not until Mexico's central government began to impose stricter controls did the Texans resist. Reinforced by disaffected Mexican anticentralists (federalists), they became bolder, ultimately declaring their independence. In the end, Stephen F. Austin, who had painstakingly charted Texas's political relations with Mexico City, solemnly acknowledged that resistance was the only recourse of a people who believed they were "in danger of becoming the alien subjects of a people to whom they deliberately believed themselves morally, intellectually, and politically superior."[23]

To sustain their cause, they dispatched recruiters to New Orleans and into the western and southwestern U.S. states, promising generous land bounties. Those who joined up arrived in Texas in the aftermath of the fall of the Alamo and the Goliad "massacre," restless migrants from Tennessee and Kentucky fired with a determination to "make Texas" in the same way their forebears had "made" the trans-Appalachian country. Modern historians have sometimes depicted the Texas rebellion as the work of American conspirators, among them Jackson, who tried to bully the Mexican government into selling the Prairie Rose. But the internal dissensions, rivalries, and ethnic antagonisms in Texas were symptomatic not of a war made in Washington but of a chaotic struggle on the periphery.[24]

The Dispossessed

Already persuaded that civilization required domination of nature, which the Spaniards and the Portuguese had been unable to accomplish, Americans distinguished themselves in yet another way from their southern neighbors. They became even more fixed in their convictions that the remaining Indian tribes east of the Mississippi must not retard the westward sway of the nation. Americans professed a civilizing mission toward the Indians and even dispatched agents to transform at least some of them into citizens, but the harsh methods employed unarguably contradicted the intent. Henry Adams was not alone in noting that Jefferson's plan to turn Indians into farmers involved plunging them into debt with the lamentable result of driving them off the land. "The contradiction," observes a student of Indian removal, ". . . had to be sustained; the federal government had to meet world opinion with a policy of benevolence while also meeting its citizens' desire for land."[25]

Natural rights devolved on the individual but not on the Indian, argued one Jeffersonian, Henry H. Brackenridge, because the Indian did not cultivate the soil. Most Indians moved on as the line of settlement inched westward. Since the Battle of Fallen Timbers in 1794, they had fought a losing battle against the white advance in the western country. On the eve of the War of 1812, Tecumseh, a remarkable spokesman for both northern and southern Indian grievances, fashioned a momentary alliance of the major tribes with the British in anticipation of a renewed Anglo-American conflict, but the outcome was a series of losses commencing with William Henry Harrison's victory in the Indiana territory and culminating with Jackson's savage campaign in the southeast during the war. The Hero of New Orleans followed with a military reprise in his invasion of Spanish Florida in the spring of 1818.[26]

Here and there, even on the frontier, whites and Indians sometimes managed to tolerate one another, particularly where the Indian seemed to be adapting to the ways of the colonizers. White men lived in Indian communities to instruct in crafts and skills; Indians worked in white settlements.

Tecumseh's pan-Indian overtures did not appeal to significant numbers of Cherokees, Choctaws, Chickasaws, and Muscogees, because they dared not risk war with the encroaching whites. Some tried to adjust to the intruding white culture. Among the Cherokees, accommodation made to the customs, laws, and religion of the conqueror (including the practice of slavery) went farther than a few of the most ardent assimilationists had prophesied. When the state of Georgia launched its drive to open up Cherokee lands to white development and pillage, the Cherokees resisted and found momentary comfort in the deceptively broad support for their cause.[27]

At bottom, however, most Americans of this era found little reason to believe that Indians could ever be assimilated. Even their defenders were ambivalent when confronted with counterarguments that Indian preferences were rarely considered in these discussions. Miscegenation, of course, would have accomplished the assimilationists' goals, but this solution came along almost contemporaneously with state laws prohibiting Indian-white marriages. Eighteenth-century rationalist beliefs that Indians were capable of becoming "white" through education, training, and acceptance of European ways weakened in the face of persistent arguments "that the Indians were innately and ineradicably 'redmen'" and could never be changed by putatively benevolent policies.[28]

Considerations of Indian removal, which commenced with congressional debates in the 1820s and escalated into a dramatic confrontation between President Jackson and Chief Justice John Marshall in the early 1830s (in a case involving encroachment on Cherokee lands in north Georgia), inevitably reverted to these fundamentals. When the Supreme Court declared in favor of the Cherokees, Jackson arrogantly refused to abide by the decision, resolving to settle the matter by a politically expedient and, to the president, just solution—removal of southeastern tribes to faraway territories in present-day eastern Oklahoma. "Philanthropy could not wish to see this continent restored to the condition in which it was found by our forefathers," Jackson wrote, expressing a widely held view of Indian removal. "What good man would prefer a country covered with forests and ranged by a few thousand savages to our extensive Republic, studded with cities, towns, and prosperous farms . . . , occupied by more than 12,000,000 happy people, and filled with all the blessings of liberty, civilization and religion?"[29]

The exclusionary doctrine applied as emphatically and systematically to black Americans, as well. Tocqueville despaired of the racial situation in the United States, predicting slavery's inevitable demise yet warning that the aftermath would be racial war. This was a starkly pessimistic view, given the prospects of the immediate postrevolutionary era, as northern states had passed antislave laws. When the slave trade ended by constitutional stipulation in 1808, the older environmentalist belief that *conditions*, not biological, traits explained "black inferiority" had already weakened before a tide of racial animosity against free blacks in the North and the articulation of proslavery arguments, expressed tentatively as apology, in the South. Reformers now spoke of emancipation and removal. Former president Madison proposed a gradual emancipation plan in 1819 and resettlement of freed persons in the West when the question of Missouri's admission as a slave state provoked a divisive sectional quarrel. This was an unworkable solution, given the rapid expansion of plantation economies into the Old Southwest. Jefferson's political constituency resided in a coalition of middle Atlantic and southern states, where many of the country's legendary yeoman farmers lived, certainly, but also where export agriculture (dominated by cotton) thrived and the ideology of slave society deepened its hold. The southern slave economy exhibited irrational traits that contributed to economic backwardness because capital was reinvested in land and labor.[30]

Removal of emancipated slaves to the west was unacceptable for another reason even less susceptible to political resolution—white racism in the North, which intensified after the War of 1812. Few southerners were troubled about the contradiction over expressions of democratic values for whites and the drawing of a color line in a slave society. Acceptance into the democratic community of the North was more problematical, given the violence directed at free blacks among urban working people and the growing acceptance of "scientific" evidence of black inferiority among intellectuals and community leaders. In the hierarchical society of eighteenth-century British North America, blacks occupied a lower rung on the evolutionary human ladder. In the democratic society of the United States, they were not one of the "ins" so they necessarily fell into the category of "outs."[31]

This racism found expression in the American Colonization Society, which drew its strength from social conservatives persuaded that "christianized" former slaves could be resettled in Africa, where, it was argued, the transplanted converts would "redeem" that continent. Liberia was founded by emancipated American slaves in the early 1820s. Others went to Haiti, where they resisted efforts by the Haitian government to remake them into small farmers and agricultural laborers. Colonizationist schemes appealed to those who believed that "slavery was an anomalous institution that did not fit the basic American social pattern" and who held the presumably unchangeable belief that "American society . . . was a corporate entity into which the black group had never been and never could be incorporated."[32]

As a proportion of the slave population, however, the numbers of emigrants were quite small. Most free blacks were uncooperative in these ventures, which served to reinforce a racist dynamic that appeared in proposals to extend slavery into the Indian territory or in property qualifications for voting that applied to black but not white voters. It is thus unsurprising that Tocqueville wrote of the prospects for blacks in the United States in apocalyptic terms. Race was an "American" topic that ill fitted (as he acknowledged) his description of a "democratic" society. Slavery's abolition, he believed, was inevitable, but racial strife imperiled the nation: "In those parts of the Union in which the negroes are no longer slaves, they have in no wise drawn nearer to the whites. On the contrary, the prejudice of the race appears to be stronger in the States which have abolished slavery . . . and nowhere is it so intolerant as in those States where servitude has never been known."[33]

The Monarchical Neighbor

The American impact on the Canadas was subtler. In the Canada Act of 1791 the British government acknowledged the ethnic divisions between French Quebec and the English conquerors, who gained representative government with the creation of Upper Canada. In Lower Canada French civil law and the established Roman Catholic Church prevailed. The rest of British North America was a "strange constitutional *mélange*": Newfoundland (a crown colony); Prince Edward Island, New Brunswick, and Nova Scotia (royal provinces with elective assemblies); Rupert's Land (governed by a charter company); and the distant northwest (with neither constitution nor precise southern boundary). The cultural makeup was equally varied. Not only were there English and French but cultural and ethnic offshoots—Acadians, American–regional British mixtures, Highland Scots, Irish, Indians, and descendants of Indian-European unions *(métis)*. Most Upper Canadian settlers were from the United States and thus suspect in the eyes of the British governor, John Simcoe, who sought to recreate eighteenth-century England in Upper Canada but sensibly recognized that population increase and economic development were the best ways to prevent absorption into the rambunctious republic to the south.[34]

Simcoe welcomed fleeing Loyalists from the United States and granted them generous land concessions, a policy aimed at preventing absorption of the province into the United States during the War of 1812. During the conflict, both French Canadians and "new Loyalists" joined forces to halt the U.S. invasion. (The fundamental reason for Canada's successful defense was stupidity and bungling by U.S. commanders.) After 1815, the British government encouraged Canadian colonization, but the scheme encountered numerous obstacles, among them the disturbing reality that most of the likely emigrants preferred to settle in the United States. Some fell on hard times; others pleaded for assistance from British officials, and some eventually settled in Canada. In the 1820s, the British underwrote another group of emigrants, most of them economically impoverished Scots and Irish. Many of these, the historians of this migration observed, readily sold their provisions and supplies and went to the United States, where they joined families or took jobs on road and canal projects.[35]

Already Canada was experiencing heightened social agitation born of resentment over Tory-Anglican privilege. In the next decade, reformers, many of them Methodists influenced by the greater religious tolerance and democratic sentiments in the United States, began to agitate for fundamental change in governance. In English Upper Canada, they found a volatile leader in William Lyon Mackenzie (the "firebrand"), who railed against the favoritism and the monopolization exercised by the oligarchy under what was styled the Family Compact. In the spirit of Andrew Jackson's attack on the "monster bank," Mackenzie (who was elected mayor of Toronto and regularly sent to the Assembly) assailed Tory-Anglican privilege and, increasingly, spoke of American "solutions" to Canadian problems. In French Lower Canada, the spokesman of the disaffected was Louis-Joseph Papineau, Speaker of the Assembly, a landowner who meshed socially conservative views with denunciations of the political alliance fashioned by French-Canadian and British officials. Rebellions erupted in both provinces in 1837. The violence prompted more emigration southward, initially by fleeing rebels and, later, by Canadians who joined in the great migrations across the United States in the forties and fifties.[36]

The Political Economy of the New World's First Republic

A democratic consciousness may have enveloped community and town in Tocqueville's America, but among men of wealth and power the reality was an industrial consciousness, a fusing of republican and capitalist beliefs with the inherited power of the state as agent of large-scale economic change. Driven by the twin forces of colonial assemblies' demands that tax payments be made in paper currency or specie rather than in kind and the consumer "revolution" that swept mid-eighteenth-century British America, the market was a powerful institution before independence, particularly in the North, where labor impressment and servitude had deteriorated. The market economy, which presumably drew labor voluntarily into production, was in actuality a subtler form of coercion, not as absolute as the slave system predominating in the southern states, certainly, but sufficiently powerful to encourage those who believed that government would assist in its development. In his 1825 annual message, President John Quincy Adams, with a logic comprehensible to Latin American Creoles, solemnly declared the "great object of the institution of civil government is the improvement of the condition of those who are parties to the social compact."[37]

Jefferson the philosopher extolled the agrarian and condemned the commercial world. But Jefferson's party appealed to planters, farmers, tradesmen, and professionals who hearkened to his vision of national development, and Jefferson the president sharply modified physiocratic beliefs that agriculture was the singular origin of real wealth. Although in 1820, 80 percent of the U.S. labor force toiled in agriculture, the United States was already an impressive commercial nation. Commerce and manufacturing could not be neglected on the naive presumption of an autonomous, self-sufficient agricultural domain abutting the transatlantic economy. Jefferson's agrarians had been a part of an export economy for a century. They required an expansionist foreign policy. Jefferson accommodated them, even as he confronted a broadening European conflict that threatened U.S. national security. Exploiting the precarious neutrality of his Federalist predecessors, he ran the risk of war and incited dangerous political divisions within the country to fashion for the United States a distinctly national vision of empire: a balanced economy, vigorous pursuit of markets, and continental expansionism. His policies may have helped to bring on a war for his successor, but in leaving office he noted proudly that his policies "hastened the day when an equilibrium [existed] between the occupations of agriculture, manufactures, and commerce."[38]

In an era when Jeffersonian and Hamiltonian beliefs about political economy and the role of the central government (and the states) in national and regional development seemed to be coalescing and when the prospects for economic growth appeared stronger than ever, indicators of an emerging propertyless labor force in the cities were naturally viewed as aberrations. After all, the United States, a determined adversary of both the British-dominated Atlantic economic system and the Napoleonic continental system, had fashioned an *American* system, identified largely with a Westerner, Henry

Clay of Kentucky. Clay rejected the "cautious constitutionalism" of Presidents James Madison and James Monroe in favor of the "big dreams of Jefferson and [Secretary of the Treasury Albert] Gallatin."[39]

In its triune structure of a national bank, internal improvements, and a protective tariff, the American system constituted a blueprint for national economic development. The United States could draw on foreign capital to expand its factory system, take advantage of the post–Napoleonic-war downturn in the North Atlantic economy, and become an important player in the industrial revolution. Its agricultural productivity, particularly in cotton, sugar cane, and tobacco, had achieved comparative advantage by 1800. Commercialization of agriculture not only brought U.S. farmers into the Atlantic economy but transformed rural society and culture.[40]

The United States may have entered the industrial revolution late, but it had tremendous advantages over its European rivals. Unlike their European competitors, U.S. industrialists did not have to circumvent urban guild organizations to link rural laborers and handicrafters to supplies and ultimately to a market. They could readily shift to crude but promising home manufacturing and move it west or into the cities. They could draw on a domestic and immigrant labor force. They could obtain financing through credit and look to developing, state-supported canal, turnpike, and, later, railway systems for transportation. Expanding market demands, sources of capital, political encouragement and support, transportation and technology, and a capable labor force explain much about this rapid economic transformation, but there were other, less appreciated "frontiers of change." American culture and society provided a qualitative sustenance. "Innovators had to succeed in the market," the economic historian Thomas Cochran concedes, "but their successes are a measure of results rather than causes. The statistics . . . can only suggest what happened, not why it happened."[41]

Government promotion of national economic development, articulated by Jefferson and refined by Clay, naturally found favor among young political leaders whose philosophies and ambitions accorded with Whig party credos. As the American system came to be identified with closer political connection to the promoters of canals and turnpikes, the national bank, the tariff, and, especially, the men of wealth who allegedly benefited, Jacksonians discovered a political issue bound to appeal to those who were being left out. The economic philosophy that sustained the American system derived from liberalism, but its application, Jackson charged in his veto of the Bank Recharter Bill in 1832, permitted "the rich and powerful . . . [to] bend the acts of government to their selfish purposes. Distinctions in society will always exist under every just government . . . , but when the laws undertake to add to these natural and just advantages artificial distinctions, . . . the humble members of society—the farmers, mechanics, and laborers . . . have a right to complain."[42]

The "New American"

The social legacy of this economic transformation was both blessing and curse. It doubtless promoted social leveling, which Americans applauded, but it ushered in an economic individualism that altered eighteenth-century community bonds and the character of family life. There was seemingly unparalleled opportunity in the West, for both speculator and settler, but the changing economic character of the Northeast was a portent of nineteenth-century urban life. In the sixty years after 1760, a dramatic transformation of Massachusetts occurred in the creation of linkages between countryside and city, bringing "much of urban society to country villages, making their old cultural isolation obsolete."[43]

But a parallel development to the flourishing of "supra-local perspectives" or a more committed citizenry was another urban society with a less promising future. The factory system, which began to dominate manufacturing after the War of 1812, exploited the advantage of economies of scale to devastate the household manufacturing that had blossomed in the years after the revolution. The alteration transformed families from small producers and working entrepreneurs into poorly paid laborers, with debilitating social consequences. A steam-powered cotton manufacturing plant in Rhode Island, established in 1790 by the English immigrant Samuel Slater, employed nine children, aged seven to twelve. Two decades later, the country had eighty-seven cotton mills, which operated with a labor force of four thousand workers, thirty-five hundred of them women and children.[44]

Modernization may have dramatically altered the role of women and children in the workforce by shifting production from the home to the factory, but such a change did not sever other timeless marital bonds. Though women's labors had been crucial to colonial prosperity and to the factory system of the early nineteenth century, their role was considered secondary to that of men in the economic life of the country. Unless single and eighteen years of age or widowed, a woman's earnings and her property belonged to her spouse. Enhanced social status through achievement in the workplace was rare because employers set women's wages in accordance with the prevailing belief that men were their providers. American mores reinforced a cult of domesticity, even after textile production had shifted from the home into the factory and mothers began sending their daughters to the mills. In the mill towns, however, the daughters remained under public scrutiny, their virtue protected, a consequence Chevalier attributed to the "manners of the English race. . . . The Protestant education, much more than our [French] Catholic discipline, draws round each individual a line over which it is difficult to step."[45]

Conditioned by what they knew of labor's predicament in Europe, foreign visitors instinctively praised the American's higher standard of living, from the amount of food on the table in workingmen's boardinghouses to the similarity of dress between young tradesmen and their bosses. In the same era, urban skilled workers complained of rising living costs and the impossibility of making ends meet. In March 1834, the General Trades' Union of New York City proposed the creation of a national union to address conditions that resulted in "the most unequal and unjustifiable distribution of the produce of labor, thus operating to produce a humiliating, servile dependency, incompatible with the inherent, natural equality of men."[46]

Social historians sometimes attribute the disparity between what European visitors described and the sordid realities of urban working-class life as yet another indicator of harsh conditions imposed by industrialists, the estrangement between boss and worker over control of the workplace, and heightened middle-class insensitivity to the workers' putative sacrifice to the community in forgoing self-improvement. What they may be missing are subtler explanations. Disproportionately large numbers of those men and women who labored in manual work in the 1830s were single, unattached young migrants from farming communities or from Europe. Unlike the heads of working families, they could afford to spend significant amounts of their income on food and clothes and thus look as if they were headed up the social ladder. Once married, however, they faced more precarious circumstances. Even as work became more complex, the social definition of its worthiness had simplified into a division between those who labored with their hands and those who used their minds. Many of those in the latter category, of course, started out at modest wages in highly competitive jobs, but their prospects for moving up or starting their own businesses were good. They did not readily fit into the late-eighteenth-century category of wealthy, socially prominent merchant elites, but neither did they belong with the skilled (and certainly not the unskilled) workers of the cities. Those who spoke ecstatically of free labor had few doubts that it was not slave labor, and they rhapsodized about the United States as the "poor man's best country." But even as they denounced European industrial models they readily slipped into European stigmatizations of those who labored with their hands.[47]

Such thinking prompted reformers not to address social inequities but to visualize a society that contrasted with the one already emerging among the urban working poor. Children of working-class or farm families may have continued to labor under miserable conditions with few chances for realistic social advancement, but among the emerging middle class prospects were different. New ways of thinking about marriage and the family provided a sketchy definition for what Carl Degler has properly termed the modern family, in which family size diminished, partners demonstrated tenderness and respect, women acquired greater influence within the home and heightened stature in society, and childhood was a distinctly important experience requiring special attributes of parenthood. Men were the providers and the links between the family and the outside world. Unlike the eighteenth-century model, the family of the 1830s was no longer a patriarchy where fathers ruled wives and children, arranged marriages for their daughters and "positions" for their sons, and continued to advise them for the remainder of their lives. Among the rich, the old ways persisted, but the new family social pattern called for a break with the nuclear family of one's birth and its recreation at adulthood. What happened to you in life was your responsibility. Thus was reinforced the prevailing wisdom of self-identity and self-determination.[48]

The cumulative effect of these changes—from the diminished importance of the family in community and politics to the uprooting of once-settled people in search of new opportunities—was to alter individual relationships with formerly cherished social institutions (family, community, church) that Americans now supplemented with voluntary associations. One could choose his or her social relationships—church, business and professional organization, scientific and cultural groups, or one of the moral improvement associations that by mid-century swept the social landscape. In these myriad new social institutions and associations, created not by government but by private groups, Americans found not only a way to ameliorate a plethora of social ills (drunkenness, gambling, cursing, and breaking the Sabbath) but also a way to reinforce their commitment to national moral regeneration through vigorous proselytization. The names of these voluntary organizations attest to a public moral purpose: American Temperance Society, American Sunday School Union, American Home Mission Society. Collectively, they constituted a "Benevolent Empire."[49]

Continental expansionism was an expression of the empire of means, and government played a central role in its attainment. The second vision of empire, often identified in American mythology, had as its ultimate goal the integration of society within the polity. To this end, government often played a crucial role, but to assure success it depended for help on other social institutions (schools, churches, the family), a willingness to meet demands and expectations of the citizenry, and sufficient resources to satisfy their demands. In the integration of often disparate and conflictive social groups in the postrevolutionary era and in the molding of a citizenry, the United States was notably more successful than Haiti or Spanish America.[50]

Tocqueville's America contained its social inequities, for women, blacks, and Indians did not share the full benefits of the democratic society. Tocqueville recognized that democracy meant equality under the law and in the holding of political rights. More critically, it required the absence of a "radical inequality" in those social *relationships* whereby one person felt or was made to feel inferior and, even if worthy, could not change things. The democratic society Tocqueville eulogized had displaced an eighteenth-century hierarchical, corporatist structure and its graduated ranks with one of seamless patterns where the individual encountered no insuperable barriers in a self-determined quest for achievement and success. Those deemed unworthy were excluded, driven out, exterminated, enslaved, or so beaten down that they could be shaped into whatever those who ran the country's economic engines or dominated its communities needed—a mass army of followers from whom much was demanded and who were expected to be grateful for the little they got in return.

In his provocative study of the making of national identity in the sequential ages of Jefferson and Jackson, Major L. Wilson skillfully probes the myriad ways Americans blended their faith in freedom, their convictions about progress, and nostalgic reminders from their revolutionary experience to fashion an explanation for who they were and where they were going. Nostalgia and reflection convey fundamentally different values. Untroubled by ambiguity and contradiction, a people found reassurance. If Americans of the era had paused to look within themselves closely to the degree to which they gloried in what they were doing, and to ponder the dangers to their once-valued corporate and community identities, they might have been better prepared for the storm that broke in the next generation. The signals were everywhere yet they were subsumed in the optimistic view that Americans would find a way to reconcile any threat, that they possessed—to exploit Wilson's phrase—"space, time, and freedom" to meet any challenge.[51]

A linear perspective on U.S. history suggests that the mid-century crisis of union and the collapse into civil war could have been avoided or at least mitigated if U.S. leaders had taken another route or if society had lived up to the revolutionary promise by including the dispossessed into the society of those deemed worthy. Such inquiries help us to understand but not to explain the age. Explanation requires an appreciation of the chaotic patterns of the revolutionary years, which simultaneously conveyed *both* reassuring and disturbing portents—forces that lingered for three-quarters of a century, to explode in predictable and unpredictable ways.

II

Bolívar's America

In the relatively short span of half a century, the United States had created what Europeans not only had failed to achieve but deeply feared: a democratic society. The United States was no longer the singular republic of the New World, yet its political and social accomplishments set it apart. By comparison, Tocqueville attributed Latin Americans' failures to an inability to sustain democratic institutions. Theirs was not the want of resources or physical expanse to develop: "In what portion of the globe," he wrote, "shall we meet with more fertile plains, with mightier rivers, or with more unexplored and inexhaustible riches, than in South America?" In the aftermath of its war of independence, the United States had severely reduced its landed army; the new republics to the south had not and now suffered: "They make war upon each other when they have no foreign enemies to oppose; and the Anglo-American democracy is the only one which has hitherto been able to maintain itself in peace."[1]

Years before the final victory of the Spanish-American patriots, North American observers came to contradictory judgments about the prospects for democracy in Latin America and the fashioning of hemispheric unity. Jefferson, whose *Notes on the State of Virginia* was well received among Spanish-American literati, informed Congress that Mexicans required a liberation of the mind before they could savor the blessings of freedom. John Adams scoffed that democratic government was no more appropriate for Spanish America than "birds, beasts, or fishes." In the early 1820s, as publicists in the United States wrote expansively about continental solidarity, Edward Everett of the prestigious *North American Review* warned about a thoughtless rush into alliance with South American revolutionaries: "We have no concern with South America; we have no sympathy, we can have no well founded political sympathy with them. We are sprung from different stocks. . . . Not all the treaties we could make, nor the commissioners we could send out, nor the money we could lend them, would transform their . . . Bolívars into Washingtons."[2]

Order Out of Chaos?

Save for the unflattering personal comparison, Bolívar would have agreed with these somber assessments. Troubled by the factionalism and civil strife of the decade, he summed up the deplorable legacy of the revolutionary struggle in bitter lamentation. The war of continental liberation had ended in triumph, but it had also brought the anarchy Bolívar now condemned. In the course of a continental struggle he had fashioned a military alliance of disparate racial and social classes; the victory won on the battlefield had dissolved amid the feuding of rival chieftains and opportunists. Latent demons devoured him. Liberated Colombians were as fractious and divided as ever. Only large states survived the chaos of revolution. He feared the expansive reach of Iturbide's Mexican Empire (which extended southeastward into Central America), the aggressive designs of the United States, and the "Africans of Haiti whose strength is mightier than primeval fire." He despaired about the hatreds within a Colombian nation not yet formed—"one part is savage, another slave, and most are enemies of each other." In 1825, the year in which Bolívar had urged the formation of a defensive league among the liberated Spanish colonies, he had predicted that the local conflicts plaguing the independent republics would culminate in ways "no human calculation or foresight can hope to predict."[3]

His dilemma was largely of his own making. Believing that the political future of the new republics lay in the surviving elements of the prerevolutionary social order, particularly in the cities, he discounted the new claimants for power within the military and among the rural chieftains. Bolívar had been able to fashion his revolutionary army principally because he drew from a rural constituency. When he arrived in Lima or Bogotá in command of a force that challenged the domination of urban social elites, they instinctively turned against him, sometimes making common cause with the disgruntled military chieftains "dissatisfied with the meager place reserved for them in the Bolivarian order."[4]

In many ways, Argentina and Mexico in the 1820s serve as appropriate metaphors for charting the political chaos of postrevolutionary Spanish America. The political architect of liberal Argentina in the 1820s was Bernardino Rivadavia, who strengthened the economic links between Buenos Aires and Europe and dreamed of transforming the city into a South American Paris. Argentine nationhood had to be molded with European people as well as ideas and practices. For a moment, later generations averred, Argentina had stood poised to join the modernizing nations of Europe. But the country was not ready.[5]

As the 1820s came to an end, however, the domination of porteño "Unitarians" had provoked a growing opposition within Buenos Aires Province. The provincial "Federalists" shared the unitarian disdain for the remote interior provinces but deeply resented the haughty and imperious ways of the *unitario* elite. The rift between them was as much social and cultural as economic, though the Federalists saw themselves as the defenders of democracy as opposed to a "money aristocracy" that had mistakenly sold the country's birthright for foreign loans. The most vocal Federalists were Manuel Moreno and Manuel Dorrego, who crafted a political constituency among provincial landowners and maintained discreet ties with the British and with the city's *nouveaux riches*. In August 1828, Dorrego became governor of Buenos Aires Province and promptly infuriated the unitarios by signing a treaty with Brazil agreeing to Uruguayan independence. Three months later, the porteños decided to settle matters in an unconstitutional manner: by force of arms. Their army easily routed that of Dorrego, who had to flee for his life. When pursuers finally caught up with him, the vengeful *unitarios* executed him. The act was a murderous portent of what lay in the Argentine political future. A decade that had begun in one political crisis now ended in a second convulsion. At both moments, one authoritative and determined man intruded to restore order: Juan Manuel de Rosas.[6]

Mexico followed a similar pattern of political discord, though its prospects after the collapse of Iturbide's imperial experiment were more promising. Unlike Argentina, where U.S. interests were largely commercial, Mexico appeared to be susceptible to Washington's political guidance and, especially, to the republican proselytizing of the first U.S. minister to the republic, Joel Roberts Poinsett. Inspired by the Mexican choice of a federalist structure that appeared to be modeled on that of the United States, and confident that he could influence the course of Mexican politics, Poinsett plunged into the bitter feuding among liberals and conservatives, federalists and centralists, and the activist lodges of Scottish Rite Masons and York Rite Masons (*escoses* and *yorkinos*). When yorkino lodges sprang up throughout the country, Poinsett instinctively believed that Mexican political culture was replicating that of the United States after the passing of the Federalists. After all, the prevailing *laws* stipulated that Mexicans were citizens and no longer a people differentiated by the traditional racial divisions.

But the political convulsions of the decade and the realities of a society still riven by caste and color noticeably diminished Poinsett's early enthusiasm. Departing Mexico in 1829 after an embarrassing effort to harass the Mexican government into selling Texas, Poinsett penned a devastating assessment of Mexican society. Lucas Alamán averred that most Mexicans were not yet ready for democracy, identifying the Indian as the most formidable obstacle to the country's social development. Poinsett attributed Mexico's lamentable condition to the heritage of the conquest and, particularly, to the refusal of ordinary whites to work. "Here . . . is wanting that portion of a community which forms the strength of every nation, but especially of a Republic, a free and virtuous peasantry." His pessimistic assessment set the standard for two generations of U.S. observers of Mexico.[7]

The Caribbean Cockpit

The political convulsions of the 1820s were a somber portent of independent Spanish America's political future, as the testimony of contemporaries verified, but both North and Latin American commentators' deepest fears concerned the Caribbean. Bolívar often mused about the Caribbean, where ideology, racial fears, and black rebellion had combined to produce a frightening metaphor for slave liberation. Preventing "another Haiti" made Bolívar a kindred spirit of North Americans who derided his presumption of leadership of a continental defensive alliance of former Spanish colonies.[8]

But Bolívar did not share his North American contemporaries' acquisitive instincts toward Spanish Cuba. Mexican and Colombian firebrands spoke rashly about Cuban liberation. North Americans mused about the strategic and economic imperatives of domination, but they had more potential allies in Cuba than did Bolívar. In 1810 discontented Cuban Creoles had remained loyal because they had wrung some important concessions from the Spanish Crown. At the same time, fearful of what they had learned from abolitionist discussions in the Spanish Cortes, they made clear their determination to preserve Cuban slavery by presenting the U.S. consul with an annexation proposal. The bearer of this document, José de Arango y Nuñuz del Castillo, articulated their reasoning. "We admire your institutions, your laws, and your form of government; we see that they procure your prosperity and your happiness."[9]

More critical for the Spanish government, of course, was preserving the imperial hold on Cuba. Resolving to placate disaffected Cubans, the Spanish enthusiastically continued an earlier policy of phasing out communal haciendas and the hereditary *señorios* (large estates), turning them into individual holdings and in the process unleashing a frenzied development in rural society. A more consequential legacy was the impetus that these economic decisions provided for those who planned for the expansion of the Cuban sugar plantation economy. Sensing opportunities to capitalize on the waning of slave plantation agriculture in the British and the French West Indies and troubled over British abolitionist pressures against a presumably demoralized and unprogressive metropolitan state, Cuba's planter elites looked to the aggressive liberal republic on the mainland for inspiration. With slavery under assault elsewhere in the West Indies, they admired a government that reconciled the principle of liberty with the institution of slavery. In 1823, they made another proposal for annexation, which elicited a fundamental statement on U.S. policy toward Cuba from Secretary of State Adams: "There are laws of political as well as of physical gravitation," Adams wrote to U.S. Minister to Spain Hugh Nelson concerning the Monroe administration's rejection of annexationist overtures from discontented Cuban Creoles. "If an apple, severed by a tempest from its native tree, cannot choose but fall to the ground, Cuba, forcibly disjoined from its own unnatural connection with Spain, and incapable of self-support, can gravitate only towards the North American Union, which, by the same laws of nature, cannot cast her off from his bosom."[10]

The Perils of Abolition

The Haitian symbol troubled Bolívar. His dream was an egalitarian society, but the experience of war and the requirements of mobilizing black slaves and pardos in the waging of continental war had taught him that victorious Creoles could not create united nations from slave societies. Everywhere in liberated Spanish America (except, perhaps for Mexico, Central America, and Chile, where abolition came relatively easily by decree from the new governments), there were prophecies of doom occasioned by the incorporation of blacks and coloreds into society. At the same time, rival political factions from Venezuela to Buenos Aires armed black troops to achieve their goals. The reasons for voicing such apocalyptic predictions may have had less to do with genuine fears of social conflict than with the prevailing contradictions within societies whose leaders professed egalitarian beliefs yet wished to preserve the old privileges. Or perhaps, equally compelling, the old order had been so visibly weakened that what had survived could not be sustained.[11]

Indians, who had occupied a special status within Spanish America, had little professed desire to be incorporated into the new social order, where in any event they would have occupied an inferior status. Creoles acknowledged that the revolutions had removed caste distinctions and, here and there, recognized the military accomplishments of pardos and mestizos, but privately expressed apprehension over their presumptions to political office. Yet those of mixed caste who gained power and could have used it to advance a social mission to fulfill the egalitarian promise were reluctant to do so. Indians, who were far more numerous than blacks, fought in the campaigns, but most of Bolívar's generation presumed they would make few demands for social equality after independence. Optimistic Creoles, such as the New Granadan José Manuel Restrepo (writing about the racial strife in Popayán), believed that with abolition the danger of racial disturbance would subside. By the end of the fighting, however, Bolívar had abandoned some of his wartime professions of faith in the role of the liberated slave. He joined the ranks of apprehensive Creoles in warning about a *pardocracia*—rule by the mixed-race progeny of people to whom the Spaniards had sold "certificates of whiteness" in the late colonial era and who now seemed to be in control of Ecuador. "We shall have more and more of Africa," he wrote Santander in one of his many statements about racial dynamics in the new republics. "I do not say this lightly, for anyone with a white skin who escapes will be fortunate."[12]

Such apocalyptic visions of the Africanization of society and rebellion from below, white British West Indians believed, could not come to pass in places where amelioration of slave conditions existed, where Christianity had penetrated, and where Africans and their descendants adapted to Caribbean culture through a process of creolization. In incremental stages, the free colored of the British West Indies acquired enhanced civil status as colonial legislatures removed legal discriminations. By the 1830s, the free colored in Britain's West Indian dominions possessed a "juridical position equal to that of whites."[13]

Cultural alterations creolized British West Indian society but created neither uniformity of view nor harmony. Those who changed the most were slaves, the least, whites. The social distinctions of plantation economies remained. Whites looked to the mother country for their identity, creolized blacks, to the West Indies. The colored may have taken their *cultural* identity from England, but their physical bondage to the islands made them a people without a country. In a manner that befuddled all except the slaves and their leaders, the British West Indies suffered periodic slave discontent and three serious rebellions between 1815 and 1832—on Barbados (1816), at Demerara (1823), and on Jamaica (1831–1832)—in which Creoles dominated and the ideological impact of the Haitian revolution appeared slight. West Indian planters attributed these uprisings to the misguided stirrings of the British Anti-Slavery Society, which revived in the mid-1820s as the Society for the Mitigation and Gradual Abolition of Slavery and subjected Parliament to a relentless propaganda campaign, and to their kindred spirits, philanthropists and missionaries, who were social conservatives but nonetheless saw themselves as redeeming forces in a crusade.[14]

Both arrogantly presumed they were "guiding" the West Indies toward peaceful emancipation. Pressure from London, whether through a program of punitive fiscal policies or of direct intervention, they confidently believed, would bring the fearful West Indian planters to accept the inevitable. One of the most effective publicists for emancipation was James Cropper, a Quaker and Liverpool merchant who subscribed to Adam Smith's principles infused with moral purpose: "Slave labor was . . . a moral and economic anachronism that could be abolished most effectively by free-market forces."[15]

In the West Indies, rebel leaders had already adapted religious instruction to a rebellious purpose. In its transmuted form and, especially, among those where evangelical revivalism took root, Christianity provided a means by which they could sustain a following among slaves gathering in secret meetings of the faithful. Religion was not central to these risings, however. Leaders often came from among those who were free and had even been the recipients of white beneficence but who accurately calculated that they could never aspire to full equality as long as slavery existed. In Jamaica, the violence had come in the aftermath of the precipitate actions of whites, who gathered to protest the assembly's grumbling acquiescence in imperial demands on civil rights for free blacks and coloreds. Among the islanders there had circulated another story that the king would shortly emancipate the slaves. An outraged white assembly met in the fall to consider proposals for ameliorating the slave laws; some whites spoke of rebellion and threatened to appeal for annexation by the United States. Probably few of the slaves knew about events in England, but they could see the feverish white reaction to pressure from Parliament and sensed the prospects for freedom. They gathered in chapels and meetings with the expectation that emancipation was at hand.[16]

One of the leaders of the ensuing revolt, Sam Sharpe, apparently believed that white fear of an uprising might be enough to wrest concessions. But whatever prospects existed for a peaceful solution ended whenever separate groups of slaves began firing several estates. The revolt itself was short-lived and ruthlessly put down. Twelve whites and several hundred slaves died, some killed by soldiers or militiamen and others by spontaneous and random execution. In Montego Bay, whites flogged captured blacks until they died. They destroyed dissenters' chapels. Blacks were poorly armed and divided into splintered groups. They had erred in believing that royal troops would not take up arms against them; they also did not anticipate the savagery of whites, who blamed the rebellion on dissenting missionaries, in their reprisals. "Shooting is . . . too honourable a death for men whose conduct has occasioned so much bloodshed, and the loss of so much property," proclaimed the *Courant* in denouncing the missionaries' role.[17]

Sharpe died by hanging at Montego Bay on May 23, 1832, affirming at the end: "I would rather die on yonder gallows than live in slavery." A week later, the House of Commons established a committee to study and report on measures for the abolition of slavery in British dominions.[18]

"Those Who Serve a Revolution"

The violence accompanying the movement for abolition in the Caribbean reminded Bolívar of the convulsions raging about him. He often expressed frustrations similar to those voiced in the postrevolutionary United States, but he had diminished faith in the rule of law as a moderating power in the disorder engulfing Colombia. A year before his death, he bemoaned the destructive, localized conflict tearing asunder the Colombian republic, then a fragile federation of Venezuela, Ecuador, and Colombia created a decade before. The reality that "force is dissipated by distance" offered only partial explanation for Colombia's political debilities. He attributed the national malaise to failure of leadership. Government lacked credibility because those who held power had proved incapable of exercising power, the nation lacked a unifying ideology because they could not articulate one.[19]

His own faith perished with the failure to achieve that unity. His name and cause were admiringly invoked as secular prophet and dreamer from Mexico to Chile, yet in every place where his creative handiwork appeared (for example, in the Bolivian constitution or the proposal for a Federation of the Andes), he was denounced as a usurper or defied by those whom he had freed from monarchical tyranny. Peruvians violated the Colombian frontier. In Venezuela, Páez proved unable to quell the bandits of the llanos and in desperation called out the militia, which brought protests from some of the civil governors and prompted the Colombian parliament to call him to Bogotá for a dressing-down and a stern reminder of constitutional limits on executive power. Páez returned to Venezuela, threatening secession. When the Liberator rode into Caracas to deal with the recalcitrant llanero, he was hailed with cries of "Viva Bolívar, Viva Páez, Viva Colombia!"[20]

Bolívar left the city momentarily reconciled with Páez, his tormented mind filled with stories about the machinations of Santander and the perils confronting Colombia. In the aftermath Venezuela plunged into chaotic politics that disturbed even the fierce Páez. As Bolívar's mood became more despairing of the Latin American condition, he privately acknowledged the futility of what he had strived to bring about but seemed all the more determined to pursue a singular course. In spring 1828, following the government's suppression of a revolt, he railed against his old ally, Santander, and the liberals' abandonment of the ideal of the virtuous republic. Citing Montesquieu as authority, he averred: "As it has never been possible to reform a people corrupted by slavery, nations, too, need conquerors only, never liberators."[21]

Bolívar's predicament was mostly of his own making, though he instinctively attributed the political malaise, as he had written in the Jamaica letter of 1815, to those debilities inherited from the centuries of Spanish rule. Responding to the conservative impulses that attributed the disorders everywhere in the new states to inappropriate liberal measures, he accepted a dictatorship in 1828 to preserve the republic. Despondent over the political condition of Colombia, he was driven in his last years to fashion schemes of regional and even continental unity (limited, of course, to the former Spanish colonies) as a desperate effort to fashion some order out of the chaos engulfing his world. In large part, the fragmentation of Colombia was an inevitable consequence of Bolívar's delusion about the prospects of creating a virtuous republic in a "world that was racially heterogeneous, economically divided, and—with the exception of the *criollo* elite—had no previous sense of community of any kind."[22]

In 1830, not yet fifty, he died, a victim of tuberculosis and the emotional torment of a man hailed as a liberator and then scorned by those whom he had led to freedom. A few weeks before his death he scribbled an epitaph for a continent: "America is ungovernable. Those who serve the revolution plough the sea."[23]

Governance

Latin America's postrevolutionary generation confronted not only a decay in the moral order but a failure of public-spiritedness. Few of those who presumed to exercise the authority formerly held by viceroys were able to cope with factionalism, regionalism, and, more than anything, the rise of chieftains *(caudillos)* who knew nothing of constitutionalism and exercised power by sheer will and determination: Antonio López de Santa Anna in Mexico, Rafael Carrera in Guatemala, José Antonio Páez in Venezuela, and Juan Manuel de Rosas in Argentina, among others.[24]

Niccolò Machiavelli's *The Prince,* not John Locke's *Two Treatises on Government,* was more germane to their predicament. Bereft of the monarchical authority they had once excoriated, leaders of the new governments now found themselves not so much inheritors of power as victims in a prolonged conflict among families, regional chieftains, and cities. Had their cultural heritage determined their future? Or had they failed to create political institutions to supplant those they had weakened or destroyed? Emerging social patterns drew their form only partially from those imagined at the outset of the long and violent conflict. Institutions, weakened by the years of conflict, were a fragile base for crafting republican societies. "The government is maintained by the influence and the power of those leaders that have made independence," wrote General O'Leary. "Institutions alone have no force. The people is an easily managed machine too ignorant to act for itself. Public spirit is non-existent."[25]

Contemporary North Americans blamed the Latin American situation on the failure of the liberators to establish political institutions capable of surviving the discord that generally follows wars of independence. Viewed in the context of a fifteen-year span, the early judgments on Latin American prospects offered a more sympathetic and sophisticated assessment. The central government was too weak to act as the principal agent in the creation of an integrated society, a condition noticeably exacerbated by the financial and budgetary restraints and by the physical damage wrought by many years of conflict. But the problems encountered by the new governments were further complicated by other uncertainties. Latin America's wars for independence were also civil wars. The militarization of society was one legacy. Another was the lack of assurance that those who had borne arms in the cause—blacks, mestizos, pardos, and Indians—would remain loyal to civilian authority. Creoles had managed to freeze the social question late in the struggle, creating a momentary unity of purpose. Once the warring ended, and the Creoles made it clear that they intended to preserve many of the features of the colonial social structure, the acquiescence of the castas in the new regime was everywhere an uncertainty.[26]

Legitimacy of government thus depended heavily on the ability of the state to maintain itself by forceful means. Using the military as an instrument of authority, even at the local level, meant that the character of public life took its shape from military, not civilian, institutions. An early task for the new governments, then, was the creation of a state more imposing than the military that was presumably bound to preserve it.

Mexico and Chile represented two polar extremes in the experience of the postindependence governments. The Mexican republic inherited the most debilitating characteristics of the Bourbon military reforms. In order to pacify the northern frontier and protect against French and Russian intruders, the Spanish had created a military organization and, to assure its loyalty, had granted its officers special privileges with the *fuero militar*. From the first decade of independence until the 1850s, the army became a decisive political force in the life of the republic, despite both a constitution that reserved the power to declare war to the legislature and the deep-seated antagonism of civilian political leaders. In the aftermath of the anti-Iturbide rising, however, the new republican government permitted rebel leaders to retain their rank, leaving the capital with an inordinately large number of officers and prompting the meddling and judgmental Poinsett to observe: "In a republic without virtue and a large standing army, there is always danger. I have represented forcibly to these people that they cannot assemble a large force on any one point without great danger to the liberties of the country."[27]

There were, of course, subtle but important differences in the role of the military in various countries. Despite Santander's 1817 comment that the army must be sustained to safeguard against the enemies of independence, in both Venezuela and Colombia the military fell into disfavor, a sentiment explained by public antipathy to wartime excesses and the apprehensions of civilian political leaders. Resentment among officers over perceived ill-treatment was widespread. Apprehension about their interference among political figures ran deep. On the eve of Venezuelan secession from Colombia in 1829, the Colombian minister of the interior, José Manuel Restrepo, blamed the country's troubles on Bolívar's habit of rewarding ambitious and greedy officers. Within a few years, however, the generals had been curbed. Chile experienced greater anarchy than Mexico in the 1820s—five revolutions in the last three years of the decade—but in the following decade the "Portalian Republic" purged the officer corps of liberals and others who threatened the state. Portales cut the regular army to three thousand and, to guard against political ambition among its officers, established a civilian militia.[28]

Undeniably, a degree of social democratization accompanied the making of a peacetime regular army, but, for the most part, the postwar military officer corps came from the older families or from those who aspired to join them. Though nominally obligated to protect the state, the ultimate expectation was preservation of the social structure that had largely survived the revolutionary turmoil. Before the wars of independence, the Spanish military, reorganized and determined to carry out the new imperial policies, had frustrated the Creoles' agenda. Even in victory, the new rulers of Latin America were uncertain as to the military's demands for preserving its loyalty. The price of maintaining a relatively costly military structure in years of economic distress meant inevitably high burdens on the national budget. There was always the risk that political opportunists would find a weak government an easy prey or respond to demands from disaffected groups to topple an unpopular regime. Or, in a reversal of roles, a backcountry general discontented over his social status might unleash his illiterate troops in a campaign of plunder, to remind the propertyholders who held real power.

Militarism, where the regular army constitutes a distinct social and political group, may be an inappropriate description for what prevailed in postindependence Venezuela (and, by implication, in much of the rest of Latin America). But there is little doubt about the militarization of postindependence Latin American society, where internal strife, regional feuds, and pervasive uncertainty among political leaders and opportunists meant that weak governments might have to rely on the use of force to impose their will or to survive. Such a choice meant rewards to men who commanded the loyalties of other men. The militarization of society not only was a sign of the weakness of civilian authority but, more ominously, conveyed the impression that the new governments did not intend to fulfill their pledge of a more egalitarian social order. One reason for the retreat from these professions lay in the apprehension, acknowledged by revolutionary leaders throughout the Americas but more pronounced in Latin America, that society could not survive prolonged conflict, a fear that the future might be more calamitous than the past. Reasons for such pessimism varied but were ultimately linked to blacks or the castas and horrifying memories of the war's early years, a warning Bolívar issued in his last years to justify his dictatorial rule.[29]

North American leaders had created the United States by bonding autonomous colonies; Bolívar and his comrades had removed the head of a patrimonial society but they had not created nations. There was neither social revolution nor a fundamental political transformation, except in the sense that national governments took form and imposed a new bureaucracy that had to contend with a privileged elite and a generation of opportunists. The new political order decreed new constitutions, promulgated laws, and divided generally into two broad alignments: those who held traditional social philosophies, defended the high church, and tolerated unreconciled monarchists; and those who espoused the views of intellectuals and professionals and were distrustful of the church. Traditional historiography designates the former as "conservative" and the latter "liberal" in order to explain the makeup of conservative and liberal parties. Liberals and conservatives divided primarily not on ideological but on religious issues. Liberals were more disposed to North American and European political and economic models, especially where the litmus test was individual liberty and opportunity. Until mid-century, generally, liberals suffered more from internal tensions exacerbated by the apparent irreconcilability of their determination to advance individual liberty and their willingness to use state power against corporate entities under the pretext of defending individual liberty.[30]

For the most part, liberal and conservative leaders of Latin America had more in common than once believed. What mattered most in differentiating among them lay in what Frank Safford has identified as "location" in the political culture. In this design, economic function as determinant of political values is less revealing as a political measure than one's place and relationships in a social ambience that was more fluid than once believed. Landowners, clergy, and the military sometimes acted in concert, sometimes not. One does not have to be a Marxist to acknowledge the "class" interest that presumably linked the rural landowner who produced for the export market and the urban merchant and lawyer. Where conflict occurred, it rarely did so along narrow lines of economic interest. Conservatives were largely men who grew up in a town that had benefited economically and educationally in the colonial era; liberals occupied "peripheral social locations." They had to earn their way into the elite by dint of sacrifice and talent rather than by inheriting familial status. Though such a scheme must be modified from country to country and, especially, within each country, it has the persuasiveness offered by fundamental principles of spatial geography. Economic interests mattered in politics. What mattered more were one's relationships with those near and far. What could matter a great deal more were one's links to those who had power and influence.[31]

Despite these reservations, the presumed common admiration of liberal and conservative groups for European economic and cultural models and the undeniable social reality of a widening gulf between an elite minority and an increasingly impoverished majority provide a modern generation of Latin Americanists with seemingly persuasive evidence that Latin America's political leaders made the wrong choices at independence. Turning their backs on the communal, self-subsistence, and traditional "folk cultures" of the continent, they imported what they needed to forge nationhood. By using the power of the state to force alien notions of individual liberty and capitalist practices on peoples who ill understood them, and certainly benefited little from them, these elites systematically destroyed one world while professing to create a better one. The Argentine historian Hector Iñigo has summed up the case against the liberal formula for modernizing nineteenth-century Latin America in one devastating sentence: "Liberalism promised a theoretical garden of happiness which historically became a jungle of poverty."[32]

Growth or Development?

Weakened by internal dissension and conflict, the new states confronted harsh economic realities that militated against national integration and unity. The lofty plans of Latin America's first generation of leaders to shape national economic policy systematically collapsed before the twin forces of metropolitan economies (predominantly British and, later, North American) and regional economic groups intent on preserving their autonomy. The war devastated livestock production and mining and scattered the labor force. In the aftermath, the two groups with investing capital—the church and merchants—were reluctant to shift their monies into industry. What local manufacturing survived the war quickly fell before the onslaught of cheaper imported goods. Latin America thus entered independence with its economic future mortgaged to the land for production of export staples and a servile labor force for agricultural work.[33]

Colonial familial networks, rooted in the age of conquest, survived the dramatic changes in political life. The old families, deprived of the corporate institutions, shifted their attention to controlling the state bureaucracy and ex-

ploiting their power to dominate the political process. Every region had its notable families, and some managed to retain and even expand their influence,
but the political reach of landowners and their role as a class in economic policy should not be exaggerated. A rural social structure of estancia and small
plot, of *hacendado* and *peón*—characterizations denoting hierarchy, power,
and rigid control—is a generalization often employed to describe virtually
every region of Latin America in the nineteenth century, yet on closer inves-
tigation each reveals patterns of development infuriatingly complicated and
complex.[34]

By mid-century, national economies weakened even further before external forces, and once-hostile political elites appeared to be forging a consensus about economic development. Modern scholars are often tempted to view
the first decade of independence as one of critical (and deterministic) choices
for those who governed and, further, to interpret national consolidation as a
struggle between those who "sold the country out to foreigners" and adopted
foreign models (thus preventing economic diversity and encouraging underdevelopment) and those who labored to preserve national identity and sound
economic policy. Among both groups were other divisions—"good" caudillos
and "bad" caudillos—that complicated the process of national development,
depending on which country is studied and how strongly the researcher ad-
heres to counterfactual arguments.

Despite the appeal of *dependentista* analysis, certain generalizations about
Latin America's economic trajectory from the 1820s until mid-century are indisputable. The shift to export commodities (particularly coffee and sugar in
Brazil and Cuba) was a response to markets for these products in Europe, not
a dictate from metropolitan economies to peripheral ones. Great Britain, the
external economic power in Latin America during the nineteenth century, especially in the Caribbean and Brazil, often used its military power not to reinforce dependency. But, as demonstrated in the assault on the slave trade to
Cuba and Brazil, the intent was "to ruin the planters of Brazil and Cuba by refusing to buy their products and by trying to cut off their supply of slave labor."[35]

Latin American economic expansion was not simply a choice of reallocat-
ing resources from domestic to foreign production (as comparative-costs theory assumes) but one of selling a surplus product for which there was little internal demand. Development of these resources varied in complexity from
place to place. In every case, external factors were important, but they did not
determine Latin America's economic future. Commercial liberalization, so

appealing to the first generation of Latin American leaders, proved a chimera. In ridding themselves of a restrictionist Spanish mercantilism, they imagined a dramatic explosion of Spanish-American exports. Sadly, their dreams vanished in the reality of British traders coming to sell rather than buy and of wary domestic investors. Bolívar was one of them. "We own too many properties and farms and houses which tomorrow will tumble in an earthquake," he wrote his sister, "but had we in England a hundred thousand pounds safely assured in the bank, we would enjoy an income of 3 percent per annum."[36]

Scholars often identify Paraguay and Peru as excellent sources of dependentista evidence of the right-and-wrong litmus test in routes to modernization. Paraguay at 1850 stood as a still relatively isolated backwater in Latin America, yet the long years of rule under Dr. Francia (1815–1840) had provided the people with a strong sense of national identity and economic self-determination. Peru's route to modernization after 1850, it is argued, is littered with evidence of a conspiracy by the oligarchy to bind the country and its oppressed masses to liberal orthodoxy and the tyranny of free trade. "No other economy of Latin America," writes Paul Gootenberg, "matched Peru in the fervor, simplicity, and tenacity of its liberal orthodoxy. And no country appeared so thoroughly dominated by the liberal politics of its export elites."[37]

On closer evaluation, the facile presumptions made about each during the formative postindependence years provide little validation of the statement that Paraguay was the preferable model of development or that Peru became an export-oriented economy because its first generation of rulers planned things that way. What Francia achieved was not an "autonomous revolution" but Paraguayan immunity from the economic anarchy of Buenos Aires. He excluded foreign capital, foreign exports, and those foreign views he considered harmful. Meaningful economic development could not be carried out under these circumstances.[38]

Peru's postindependence leaders *were* protectionists. They fashioned a national economic policy to counter the twin debilitating forces of an onslaught of British, French, and North American commercial penetration and the political chaos of the age—twenty-four major political crises from 1821 to 1845. As in Mexico, bureaucrats and caudillos fended off liberal strategists but became just as dependent on moneylenders. In the uncertain economic and political climate, Peru's nationalists—an improbable coalition of domestic shopkeepers, artisans, landed oligarchs, officials, and caudillos—could not preserve the old protectionist traditions. They created a "viable nationalist movement but, ultimately, not a viable nationalist state."[39]

Chaos and the Limits of Choice

The failure to create a viable state has often been attributed to the intrusive power of the North Atlantic economies or the adoption of inappropriate foreign models by elites. A less deterministic but more persuasive argument incorporates the dynamics of chaos into evaluations of the legacy of revolutionary Latin America. Viewed from a linear perspective, the disorder of postrevolutionary Latin America is often perceived as a violent attempt by the dispossessed and the disinherited to claim their rightful place in the new order. That liberal and conservative elites were often in fundamental agreement about the preservation of order in such unsettled conditions is indisputable. Their differences were largely tactical, not strategic. Their views of progress and the role of the state in the economy differed, certainly, but the dilemma they confronted was more complicated than one of choosing between foreign and indigenous cultural and political models. The social and political dynamics of postrevolutionary Latin America responded to different forces.[40]

Because they were a vital force in managing political chaos, the caudillos thus played a critical role in the development of postindependence Latin American states. Two such leaders, Juan Manuel de Rosas and Antonio López de Santa Anna in Argentina and Mexico, respectively, provide illustrative examples of this process. The role of Rosas in Argentine history is ambiguous. Alternately damned as the leader who single-mindedly destroyed the Happy Experience of Rivadavia and praised as the necessary man to restore order after the calamitous porteño luminaries of Argentina's Generation of '37, Rosas inaugurated a more systematic and calculated form of the gaucho terrorism personified in Juan Facundo Quiroga.[41]

Rosas was no gaucho, however, but a Buenos Aires provincial caudillo who became a governor and proved in the civil conflict of 1829 that he could command popular, anarchic forces and restore order. When he left the governorship of Buenos Aires, the disorder returned. In 1835 he resumed the governorship with the approval of a legislature and a society emotionally devastated by convulsions since the May 1810 revolution. For the next seventeen years, he ruled as virtual dictator. Rosas was popular, a landowner who served landowning interests yet strengthened his own following by parceling out land to military and civilian followers and to those who took part in the Desert Campaign against the Indians. Afterwards 90 percent of the land certificates wound up with the expanding *estanciero* class. In his relentless quest for power and his mercurial style, he often rewarded and persecuted the same social groups. Always, the rationale was the preservation of order. "Our revolution," he declared in 1836, "was not a rebellion to replace legitimately constituted authority, but an attempt to fill the void left when that authority vanished, leaving the nation without leadership." This represented the sentiment of a man determined to bring order out of chaos.[42]

Such acquiescence in dictatorship was a tacit admission that transplanted European political models ill-fitted the Argentine situation. What was required, a contemporary Federalist paper noted, was a policy born of a quarter-century's "experience . . . of violent social change" and of "exact knowledge of events and men," and "not of dreamy idealism of an absolute theory, ever inapplicable to the special circumstances of each society."[43] Had Argentina's rural peoples and gaucho culture found a leader to articulate the true Argentine identity and offer an alternative to that expressed in the writings of the Generation of '37? Even Sarmiento, who viewed Rosas and all caudillos as enemies of progress and civilization, believed the caudillo was "the mirror which reflects in colossal proportions the beliefs, the necessities, the concerns and customs of a nation in a given moment in history."[44]

This was an implicit recognition that Rosas was the "necessary gendarme" who instinctively understood how to contain the chaos endemic to the militarized society. Rosas's rule was not a break with the immediate past but a continuation of unitario centralism and repression under the rubric of federalism. The porteños had extended universal male suffrage, talked glowingly of recreating Paris in the Rio de la Plata, and mercilessly persecuted vagrants and gauchos. Rosas made a mockery of the vote through his control of the bureaucracy, the police, the army, and a paramilitary group known as the *mazorca* (literally, "corn," but pronounced the same as *más horca*, "more hanging"). Nationalism to Rosas was inimical unitario doctrine, but he offered no alternative vision. Society, not nation, was his obsession. In late 1835, endowed with dictatorial powers, he catalogued its condition in Hobbesian phrases: "Society was in a state of utter dissolution: gone was the influence of those men who in every society are destined to take control; the spirit of insubordination had spread and taken widespread roots. . . . The inevitable time had arrived when it was necessary to excercise personal influence."[45]

Rosas was popular, but his caudillo state was not the creative force behind Argentine nationalism. Rather, the state under Rosas was the mechanism by which his successors pacified the interior, devastated Indian communities, and hounded the gaucho into the captive labor force of the *estancieros*. Despite his use of the machinery of terror and dominance of the bureaucracy, Rosas was absolute only in Buenos Aires Province. Beyond its borders, the capacity or even the willingness of the regime to enforce total control over society weakened. In the early 1850s, following a crisis with Brazil, a defiant caudillo from Entre Ríos raised an army and brought him down. The dictator shared with Bolívar a fascination for the gentlemanly life of the English countryside. Unlike the Liberator, he was able to achieve it.[46]

Mexico in 1830 exhibited most of the disorders that had plagued Argentina in the 1820s. After a decade of political turmoil, it had a conservative, centralist government led by Anastasio Bustamante and Lucas Alamán. One of the insurgents, Carlos María Bustamante (who wrote an eight-volume historical account of the era), had grown so disillusioned with the political turmoil that he welcomed the new regime as the only recourse to restore order. "The people is a ferocious and ungrateful beast which is not easy to subdue once it has lost respect for the powers that be."[47]

But the conservatives in power proved no more capable than their predecessors in containing the "ferocious and ungrateful beast." They governed ineffectually over a congeries of regions, each with its local chieftains and without sufficient revenue to sustain a viable policy. The government could not compel the church, the landowners, or the states to lend support. It could not rely on the military to police the bandits and marginals of society. On the northeastern frontier, it tried to reverse earlier policies of generous land grants to North American settlers and precipitated another crisis. In the southern state of Guerrero, a popular cacique, Juan Alvarez, forged an alliance with disgruntled Indians, promising them a return of lands seized by whites. These rural conflicts went beyond struggles over land, however. Local leaders such as Alvarez (a guerrilla in the war of independence) drew on a long tradition of resistance to central authority to mobilize local peoples over such conflictive issues as taxation, local autonomy, and rental of municipal land. These outbursts on the periphery set the pattern for Mexican politics in the postcolonial era.[48]

Into this turmoil strode the Crimson Jester of Mexico, Antonio López de Santa Anna, who had brought down Iturbide in 1822 and, a decade later, entered the capital as triumphant as any monarch. Mexico's most enigmatic caudillo then promptly turned over administrative power to his vice president, Valentín Gómez Farías, who launched an ambitious program to reduce the power of the church and the size of the military. Within a year, Santa Anna returned to power, overturning his own government and vowing to overcome the "empire of anarchy" by installing a centralist regime "at the critical and precise moment in which society was approaching its dissolution."[49]

Presumably a liberal, he was in power anathema to them, negotiating loans with the clergy and forging an alliance with the army and with powerful hacendados. With their backing, he moved in late 1834 to seize state treasuries and to dismantle the federalist system created by the 1824 constitution. The "empire of anarchy" found new life throughout Mexico—in the south with Alvarez's revolt against Santa Anna, in Zacatecas with a federalist governor's denunciation of dictatorship, and in Texas with the rebellion of the northern frontier against the center. Santa Anna had two followings: one in the nation, the other in Veracruz. In the former stood officers, civilians, clergy, proprietors, and moneylenders who were loyal to him when it served their interests. In Veracruz men followed him for personal reasons. Alvarez's constituency was local. He often boasted, "Merely a gesture from me is an order for them."[50]

But Alvarez's was a regional power. Santa Anna could invoke men to arms in the name of the patria. When he marched north to suppress the Texas insurgency, he arrogantly informed the British and French ministers that U.S. aid to the rebels would prompt him to march on Washington and raise the Mexican flag above the Capitol building. The loss of Texas momentarily diverted the centralist agenda and Santa Anna's career. In 1838 he again strode across the Mexican political stage, this time in the defense of Veracruz during the "Pastry War" with the French. In the forties his political fortunes rose and fell with the political crisis and the war with the United States. Openly nourishing conservative beliefs about the restoration of monarchy in a country wracked by social discord, Santa Anna endorsed elitist notions of popular governance. He strengthened the military.[51]

Throughout the land there was defiance. In 1842, Sonora, Baja California, Pueblo, and Oaxaca declared against centralism. In 1847, a caste war erupted in Yucatán. The Indians verged on victory over the hated whites, who declared independence and in 1848 (only a few weeks after the U.S. Senate's approval of the Treaty of Guadalupe Hidalgo, which ended the war with Mexico) offered the province to Spain, Great Britain, and the United States, Mexico's conqueror. In the northern states, Indians driven south by the U.S. invaders ravaged mining camps, villages, and haciendas. Mexico's humiliation in that conflict should have been Santa Anna's, but in 1853, responding to Alamán's pleas that he restore order, Santa Anna returned to power for the last time. Two years later, a coalition of liberal civilians and caciques, among them his old nemesis, Juan Alvarez, finally brought him down.[52]

Subsumed in these visible ideological and political conflicts was a grim re-

ality that confounded the liberals and conservatives, federalists and centralists: the political models each proposed offered inadequate means by which
to govern a country in which social and political divisions were exacerbated
by deeper and more insidious conflictual patterns. With the loss of almost half
of their nation's territory to the northern colossus, some Mexicans found a
scapegoat for these social ills. Others recognized a more fundamental problem, however. Poinsett's words about the want of a "community" rang as true
in 1847 as they had almost twenty years earlier, particularly to those who persisted in looking at the Mexican condition from the perspective of Washington, D.C., or even of Mexico City. The lot of Mexico's indigenous people remained miserable. A few liberals (among them Melchor Ocampo) dared to
criticize the immorality of debt peonage, but the shared horror of social convulsion often united liberal and conservative in a symbiotic pact. Aggrieved
Indians knew that protection of their interests lay with local caciques like Alvarez, not liberals who spoke of reforms.[53]

North American scholars have largely attributed the political malaise of
Mexico and most of Latin America's republics to a variety of conditions: the
leaders' obsession with internal order, the preservation of a hierarchical social order, the fragility of political institutions, and the shallow roots of republican traditions among peoples accustomed to deference. This is another
way of saying that republican Spanish America was crafted according to organizing principles of monarchical Spanish America—from the top down but
without the unifying bonds of a patrimonial elite or a consensus about fundamental principles of republican governance. Creoles who had commenced a
revolution to assume control of a vulnerable and weakened Spanish bureaucracy now found themselves beholden to the military, the strongest institution
in the new state structure, to restore order in a world they had made disorderly. And they had to do so with neither an acknowledgment that they must
share power if they were to survive nor a comprehension that the disorder they
found everywhere about them might not be susceptible to the political solution prescribed by eighteenth-century liberalism.[54]

In countries riven by uncertainty and apprehension of discord, the yearning for order was paramount among those disturbed by social tensions. But
the primacy of order in the agenda of those who held power retarded but did
not undermine the process of democratization. Belief in popular sovereignty
and equality was widely accepted, though in practice abused. The survival of
slavery and Indian tribute, property restriction, and indirect elections served
to limit the power of the vote. In any event, given the passivity of the electorate,

the cumulative impact of a broadening suffrage was not so critical to leaders as the somber acknowledgment that the political culture incorporated new groups that they must appease or control.[55]

Liberal philosophy argued for the former course as fundamental to progress, but the leaders chose the latter.

12

The Americas at 1850

In 1865, at a moment of apparent triumph for North American liberalism and national unity, the Chilean radical Francisco Bilbao wrote a laudatory description of the United States as the "foremost of nations." In the 1820s, the Western hemisphere's first republic had inspired a generation of Latin American liberals in their labor of crafting independent governments. Its aggressive continentalism in North America (achieved largely at the expense of a Latin American nation), the professed disdain of its leaders for Latin culture and society (often expressed in blatantly racist characterizations), and its pursuit of tropical empire in the Caribbean and Central America in the 1850s seemed aberrations for those who agreed with Bilbao (see map 5).

The United States had achieved unity amid chaos. In the federal government's use of power in what might properly be called a "war against the states," it had created the leviathan state, something eighteenth-century revolutionaries had condemned as menacing but which liberals believed fundamental for assuring the triumph of those modernizing forces they had always championed. A generation earlier, the ugly side of majoritarian rule manifested itself in numerous ways, from trampling on the rights and sensibilities of minorities to the brutally racist character of U.S. expansionism. This was the "overpowering" force Tocqueville alluded to in *Democracy in America.*

5. The Americas, 1850.

But liberalism acknowledged that such excesses could be contained even as the state encouraged the creative, orderly forces in society.[1]

Contrary to the democratic ideal and its inherent faith in community and tradition, liberalism now embraced individual freedom, expressed as a contractual relation voluntarily made with others, and, ultimately, with the state. As Adam Smith had postulated, liberalism was intimately linked to capitalism and commerce. It challenged community traditions, which perpetuated ascriptive values and thus retarded the liberation of the individual. Within a generation, Latin American leaders would be pointing to the noticeable economic progress and material achievements of the United States to justify their some-

times brutal use of power in the crafting of the modern nation-state, and their defilement of community and folk culture in the name of progress. Liberal ideology presumed a universality in human aspirations for a better life; liberal political economy, however, required continuing role of the few over a non-slave but subservient labor force of the many. As political thought, classical liberalism had invigorated the revolutionary cause. By the mid-nineteenth century, that commitment had withered before widespread middle-class fears of threats to the social order from the dispossessed. In the economic arena, conversely, liberalism confidently offered the prospective capitalist the assurance of a rational social order uninhibited by traditional restraints. The foundation of the liberal state, Marx noted, thus rested on a "double freedom": "The free worker was expected to offer social and political deference without claiming economic dependence."[2]

One task was the redefinition of *nation* and *nationalism* to accommodate the agenda of the state. In an era when liberals still recoiled in horror from the implied (and in Europe, violent) challenge to their hold on power by the wave of popular outbursts and uprisings that swept Europe in 1848, the meaning of *nation* and *nationalism* underwent a subtle transformation. Unlike the French Revolution's democratic exaltation of nation (or the early-twentieth-century principle of self-determination), nationhood in the mid-nineteenth century was intimately linked to the nation-state's commitment to industrial progress. Countries had to achieve a quantifiable measure of economic attainment to meet the test for nationhood. That threshold satisfied, there existed three remaining essential criteria: association with a state, usually one with a long past; a cultural elite who could articulate national identity in their writings; and, most distressingly, a capacity for conquest, a trait distinguishing those peoples who possessed a collective sense of purpose from those who did not.[3]

Despite the survival of independent states, the Americas at 1850 displayed many of the contradictions a generation of imperial reformers had categorized a century earlier. A political revolution had occurred, the social structure had been shaken, and economies had been loosened from imperial restrictions, certainly, but the legitimacy of government remained tainted by corruption, and the revolutionary promise of inclusivity was not yet fulfilled. In monarchical societies, not everyone was equal but all were subjects; in republics, not everyone was equal and not all were citizens. In the two largest independent nations of the hemisphere, the United States and Brazil, defenders of slavery often invoked the liberal credos of civilization and progress to justify perpetuation of the institution. By almost every measure, racial distinctions, now increasingly reinforced by pseudoscientific half-truths, were as entrenched as ever.[4]

What made the Americas at 1850 different from the hemisphere of the mid-eighteenth century was the myriad of independent nation-states, novel political forms, and, perhaps most significant, the maturation of societies where status seemed to depend less on ascribed than on achieved qualities. But the irrationalities condemned by nineteenth-century liberals as obstacles to progress had not been supplanted. Though weakened by the emergence of liberal nation-states, they, too, had persevered. Their vitality complicated rational assessments of the Americas at 1850, but they did not prevent a reformulation of the eighteenth-century justification for the hierarchical society based not on inequality but equality of opportunity—the conviction that entry into the middle class was open to all except those who lacked intelligence or were so debilitated by race or heritage that they were justifiably doomed to their lot.[5]

In Latin America and in the Caribbean, proponents of a new liberal economic order confronted different problems but shared with their North American counterparts the challenges posed by fragmentation and the demands of historically suppressed groups. In an era when economic liberalism called for drastic limits on the intrusion of the state in the economy, so as to permit capital and labor to seek out the best opportunities and wages without institutional constraints, political aspirants could not ignore the warnings of Thomas Malthus and David Ricardo about contradictions within national economies and stresses in the system. As population and capital grew, the internal pressures brought subsistence wages, lower profits, and a rise on land rent. Relief for industrial nations came from importing greater amounts of food and resources from those countries that possessed a comparative advantage in agriculture and low-wage labor. The labor force could be internationalized. Wealth depended on trade, not gold or silver. A Brazilian finance minister summed up the conventional wisdom: "The economic ideal of a country should not be to import little, but to import and export much."[6]

The reconciliation of competing and fractious national elites to such an agenda was problematical but, presumably, could be resolved by giving each a share. But how could diverse domestic populations be integrated into the new international economic order without the authoritative use of state power?

The Fracturing of Tocqueville's America

The United States at 1850 was a country victorious over Mexico and triumphant in its historic quest for continental domination, yet its political culture was riven by division and suspicion. Employing the specious reasoning that Mexico was responsible, President James K. Polk had sought war in 1846 in order to unite a nation in a putatively defensive struggle. Midway through the conflict, irritated by the public attention given to the country's commanding generals and, more likely, determined to isolate those persistent Whig critics who called this a war on behalf of the southern slavocracy, the president authorized an offensive campaign in central Mexico—an ambitious drive to seize the Mexican capital and compel a humiliating surrender and, his critics charged, to bring about the annexation of all Mexico to the United States. In the end, he got a treaty he really did not want, approved by a Congress that had dutifully condemned the offensive war as morally indefensible but nevertheless had funded it. The most lasting historical consequence of this conflict (other than the fact that the final one-third of the continental United States was carved out of one-half of Mexico) was the debate precipitated by a proposal from a young Pennsylvania congressman, David Wilmot, who offered a resolution stipulating that slavery would not be permitted in any of the territory acquired in this war.

From this defining moment, modern historians generally agree, the United States plunged toward inevitable civil war. A decade after Wilmot's proposal, the republic and the democratic society extolled by Tocqueville stood perilously close to rupture. In 1776, the only uncompromisable issue had been independence. In 1850, the United States, which had depended on compromise to create and sustain a government, entered a decade in which political compromise became moral betrayal, the expansionist impulse identified with Manifest Destiny (expressed in volatile tones of "Young America") became synonymous with states' rights southerners who expatiated on tropical empire and the export of slave empire into Cuba and Nicaragua, and political parties, once so promising in their role in the political culture, fractured. Expansionism, once inspired by such Jeffersonian phrases as the "empire of liberty" early in the century, had by the 1850s metamorphosed into a racialist doctrine disseminated in the penny press and touted by politicians as the driving spirit in forging American civilization.[7]

In November 1860, the northeast and Great Lakes states of the country elected a president; one month later, the southern states began to secede. Presumably, this was a moral dispute between those who believed in the liberal precept of human rights to the value of one's labor and those who accepted the notion that property rights were preeminent. Expressed in often rancorous debate at every political level, the issue crystallized in the 1850s in the hue and cry over the extension of slavery into the territories, a conflict in which the Northeast would abandon its historic defense of southern states' rights and rally to the westerner's demand for "free soil, free labor." As a political slogan, "free soil, free labor" postulated defiance of the slavocracy in the lands acquired in the Mexican War. As ideology, the slogan enveloped not only opposition to southern political power but devotion to union and a moral condemnation of slavery (yet often allowed severely racist sentiments). Adopted by the Republican Party, "free soil, free labor" expressed a conviction that slavery and national progress were mutually exclusive.[8]

Two societies, both the legacy of dynamic social and economic changes over more than three decades, had emerged in the United States. One was the democratic society extolled by Tocqueville two decades earlier, which had become essentially formless by the end of the Mexican War. This new society, nurtured in the years after the War of 1812, evolved slowly and matured just as the country's national political system plunged into the riveting sectional crises of the decade. It had benefited from continentalism and state-making, whatever the contemporary doubts, confusions, and uncertainties about "manifest destiny" that reverberated on Capitol Hill. United by its hostility toward the Indian and the Catholic immigrant, militantly nationalistic in the 1840s, its constituents sharply divided over the pivotal issues of the following decade.

This society had fanned out from the eastern seaboard, dispersing its peoples and values in countless ways, acquiring lands in the western country and socializing political authority in its wake. Feared by the Founders, it had captivated Tocqueville, who instinctively sensed its pervasive impact and alerted a generation to a little-appreciated truth: "The nature of society explains the stability of government, and freedom is preserved not by the forms and structures of political institutions but instead by the peculiar habits, attitudes, and values of a people."[9] The "other America"—a heterogeneous mix of marginals, dispossessed, Indians, blacks, and immigrants—was propertyless and poor. In an era (1830–1850) when 90 percent of free adults were literate and book production mushroomed 800 percent, the distance between the wealthy and the poor noticeably increased. The bottom 50 percent of the population controlled 1 percent of national assets.[10]

Though the former had benefited from national expansionism and the democratization of society, both had become increasingly defiant of authority. Governments at every level had increased in size, yet, paradoxically, their capacity to wield influence had actually diminished. The hold of the center over the periphery—sometimes manifested through presidential intrigue, special agents, or, as in the negotiations with Spain over the Floridas or with Mexico over Texas and California, through the use of military threat—was fragile but maintained. As long as Congress dictated the rules by which a continental empire was acquired and developed and took form as new territories and states, then the Old North and Old South could impose their will. Political parties unified the country because they represented geographical constituencies, not ideological or social interest combinations.[11]

In the 1850s, the grip of the center weakened as the political system fragmented and the successors of the Founders abandoned their role as defenders of order and protectors of liberty. Corruption prevailed in national and state politics. When former secretary of war William Marcy returned to Washington, D.C., as secretary of state in the Democratic Franklin Pierce administration, he noted the dramatic change: "In social life there is great extravagance, . . . [for] the treasury doors have been opened so often that they appear to yield to the slightest pressure, & turn easily & smoothly on their hinges."[12] In the aftermath of the Mexican War, in which both of the "Two Americas" had participated, the martial spirit persevered, demonstrating its power in the more aggressive foreign policy of the decade but also manifesting its debilitating impact on civil society in myriad cultural and social confrontations. These two dynamic constituencies loomed over the political canvas throughout the decade, and their presence complicated the debate over slavery and its extension into the territories. Northern Free-Soilers determined to benefit from the promise of a "larger liberty" were instinctively antislave but also held anti-Negro and anti-immigrant sentiments. In this explosive social context, traditional parties weakened as the sectional antagonism deepened. The Whig Party collapsed from a combination of powerful factors. Its most obvious liability was its historic stake in the American system, with its political compromise on the slave issue, but a less appreciated consideration was the heightened social tensions between overwhelmingly Protestant nativists and the 2.9 million immigrants, predominantly Catholic, who entered the country in the decade after 1845. An anti-Catholic, anti-immigrant movement, the Know Nothings, became a new political force, the American Party.[13]

The metaphor for Free-Soilers and states-righters was Bloody Kansas, where violent conflict between pro- and antislavery settlers raged in 1855 and 1856. Others perceived in the struggle over slavery an opportunity to rekindle the democratic promise of the revolution. Subsumed within the political issue of slavery in the territories, which galvanized northern racists as much as abolitionists, was a compelling belief that a dynamic, expansionist slave system threatened the country's future. "Slavery is here. It is not a stationary matter. It goes on developing itself, more and more, from day to day," lamented Charles Francis Adams. Lincoln was more eloquent in his public despair over the perils: "On the question of liberty, as a principle" he intoned, "we are not what we have been," for the determination those "political slaves of King

George" had shown to war for liberty had "become extinct, with the *occasion*, and the *men* of the Revolution."[14]

In the chaotic political climate of 1860, four parties projected different agendas but were equally persuasive in the strength of their appeal. Capitalizing on the division among Democrats, the young Republican Party forged a victorious coalition of businessmen, abolitionists, and Free-Soilers. In one of the most corrupt elections in the country's history, they made Abraham Lincoln the sixteenth president of the United States. The devastating civil war that erupted six months later settled the debate over chattel slavery. But it did not reconcile those who clung to the revolutionary aspirations for the egalitarian society. In the nation so admired by Bilbao in 1865, the preservation of union signaled more than repression of defiant slaveholders. The victory heralded the birth of the leviathan state and the rebirth of alliance between social conservative and economic liberal, both necessary for disciplining a generation and forging a modern industrial nation.[15]

The Caribbean at Mid-Century

The Caribbean at 1750 was a European slave-plantation archipelago on the eve of calamitous rebellion. At 1850, it was both slave and free, colonial and independent. The plantation economy survived rebellion and emancipation; immigrants had arrived to supply a labor force when ex-slaves carved out their own small holdings. In 1848, following a long debate, the French government decreed slave emancipation, leaving only the Dutch and the Spanish possessions as outposts of a once-vigorous Caribbean slave society. Abolition of slavery came in the Danish West Indies in the same year; in the Dutch West Indies in 1863; in Puerto Rico in 1873; and in Cuba in 1886. Except for the Spanish Caribbean, the process was similar: the diminishing economic role of colonial slave societies paralleled a weakening political influence. In the aftermath of abolition, however, those who had suffered the most from slavery found themselves marginalized in the new social and political order.[16]

The Caribbean's two independent governments, Haiti and the Dominican Republic, were riven by political feuding and weakened by economic subordination to the Atlantic economy. In 1844 Dominican rebels expelled Haitian occupiers and declared their independence. The new republic's fragile politics reverberated with fears of another Haitian invasion. Five years later, Haitian leader Faustin Soulouque precipitated an international crisis when he threatened to reclaim the eastern portion of the island. The beleaguered Dominicans looked to rival European and North American powers for protection and, when the Haitians became more menacing, the Dominican congress resolved to grant France a protectorate over the republic. The Dominican president approached the British and U.S. governments with similar proposals. As a last resort, the Dominican leader turned to Spain. In April 1849, the Haitians invaded but were repulsed after a fierce battle.[17]

The conflict persisted intermittently throughout the 1850s, subsiding with the end of Faustin Soulouque's rule in 1859. Throughout, Haitians tried to arouse the U.S. government to the dangers of European meddling in the Dominican Republic, but Washington was more interested in advancing its own interests. Ambitious Yankee promoters were already descending on the Spanish-speaking portion of Hispaniola and currying favor among its political factions. In 1861, as the United States plunged into civil war, the Dominican political leader Pedro Santana invited the Spanish to reoccupy their former colony. Haiti soon became a refuge for Dominican guerrillas and exiles. With the parallel French, Spanish, and British pressure on the newly installed civilian government of Benito Juárez in Mexico, Haitians again found themselves threatened. In these perilous circumstances, the Haitian government proved less defiant than its people. Submitting to a Spanish demand to acquiesce in the Spanish reoccupation of the eastern portion of the island and to cease their support for Dominican rebels, Haitian authorities found themselves confronting an angry populace. They imposed martial law to contain it.[18]

In the United States, the Haitian cause was more successful. Racial antagonism and placation of the slave South had prevented U.S. diplomatic recognition for more than fifty years. With the secession of most of the slave states, that was not long an impediment. Once the Union was committed to the eradication of slavery within the United States, Lincoln believed, freed slaves could be colonized in Haiti or Central America. (He persisted in these views until the last year of the war, when colonization was no longer a practical alternative.) Recognition of Haiti was a pragmatic, not a moral, issue. But the debate revived many of the old racial fears and stereotypes. Brenda Plummer cogently summarizes its meaning when she notes that for opponents of recognition Haiti was a "republic without virtue, that is, a republic without whites." Though the advocates never persuaded the opposition of the moral link between a war against southern slavery and the necessity of recognizing the government of a people who had waged the first successful war against New World slavery, the cause of Haitian recognition triumphed. Economics and politics dictated it. Haiti was consumer of U.S. products and possible destination of colonized blacks.[19]

At 1850 the bonds between Caribbean and U.S. slavery appeared stronger than ever. Cuban planters and slaveowners, their apprehensions deepened by Spanish acquiescence in British seizures of slave ships and a slave conspiracy known as La Escalera, had fashioned closer ties with the slave society to the north. Joined by businessmen, property owners, and discontented intellectuals, they established an annexationist society in New York that disseminated propaganda, lobbied Congress, and provided proannexationist speakers for public forums. The society's counterpart in Cuba was the Club de la Habana, which approached the Polk administration to advocate Cuban annexation in 1848, a year in which the United States also received an annexationist proposal from secessionist whites in Yucatán. In successive invasions from 1849 to 1851, proannexationist southern filibusters joined expeditions led by Narciso López, a Venezuelan exile turned Cuban rebel with strong ties to several powerful southern politicians. The last invasion, in summer 1851, proved disastrous—López was captured and publicly garroted, and many of his North American followers were shipped off to Spanish prisons. Two years later, the Democratic Franklin Pierce administration, responding to the aggressive instincts of Young America, offered to purchase the island. When that failed, the administration tried to intimidate the Spanish government into ceding the island. Outspoken northerners squelched that effort, but the notion of distracting public attention from the domestic crisis over slavery with an aggressive foreign policy persisted through the decade. On the eve of civil war, one of the final efforts to placate the South came from Democrats proposing the annexation of a slave Cuba.[20]

Cuba's vulnerability to foreign pressures and the outspokenness of its proannexationist elements persuaded a generation of U.S. leaders that Spain's grip on the island was fragile and, as Secretary of State John Quincy Adams had predicted, Cuba would inevitably fall into the North American government's outreached hand—not as an outpost of slavery, obviously, but clearly within the United State's grasp. Cuba's liberation would evolve under a powerful but benign U.S. guidance. Such arrogance blinded U.S. leaders to the Spanish capability to perpetuate colonial rule by placating disaffected Cuban Creoles. In the uncertain years of the late forties and early fifties, the governor-general clamped down on the annexationist press. More effective was a threat that had been used during the wars of independence: Spanish officials warned Cuban Creoles that their support of annexation would prompt an emancipation decree from Madrid. "The terrible weapon," wrote the governor-general, "could . . . prevent the loss of the island, and if the inhabitants convince themselves that it will be used, they will tremble and renounce every illusion bringing upon themselves such an anathema."[21]

As long as Cuban Creoles could be placated with promises, their enthusiasm for annexation to the United States waned. Spanish policy followed a cyclical pattern, however. After the U.S. Civil War, a reformist Cuban Party demanded further concessions. Rebuffed, Cuban Creoles again raised the flag of revolution in 1868. A few weeks later, a trio of revolutionary leaders dispatched a petition for admission as a state. But the Creoles were deluded. Seeing themselves in a position similar to that of rebellious Texans in the mid-1830s, they persuaded themselves that a separatist movement in Cuba, if successful, could negotiate admission of the island as a state in the Union. The U.S. reaction to *white* Cuban Creoles, they believed, would be similar to the attitude it had displayed toward Texans in the mid-1840s. But where Cuba was concerned, North American thinking had always followed a pattern the Cuban Creoles found unacceptable. Cuba might be annexed as a territory but not with the intention of passing through territorial status to statehood. The distinctions were still apparent at the end of the century, when a conquering U.S. military invaded Cuba, installed a military government, and revived talk of annexation among Cuban Creoles fearful of the social changes identified with *Cuba Libre*. They were still adamant about statehood, wrote a U.S. observer, Forbes Lindsay, who added: "A large majority of the native population of Cuba have negro blood in their veins. Practically one hundred percent of the people confess the Roman Catholic faith and Spanish is the mother tongue of the same proportion. Would the American nation agree to the construction of a sister state out of such material?"[22]

In the British Caribbean, the postemancipationist insular society appeared to replicate a bipolar evolution, where former white slaveowners sought to preserve the rigidly stratified social order and met continuing resistance from an egalitarian *demos* of the emancipated. In actuality, its character followed chaotic patterns of development. In some places, the rigid social structure of the slave era survived virtually intact. The plantation economy persevered; new forms of indentured labor, mostly satisfied by immigration, appeared. Some emancipated slaves lived in a subsistence peasant economy; others served as a wage labor force. Mulattoes sometimes fashioned alliances with blacks; in other instances, they distanced themselves from the emancipated in order to maintain distinctions in the social hierarchy. Everywhere there was uncertainty about what the emancipated majority wanted.[23]

The contemporary British historian and essayist Thomas Carlyle, who

doubted that working people had any entitlement to leisure, arrogantly stated
that for the emancipated in the British West Indies freedom meant the right to
lounge under a tree and eat pumpkins, but the owners of the land producing
that pumpkin had the right to compel that person to labor. Carlyle was correct
only in the sense that the meaning or freedom for the emancipated was different. They did not disdain work; on the contrary, what they sought was an
economic alternative to plantation labor. Given their experience, it was a rational choice. But in the political context in which they challenged prevailing
assumptions, there was only a slight prospect of success. They not only worked
hard on their own plots, but they worked hard *on the plantations*. Perhaps, as
Sidney Mintz has suggested, they believed in the possibility of a new society,
not Western but African, a society drawing its strength from four hundred
years of deprivation and struggle by ten million people. The society they imagined, of course, was not the same as that planned for them by their former masters, nor could their putative European liberators—missionaries and abolitionists—accept the notion that freed peoples preferred a future modeled on
their African past.[24]

Place as much as circumstance often greatly affected the lot of the emancipated. In the Leeward Islands, the status of the ex-slaves under the law improved considerably, but the social inequality predicated on race remained.
On Barbados, where whites dominated and former slaves lacked access to
arable land, planters easily maintained their domination over a captive labor
force. Similar forms of coercion served the planters of Antigua, though in the
decade after 1845, sixty-seven free villages with more than fifteen thousand
inhabitants flourished. In Jamaica, Guyana, and Trinidad, larger and with
greater amounts of unoccupied land, emancipation inspired an exodus from
the plantation to escape planter control. Guiana's fifteen thousand ex-slaves
were landless in 1838; four years later, they owned seven thousand acres on
the coast. By the end of the forties, the Afro-Guyanese population possessed
four hundred estates and ten thousand houses.[25]

In Jamaica, the fortunes of the emancipated were different. As the bar-
gaining power of plantation laborers declined, white planters and local authorities conspired against them when they demanded title to uncultivated
land. Subsistence agriculture without a parallel need to work for wages had
no place in the economic calculations of Jamaican planters. Neither would
they permit renters to grow crops for export. As the economic prospects of the
island grew more precarious, the emancipated grew more defiant. In 1865, a
group of distressed holders of small plots petitioned Queen Victoria for the

right to cultivate subsistence crops on uncultivated Crown lands, pledging they would pay for the land in installments. The response, drafted by a veteran colonial officer, Henry Taylor, informed the petitioners that their "prosperity" depended "upon their working for Wages, not uncertainly, or capriciously, but steadily and continuously, at the times when their labour is wanted, and for so long as it is wanted."[26]

A few weeks later, following a violent confrontation between freedmen and militiamen, they joined other discontented in the Morant Bay rebellion. It was ruthlessly and decisively stifled. A short time later, vowing to safeguard public order, the planter-dominated Jamaican Assembly resolved to dissolve and return the island to Crown colony status. The act was a muted but unmistakable surrender of those who believed they could preserve the "old Jamaica" without slavery and who had little faith that "free labor," heralded by metropolitan abolitionists, bore any relevance to Jamaican realities. The refusal of the emancipated to labor in a declining plantation economy revived older notions that not everyone could be acculturated to the economic incentives of the market and those who could not were undeserving of the right of self-determination. This reasoning represented the harsher element of liberal ideology that rejected arguments that all peoples, regardless of their color or experience, could be shorn of those debilitating human features that impeded their social progress.[27]

Unlike their counterparts in the British Caribbean, those emancipated in the French Caribbean, who had benefited from the activities of the metropolitan coalition of workers, liberals, and radicals of 1848, were able to use their majoritarian numbers to participate in their governance. It was a short-lived victory, however. In the restoration of Bonapartist France in the 1850s their privileges were sharply curtailed. By the end of the decade, French ships were crossing the Atlantic with "liberated" Africans destined to pay for their freedom as involuntary laborers on West Indian plantations. As the modern Bonaparte, the leader of France dreamed and plotted the resurrection of French influence in the New World—in the isthmus, in Mexico, and in the Confederacy.

Latin America: A New Generation
Latin America at mid-century projected a more promising future. Its postwar economies, ravaged by fifteen years of savage conflict, had recovered. Its political condition, once the despair of not only foreign observers but the revolutionary heirs themselves, had improved, reflecting the determination of a younger generation to rid their countries of the last vestiges of colonial insti-

tutions. Some of the explosive political issues of earlier years (for example, the church-state relationship) still divided elites, but the passions of the 1820s and 1830s had subsided. Liberals and Conservatives, once fratricidal enemies, appeared to be reconciling most of their fundamental differences. Doubts about the political and especially the economic prospects for the continent lingered, of course, but not all shared the Argentine Juan Bautista Alberdi's pessimism when he wrote: "When our parents were twenty-five they had already liberated a whole world."[28]

The liberal renaissance in mid-nineteenth-century Latin America is more easily described than explained. The progressive dynamics of the era—the accelerated pace of change, the weakening of lingering colonial traditions and privileges, the heightened economic prospects for Latin American exports, the receptivity to new ideas, and the determination of a younger generation to transform politics—are indisputable, though their impact varied from place to place. At the same time, as modern critics of the Latin American condition point out, the democratic impulses of mid-century liberal reformism were not only weak but limited. Far more consequential, they argue, were such things as the erosion of corporate protection of indigenous peoples, the mortgaging of Latin American economies to a dominating North-Atlantic economic system, and, most damnable, the readiness with which liberals accepted elitist and authoritarian political systems in the name of order and progress. Had Latin America's leaders chosen domestic rather than external models for progress, these critics further contend, the legacy would have been much less depressing.

Liberalism's prospects depended less on choices than on circumstances. The universal liberal political model was constitutional government safeguarded by a military loyal to civilian rule. In this context, social and cultural renovation would inevitably follow. But the realities—the gloomy prospects of a "prosperous and innovative rural democracy" flourishing in Mexico or New Granada (Colombia) or Argentina—meant that Latin American liberalism would undergo a "profound mutation." Its character varied from place to place.[29]

Central America, which escaped most of the ravages of the long war of independence, may serve as illustration of the promise and of the often frightful costs of liberal progress. Modern scholars, explaining Central America's monocultural economy in the twentieth century, often erroneously characterize its postindependence economy as dominated by the hacienda and the liberal agenda as an insidious plot to create an agroexport economy at the expense of its indigenous people. In this context, the conservative role was necessarily not only to oppose liberal plans of centralization but to protect indigenous cultures from the repressive forces of Europeanization. The reality was more complicated. Central America's postrevolutionary economies were more diverse than commonly believed; its liberal politicos probably retarded economic progress by their incessant warring. Their conservative enemies, admired by modern Central Americanists for their determined shielding of indigenous peoples (especially in Guatemala) from the ravages of liberal labor codes, were also culpable for their role in the fashioning of monocultural economies and the repressive state regimes of the late nineteenth and early twentieth centuries.[30]

In the 1820s, liberals crafted a union (the United Provinces) of five former Spanish colonies—Costa Rica, Nicaragua, Honduras, El Salvador, and Guatemala—and looked to foreign models in their political agendas and to immigrants to develop modern isthmian economies. Their political leader was the Honduran Francisco Morazán. In the following decade, isthmian liberals began to implement their ambitious plans. In Guatemala, the liberal design for development appeared to offer the most promise. In a country desperately poor and largely populated by non-Spanish indigenous peoples, liberated president Mariano Gálvez managed to allay the apprehensions of some of the traditional elites, but his program alienated most of the lower classes, the church, and those displeased with the dismantling of old Spanish institutions. Ultimately, they found a leader in Rafael Carrera, a mestizo who understood little about economies but alertly recognized the weakness of the liberal state in a traditional society. He took power in 1837 and survived in power for almost two decades, presiding over a restorationist social revolution that revived church power, returned communal lands to Guatemala's indigenous peoples, and even reinstituted Spanish labor laws.[31]

The political instability that accompanied the warring between states loosely joined in the United Provinces (123 battles from 1824 to 1842) certainly impeded efforts to integrate isthmian economies, but the chaos of the era provided the opportunity for creative activity that helps us to understand how and why the isthmian economy of the late nineteenth century took shape. As regional economic integration weakened and the federation collapsed, the national economies began to shift toward an export economy. Progress depended on several factors: attentiveness to public roads, encouragement of investment, internal stability, and geographic factors. Costa Rica fared much better than Nicaragua or El Salvador, where elitist political warring continued. From independence until the 1850s, the intermittent conflict between rival elites in León and Granada permitted Nicaragua's rural peoples, Indian and mestizo, to benefit from the urban political anarchy and build their own communities. Unlike Nicaraguan patriarchs, who coveted their land and required their labor if Nicaragua was to develop an agroexport economy, these rural peoples expressed little interest in liberal economic agendas or the Enlightenment rhetoric espoused by urban elites.[32]

In the late 1840s, as California gold fields beckoned generations of North (and South) Americans, Nicaragua and the Colombian isthmus of Panama attracted developers, promoters, and transients. The strategic and economic implications of a transisthmian passage in these two venues heightened the international politics of the region. In 1846, the Polk administration negotiated a canal treaty with Colombia by whose terms the United States agreed to guarantee the neutrality of the isthmian passageway. Under its provisions, a U.S. company built the Western hemisphere's first transcontinental railroad. Four years later, following a series of incidents, the U.S. and British governments, rivals in Central America, pledged themselves to joint efforts in developing a transisthmian route.[33]

As in the past, the isthmus was again an international battleground, but little in their history prepared Central Americans for the invasion of Yankee filibusters in the 1850s. For Nicaragua, the experience was devastating. Midway through the decade, Nicaragua's president was William Walker, a Tennessee filibuster who had migrated to California, failed in an effort to take over the Mexican state of Sonora, and then sailed for Nicaragua, where political conflict between Liberal and Conservative elites had erupted into civil war. In Walker and his followers, the Liberals found a momentary ally, but the "grey-eyed" man of destiny just as quickly turned on his Nicaraguan allies. He waged a savage war and, for a year or so, ruled over a defiant people. His was a generation of Jacksonian Democrats who spoke of recreating the slave plantation society in the tropics. A decade before he penned his encomium to the United States, the Chilean radical Francisco Bilbao identified Walker as the embodiment of the U.S. menace to a continent: "Walker is the invasion, Walker is the conquest, Walker is the United States . . . [and] the prophetic voice of a filibustering crusade which promises to its adventurers the regions of the South and the death of the South American initiative."[34]

Spearheaded by the fiercely independent Costa Ricans, who had fought Morazán and the isthmian union, a momentarily unified Central America drove Walker from power. Returning as a heroic adventurer to a bitterly divided motherland, Walker was lionized when he appeared in public. He wrote a book about his exploits in Nicaragua. Shortly after its publication, he put together another expedition, sailed from New Orleans, and landed on the north Honduran coast. Confronting strong resistance, he escaped, taking refuge aboard a British warship. The British officer was more politic than compassionate: he turned Walker over to the Hondurans, who executed him. A former Nicaraguan accomplice wrote his epitaph: "God will condemn his arrogance and protect our cause."[35]

In several important respects, the successive experiences of Guatemala and Nicaragua from the 1830s to the 1850s were symptomatic of the fundamental flaws some historians have attributed to the liberal triumph in the postindependence era in Latin America. In their zeal to achieve progress, they had erred tragically by imposing inappropriate economic models on traditional cultures. Arrogantly, they had defined the interests of the nation to accommodate the priorities of the nation-state and not the fundamental needs of those who composed the nation. Though the bill of indictment reads differently, a generation of North American leaders withstood similar accusations of betrayal of the public trust and the revolutionary promise. Radicals called for a moral cleansing of the body politic. In some fundamental ways, these and parallel charges were reverberations of the prerevolutionary era.[36]

Perhaps no Latin American country paid a higher price for the triumph of liberalism than Mexico. The war with the United States had not only culminated in the loss of fifty percent of the nation's territory but had also revealed its political and social weaknesses. During the conflict, sisal producers in Yucatán had tried to secede and had unintentionally provoked a rebellion among Cruzob Mayans against whites, plunging the province into a caste war. Monies from the Treaty of Guadalupe Hidalgo enabled the central government to quell the separatist insurrection. But the humiliation of the U.S. invasion and of defeat persuaded both liberals and conservatives that Mexico must be transformed. Liberals such as José Luis Mora, who had often extolled the United States as the model republican society, now belatedly recognized that Mexico could never achieve liberal goals by imitating the U.S. variety of liberalism. The European liberal tradition was more relevant. For the conservatives, of course, the regeneration of the nation required purging the country of republicanism and restoring monarchy.[37]

Liberals had their own sweeping agenda for national restoration and progress. A modern nation required not only a shedding of debilitating traditions but the creation of a new political order. They confronted a dual enemy. The first was the entrenched combination of clerical, military, and social conservative forces that had effectively stymied liberal purists for a generation. In the years after the humiliating defeat by the United States, Mexican liberals recovered their sense of purpose and, after the overthrow of Santa Anna in 1855 by the revolution of Ayutla, gained power. In a flurry of political legislation known in Mexican history as La Reforma, a triad of liberal leaders—Benito Juárez (a Zapotec from Oaxaca), Miguel Lerdo de Tejado, and Melchor Ocampo—profoundly altered the relation between state and society. In a series of laws, Reforma Mexico abolished ecclesiastical and military privileges and severely limited corporate ownership of land. A new constitution in 1857 was federalist in tone but gave the central government far more authority than the fundamental law of 1824. Its silence on religion, coupled with the direct threat to clerical authority, brought denunciation by the church and the threat of excommunication to any Mexican taking an oath of office under the new law.

Moderates such as Ignacio Comonfort, who agreed to stand for the presidency under the new constitution, tried valiantly to reconcile Mexico's alienated churchmen and military officers but failed. When the military revolted, Comonfort fled to the United States. As chief justice, Juárez was next in line for the presidency, but he now confronted a menacing alliance of central highlanders, hacienda owners from the central valley, and communal Indians who had lost titles to lands under Reforma legislation. In 1858, Mexico collapsed into civil war. In this conflict, Juárez put together a coalition of mestizos, opportunistic businessmen, and landowners from the far north. Desperate for U.S. support and money to satisfy its European creditors, Mexico agreed to cede vital transit rights across the Isthmus of Tehuantepec to the United States. A band of suspicious Republicans in the U.S. Senate prevented the measure from becoming law, but this episode revealed the precariousness of the liberal cause in Mexico.

Juárez finally triumphed just as Lincoln was assuming the presidency in 1861. It was a Pyrrhic victory for Mexico's liberals, who now had to face the nation's second enemy: European creditors in Great Britain, France, and Spain, whose governments dispatched a punitive expedition to the port of Veracruz in the fall of 1861. Spain and Britain quit this venture, but the French had more ambitious plans. Conspiring with a gaggle of Mexican conservatives bent on placing a Hapsburg prince on a restored Mexican throne, Napoleon III sent his troops into the Mexican highlands. Repulsed at Puebla in May 1862, they returned the following year, drove all the way to the Mexican capital, and installed Maximilian as emperor of Mexico.

For three years the juaristas waged a relentless and often savage guerrilla war. Victorious in 1867, Juárez recreated the liberal state, gradually but systematically transforming it into a more powerful institution to provide order and discipline to a generation shattered by war. The decision was justified, he believed, by the disorder caused by bands of roving, disbanded soldiers in rural Mexico. But the fundamental character of the new political order had taken form in the tumultuous fifties, when Reforma Mexico's victorious liberals had their first realistic opportunity to weaken the nation's corporatist social order and to chart their design for the leviathan state. Young, determined to modernize Mexico, and professing European middle-class homilies about republican government and liberal economic policies, they included soldiers, scattered industrialists and merchants, petty bureaucrats, disgruntled landowners, and hordes of lawyers. Conservatives vilified Indian Mexico as barbarous, but their liberal enemies, ultimately ensconced in positions of power, turned their backs on their peasant allies. Their "primary goal was to lay the foundation of the secular Mexican nation-state."[38]

Elsewhere, the liberal challenge to the old order in the 1850s brought no civil war as savage as that experienced by Mexico, but the political strife prompted liberals to rethink their priorities. In Colombia (called New Granada and the Granadine Republic from 1830 until 1863), Santander's liberal regime in the 1830s had rid the country of the militarism still plaguing other republics but did not pacify the nation's regionalist chieftains. As the forties commenced, Colombia was embroiled in a succession of conspiracies, uprisings, and plotting known as the War of the Supremes. One legacy was a political reordering in the form of Liberal and Conservative Parties, which represented social rather than ideological divisions.

As long as elites moderated their passions, the political culture retained a cosmetic stability. But in the aftermath of the 1848 revolutions in Europe, Colombia's liberals, though divided over such fundamental issues as the role of the state, the church, and the military, enacted a series of sweeping reforms—abolition of slavery, absolute freedom of the press, universal male suffrage (and even limited women's suffrage), laissez-faire economic policy, and the conversion of communal Indian property to individual holdings. In the late 1850s, Conservatives returned to power but fell in a revolt of 1860. Restored Liberals weakened the central government even more with the constitution of 1863. When disorder and local revolt followed, the opportunistic among them drew a basic conclusion about power and the state. A doctrinaire Liberal of the 1850s, Rafael Nuñez, disillusioned with the socially corrosive impact of Liberal policy, crafted a political understanding with rival Conservatives. As president in the 1880s, Nuñez ended the Liberal era by replacing the 1863 constitution with a document that centralized power and negotiated a new understanding with the church.[39]

The Venezuelan liberal interlude of the 1850s did not produce such deep ideological fissures, yet the nation collapsed into dictatorship and became a more powerful state. From the early 1830s until the late 1840s, Venezuela was the classic caudillo nation of José Antonio Páez, who ruled firmly but benignly. Liberal reforms permitted by Páez took hold because the upper class, whose interests he resolutely defended, generally supported them. But in the troublesome late forties, when an economic crisis splintered agriculturists and merchants, Venezuela's Liberals overturned the Conservative Oligarchy, as the Páez era was called, and instituted a Liberal Oligarchy. The military played a critical role in sustaining Liberal regimes in the 1850s, one of several anomalies in the Venezuelan political record. They satisfied the country's agro-exporters with distinctively illiberal economic measures, but not even the military presence in government was able to quell resurgent racial and class hatreds—animosities born in the war of independence and dormant for a generation.

A momentary coalition of Conservatives and alienated Liberals brought a new regime to power, but the ousted Liberals immediately staged their own rebellion (known as the Federalist War) in 1858. In the anarchy that ensued, the ranchers of Guarico Province petitioned for the return of Páez from exile in the United States. The old caudillo assumed virtually dictatorial power, as had Bolívar in his last years, but in the different political circumstances he was less the authoritative ruler of a divided nation than a negotiator among its factional chieftains. When the civil war ended five years later, Páez again went into exile, and the victorious Liberals crafted a Federalist constitution that resembled the Liberal document of Colombia. The social disorder that followed persuaded a generation of Venezuelan Liberals that progress required the vigorous use of central power.[40]

In the Southern Cone, both Argentina and Chile traveled troubled routes to modernity. Argentina's first generation of Liberals had fashioned a revolution but they had not united a nation. Exiled, persecuted, and embittered by Rosas's dictatorship, they heartened with the overthrow of the dictator in 1852. Rosas's downfall, however, served only to revive the old federalist-unitario feud. When the confederate government produced a new constitution in 1853, a document modeled on that of the United States, Buenos Aires refused to approve it. A generation before, the political strife between the city and the interior had enabled Rosas to impose his authoritarian rule. In the 1850s, however, Argentine liberals (such as Juan Bautista Alberdi) wrote eloquently about building a new nation—"to govern is to populate," Alberdi declared, anticipating Argentina's preference for European immigrants. The unitario-federalist clash produced two brief civil wars at the end of the decade—the first, a victory for the confederation, the second, for Buenos Aires—but in the aftermath Buenos Aires joined the Confederation and Bartolomé Mitre (governor of Buenos Aires Province) became the first president of a united Argentina.[41]

The makers of modern liberal Argentina were sometimes as violative of individual rights as the dictator Rosas. Indeed, their success depended on the centralizing policies of Rosas, for control of the state enabled his triumphant enemies to impose economic policies that discouraged political participation. Corruption and violence as much as ideology characterized liberal rule. Mitre ruthlessly persecuted the gauchos. In 1865, Argentina joined Brazil and Uruguay in waging war against Paraguay. As had Juárez and Lincoln, the Argentine leader used the circumstance of war as justification for disciplining the internal enemies of the state. Three years later, Mitre turned over power to a political adversary, Domingo Sarmiento, admirer of U.S. educational traditions and biographer of Abraham Lincoln. In the following decade Argentina's modernization appeared to be following a course parallel to that of the United States: building of railroads, a desert war against Indians, large-scale immigration of laborers, harsh discipline for native workers, and dynamic growth in farming and especially ranching. Unlike their North American counterparts, Argentina's modernizing elites intentionally chose European cultural models, thinking them more appropriate than the gaucho tradition. That choice would haunt their twentieth-century successors.[42]

For a generation, Argentina's internal divisions stood in sharp contrast to the disciplined and purposeful order evident in neighboring Chile. After the tumultuous twenties, Chile acquired a new constitution in 1833, and its landed oligarchies, in return for political sustenance of a rigid rural social structure, acquiesced in the creation of a strong central government. Throughout the thirties, it was dominated by one of the nation's most admired strongmen: Diego Portales. Though never president, Portales effectively made the Chilean presidency into the most powerful executive office in the New World. On the west coast of South America, Chile projected an assertiveness and an imperial ambition that rivaled the continentalism of the United States. Within the country, Portales preserved oligarchical rule by tolerating minimal dissent and voting fraud. The purpose of effective government was preservation of the social order, which, to employ one of Portales's aphorisms, was "maintained . . . by the weight of the night, and because we do not have men who are subtle, capable, or prone to take offense."[43]

Portales fell to an assassin's bullet in 1837, but the Portalian state persevered. Chile won an impressive victory in a confrontation with Peru and Bolivia, the economy continued to improve, and by the end of the 1840s, the nation's reputation for political tranquillity and progress was unrivaled by any Latin American nation. After the Mexican war, Chilean leaders were outspoken in their warnings about the menace of "Anglo-Saxon imperialism"; their condemnations were explained partly by Chile's pretensions to leadership in a new South American security system, partly by the harsh treatment suffered by Chilean migrants to California gold fields. The Chilean minister to the United States expressed the national mood when he wrote about North Americans: "What today they are doing to Mexico by taking over California, they will do to us tomorrow for frivolous reasons if it occurs to them."[44]

But the real danger to the Portalian state came from within Chile. The most blatantly threatening denunciations came from radical Chilean liberals, who organized the Society of Equality. Its best-known proselytizer was Bilbao, who had shocked the Chilean elite with his writings and suffered expulsion in the mid-forties but was back in the country in 1850. With Bilbao in charge, the society began disseminating tracts, organizing demonstrations, and generally mobilizing opposition to the regime. President Manuel Bulnes felt sufficiently threatened to order the dissolution of the society. When Bulnes virtually imposed his successor, Manuel Montt, through a rigged election, the resulting protest sparked rebellion in 1851 and again 1859. The violence, which occurred primarily in the south and the north, demonstrated the first effective challenge to the Portalian state and the tradition of strong executive power wielded in Santiago. Its purpose had powerful social implications for rural Chile. As Benjamín Vicuña warned at mid-decade, the uprising was necessary in order to "rescue our rural classes from abject servitude" and, as another contemporary observed, to rid Chile of a rural society that had "two rival classes, almost two races, that are becoming increasingly antagonistic."[45]

Throughout the Americas at mid-century, the political crises of nation-states—crises of legitimacy as well as of authority—revealed the permanency of eighteenth-century traditions and aspirations in an era when a generation identified progress with rational economic choices. National identity was not a rational calculation, however. The nation-states of the New World had not yet infused their legitimacy with what they desperately required—the abiding national spirit of peoples who had made possible their independence but whose loyalties remained doubtful. Nationalism expressed in official ideology or movements may not express the sentiments of those who appear loyal or supportive. Most certainly, nationalism cannot be equated with the beliefs, the interests, or the needs of common people.[46]

Epilogue

Early in this study I concluded that understanding a revolution is an easier task than explaining why a revolution occurs. On completing it, I am persuaded that revolution is more easily explained if one is permitted to define what a revolution is. None of the three revolutions I have surveyed conforms sufficiently to any of the prevailing theories of revolution identified in history or in the social sciences so as to explain why they occurred or followed a particular course. The modern historiography of the American Revolution, richer and more contentious than that of the Haitian or Spanish-American revolutions, has swung between seemingly incompatible ideological and structuralist interpretations. Each of the three revolutions has been described as restorationist or, alternatively, as modern. Social historians correctly point to the contradiction between the promises of liberation of the individual and the creation of new restraints in the postrevolutionary order. The revolutionary agenda is often a shorter list than the modern bill of indictment.

The relevance of these revolutions and wars of independence for our time has less to do with what they achieved or failed to resolve than with other commonalities. Contradictions abounded in both eras. In the late eighteenth century, as is occurring in the late twentieth, government was deemed unnecessarily intrusive and woefully ineffectual; society, too materialistic and too restrictive; capitalism, unjust and liberating. In a world of such contradictory dualities, it is easy to understand why the young people of Concord marched off to fight in the American Revolution wanting only to restore a mythical community described by their grandparents or why young Americans in the 1990s, better educated than their parents, often say they will settle in life for the lifestyles of their parents. In the late eighteenth century as in the late twentieth, the promise of reward through achievement coexisted with the reality of denial because of color or gender or economic circumstance.

Both ages exhibit two other commonalities—chaos and complexity—characteristics which do not explain why revolutions occur or what can be done to prevent them but help us to understand why the violence follows certain patterns and, just as important, why the postrevolutionary governments behave in ways that appear to contradict the revolutionary purpose. These are the measures I have applied in this study. What explained the character of these revolutions, I believe, was their chaotic form. What explained their triumphs was the creativity made possible by chaos. What explained their failure was the inability to contain that chaos. What explained the choices of postrevolutionary leaders was their determination to channel the chaotic forces unleashed by war or, if fearful of what they portended, to crush them.

Such an approach suggests that I believe events dictate human choices and that people cannot make their own history. On the contrary, I argue that people at every level played a determining role in the revolutionary age. But it was not so much their ideological conviction or material condition that dictated their choices as the opportunity provided by the chaos of the times. Leaders of the American Revolution often fumed about the diminished authority or the decline of revolutionary faith and commitment, but the revolution that occurred in the "hearts and minds" of people, to use John Adams's phrase, would not have been possible except in the chaotic circumstances of those years. George Washington was an able commander because he conformed to European-style military discipline; he won the war in the Pennsylvania countryside because he adapted to its chaotic patterns. Hidalgo failed, undeniably, because his Creole allies turned against the army he mobilized with the Grito de Dolores, but Hidalgo's movement collapsed because he could not control his followers. Bolívar succeeded as military leader because he was able to direct the destructive power of country warriors in a chaotic war; he failed as postrevolutionary leader because he could no longer survive in a chaotic world. Toussaint-Louverture failed when he tried to restore the plantation economy in Haiti; he succeeded, however, when he acknowledged that despite the chaos of the black rebellion, the slaves had a singular purpose—the end of slavery, whatever the cost.

The achievement or, conversely, the denial of the revolutionary promise has inspired more than scholarly controversy. For the revolutionary generation in the Americas, as well as for that of our own times, the contradictions that abound prompt demands for political resolution. The abiding issue of the revolutionary age was the relation of the individual to the state and to society; today it is the social question, the obligation of the state and the society to the individual. If revolution was the only means to alter the first, it is sometimes argued, then perhaps revolution is necessary to address the second.

Perhaps, but only if it can be proved that revolution made possible the first.

Notes

Introduction

1. "The fact that the word 'revolution' meant originally restoration, hence something which to us is its very opposite," observed Hannah Arendt, "is not a mere oddity of semantics. The revolutions of the seventeenth and eighteenth centuries, which . . . appear to show . . . the spirit of the modern age, were intended to be restorations." *On Revolution* (New York, 1963), 36.

   The introduction of the adjective *modern* to *revolution* requires further refinement. As Eugene Genovese explains: "Modern revolutionary movements, beginning with the moderate ideology of the leaders of the American Revolution and especially with Jacobinism in both its French and Haitian forms, took a new turn, notwithstanding the substantial measure of historical continuity they represented. They introduced considerable rationalism into older ideas and projected a more realistic view of human nature and action. Specifically, their break with the ideas of supernatural deliverance enormously reinforced the demand for the assertion of human will and significantly reduced . . . the tendency toward Manichaean fanaticism. Such movements have thrown up messiahs and sometimes almost deified them, but they have generally responded to charismatic leaders with a degree of realism and restraint hardly possible for those following a prophet and a revelation. This shift . . . away from the tradition of revolutionary millenarianism has created unprecedented room for autonomous popular action; it has, in fact, required that action even while creating new methods of restraint and repression." Genovese, *From Rebellion to Revolution: Afro-American Slave Revolts in the Making of the New World* (New York, 1979), 122–23.

2. John Dunn, *Modern Revolutions: An Introduction to the Analysis of a Political Phenomenon* (Cambridge, 1972), 232. In defining the attributes common to all

revolution, Peter Calvert strives to be both precise and encompassing: revolution is "*sudden, . . . violent . . . political succession, . . .* [and] *change.*" *Revolution and Counter-Revolution* (London, 1990), 15–16. This is a definition that applies to every revolution yet satisfactorily defines none of them. Hannah Arendt employs the existence of violence in revolution to make the point much better: "Revolutions and wars are not even conceivable outside the domain of violence. . . . To be sure, not even wars, let alone revolutions, are ever completely determined by violence." *On Revolution,* 9.

Revolution was not the only word to alter in meaning in this era. Words such as *equality, republic,* and *democracy* filled the oratory and pamphlets of the day. In the context of a heady transatlantic political debate they conveyed one meaning for those who try to understand the revolutionary era, yet, as Raymond Williams points out, they acquired sometimes very different meanings for those who lived in that age. Five key words—*industry, democracy, class, art,* and *culture*—underwent fundamental change in meaning from the late eighteenth to the mid-nineteenth century. "The changes in their use, at this critical period, bear witness to a general change in our characteristic ways of thinking about our common life; about our social, political and economic institutions; about the purposes which these institutions are designed to embody; and about the relations to these institutions and purposes of our activities in learning, education and the arts." Williams, *Culture and Society,* 1750–1950 (New York, 1958), xiii.

3. Robert R. Palmer, *The Age of the Democratic Revolution: A Political History of Europe and America, 1760–1820* (2 vols., Princeton, 1959, 1964), 1:21.

4. Walter LaFeber, *Inevitable Revolutions: The United States in Central America,* 2nd ed. (New York, 1993; orig. pub., 1983), 16. As a comparativist, I agree with LaFeber's observation that the meaning of revolution may be strikingly different in different places and that it is critical to understand why those differences exist. I do not believe that U.S. policy inevitably creates the kinds of revolution the United States seeks to prevent. As George III and George Washington both discovered, tolerating defiance can sometimes embolden an aggrieved party. Fidel Castro once commented that, given the kind of revolution that Cuba must have, the United States would have to oppose it. There could be no accommodation.

5. On the centrality of political dynamics in explaining revolutionary change see Charles Tilly, *From Mobilization to Revolution* (Reading, Mass., 1978). On the relation between modernization and revolution, see Charles Tilly, "Does Modernization Breed Revolution?" *Comparative Politics* 5 (1976): 425–47.

6. Sidney Mintz, "Can Haiti Change?" *Foreign Affairs* (Jan.-Feb. 1995), 73.

7. Carville Earle, *Geographical Inquiry and American Historical Problems* (Stanford, 1992), 7. See also Michel Foucault (Colin Gordon, ed.), *Power/Knowledge: Selected Interviews and Other Writings, 1972–1977* (New York, 1980), 63–77; Robert Sack, "Geography, Geometry, and Explanation," *Annals of the Association of American Geographers* 62 (1972): 61–78; and Andrew Sayer, "The Difference That Space Makes," in Derek Gregory and John Urry, eds., *Social Relations and Spatial Structures* (New York, 1985), 49–66.

For a suggestive interpretation of the meaning of universalist-particularist conflict in modern times see Immanuel Wallerstein, *Geopolitics and Geoculture: Essays on the Changing-World System* (Cambridge, 1991); the response by William McNeill, "Wallerstein's Vision of Past and Future," *Diplomatic History* 18 (Spring 1994): 269–76; and the sophisticated discussion in Peter Novick, *That Noble Dream: The 'Objectivity Question' and the American Historical Profession* (Cambridge, 1988), 458–59, 466–71, 582–85.

8. One example of unanticipated consequences in the eighteenth century found reinforcement in Adam Smith's 1776 book *The Wealth of Nations*. Modern commentators, John Hall observes, too often attribute the "market revolution" of the age to enlightened and rational decisions by proprietors, merchants, and manufacturers. The reality, as Smith himself pointed out, was "a revolution of the greatest importance to the public happiness . . . brought about by two different orders of people who had not the least intention to serve the public." Hall, *Liberalism: Politics, Ideology, and the Market* (Chapel Hill, N.C., 1987), 42.

Commenting on the irregularities in Latin American history, Willam B. Taylor writes: "Latin America has been at the same time united and fragmented by its European history. Latin America does have a shared history of three centuries of Iberian colonization, enclave economies, and . . . a common marginality to an emerging world economic system. But these are not homogeneous or timeless traits. Iberian institutions and demands did not spread uniformly or penetrate everywhere at once. The cities of Latin America have been self-consciously Europeanizing centers of authority, exchange, and values but their control over the vast countryside has been intermittent and uneven." Taylor, "Between Global Process and Local Knowledge: An Inquiry into Early Latin American Social History, 1500–1900," in Olivier Zunz, ed., *Reliving the Past: The Worlds of Social History* (Chapel Hill, N.C., 1985), 117.

9. "In science as in life," James Gleick has written, "it is well known that a chain of events can have a point of crisis that could magnify small changes. But chaos meant that such points were everywhere. They were pervasive." *Chaos: Making a New Science* (New York, 1987), 23; see also 38–39, 48–49, 94–95, 303–15; Andrew Abbott, "Transcending General Linear Reality," *Sociological Theory* 6 (1988): 169–86; and D. R. Hofstadter, "Metamagical Themas," *Scientific American* 245 (Nov. 1981): 22–43.

Peter Calvert notes the relevance of chaos theory in the study of revolution when he writes, "Scholars who have sought to understand the phenomenon [of revolution] better have characteristically concentrated on the causes, the social forces generating support for revolutionary movements. This is the most difficult angle of approach. The magnitude of the research implied and the number of variables to be precisely identified are immense. The smallest error can have the most important consequences in assessing a movement whose active phases are normally compressed into a period of no more than a few weeks." *Revolution and Counterrevolution*, 118.

10. See M. Mitchell Waldrop, *Complexity: The Emerging Science at the Edge of Order and Chaos* (New York, 1992), 11–13, 184–85, 351.

Students of revolution often make a distinction between rebellion and revolution, the first presumably "restorationist" and inspired by irrational, religious motives, the second a modernizing transformation that draws heavily on secular values. Yet, as Perez Zagorin points out, "The conception of a future new order as the goal and justification of revolution also appears, both in the religious millenarianism and in the secularized form of rationalistic and natural-rights doctrine. . . . Ideologies of the normative past can lead, despite their backward-looking orientation, both to highly innovative demands in rebel programs and to large-scale change." Zagorin, "Prolegomena to the Comparative History of Revolution in Early Modern Europe," *Comparative Studies in Society and History* 18 (1976): 171.

On the pertinence of "latent events" and their disturbing effects on the rich and abundant historiography of the American Revolution, Bernard Bailyn writes, "The political and ideological background of the American Revolution has been studied by more people over a longer period of time than any other topic in American history. But old historical problems do not preclude new solutions: indeed, they require them, for historical explanations are delicate contrivances, capable of being fundamentally upset by small bits of information and transformed by shifts in historians' angles of vision." *The Origins of American Politics* (New York, 1970), 3.

11. Gordon Wood, *The Radicalism of the American Revolution* (New York, 1992), 365, 368. See also Alfred Young, introduction to Young, ed., *Beyond the American Revolution: Explorations in the History of American Radicalism* (De Kalb, Il., 1993), 3–24.

12. Jorge Domínguez, *Insurrection or Loyalty: The Breakdown of the Spanish Empire* (Cambridge, Mass., 1980), 245.

13. Luís Villoro, *La revolución de independencia: Un ensayo de interpretación* (Mexico City, 1953), 12. "History is made by men's actions," writes Eric Hobsbawm, "and their choices are conscious and may be significant." Yet the greatest of all revolutionary strategists, Lenin, was lucidly aware that during revolutions planned action takes place in a context of uncontrollable forces." Hobsbawm, "Revolution," in Roy Porter and Mikulas Teich, eds., *Revolution in History* (Cambridge, 1986), 12.

1 The Tense Society

1. For much of this account of the British occupation of Havana I have relied on Hugh Thomas, *Cuba: The Pursuit of Freedom* (New York, 1971), 1–11; Louis A. Pérez, Jr., *Cuba and the United States: Ties of Singular Intimacy* (Athens, Ga., 1990), 1–9; and Richard Pares, *War and Trade in the West Indies, 1739–1763* (Oxford, 1936), 574–80. See also Archivo Nacional de Cuba, *Papeles sobre la toma de la Habana por los ingleses* (Havana, 1948).

2. Peggy Liss, *Atlantic Empires: The Network of Trade and Revolution, 1713–1826* (Baltimore, 1982), 33.

3. Quoted in ibid., 38. See also Francis Jennings, *Empire of Fortune: Crowns, Colonies, and Tribes in the Seven Years' War in America* (New York, 1988), 172.

4. "Unlike English, Irish, and Scots, the Americans were armed and were more or less trained for war," writes John Shy in his history of the British military in North America. "Perhaps these militiamen were not very impressive when enlisted or drafted to fight the French or Indians, but they were at their best when fending off what they took to be an immediate threat to their liberty or property." *Toward Lexington: The Role of the British Army in the Coming of the American Revolution* (Princeton, N.J., 1965), 43; see also 18–21.

5. Jack Sosin, *Whitehall and the Wilderness: The Middle West in British Colonial Policy, 1760–1775* (Lincoln, Neb., 1961). For the transformation in Indian-white relations in one colony, see the engaging multidimensional study of Tom Hatley, *The Dividing Paths: Cherokees and South Carolinians Through the Era of Revolution* (New York, 1993).

6. Stephen Saunders Webb, *The Governors-General: The English Army and the Definition of Empire, 1569–1681* (Williamsburg, Va., 1979), 465. "At the time," writes Shy of the political debate going on within England about the empire, "many Americans and some Englishmen [were] deceived . . . into thinking that a liberal colonial policy was a political possibility. But actually issues, including American issues, were seldom more than the excuse for previously determined factional divisions." *Toward Lexington,* 50–51.

7. For an analysis of the efficient working of the British Empire and, especially, the role of colonial interest groups, see Alison Gilbert Olson, *Making the Empire Work: London and American Interest Groups* (Cambridge, Mass., 1992).

8. T. H. Breen, "An Empire of Goods: The Anglicization of Colonial America, 1690–1776," *Journal of British Studies* 25 (Oct. 1986): 474. See also John J. McCusker and Russell R. Menard, *The Economy of British America, 1607–1789* (Chapel Hill, N.C., 1985); Bernard Bailyn and Philip Morgan, eds., *Strangers Within the Realm: Cultural Margins of the First British Empire* (Chapel Hill, N.C., 1991); James F. Shepherd and Gary Walton, "Trade, Distribution, and Economic Growth in Colonial America," *Journal of Economic History* 32 (1972): 128–45.

9. Joyce Appleby, "The Social Origins of American Revolutionary Ideology," *Journal of American History* 64 (Mar. 1978): 950. See also Breen, "Empire of Goods," 486–89. The "subversive implications" of the consumer revolution were not immediately apparent. "To the time of the Revolution," Michael Zuckerman writes, "Americans who thought explicitly about such matters were unable to envision an alternative to the imperatives of restraint and regulation because they could not see how the release of the individual from deference to the demands and expectations of his neighbors could result in anything but chaos" James A. Henretta, Michael Kammen, and Stanley Katz, eds., *The Transformation of Early American History, Society, Authority, and Ideology* (New York, 1991), 178.

10. "Two abstractions—nature and freedom—formed the basis of the Americans' conception of government," argues Joyce Appleby, "and both of them owed their eighteenth-century reworking to social changes wrought by the market." *Liberalism and Republicanism in the Historical Imagination* (Cambridge, Mass., 1992), 120–21.
   The dispute over the social legacy of the market economy and the consumer revolution in the countryside is explored in Breen, "Empire of Goods," 467–99; James Henretta, "Wealth and Social Structure," in Jack P. Greene and J. R. Pole, eds., *Colonial British America: Essays in the New History of the Early Modern Era* (Baltimore, 1989), 266–71; Henretta, "The Transition to Capitalism in Early America," in Henretta, *Transformation of Early American History*, 220–27; and Allan Kulikoff, *Tobacco and Slaves: The Development of Southern Cultures in the Chesapeake* (Chapel Hill, N.C., 1986), 10–13, 76–77, 202–3, 388–89. See also the cautionary note in Thomas Bender, *Community and Social Change in America* (Baltimore, 1982; orig. pub., 1978), 66–67.

11. Abbot Emerson Smith, *Colonists in Bondage: White Servitude and Convict Labor in America, 1607–1776* (Gloucester, Mass., 1965; orig. pub., 1947), 3–7; James Schouler, *Americans of 1776: Daily Lives in Revolutionary America* (Bowie, Md., 1990; orig. pub., 1906), 16–19. For an estimate of the numbers of servants, convicts, political prisoners, and vagabonds imported into British America from 1580 until 1775 see Richard S. Dunn, "The Recruitment and Employment of Labor," in Greene and Pole, eds., *Colonial British America*, 159. The most persuasive statements of an older, now somewhat discredited thesis about slave labor may be found in Evsey D. Domar, "The Causes of Slavery or Serfdom: A Hypothesis," *Journal of Economic History* 30 (1970): 18–32; and H. J. Nieboer, *Slavery as an Industrial System: Ethnological Researches*, 2nd ed., rev. (New York, 1971; orig. pub., 1910). Both of these authors argued that "open resources" made involuntary labor necessary because the relative inexpensiveness of land reduced the supply of freeworkers and made the use of bound workers more attractive. In the past generation, however, this view has come under sharp attack, principally because it fails to explain why slavery prevailed in some areas (for example, plantation agriculture) but not in others. See Stanley Engerman, "Some Considerations in Relation to Property Rights in Man," *Journal of Economic History* 33 (1973): 56–59; and Orlando Patterson, "The Structural Origins of Slavery: A Critique of the Niebohr-Domar Hypothesis from a Comparative Perspective," in Vera Rubin and Arthur Tuden, eds., *Comparative Perspectives on*

Slavery in New World Plantation Societies (New York, 1977), 12–34. On the mulatto population see Joel Williamson, *New People: Miscegenation and Mulattoes in the United States* (New York, 1980). For the controversial argument that white freedom depended on black slavery, see Edmund S. Morgan, *American Slavery, American Freedom* (New York, 1975); see also Morgan, "The World They Made Together: Black and White Values in Eighteenth-Century Virginia," *New York Review of Books* (June 16, 1988): 27–29.

12. David Hackett Fischer, *Albion's Seed: Four British Folkways in America* (New York, 1989), 785–816.

13. Both quotations are in Shy, *Toward Lexington*, 60. On the Cherokee War in South Carolina see Hatley, *Dividing Paths,* 119–40, who characterizes this conflict as "a game—a man's game for the most part—where political stakes on both sides hinged on remembered notions of prestige and place and destiny. The consequences of the persistent warfare and confrontation pulled in everyone—women and children, hostages and slaves, warriors and soldiers" (ibid., 119).

A small number argued for miscegenation, which was, according to D. W. Meinig, "inevitably widespread . . ., as an obvious means of ameliorating the collision of cultures." Meinig, *The Shaping of America: A Geographical Perspective on 500 Years of History,* vol. 1: *Atlantic America, 1492–1800* (New Haven, 1986), 210. On "Indianized" colonists see James Axtell, *The European and the Indian: Essays in the Ethnohistory of Colonial North America* (New York, 1981), 276–29, 306–12; and the comment by Annette Kolodny, "Among the Indians: The Uses of Captivity," in *New York Times Book Review* (Jan. 31, 1993): 1, 26–29.

Gregory Nobles summarizes the dilemmas of metropolitan officials striving to control the environment, Indians, and especially the white settlers on the frontier in "Straight Lines and Stability: Mapping the Political Order of the Republic," *Journal of American History* 80 (June 1993): 28.

14. Meinig, *Atlantic America*, 285–87; Francis Jennings, "The Indian Revolution," in Alfred Young, ed., *The American Revolution: Explorations in the History of American Radicalism* (Dekalb, Ill., 1976), 322–23, 333–37; J. Leitch Wright, Jr., *Anglo-Spanish Rivalry in North America* (Athens, Ga., 1971), 116–17.

15. "Hints respecting the Settlement of our American Provinces," quoted in Shy, *Toward Lexington*, 65.

16. Richard A. White, *The Middle Ground: Indians, Empires and Republics in the Great Lakes Region, 1650–1815* (New York, 1991), 227.

17. Meinig, *Atlantic America*, 206.

18. Quoted in White, *The Middle Ground*, 340. In the aftermath of Pontiac's uprising, writes White, backcountry whites sought revenge for Indian killings. "They murdered Indians in such large numbers that [a British official] warned it was not safe for any Indian to come near the Pennsylvania frontier" (ibid., 345).

19. Bernard Bailyn, *Voyagers to the West: A Passage in the Peopling of America on the Eve of the Revolution* (New York, 1986), 3–57; Bailyn, *Faces of Revolution: Perspectives and Themes in the Struggle for American Independence* (New York, 1990), 166–67.

20. Rhys Isaac, "Evangelical Revolt: The Nature of the Baptists' Challenge to the Traditional Order in Virginia, 1765–1775," *William and Mary Quarterly,* 3rd Ser., 31 (1974): 363; Kulikoff, *Tobacco and Slaves,* 348–49; Sylvia Frey, *Water from the Rock: Black Resistance in a Revolutionary Age* (Princeton, 1991), 14–17, 26–29.

21. Richard Hofstadter, *America at 1750: A Social Portrait* (New York, 1971), 271–72. See also Patricia Bonomi, *Under the Cope of Heaven: Religion, Society, and Politics in Colonial America* (New York, 1986); and David S. Lovejoy, *Religious Enthusiasm in the New World: Heresy to Revolution* (Cambridge, Mass., 1985).

22. Bernard Bailyn, *The Origins of American Politics* (New York, 1970), 40–41, 56–57. In formulating this view, Bailyn drew heavily on Caroline Robbins, *The Eighteenth-Century Commonwealthman* (Cambridge, Mass., 1959). See also Anthony Pagden, *Lords of All the World: Ideologies of Empire in Spain, Britain, and France* (New Haven, 1995), 84–85, 160–61.

23. "In fact," writes John Shy, "the North American army was not originally established either to defend colonial society or to control it. In time, to be sure, it was called on to do both" (Shy, *Toward Lexington*, 83; see also 66–69, 78–79).

24. Quoted in Edward Countryman, *The American Revolution* (New York, 1985), 78. See also Pauline Maier, "Popular Uprisings and Civil Authority in Eighteenth-Century America," *William and Mary Quarterly* 27 (Jan. 1970): 6–9, 20–21; Gary Nash, "The Transformation of Urban Politics, 1700–1765," *Journal of American History* 60 (1973): 620–21; and Paul Gilje, *The Road to Mobocracy: Popular Disorder in New York City, 1763–1834* (Chapel Hill, N.C., 1987), 5–7, 24–25.

25. A Philadelphian described their despair: "One half of the world are ignorant how the other half lives; . . . while the slightest inconveniences of the great are magnified into calamaties, while tragedy mouths out their sufferings in all the strains of eloquence, the miseries of the poor are disregarded. . . ." Quoted in Joseph Ernst, "'Ideology' and an Economic Interpretation of the Constitution," in Young, ed., *The American Revolution* 181. See also the essay by Gary Nash in ibid., 30–31; and Gordon Wood, *The Radicalism of the American Revolution* (New York, 1992), 244–45.

26. "By any reckoning of average," write Oscar and Lilian Handlin, "they should all have perished, or they should have fled the cities, or they should have risen in desperate rebellion." *A Restless People: Americans in Rebellion, 1770–1787* (Garden City, N.Y., 1982), 42. On the diminished size of agricultural holdings, see James T. Lemon, *The Best Poor Man's Country: A Geographical Study of Early Southeastern Pennsylvania* (Baltimore, 1972), 87–94; and Kenneth Lockridge, "Land, Population and the Evolution of New England Society, 1630–1790," *Past and Present* (April 1968): 62–80.

27. Maldwyn Jones, "The Scotch-Irish in British America," in Bernard Bailyn and Philip Morgan, eds., *Strangers Within the Realm: Cultural Margins of the First British Empire* (Chapel Hill, N.C., 1991), 296–99. By the mid-eighteenth century, the once-popular notion of transforming Indians into "civilized" Europeans had diminished, as had perceptions of the Indian as a "noble savage." On the eve of the American Revolution, Anglo-Americans no longer believed the Indian worthy of incorporation into white society. See Axtell, *The European and the Indian*, 266–67; and Alden T. Vaughn, "From White Man to Redskin: Changing Anglo-American Perceptions of the American Indian," *American Historical Review* 87 (Oct. 1982): 917–53.

28. Richard M. Brown, *The South Carolina Regulators* (Cambridge, Mass., 1963), 140–42; Marvin L. Michael Kay, in Young, ed., *American Revolution*, 73–75.

29. "Woven into Otis's offensive," writes Gary Nash, "was the theme of resentment against wealth, narrowly concentrated political power, and arbitrary political actions which affected Boston's ordinary people" (Nash, in Young, ed., *American Revolution*, 23; see also Nash, "Transformation of Urban Politics," 612–13; and Maier, "Popular Uprisings," 28–29.

30. Quoted in Walter Cosner, Jr., et al., *Resistance, Politics, and the American Struggle for Independence, 1765–1775* (Boulder, Colo., 1986), v. When Samuel Chase of Maryland attacked the Stamp Act, his detractors denounced him as a "foul mouthed and inflaming Son of Discord and faction—a common disturber of the public tranquility." In his reply, Chase denounced them as "despicable pimps and tools of power, emerged from obscurity and basking in proprietary sunshine." Broadside, *To the Publick* (Annapolis, 16 July 1776), quoted in Merrill Jensen, *The American Revolution Within America* (New York, 1974), 18.

31. "The decision to use the taxes to pay for British regulars in America and to make governors and judges independent of the colonial legislatures realized all the old fears," Richard Bushman notes. "The horror of a rapacious band of alien officials ravaging the province, the danger foreseen for seventy-five years, seemed about to be enacted." Bushman, *King and People in Provincial Massachusetts* (Chapel Hill, N.C., 1985), 177.

32. Peter Shaw, *American Patriots and the Rituals of Revolution* (Cambridge, Mass., 1981), 228–29, carefully distinguishes between "ritualized and merely collective action." The former was less destructive; crowds were more restrained. Spontaneous outbursts usually brought about much more damage, but as an explanatory factor in the making of revolution, ritual crowd violence, subject to social controls, was much more influential.

33. For a discussion of the hardships imposed by the Navigation Acts on British America see Immanuel Wallerstein, *The Modern World System III: The Second Era of Great Expansion of the Capitalist World Economy, 1730–1840s* (San Diego, 1989), 196–99.

34. The rich in New England and the middle colonies, wrote David Ramsay in his postrevolutionary history, took little part in the patriot cause, "but the reverse took place in the southern extreme of the confederacy. There were in no part of America, more determined whigs, than the opulent slaveholders." Quoted in Russell R. Menard, "South Carolina Lowcountry," in Ronald Hoffman, et al., eds., *The Economy of Early America: The Revolutionary Period, 1763–1790* (Charlottesville, Va., 1988), 274. See also Marc Egnal and Joseph Ernst, "An Economic Interpretation of the American Revolution," *William and Mary Quarterly,* 3rd Ser., 29 (Jan. 1972): 22–28; and Albert H. Tillson, Jr., *Gentry and Commonfolk: Political Culture on a Virginia Frontier, 1740–1789* (Lexington, Ky., 1993).

35. Egnal and Ernst, "Economic Interpretation of the American Revolution," 28–32.

36. Quoted in Gary Nash, *The Urban Crucible: Social Change, Political Consciousness, and the Origin of the American Revolution* (Cambridge, Mass., 1979), 199. See also Gilje, *Road to Mobocracy,* 50–53. Gage's moderation in the Stamp Act crisis may have been the result of his having inadequate forces to contain the disorder. "During these Commotions in North-America," he reported in early 1766, "I have never been more at a Loss how to Act, to perform the Duty which I owe to my King and Country, and at the same Time prevent any Cause of Clamor against Military Power and Influence" (quoted in Shy, *Toward Lexington,* 215).

37. Bailyn, *Origins of American Politics,* 66–67, 80–81, 86–87, 96–99, 104–5; on the fragility of the colonial aristocracy in the prerevolutionary decade, see Wood, *Radicalism of the American Revolution,* 120–22, 160–61, 170–71. Though the colonial councils were composed of prominent people, their utility to governors varied greatly because they could not be readily transformed into subservient bodies. The dynamics of British North American political culture did not permit it. See Jackson Turner Main, *The Upper House in Revolutionary America, 1763–1788* (Madison, Wis., 1967), 94.

38. George Rudé, *The Crowd in History, 1730–1840*, rev. ed. (London, 1981), 54–57.

39. Quoted in Robert R. Palmer, *The Age of the Democratic Revolution* (2 vols., Princeton, 1959, 1964), 1:172. For a suggestive comparison of mobs in England and British America, see Gordon S. Wood, "A Note on Mobs in the American Revolution," *William and Mary Quarterly* 23 (Oct. 1966): 635–42.

40. As Sir Lewis Namier pointed out, "In 1760 Great Britain had not yet reached a stage at which it would have been possible to remodel the Empire as a federation of self-governing States under a Crown detached from the actual government of any of its component parts." *England in the Age of the American Revolution*, 2nd ed. (New York, 1961), as quoted in Robert W. Tucker and David Hendrickson, *The Fall of the First British Empire* (Baltimore, 1982), 406–7. See also John Phillip Reid, *Constitutional History of the American Revolution: The Authority to Legislate* (Madison, Wis., 1991).

41. Bailyn, *Origins of American Politics*, 153.

42. Charles A. Beard and Mary R. Beard, *The Rise of American Civilization* (New York, 1934), 219–20. Burke spoke to the volatile issue of taxation and its importance: "Leave America to tax herself," he warned, "but if, intemperately, unwisely, fatally, you sophisticate and poison the very source of government by urging subtle deductions and consequences odious to those you govern . . ., you will teach them to call that sovereignty itself into question." The inevitable outcome of such measures was rebellion: "If that sovereignty and their freedom cannot be reconciled, which will they take? They will cast your sovereignty in your face. Nobody will be argued into slavery." Quoted in Paul Rahe, *Republics Ancient and Modern: Classical Republicanism and the American Revolution* (Chapel Hill, N.C., 1992), 555.

43. Quoted in Beard and Beard, *Rise of American Civilization*, 221; see also Shy, *Toward Lexington*, 318–19.

44. Quoted in Tucker and Hendrickson, *Fall of the First British Empire*, 284–85.

45. Quoted in ibid., 293. When Gage informed his superiors that the pacification of New England would require twenty thousand men, they responded by recommending that he build a loyal corps from the "friends of government in New England." Quoted in David Hackett Fischer, *Paul Revere's Ride* (New York, 1994), 76.

46. Hutchinson to Hillsborough, March 12, 1770, in K. G. Davies, ed., *Documents of the American Revolution, 1770–1783* (Shannon, Ireland, 1972), 2:59–60. Preservation of the social order could hardly be assured, Bailyn writes, "where authority was questioned before it was obeyed, where social differences were considered to be incidental rather than essential to community order, and where superiority . . . was scattered broadly throughout the populace" (Bailyn, *Origins of American Politics*, 319). A student of Massachusetts revolutionary crowds notes that their "social composition . . . changed according to the nature of the action." Dirk Hoerder, *Crowd Action in Revolutionary Massachusetts, 1765–1780* (New York, 1977), 374.

47. Merrill Jensen, ed., *Tracts of the American Revolution, 1773–1776* (Indianapolis, 1967), 273.

48. Quoted in Jensen, *American Revolution Within America*, 40–41. A British traveler in the colonies wrote later that he was continually "harassed and persecuted beyond measure, by the demagogues of this revolutionary faction." Few in the British ruling classes, he wrote, had any notion of the "illiberality of conduct of the Americans, and the barbarous treatment practiced by them upon those unhappy persons who have had the misfortune of falling into their hands." John Ferdinand Dalziel Smyth, *A Tour in the United States of America* . . . (2 vols., New York, 1968; Orig. pub., 1784), 2:188–89.

49. Richard D. Brown, *Revolutionary Politics in Massachusetts: The Boston Committee of Correspondence and the Towns, 1772–1774* (Cambridge, Mass., 1970), 244–47; Robert Gross, *The Minutemen and Their World* (New York, 1976), 50–51.

50. Quoted in Maier, *From Resistance to Revolution*, 273.

51. Quoted in ibid., 274.

52. Quoted in Mary Beth Norton, "The Impact of the American Revolution," in Norton, *Major Problems in American Women's History* (Lexington, Mass., 1989), 102.

53. Quoted in John C. Miller, *Origins of the American Revolution* (Boston, 1943), 401.

54. Wood, "A Note on Mobs," 639.
    This "absence of resistance" was indeed significant, but explaining it is another matter. In a persuasive work on the workings of the British empire, Jack Greene assumes that the use of force by imperial authority to assure compliance with policy "would have constituted an admission of the absence or breakdown of authority" and, further, a denial that "local sanction from the peripheries was essential to endow any position of the center with constitutional authority." Greene, *Peripheries and Center: Constitutional Development in the Extended Politics of the British Empire and the United States, 1607–1788* (Athens, Ga., 1986), xi; see also 40–41, 50–52, 74–76.

55. Shy, *Toward Lexington*, 372–74, 396–97, 420–21, 423–24.

2 A People at War

1. Quoted in Michael Zuckerman, *Peaceable Kingdoms: Massachusetts Towns in the Eighteenth Century* (New York, 1970), 249.

2. The Adams quotations are from Henry Steele Commager and Richard Morris, eds., *The Spirit of 'Seventy-Six: The Story of the American Revolution as Told by Participants* (New York, 1975), 76; and David Hackett Fischer, *Paul Revere's Ride* (New York, 1994), 279. For a chronology of the American war of independence, see John Ellis, *Armies in Revolution* (London, 1973), 42–45.

3. Quoted in John C. Miller, *Origins of the American Revolution* (Boston, 1943), 419. On the *rage militaire*, see Charles Royster, *A Revolutionary People at War: The Continental Army and American Character, 1775–1783* (Chapel Hill, N.C., 1979), 25–53.

4. Quoted in Gordon Wood, *The Creation of the American Republic, 1776–1787* (Williamsburg, Va., 1969), 75. See also Forrest McDonald, *E Pluribus Unum: The Formation of the American Republic, 1776–1790* (Boston, 1965), 108–9; Emory G. Evans, "Planter Indebtedness and the Coming of the Revolution in Virginia," *William and Mary Quarterly*, 3rd Ser. 19 (1962): 511–33.

5. Quoted in Miller, *Origins of the American Revolution*, 459.

6. Quoted in Royster, *Revolutionary People at War*, 24. See also John R. Galvin, *The Minute Men—The First Fight: Myths and Realities of the American Revolution*, 2nd ed., rev. (Washington, 1989, orig. pub., 1967), 39.

7. Quoted in H. L. Keenleyside, *Canada and the United States* (New York, 1929), 28; see also Philip Lawson, *The Imperial Challenge: Quebec and Britain in the Age of the American Revolution* (Buffalo, 1989); Reginald Stuart, *United States Expansionism and British North America, 1775–1871* (Chapel Hill, N.C., 1988), 11–13; and Hilda Neatby, *Quebec, the Revolutionary Age, 1760–1791* (Toronto, 1966).

8. William John Eccles, *France in America* (New York, 1972), 237–38; see also 224–35; Donald W. Meinig, *The Shaping of America: A Geographical Perspective on 500 Years*

of History, vol. 1, *Atlantic America, 1492–1800* (New Haven, 1986), 278–79; Immanuel Wallerstein, *The Modern World System*, vol. 3, *The Second Era of Great Expansion of the Capitalist World-Economy* (San Diego, 1989), 208–9; H. Blair Neatby, "Canadianism—A Symposium," Canadian Historical Association, *Report* (1965), 74; and Gustave Lanctot, *Le Canada et la Révolution americaine* (Montreal, 1965).

9. Quoted in Pauline Maier, *From Resistance to Revolution: Colonial Radicals and the Development of American Opposition to Britain, 1765–1776* (New York, 1972), 257.

10. A. W. Peach, ed., *Selections from the Works of Thomas Paine* (New York, 1928), 23, as quoted in Miller, *Origins of the American Revolution*, 467. Theretofore, David Wooten observes, "republicanism" had been an opprobrious term, but "overnight, Paine revolutionized the political vocabulary of America, and made 'republican' a term of approval." Wooten, "Introduction: The Republican Tradition from Commonwealth to Common Sense," in Wooten, ed., *Republicanism, Liberty, and Commercial Society, 1649–1776* (Stanford, 1994), 18.

11. Quoted in Miller, *Origins of the American Revolution*, 485.

12. Edward Countryman, commenting on their role, observes that their participation in the revolution concerned urban radicals, "but by then the Revolution was no longer their exclusive property, if ever it had been. And because it was not, it was all the more a revolution." Countryman, "'Out of the Bonds of Law': Northern Land Rioters in the Eighteenth Century," in Alfred Young, ed., *The American Revolution: Explorations in the History of American Radicalism* (De Kalb, Ill., 1976), 61.
    For this account of the social turmoil in 1775–1776, I have relied on Rhys Isaac, *The Transformation of Virginia, 1740–1780* (Williamsburg, Va., 1982), 256–59; Edward Countryman, *American Revolution*, 114–22; Allan Kulikoff, *Tobacco and Slaves: The Development of Southern Cultures in the Chesapeake, 1680–1800* (Chapel Hill, N.C., 1986), 300–3; Richard Bushman, "Massachusetts," in Richard Jellison, ed., *Society, Freedom, and Conscience: The American Revolution in Virginia, Massachusetts, and New York* (New York, 1976), 121–24; Leopold Launitz-Schurer, Jr., *Loyal Whigs and Revolutionaries: The Making of the Revolution in New York* (New York, 1980), 188–89; and John S. Pancake, *This Destructive War: The British Campaign in the Carolinas* (Tuscaloosa, Ala., 1985), 78–79.
    Eight states provided for blacklisting and banishing loyalists, who incurred the death penalty if they returned; and every state allowed confiscation of property. The estimated number of loyalists is 20 percent (500,000 out of a population of 2.5 million), but they were probably as many as one-third of those active in revolutionary-era politics. For a representative personal account of their activities, see Catherine S. Crary, ed., *The Price of Loyalty: Tory Writings from the Revolutionary Era* (New York, 1973); and William H. Nelson, *The American Tory* (Boston, 1961).

13. Alfred F. Young, *The Democratic Republicans of New York: The Origins, 1763–1797* (Chapel Hill, N.C., 1967), 12–13. For a psychological measure of determining loyalist and patriot choices, see N. E. H. Hull, Peter C. Hoffer, and Steven L. Allen, "Choosing Sides: A Quantitative Study of the Personality Determinants of Loyalist and Revolutionary Political Affiliation in New York," *Journal of American History* 65 (Sept. 1978): 344–66.

14. Quoted in Paul A. Gilje, *The Road to Mobocracy: Popular Disorder in New York City, 1763–1834* (Chapel Hill, N.C., 1987), 67.
    Revolutionary pamphleteers circulated their incendiary tracts among men, but with the onset of economic boycotts, women became more involved in the anti-British campaign. "The emergencies of the war," writes Linda Kerber, "pulled women into

political relationships and forced them to make political choices." Kerber, "The Limits of Politicization: American Women and the American Revolution," in Jarezlaw Pelenski, ed., *The American and European Revolutions, 1776–1848: Sociopolitical and Ideological Aspects* (Iowa City, 1980), 57. See also Kerber, *Women of the Republic: Intellect and Ideology in Revolutionary America* (Williamsburg, Va., 1980), esp. 26–31, 48–50, 54–57, 86–87, 282–85.

15. Quoted in Steven Rosswurm, *Arms, Country, and Class: The Philadelphia Militia and "Lower Sort" During the American Revolution, 1775–1783* (New Brunswick, N.J., 1987), 84. See also R. A. Ryerson, "Political Mobilization and the American Revolution: The Resistance Movement in Philadelphia, 1765 to 1776," *William and Mary Quarterly,* 3rd Ser., 31 (Oct. 1974): 565–88.

16. Quoted in Sylvia Frey, *Water from the Rock: Black Resistance in a Revolutionary Age* (Princeton, N.J., 1991), 55. The proposal ultimately failed to get a majority vote, but Dunmore's decision horrified the slaveholding Virginians and provided the radicals with the opportunity of declaring themselves as the preservers of the white race. See the essay by Rhys Isaac in Young, ed., *American Revolution,* esp. 150–53.

17. Quoted in Rachel N. Klein, *Unification of a Slave State: The Rise of the Planter Class in the South Carolina Backcountry, 1760–1808* (Williamsburg, Va., 1990), 78–79.

18. Quoted in ibid., 82. See also David Ammerman, *In the Common Cause: American Response to the Coercive Acts of 1774* (Charlottesville, Va., 1974).

19. Peter Charles Hoffer, *Law and People in Colonial America* (Baltimore, 1992), 122.

20. Quoted in Merrill Jensen, *The American Revolution Within America* (New York, 1974), 104. On the socially beneficial legacy of republicanism, see Gordon Wood, *The Creation of the American Republic, 1776–1787* (Williamsburg, Va., 1969), 112–15. Sung Bok Kim, "The Limits of Politicization in the American Revolution: The Experience of Westchester County, New York," *Journal of American History* 80 (Dec. 1993): 868–89, suggests that the protracted fighting in Westchester County actually depoliticized people who otherwise might have chosen the patriot cause.

21. John Ellis, *Armies in Revolution* (London, 1973), 3.

22. Quoted in John Shy, *A People Numerous and Armed: Reflections on the Military Struggle for American Independence* (Ann Arbor, Mich., 1990), 205. See also ibid., 8–13, 200–1, 206–7; and Don Higgenbotham, *War and Society in Revolutionary America: The Wider Dimensions of Conflict* (Columbia, S.C., 1988), 164–69.

23. Quoted in Richard Morris, *The American Revolution Reconsidered* (Westport, Conn., 1967), 68.

24. John Shy, "American Society," in Don Higgenbotham, ed., *Reconsiderations on the Revolutionary War: Selected Essays* (Westport, Conn., 1978), 80–81.

25. American Commissioners for Indian Affairs to the Delawares, the Senecas, the Munsees, and the Mingos, Pittsburgh, 1776; James Hall, *Sketches of History, Life, and Manners in the West.* Both quotations are taken from Richard White, *The Middle Ground: Indians, Empires, and Republics in the Great Lakes, 1650–1815* (New York, 1991), 366; see also 367–68.

26. Bernard Sheehan, "Ignoble Savagism and the American Revolution," in Larry Gerlach, James Dolph, and Michael Nicholls, eds., *Legacies of the American Revolution* (Provo, Utah, 1978), 152. For the legacy of beliefs in "ignoble savagism" and what it justified among those spreading "civilization," see Sheehan, *Seeds of*

Extinction: Jeffersonian Philanthropy and the American Indian (Chapel Hill, N.C., 1973); Richard Slotkin, *Regeneration Through Violence: The Mythology of the American Frontier, 1660–1860* (Middletown, Conn., 1973); and Michael P. Rogin, *Fathers and Children: Andrew Jackson and the Subjugation of the American Indian* (New York, 1975). See also Jack M. Sosin, "The Use of Indians in the American Revolution: A Reassessment of Responsibility," *Canadian Historical Review* 46 (1965): 101–2; Don Higgenbotham, *The War of American Independence: Military Attitudes, Policies, and Practices, 1763–1789* (New York, 1971), 320–21; and Gregory Dowd, *A Spirited Resistance: The North American Indian Struggle for Unity, 1745–1815* (Baltimore, 1992), 60.

27. Both quotations are from White, *The Middle Ground*, 368 and 369, respectively. For the Indian experience in the American Revolution, see Colin Calloway, *The American Revolution in Indian Country: Crisis and Diversity in Native American Communities* (New York, 1995), esp. 1–2, 6–7, 26–31, 42–43, 46, 55.

28. Dowd, *A Spirited Resistance*, xv, xviii–xix, 49, 58–59; Francis Jennings, "The Indian Revolution," in Young, ed., *The American Revolution*, 341; Calloway, *American Revolution in Indian Country*, 292–95.

29. Quoted in Col. R. Ernest Dupuy and Col. Trevor N. Dupuy, *An Outline History of the American Revolution* (New York, 1975), 52.

30. Quoted in James K. Martin and Mark Lender, *A Respectable Army: The Military Origins of the Republic, 1763–1789* (Arlington Heights, Ill., 1982), 45. See also Richard Kohn, "The Social History of the American Soldier: A Review and Prospectus for Research," *American Historical Review* 86 (1981): 553–67.

In his two-volume 1793 *History of the American Revolution* (reprinted, New York, 1968), David Ramsay described militia soldiers as men who "soon wearied of military life . . . ; to exercise discipline over freemen, accustomed to act only from the impulse of their own minds, required not only a knowledge of human nature, but an accommodating spirit, and a degree of patience which is rarely found among officers of regular armies." Quoted in Martin and Lender, *A Respectable Army*, 71–72. Washington doubtless would have agreed. The war at hand, he believed, could not be won by relying on such men; *his* military experience taught differently. Soldiers were driven by fear of officers and loyalty to comrades, not by abstractions they could not comprehend or patriotism they could not articulate.

31. Charles Royster, *A Revolutionary People at War: The Continental Army and the American Character, 1775–1783* (Chapel Hill, N.C., 1980), 62–63.

32. John Ellis, *Armies in Revolution* (London, 1973), 48–49.

33. Benjamin Quarles, *The Negro in the American Revolution* (Chapel Hill, N.C., 1961), vii. See also Willie Lee Rose, "Impact of the American Revolution on the Black Population," in Gerlach, ed., *Legacies of the American Revolution*, 186–87, 190–93; and Jeffrey Crow, "Slave Rebelliousness and Social Conflict in North Carolina, 1775–1802," *William and Mary Quarterly* 37 (Jan. 1980), 80–102.

34. Quoted in Bernard Bailyn, *The Ideological Origins of the American Revolution* (Cambridge, Mass., 1967), 236. See also J. Franklin Jameson, *The American Revolution Considered as a Social Movement* (Princeton, 1967; orig. pub., 1926), 22–23; and Gordon Wood, *The Radicalism of the American Revolution* (New York, 1992), 54.

35. Quoted in Frey, *Water from the Rock*, 78.

36. Quoted in Winthrop Jordan, *White over Black* (Chapel Hill, N.C., 1968), 303. See also Quarles, *The Negro in the American Revolution*, viii, 196–200.

37. Quoted in Allan Bowman, *The Morale of the American Revolutionary Army* (Washington, D.C., 1943), 14. See also James Kirby Martin, "A 'Most Undisciplined, Profligate Crew': Protest and Defiance in the Continental Ranks, 1776–1783," in Ronald Hoffman and Peter Albert, eds., *Arms and Independence: The Military Character of the American Revolution* (Charlottesville, Va., 1984), esp. 122–25.

38. Quoted in John S. Pancake, *This Destructive War: The British Campaign in the Carolinas* (Tuscaloosa, Ala., 1985), 48. See also James K. Martin and Mark Lender, *A Respectable Army: The Military Origins of the Republic, 1763–1789* (Arlington Heights, Ill., 1982), 76–77, 94–95; and Peter Charles Hoffer, *Revolution and Regeneration: Life Cycle and the Historical Vision of the Generation of 1776* (Athens, Ga., 1983).

   Walter Millis (in *Arms and Men*, a 1956 publication) wrote of the growing separation of soldier and citizen in the makeup of the British army, where recruiters took the "sweepings of jails, ginmills, and poorhouses, oafs from the farm . . . , [and] adventurers and unfortunates" (quoted in Martin, *A Respectable Army*, 13). But Sylvia Frey characterizes the majority as tradesmen and wage earners displaced by industrial change and in search of rations for themselves and their families. See "The Common British Soldier in the Late Eighteenth Century: A Profile," *Societas: A Review of Social History* 5 (1975): 126–27.

39. Royster, *A Revolutionary People at War*, 92, 104–5.

40. Frey, *Water from the Rock*, 106–7, 168–71.

41. Both quotations are in Royster, *A Revolutionary People at War*, 278, 280. Royster makes an important point concerning the revolutionaries' distinction between the apathetic and the neutrals: "The Americans most often mistaken for neutrals were probably revolutionaries who wanted the fruits of independence without the violence of war. . . . The danger that alarmed revolutionaries was not large numbers of indifferent Americans but Americans moved by the desire for gain without risk in a war whose outcome had long seemed certain. The prospect of losing the war because too few people wanted independence worried the revolutionaries far less than the prospect of harboring among the victors those who had awaited victory in order to exploit it." Ibid., 281.

42. Ibid., 116–19.

43. Quoted in Wayne Bodle, "This Tory Labyrinth," in Michael Zuckerman, ed., *Friends and Neighbors: Group Life in America's First Plural Society* (Philadelphia, 1982), 242.

44. Quoted in Ellis, *Armies in Revolution*, 53.

45. Quoted in Martin, *A Respectable Army*, 127.

46. Dupuy and Dupuy, *An Outline History of the American Revolution*, 118–19; Royster, *A Revolutionary People at War*, 186–89.

47. Quoted in Richard Kohn, "American Generals," in Higgenbotham, ed., *Reconsiderations on the Revolutionary War*, 120.

48. Quoted in ibid., 121–22; see also Martin, *A Respectable Army*, 186–93.

49. E. Wayne Carp, "The Problem of National Defense in the Early American Republic," in Jack P. Greene, ed., *The American Revolution: Its Character and Limits* (New York, 1987), 26–29.

50. Merrill Jensen, "A Democratic Movement," in Jack P. Greene, ed., *The Ambiguity of the American Revolution* (New York, 1968), 124–25.

51. Both quotations are from Wood, *Creation of the American Republic,* 67, 124.

52. Quoted in Jack C. Greene, *Peripheries and Center: Constitutional Development in the Extended Politics of the British Empire and the United States, 1607–1788* (Athens, Ga., 1986), 154–55.

53. Quoted in Jack N. Rakove, *The Beginnings of National Politics: An Interpretative History of the Continental Congress* (Baltimore, 1982), 121. For a thorough assessment of the revolutionary state experience and reform in internal taxation, see Roger H. Brown, *Redeeming the Republic: Federalists, Taxation, and the Origins of the Constitution* (Baltimore, 1993).

54. Wood, *Creation of the American Republic,* 359.

55. Rakove, *The Beginnings of National Politics,* 212–15. On public finance, see E. James Ferguson, *The Power of the Purse: A History of American Public Finance, 1776–1790* (Chapel Hill, N.C., 1961).

56. Quoted in Wood, *Creation of the American Republic,* 476, 477. See also Wood, "A Pluralistic Conception," in Greene, ed., *The Ambiguity of the American Revolution,* 174–79. For the politics of the era see E. P. Douglass, *Rebels and Democrats: The Struggle for Equal Political Rights and Majority Rule During the Revolution* (Chapel Hill, N.C., 1955); Merrill Jensen, *The Articles of Confederation* (Madison, Wis., 1959); and Jackson Turner Main, *Political Parties Before the Constitution* (New York, 1974).

57. Quoted in Martin, *A Respectable Army,* 196–97. Such statistics may explain why the seven-hundred-man First American Regiment, organized in 1784 to police the Northwest Territories, had a high proportion of recent immigrants—mostly Irish, Germans, and Britons. See William B. Skelton, "The Confederation's Regulars: A Social Profile of Enlisted Service in America's First Standing Army," *William and Mary Quarterly* 46 (1989): 774.

58. Edmund S. Morgan, *Inventing the People: The Rise of Popular Sovereignty in England and America* (New York, 1988), 300–303. See also Carp, "The Problem of National Defense in the Early American Republic," 30–33; and Russell Weigley, *Towards an American Army: Military Thought from Washington to Marshall* (New York, 1962), esp. ch. 1, "The Dual Military Legacy of the Revolution."

3 The Dilemmas of Victory

1. Russell Weigley, *Towards an American Army: Military Thought from Washington to Marshall* (New York, 1962), ch. 1; Marcus Cunliffe, *Soldiers and Civilians: The Martial Spirit in America, 1775–1865* (Boston, 1968), 47.

2. Quoted in Gordon Wood, *The Radicalism of the American Revolution* (New York, 1992), 177. For an assessment of the dilemmas of independence in one locale—Charles County, Maryland—see Jean B. Lee, *The Price of Nationhood: The American Revolution in Charles County* (New York, 1994).

3. Quoted in Linda Grant De Pauw, "Politicizing the Politically Inert," in William Fowler and Wallace Coyle, eds., *The American Revolution: Changing Perspectives* (Boston, 1979), 13. See also Adrian C. Levy, *The Revolutionary War in the Hackensack Valley: The Jersey Dutch and the Neutral Ground, 1775–1783* (New Brunswick, N.J., 1962), 306; and Owens Ireland, "The Ethnic-Religious Dimension of Pennsylvania Politics, 1778–1779," *William and Mary Quarterly* 30 (July 1973): 423–47.

4. Quoted in Pauline Maier, "The Charleston Mob and the Evolution of Popular Politics in South Carolina, 1765–1784," *Perspectives in American History* 4 (1970), 192. For further discussion of the settlement of the war in the South, see the essays in Ronald Hoffman, Thad Tate, and Peter Albert, eds., *An Uncivil War: The Southern Backcountry During the American Revolution* (Charlottesville, Va., 1985).

5. Rhys Isaac, *The Transformation of Virginia, 1740–1790* (Williamsburg, Va., 1982), 292–95, 310.

6. Quoted in Hannah Arendt, *On Revolution* (New York, 1963), 15. See also David Potter, *People of Plenty: Economic Abundance and the American Character* (Chicago, 1954), 94–95.

7. J. Franklin Jameson, *The American Revolution Considered as a Social Movement* (Princeton, N.J., 1967; orig. pub., 1926), 9.

8. Quoted in Lee Soltow, *Distribution of Wealth and Income in the United States in 1798* (Pittsburgh, 1990), 13–14. See also Frederick B. Tolles, "The American Revolution Considered as a Social Movement: A Reevaluation," *American Historical Review* 60 (Feb. 1954): 1–12.

9. Jackson Turner Main, *The Social Structure of Revolutionary America* (Princeton, 1965), 270–71; Walter T. K. Nugent, *Structures of American Social History* (Bloomington, Ind., 1981), 70.

10. Stuart Blumin, *The Emergence of the Middle Class: Social Experience in the American City, 1760–1900* (Cambridge, 1989), 64; Soltow, *Distribution of Wealth*, 240–41. Gordon Wood articulates a different view of the changing value of labor and, especially, notes the significance of the diminished estimation of leisure as a mark of the aristocratic class. See *Radicalism of the American Revolution*, 277.

11. Drew McCoy, as quoted in David Brion Davis, *Revolutions: Reflections on American Equality and Foreign Interventions* (Cambridge, Mass., 1990), 20. See also Nathan O. Hatch, *The Sacred Cause of Liberty: Republican Thought and the Millennium in Revolutionary New England* (New Haven, Conn., 1977); and John P. Reid, *The Concept of Liberty in the Age of the American Revolution* (Chicago, 1988).

12. Quoted in Michael Kammen, *Sovereignty and Liberty: Constitutional Discourse in American Culture* (Madison, Wis., 1988), 50.

13. Robert Wiebe, *The Opening of American Society: From the Adoption of the Constitution to the Eve of Disunion* (New York, 1984), 144; see also James Henretta, *The Evolution of American Society, 1700–1815: An Interdisciplinary Analysis* (Lexington, Mass., 1973), 168–69; and Chilton Williamson, *American Suffrage: From Property to Democracy, 1760–1860* (Princeton, 1960), 111–12.

14. Quoted in Richard Bushman, "'This New Man': Dependence and Independence," in Bushman, ed., *Uprooted Americans: Essays to Honor Oscar Handlin* (Boston, 1979), 91. See also Charles Sydnor, *American Revolutionaries in the Making* (New York, 1965; orig. pub., 1953), 110–11; Edmund Morgan, *Inventing the People: The Rise of Popular Sovereignty in England and America* (New York, 1988), 184–87; and Wood, *Radicalism of the American Revolution*, 268–70, 276–77.

15. Wood, *The Creation of the American Republic, 1776–1787* (Williamsburg, Va., 1969), 606–7.

16. Quoted in Paul Rahe, *Republics Ancient and Modern: Classical Republicanism and the American Revolution* (Chapel Hill, N.C., 1992), 334.

17. Quoted in Wood, *Creation of the American Republic,* 607.

18. Wood, *Radicalism of the American Revolution,* 186; Peter Kolchin, *American Slavery, 1619–1877* (New York, 1993), 70–71. "The 'real American Revolution,' writes Winthrop Jordan, "involved a newly intense scrutiny of colonial society, including the peculiarly un-English institution of Negro slavery." Jordan, *White over Black: American Attitudes Toward the Negro, 1550–1812* (Chapel Hill, N.C., 1968), 310–11; see also 288–89, 294–95.

19. Pauline Maier, "The Transforming Impact of Independence, Reaffirmed: 1776 and the Definition of American Social Structure," in James A. Henretta, Michael Kammen, and Stanley Katz, eds., *The Transformation of Early American History: Society, Authority, and Ideology* (New York, 1991), 214–15.

20. Allan Kulikoff, *Tobacco and Slaves: The Development of Southern Cultures in the Chesapeake, 1680–1800* (Chapel Hill, N.C., 1986), 433; Ira Berlin, "The Revolution in Black Life," in Alfred Young, ed., *The American Revolution: Explorations in the History of American Radicalism* (De Kalb, Ill., 1976), 372–77; Ronald Takaki, *Iron Cages: Race and Culture in 19th-Century America* (New York, 1990), 42–43.

21. Takaki, *Iron Cages,* 14; see also Jordan, *White over Black,* 340–41; Judith N. Shklar, *American Citizenship: The Quest for Inclusion* (Cambridge, Mass., 1991), 40–41; and Duncan J. MacLeod, *Slavery, Race, and the American Revolution* (Cambridge, 1974), 183–84.

22. Quoted in Paul Finkelman, "Making a Convenant with Death," in Richard Beeman, ed., *Beyond Confederation: Origins of the Constitution and American National Identity* (Chapel Hill, N.C., 1987), 199.

23. Quoted in ibid., 225.

24. John Shy, "Force, Order, and Democracy in the American Revolution," in Jack P. Greene, ed., *The American Revolution: Its Character and Limits* (New York, 1987), 78–79. For contrasting views on the confederation period, see Forrest McDonald, *E Pluribus Unum: The Formation of the American Republic, 1776–1790* (Indianapolis, 1979; orig. pub., 1965), who views the 1780s as chaotic; and Merrill Jensen, "The Sovereign States: Their Antagonisms and Some Consequences," in Ronald Hoffman and Peter Silbert, eds., *Sovereign States in an Age of Uncertainty* (Charlottesville, Va., 1981), 226–52, who makes the case for responsible state governments.

25. J. Hector St. John Crèvecoeur, *Letters from an American Farmer* (London, 1971; orig. pub., 1782), 58.

26. Both quotations are from Thomas P. Slaughter, *The Whiskey Rebellion: Frontier Epilogue to the American Revolution* (New York, 1986), 64, 65.

27. Quoted in Rachel Klein, *Unification of a Slave State: The Rise of the Planter Class in the South Carolina Backcountry, 1760–1808* (Williamsburg, Va., 1990), 165.
    Peter Charles Hoffer identifies this deeper concern of the young revolutionaries by comparing the reactions of George Washington (who believed he had fulfilled his public role by 1786) and Edmund Randolph to Shays' rebellion. The latter wrote: "The nerves of government are unstrung, both in energy and money, and the fashion of the day is to calumniate. . . . What then, am I to expect?" To this Washington somberly responded: "As no mind can be more deeply impressed than mine is with the awful situation of our affairs . . . so, consequently, those who do engage in the important business of removing these defects, will carry with them every good wish of mine."

Quoted in Hoffer, *Revolution and Regeneration: Life Cycle and the Historical Vision of the Generation of 1776* (Athens, Ga., 1983), 47–48.

On the importance of foreign affairs in the 1780s see Frederick W. Marks III, *Independence on Trial: Foreign Affairs and the Making of the Constitution* (Baton Rouge, La., 1973).

28. Gordon Wood, "A Note on Mobs in the Revolution," *William and Mary Quarterly* 23 (Oct. 1966): 641.

29. Wood, *Creation of the American Republic*, 369. See also Jackson T. Main, *The Upper House in Revolutionary America, 1763–1788* (Madison, Wisc., 1967), 188–91.

30. Quoted in Joyce Appleby, "The American Heritage: The Heirs and the Disinherited," *Journal of American History* 74 (Dec. 1987): 800. Reflecting the same discouraging mood, Madison wrote (in the fall of 1787) of legislative abuses "so frequent and so flagrant as to alarm the most stedfast friends of Republicanism . . . [and which] contributed more to the uneasiness which produced the Convention, and prepared the public mind for a general reform, than those which accrued to our national character and interest from the inadequacy of the Confederation to its immediate objects." Quoted in Gordon Wood, "Interests and Disinterestedness in the Making of the Constitution," in Beeman, ed., *Beyond Confederation*, 73.

31. John L. Brooke, *The Heart of the Commonwealth: Society and Political Culture in Worcester County, Massachusetts, 1713–1861* (New York, 1989), 190–93.

32. Quoted in Henretta, *Evolution of American Society, 1700–1815*, 164. On the issues leading to Shays' rebellion see Oscar and Mary Handlin, *Commonwealth: A Study of the Role of Government in the American Economy: Massachusetts, 1774–1861* (Cambridge, Mass., 1961; orig. pub., 1947), 36–47; and David Szatmary, *Shays' Rebellion: The Making of an Agrarian Insurrection* (Amherst, Mass., 1980), 38–43, 56–59, 60–64, 69, 91–102, 120–34.

33. Arthur P. Whitaker, *The Spanish-American Frontier, 1783–1795* (Gloucester, Mass., 1962; orig. pub., 1927), 58–61. For the intrigues between Ethan Allen of Vermont and the British see Michael Bellesiles, *Revolutionary Outlaws: Ethan Allen and the Struggle for Independence on the Early American Frontier* (Charlottesville, Va., 1993), 258–60.

34. Quoted in Whitaker, *Spanish-American Frontier*, 75.

35. Quoted in ibid., 44. See also 50–51.

36. Quoted in ibid., 103; see also 90–95.

37. Joshua Miller, *Rise and Fall of Democracy in Early America, 1630–1789* (University Park, Pa., 1991), 80.

38. For a stimulating discussion of the Founders' views on political life and the appropriate political models for their task, see Rahe, *Republics Ancient and Modern*, 566–67, 570–71, 584–85, 596–97.

39. Quoted in Jack N. Rakove, *Beginnings of National Politics: An Interpretive History of the Continental Congress* (Baltimore, 1982), 392.

40. Jack Eblen, *The First and Second United States Empires: Governors and Territorial Government, 1784–1912* (Pittsburgh, 1968), 44–46.

41. Quoted in Dale Van Every, *The Disinherited: The Lost Birthright of the American Indian* (New York, 1976), 86. See also Gregory Dowd, *A Spirited Resistance: The North*

American Indian Struggle for Unity, 1745–1815 (Baltimore, 1992), 90–93; Francis Jennings, *Empire of Fortune: Crowns, Colonies, and Tribes in the Seven Years' War in America* (New York, 1988), 478–79; Imre Sutton, ed., *Irredeemable America: The Indians' Estate and Land Claims* (Albuquerque, N.M., 1985), 65–66, 212–15; and Harvey Jackson, *Lachlan McIntosh and the Politics of Revolutionary Georgia* (Athens, Ga., 1979).

42. Lance Banning, *The Jeffersonian Persuasion* (Ithaca, N.Y., 1973), 89.

43. Appleby, "The Heirs and the Disinherited," 804.

44. Michael Zuckert, *Natural Rights and the New Republicanism* (Princeton, 1994), 13.

45. Isaac Kramnick, "The 'Great National Discussion': The Discourse of Politics in 1787," *William and Mary Quarterly* 45 (Jan. 1988): 6–7. See also Cecilia Kenyon, "Men of Little Faith: The Anti-Federalists on the Nature of Representative Government," ibid., 12 (1955): 3–43. In a departure from the customary historiographical debate over the Constitution, Richard C. Sinopoli contends that the ratification controversy turned on the issue of citizenship. See his *The Foundations of American Citizenship: Liberalism, the Constitution, and Civic Virtue* (New York, 1992).

46. Herbert Storing, "What the Anti-Federalists Were *For*," quoted in Michael Lienesch, *New Order of the Ages: Time, the Constitution, and the Making of Modern America* (Princeton, N.J., 1988), 139; see also 142–43. For a sustained defense of the antifederalists as social conservatives who strove to preserve community and democracy, see Miller, *Rise and Fall of Democracy in Early America*, 82–103, 136–39.

47. Lance Banning, "Republican Ideology and the Triumph of the Constitution, 1789 to 1793," *William and Mary Quarterly*, 3rd Ser., 31 (April 1974): 174. For that reason, it was inadvisable to impose too many constraints on those who governed in the name of a sovereign people (unless, of course, the "wrong gentlemen" governed). "A strict observance of the written laws is doubtless *one* of the highest duties of a good citizen," wrote Jefferson, "but it is not *the highest*. To lose our country by a scrupulous adherence to written law, would be to lose the law itself . . . thus absurdly sacrificing the end to the means." Hamilton put the issue more bluntly: "It is easy to sacrifice the substantial interests of Society by a strict adherence to ordinary rules." Quoted in Wiebe, *Opening of American Society*, 41. See also 32–33, 40.

48. But, as Jack Rakove notes, "it is striking to see how many fit the image of new men who had themselves struggled to gain—and not simply inherit—prestige and influence. Recognizing that their own rise to political power and higher social status had derived from participation in the Revolution, they were no less its products for resisting what they regarded as its excesses." Rakove, "Structure of Politics," in Beeman, ed., *Beyond Confederation*, 263–78, quotation at 279; See also Wood, *Radicalism of the American Revolution*, 253, 259; and Samuel H. Beer, *To Make a Nation: The Rediscovery of American Federalism* (Cambridge, Mass., 1993), 388.

49. Marc Egnal, *A Mighty Empire: The Origins of the American Revolution* (Ithaca, N.Y., 1988), 328–38.

50. Peter S. Onuf, "Settlers, Settlements, and New States," in Greene, ed., *The American Revolution: Its Character and Limits* 190–92. Madison (and others) believed that population increments and internal migration would favor the southern states. The Northwest Ordinances of 1784 and 1787 were designed in large part to encourage migration to a region many believed unattractive. See also the essay on the Northwest Ordinance of 1787 by Harold Hyman in *American Singularity: The 1787 Northwest*

Ordinance, the 1862 Homestead and Morrill Acts, and the 1944 G.I. Bill (Athens, Ga., 1986), esp. 19–33; and Gregory Nobles, "Breaking into the Backcountry: New Approaches to the Early American Frontier," *William and Mary Quarterly* 46 (Oct. 1989): 668–70. For the convoluted social and political intrigue in the old Southwest, see J. Leitch Wright, Jr., *Anglo-Spanish Rivalry in North America* (Athens, Ga., 1971), 138–42.

51. Quoted in Richard Norton Smith, *Patriarch: George Washington and the New American Nation* (Boston, 1993), 211. For most of this account, I have relied on Thomas P. Slaughter, *The Whiskey Rebellion: Frontier Epilogue to the American Revolution* (New York, 1986). See also George Connor, "The Politics of Insurrection: A Comparative Analysis of the Shays', Whiskey, and Fries' Rebellions," *The Social Science Journal* 29 (July 1992): 259–82.

52. Washington to Hamilton, September 7, 1792, in Worthington C. Ford, ed., *The Writings of George Washington* (New York, 1891), 12:182.

53. Quoted in Smith, *Patriarch*, 214. See also Slaughter, *Whiskey Rebellion*, 88–89.

54. Quoted in Smith, *Patriarch*, 224.

55. Quoted in Slaughter, *Whiskey Rebellion*, 221.

56. Stuart Bruchey, *The Wealth of the Nation: An Economic History of the United States* (New York, 1988), 21.

57. Lienesch, *New Order of the Ages*, 12–13; John Howe, "Republican Thought and the Political Violence of the 1790s," *American Quarterly* 19 (Summer 1967): 147–65.

58. Quoted in Bernard Bailyn, *Faces of Revolution: Personalities and Theories in the Struggle for American Independence* (New York, 1990), 258.

59. Robert Wells, "Population and the American Revolution," in William Fowler and Wallace Coyle, eds., *The American Revolution: Changing Perspectives* (Boston, 1979), 114–18.

60. Quoted in David Brion Davis, *Revolutions: Reflections on American Equality and Foreign Liberations* (Cambridge, Mass., 1990), 65.

61. Joyce Appleby, *Liberalism and Republicanism in the Historical Imagination* (Cambridge, Mass., 1992), 205. For a more detailed discussion, see Appleby, *Capitalism and a New Social Order: The Republican Vision of the 1790s* (New York, 1984), 51–53, 68–71; and Hoffer, *Revolution and Regeneration*, 74–77. On the southern elites' political security in a turbulent age, see Richard Buel, Jr., *Securing the Revolution: Ideology in American Politics, 1789–1815* (Ithaca, N.Y., 1972), esp. 77–87.

4 The Caribbean on the Eve of the Haitian Revolution

1. David Brion Davis, *The Problem of Slavery in the Age of Revolution, 1770–1823* (Ithaca, N.Y., 1975), 41–49, 82–83, 262–65.

   Until the late eighteenth century, argues David Eltis, Europeans had not counted Africans among those peoples whose enslavement outraged their moral sensibilities. They were deemed "outsiders." "When the immorality of coerced labor was finally recognized, the recognition appeared among all social groups at the same time." Eltis, "Europeans and the Rise and Fall of African Slavery in the Americas: An Interpretation," *American Historical Review* 98 (Dec. 1993): 1419.

2. Quoted in David Brion Davis, *The Problem of Slavery in Western Culture* (New York, 1966), 16.

3. "The existence of an elaborate code of laws defining slavery and policing slaves," Michael Craton notes, "does not necessarily indicate a rigorously effective slave system but more likely the reverse, a system in which the intended order has broken down and the laws are necessary to remedy flaws." Craton, *Testing the Chains: Resistance to Slavery in the British West Indies* (Ithaca, N.Y., 1982), 31; see also 48–49. For a comparison of slave laws in the eighteenth century see Elsa Goveia, "The West Indian Slave Laws of the Eighteenth Century," *Revista de Ciencias Sociales* 4 (Mar. 1960): 75–105.

4. Table I is adapted from Robin Blackburn, *The Overthrow of Colonial Slavery, 1776–1848* (London, 1988), 5. "British resources directed toward the acquisition of slaves in the eighteenth century," concludes Barbara Solow, "were very productive: they hastened the development of the New World; the rate of return on investment in the empire was enhanced; and the earnings associated with slave-produced crops enabled Britain's manufacturing sector to expand much faster than domestic demand permitted." Solow, "Capitalism and Slavery in the Exceedingly Long Run," *Journal of Interdisciplinary History* 17 (Spring 1987): 736.

5. See James A. Rawley, *The Transatlantic Slave Trade: A History* (New York, 1981).

6. The economic impact of the American Revolution on the plantation economies of the West Indies remains an issue of considerable dispute. Eric Williams, *Capitalism and Slavery* (London, 1944; reprinted, 1964), who draws heavily on the work of Lowell Ragatz, *The Fall of the Planter Class in the British West Indies, 1763–1833* (New York, 1928), identifies the loss of the mainland colonies (which supplied vital foodstuffs to the sugar economies of the British Caribbean) as the critical episode in the plantations' decline. Seymour Drescher, *Econocide: British Slavery in the Age of Abolition* (Pittsburgh, 1977), sharply questions this conclusion. Selwyn H. H. Carrington, "The American Revolution and the British West Indian Economy," *Journal of Interdisciplinary History* 17 (Spring 1987): 823–50, strongly reaffirms the Williams thesis; Richard Sheridan, "The Crisis of Slave Subsistence in the British West Indies During and After the American Revolution," *William and Mary Quarterly* 33 (Oct. 1976): 615–41, is more tentative.

7. Quoted in Franklin Knight, "The American Revolution and the Caribbean," in Ira Berlin and Ronald Hoffman, eds., *Slavery and Freedom in the Age of the American Revolution* (Baltimore, 1983), 242. Here, of course, Adams defined *slavery* and *slave* in terms encompassing the sense of dependency among British American slaveholders, a dependency that prompted Virginian slaveholders, for example, to refer to themselves as slaves.

   Caribbean dependency is often cited as deterministic in explaining the fragile development of nationhood in the region, but the application of Eurocentric experience and standards to Caribbean history, Sidney Mintz notes, has distracted scholars from the process of Creolization, which may explain much more clearly the distinctiveness of regional identity and the foundations of nationhood. Mintz, "Caribbean Nationhood in Anthropological Perspective," in Sybil Lewis and Thomas G. Mathews, eds., *Caribbean Integration: Papers in Social, Political, and Economic Integration* (Rio Piedras, P.R., 1967), 141–54.

   "West Indian history," William Green writes in a historiographical essay, "has always been written from an interdisciplinary perspective. A cockpit of conflict and a productive arena very different from that of the European metropoles, the West Indies have obliged writers of history to give close attention to social complexities, class, race, and the extraordinary economic relationships that conjoined the diverse human components of the islands." Green, "Caribbean Historiography, 1600–1900: The Recent Tide," *Journal of Interdisciplinary History* 7 (Winter 1977), 509.

8. Philip Curtin, *The Rise and Fall of the Plantation Complex: Essays in Atlantic History* (Cambridge, 1990), 9–13, 108–9; Sidney Mintz, "The Plantation as a Socio-Cultural Type," in *Plantation Systems of the New World: Papers and Discussion Summaries of the Seminar Held in San Juan, Puerto Rico* (Washington, D.C., 1959), 47; Knight, "American Revolution and the Caribbean," 7–8; Lowell Ragatz, *The Fall of the Planter Class in the British Caribbean, 1767–1833* (New York, 1928), 3. For a demurral to the argument that the British West Indies rapidly lost self-sufficiency in the quest for sugar profits, see Richard Sheridan, "The Domestic Economy," in Jack P. Greene and J. R. Pole, eds., *Colonial British America: Essays in the New History of the Early Modern Era* (Baltimore, 1984), esp. 50–53.

   African slavery in the New World (especially on the sugar plantations in the Caribbean) provided the slaveowner with the opportunity and the incentive to transform the sugar plantation into a preindustrial "plant" model. Sugar plantations became agroindustrial enterprises when they combined growing, harvesting, and processing under a singular authority. The entire operation required discipline and a labor force of skilled and unskilled mobilized for the relentless demands of production. As were later industrial operations, writes Sidney Mintz, "the system was time-conscious," a feature "dictated by the nature of sugar cane and its processing requirements." *Sweetness and Power: The Place of Sugar in Modern History* (New York, 1985), 51. Noel Deerr, *The History of Sugar* (2 vols., London, 1949–50), traces the migration of sugar cane from the eastern Mediterranean to the New World. See also Elizabeth Fox Genovese and Eugene Genovese, *Fruits of Merchant Capital: Slavery and Bourgeois Property in the Rise and Expansion of Capitalism* (New York, 1983); Richard S. Dunn, *Sugar and Slaves* (Chapel Hill, N.C., 1972); and Gabriel Debien, *Les Esclaves aux Antilles Française: XVII–XVIII Siècle* (Basse-Terre, Guadeloupe, 1974).

9. Jack P. Greene, "Colonial Identity in the British Caribbean," in Nicholas Canny and Anthony Pagden, eds., *Colonial Identity in the Atlantic World, 1500–1800* (Princeton, N.J., 1987), 259. In Jamaica, Lowell Ragatz writes, the eighteenth-century disparity suffered by whites before a burgeoning black and colored population created a "constant apprehension of servile revolt." Ragatz, *Fall of the Planter Class,* 31.

10. Because plantations ultimately came to rely heavily on *African* slave labor, Sidney Mintz warns, slavery and race appear to be inextricably linked. But "all we know about the social history of the Caribbean plantation system convinces us that the planters were . . . willing to employ any kind of labor . . . as long as the labor force was politically defenseless enough for the work to be done cheaply and under any discipline." Mintz, *Caribbean Transformations* (Chicago, 1974), 150–51. But Europeans came to view slavery as a "fate worse than death," observes David Eltis, "and, as such, . . . reserved for non-Europeans." Eltis, "Europeans and the Rise and Fall of African Slavery," 1409.

11. Robert Stein, *The French Sugar Business in the Eighteenth Century* (Baton Rouge, La., 1988), 41.

   After their expulsion from Brazil, the Dutch developed their Caribbean plantation complex in Curaçao and Suriname, which in 1788 had 591 plantations and a slave labor force of fifty thousand in a population of fifty-five thousand. Surinamese plantation prosperity was already in sharp reverse, and owners had begun to sell their properties to Dutch creditors. Absenteeism climbed to disturbing numbers. By 1813,

Harry Hoetink has estimated, almost three hundred of Suriname's 369 plantation owners were absentees. See Hoetink, "Surinam and Curaçao," in David Cohen and Jack P. Greene, eds., *Neither Slave Nor Free: The Freedmen of African Descent in the Slave Societies of the New World* (Baltimore, 1972), 60–61.

12. Stein, *French Sugar Business,* 42, and *The French Slave Trade in the Eighteenth Century: An Old Regime Business* (Madison, Wis., 1979), 9–10. For a discussion of the often precarious position of the free colored in the Caribbean see Arnold I. Sio, "Marginality and Free-Coloured Identity in Caribbean Slave Society," *Slavery and Abolition* 8 (1987): 166–82.

"The association of sugar cane, the slavery of transported Africans and the large agricultural estates commonly called 'plantations' is both intimate and ancient," Sidney Mintz has observed, ". . . but nothing says it must be grown only on plantations, or only by slaves." Quoted in Franklin Knight, "The Caribbean Sugar Industry and Slavery," in *Latin American Research Review* 18 (1983): 219–20.

Barbara Solow advances a plausible argument for the use of slave labor: "Sugar had production characteristics that gave slave labor enormous cost advantages over free labor. . . . The importance of slaves in America was not only that they could be coerced into coming when free labor did not, but when they came they did different things. More of them worked, they worked longer, they could not disperse, they attracted investment, and they produced crops for trade and export on a scale unmatched by free labor." Solow, "Slavery and Colonization," in Solow, ed., *Slavery and the Rise of the American System* (New York, 1991), 28.

13. Williams, *Capitalism and Slavery,* 24. See also Robert Miles, *Capitalism and Unfree Labour: Anomaly or Necessity?* (London, 1987), 79–80.

In the beginning, slave labor went to cotton and tobacco plantations, where slaves supplanted indentured whites. "At its inception, there was no necessary connection between cane culture and slave labor in the British settlements, nor is it at all clear that African labor was cheaper, less vexatious, superior, or . . . preferred in Barbados. It was available on easy terms at precisely the time when imports of indentured labor had become problematical and when . . . supplies of sugar in the Atlantic were falling." William Green, "Race and Slavery," in Barbara Solow and Stanley Engerman, eds., *British Capitalism and Caribbean Slavery: The Legacy of Eric Williams* (New York, 1987), 47; see also 40–41.

14. Manuel Moreno Fraginals (Cedric Belfrage, trans.), *The Sugarmill: The Socioeconomic Complex of Sugar in Cuba, 1760–1860* (New York, 1976), 17. This work appeared in Cuba as *El ingenio: Complejo economía del azúcar* (3 vols., Havana, 1978).

In the process, small tobacco farmers, who occupied some of the best lands, were pushed aside. They appealed for royal support, and the Crown granted them unoccupied lands, subsidies, and pledges to purchase their product. Some 10,000 small tobacco farmers and a rural class of free laborers thus found momentary refuge in royal protection, but the sugar aristocrats ultimately won out when the collapse of Haitian sugar production gave them another opportunity. Cuban planters invested little in technical innovation for sugar production as long as slave labor was abundant. The Cuban sociologist Fernando Ortíz describes the differing social legacies of sugar and tobacco economies in *Cuban Counterpoint: Tobacco and Sugar* (New York, 1947), 6–7.

15. "The plantation society of the West Indies," Elsa Goveia has observed, "was very different from the European society which had produced it. It tended, for example,

to create an aristocracy of wealth where European social organization tended to emphasize the aristocracy of birth." Goveia, "Comments," in *Plantation Systems of the New World* (Washington, D.C., 1959), 60.

Most comparisons of race relations in the United States and the Caribbean emphasize the undeniable and significant differences in attitudes toward miscegenation. In the United States, *colored* is virtually synonymous with *black.* In the Caribbean, however, people of color came to occupy an intermediate place in the social structure and in occupations, especially in the towns, and thus acquired a social ranking higher than that of blacks. "But this did not necessarily imply that the socioeconomic structure of the plantation society demanded such a position," Harry Hoetink contends, for "the wide variety of their occupations as well as their widespread poverty might lead to the opposition conclusion." Hoetink, *Slavery and Race Relations in the Americas: Comparative Notes on Their Nature and Nexus* (New York, 1973), 24.

16. "The idea of a society in which Negroes were released from their subordination and allowed legal equality with whites was so antithetical to the principles on which the slave society rested that it seemed to threaten complete social dissolution and chaos." Elsa Goveia, *Slave Society in the British Leeward islands at the End of the Eighteenth Century* (New Haven, 1965), 329; see also 312–15, 322–23.

17. Quoted in Jack P. Greene, "Identity in the British Caribbean," in Nicolas Canny and Anthony Pagden, eds., *Colonial Identity in the Atlantic World, 1500–1800* (Princeton, N.J., 1987), 222.

On the undeniable correlation between color and status among the slaves, Orlando Patterson acknowledges that colored slaves generally avoided the menial tasks but warns, "The data in no way suggests that Negro slaves internalized the colour ideals of the coloured group. If anything, they . . . felt little sense of racial inferiority in the face of the discriminatory behaviour toward them on the part of both the white and coloured group." Patterson, *The Sociology of Slavery: An Analysis of the Origins, Development, and Structure of Negro Slave Society in Jamaica* (Rutherford, N.J., 1967), 64.

Emilia Viotti da Costa's depiction of the extravagances of Demerara's planter aristocrats applied to other British West Indian nabobs: "In the colony, Europeans felt like exiles. And, like exiles everywhere, they tended to idealize the world they had left behind. . . . They surrounded themselves with European things, symbols of their culture, marks of affiliation: pieces of mahogany furniture, billiard and card tables made in London, decanters, tumblers, wine glasses, shades, China tea and coffee sets and dinner services, silver knives and forks, ivory-handled carving knives and forks, mirrors, clocks, pianos, and bookcases." Costa, *Crowns of Glory, Tears of Blood: The Demerara Slave Rebellion of 1823* (New York, 1994), 23.

18. Gordon Lewis, *Main Currents in Caribbean Thought: The Historical Evolution of Caribbean Society in its Ideological Aspects, 1492–1900* (Baltimore, 1987), 168, Gordon Lewis, *Slavery, Imperialism, and Freedom: Essays in English Radical Thought* (New York, 1978), 24–25; and David Watts, *The West Indies: Patterns of Development, Culture, and Environmental Change Since 1492* (Cambridge, 1987), 444–45.

19. Quoted in Richard Pares, *War and Trade in the West Indies, 1739–1763* (Oxford, 1936), 235. See also Jack Greene, *Imperatives, Behaviors, and Identities: Essays in Early American Cultural History* (Charlottesville, Va., 1992), 84–85; Lewis, *Slavery, Imperialism, and Freedom,* 47–49; and Davis, *Slavery in the Age of Revolution,* 194–95.

20. A visitor to Jamaica wrote of "the mean Shifts to which these poor Creatures are reduced. You'll see them daily about Twelve o'clock when they turn in from work, till

Two, scraping the Dunghils at every Gentleman's door for bones." C. Leslie, *A New and Exact Account of Jamaica* (1739), quoted in J. R. Ward, *British West Indian Slavery, 1750–1834: The Process of Amelioration* (Oxford, 1988), 22. On the debilitating effect of overwork and suicide as an "escape" see Gwendolyn Hall, *Social Control in Slave Plantation Societies: A Comparison of St. Domingue and Cuba* (Baltimore, 1971), 16–17, 20–21. For the biography of a runaway see Esteban Montejo (Jocasta Innesas, trans.), *Autobiography of a Runaway Slave* (New York, 1968). See also Hilary McD. Beckles, "Caribbean Anti-Slavery: The Self-Liberation Ethos of Enslaved Blacks," *Journal of Caribbean History* 22 (1988): 1–19.

21. Quoted in Michael Craton, *Sinews of Empire: A Short History of British Slavery* (Garden City, N.Y., 1974), 171–72.

22. Quoted in Williams, *Capitalism and Slavery*, 41. For the champion of liberty, the issue was less a matter of principle than the recognition that the British Empire waged colonial and commercial wars in North America, India, the Caribbean, and Africa for crucial commodities—tobacco, sugar, fish, naval stores, furs, and African slaves. From them the empire drew its wealth and strength. See Philip R. P. Coelho, "The Profitability of Imperialism: The British Experience in the West Indies, 1768–1772," *Explorations in Economic History* 10 (Spring 1973), 253–80, who argues that the economic benefits of the British West Indies in these years (deriving from ginger and government revenues) fell short by more than one million pounds of the cost of military and construction expendures and, especially, the sugar subsidy.

23. Quoted in Williams, *Capitalism and Slavery*, 50; see also 42–49.

24. On the conditions for slave revolt in Jamaica see Orlando Patterson, "Slavery and Slave Revolts: A Socio-Historical Analysis of the First Maroon War, Jamaica, 1655–1740," *Social and Economic Studies* 19 (Sept. 1970): 289–325, and his *Sociology of Slavery*, 22–23.

25. Quoted in Lewis, *Main Currents in Caribbean Thought*, 114.

26. Michael Craton, "The Planters' World in the British West Indies," in Bernard Bailyn and Philip Morgan, eds., *Strangers Within the Realm: Cultural Margins of the First British Empire* (Chapel Hill, N.C., 1991), 347. For a further discussion of abseentism and its effects see Douglas Hall, "Absentee-Proprietorship in the British West Indies," in Lambros Comitas and David Lowenthal, eds., *Slaves, Free Men, Citizens: West Indian Perspectives* (Garden City, N.Y., 1973), 106–7, 132–35; and Lowell Ragatz, "Absentee Landlordism in the British Caribbean, 1750–1833," *Agricultural History* 5 (1931): 7–24.

27. Michael Craton, "Jamaican Slavery," in Stanley Engerman and Eugene Genovese, eds., *Race and Slavery in the Western Hemisphere: Quantitative Studies* (Princeton, N.J., 1975), 249–51.
    "During the first eighty-five years of the British colonization of Jamaica," Orlando Patterson writes, ". . . we find this sorry sociological spectacle: a pseudo-society in which there were two quite distinct groups of people. . . . Both groups despised, distrusted and loathed each other. Only the impulse of greed, the chains of slavery, and the crack of the cart-whip kept them together. But such ingredients provided a poor social mortar." Patterson, "Slavery and Slave Revolts: A Socio-Historical Analysis of the First Maroon War—Jamaica, 1655–1740," *Social and Economic Studies* 19 (Sept. 1970): 293. See also Patterson, *Sociology of Slavery*, 44–47. Reviewing the latter work, William Green asks rhetorically, "How could a thoroughly evil social order involving tens of thousands of steadily resisting slaves have survived profitably for nearly 200 years?" (Green, "Caribbean Historiography," 517).

28. Blackburn, *Overthrow of Colonial Slavery*, 163–65.

29. For a comparison of maroon societies see Richard Price, *Maroon Societies: Rebel Slave Communities in the Americas* (New York, 1973). "In crucial ways," observes Michael Craton, "the Maroons were analogous to the American Indians, fighting a losing retreat against the colonial tide." Craton, "The Passion to Exist: Slave Rebellions in the British West Indies, 1650–1832," *Journal of Caribbean History* 13 (1980): 3. For an account of slaveholder practices in Dutch Guiana, see the journal of J. G. Stedman (R. A. J. van Lier, ed.), *Narrative of a Five Years' Expedition Against the Revolted Negroes of Surinam from . . . 1772 to 1777 . . .* (Amherst, Mass., 1971).

30. Gwendolyn Hall, *Social Control in Slave Plantation Societies: A Comparison of St. Domingue and Cuba* (Baltimore, 1971), 20–21, 40–41.

31. Carolyn Fick, *The Making of Haiti: The Saint Domingue Revolution from Below* (Knoxville, Tenn., 1991), 61.

32. Leslie Manigat, "The Relationship Between Marronage and Slave Revolts and Revolution in St. Domingue-Haiti," in Vera Rubin and Arthur Tuden, eds., *Comparative Perspectives on Slavery in New World Plantation Societies* (New York, 1977), 435. David Geggus, in a brief but sweeping historiographical assessment of the connection between Haitian marronage and the revolution of 1791, states: "For the Haitian school . . . it is axiomatic that the 1791 revolt was inspired and led by maroons, and that it developed out of a burgeoning swell of marronage. But this has yet to be proved." Geggus, "Slave Resistance Studies and the Saint Domingue Revolt: Some Preliminary Considerations," Florida International University, *Occasional Papers*, No. 4 (Winter 1983), 9.

33. Emilien Petit, *Traité sur le gouvernment des esclaves* (2 vols., Paris, 1777), 2:68, 69, as quoted in Hall, "Saint Domingue," in Cohen and Greene, eds., *Neither Slave Nor Free*, 172–73.

5 The Slave Rebellion

1. "Few revolutions in world history," observes David Geggus, "have had such profound consequences." Geggus, "The Haitian Revolution," in Franklin W. Knight and Colin Palmer, eds., *The Modern Caribbean* (Chapel Hill, N.C., 1989), 21. In this discussion I use "Haitian Revolution" and "Saint Domingue" Revolution interchangeably. In actuality, the term *Haiti*, an Amerindian word, was used after the declaration of independence in late 1803 and the creation of an independent state early in the following year. For a compelling fictional account of the Haitian Revolution, see Madison Smartt Bell, *All Soul's Rising: A Novel* (New York, 1995).

2. David Geggus, "Slave Resistance Studies and the Saint Domingue Revolt: Some Preliminary Considerations," Florida International University, *Occasional Papers*, No. 4 (Winter 1983): 3, 21; see also Geggus, *Slavery, War, and Revolution: The British Occupation of Saint Domingue, 1793–1798* (Oxford, 1982), 302; Herbert Klein, *African Slavery in Latin America and the Caribbean* (New York, 1986), 21–43; and Ralph Davis, *The Rise of the Atlantic Economies* (London, 1973), 125–26.

François-Dominique Toussaint Louverture (1744?–1803). Both the spelling and the meaning of *Louverture* are disputed. Toussaint himself spelled his name as "Louverture," but it often appears in English-language texts as "L'Ouverture." Its most accepted meaning is "the one who opened the way" or "the leader," but among the slaves themselves the term meant someone with a disfiguring gap between two front teeth.

Slave behavior, not only in revolutionary Saint Domingue in the 1790s but throughout the history of slavery in the Americas, David Brion Davis cautions, "may have persuaded many historians captivated by the romantic notions of slaves liberating themselves by force of arms. The frequency of insurrection has commonly been taken as reassuring evidence of slave discontent, as if no more subtle evidence were available, and as if the main result of such occurrences was not always an increase in mass executions of blacks." (D. Davis, *The Problem of Slavery in the Age of Revolution, 1770–1823* (Ithaca, N.Y., 1975), 72–73.

3. D. W. Meinig, *The Shaping of America: A Geographical Perspective on 500 Years of History*, vol. 1, *Atlantic America, 1492–1800* (New Haven, 1986), 171. Meinig identifies the *code noir* as perhaps the distinctive mark of French insular social types in the Caribbean. "French racial attitudes," Meinig continues, "were softer and more subtle, and the results showed in acculturation, miscegenation, and manumission: in a burgeoning Afro-Catholicism with its syncretic rituals and festivals, in the large numbers of mulattos and the common social recognition of many degrees of color, in the free Black planters served by their own Black servants and slaves, in the more open and intimate daily life of a vigorous creole society" (ibid.). But another scholar cautions that the intent of the code noir—to protect the property of French settlers—and its casual enforcement, especially in its prohibition of the taking of concubine slaves, may indicate a "somewhat more humane attitude" in the French West Indies rather than a distinctive contrast in the comparative lot of the slaves. See William John Eccles, *France in America* (New York, 1972), 152.

4. "Absentee plantation owners received, often without comment, annual reports of births and deaths among their slaves and animals." Robert Stein, *The French Sugar Business in the Eighteenth Century* (Baton Rouge, La., 1988), 46. Integrated into a plantation system that demanded total subjection, slaves lost their names, their familial ties, their African identity. The intent of the code noir may have been humane, but one undeniable result of French slavery was the creation of a "socially dead person." Carolyn Fick, *The Making of Haiti: The Saint Domingue Revolution from Below* (Knoxville, Tenn., 1991), 27. See also Orlando Patterson, *Slavery and Social Death: A Comparative Study* (Cambridge, Mass., 1982).

Brutality that cost lives was economically ruinous, and intelligent *colons* recognized this. "'I would be ruined if I subjected my slaves to brutal treatment,' explained a colon. 'The cruelest whites are the managers who have no responsibility for maintaining them.'" Gerard Laurent, ed., *Toussaint L'Ouverture a travers sa correspondance, 1794–1798* (Port-au-Prince, 1954), 37. My translation.

5. Michael Craton, *Sinews of Empire: A Short History of British Slavery* (Garden City, N.Y., 1974), 229.

6. Roger Norman Buckley, *Slaves in Redcoats: The British West India Regiments, 1795–1815* (New Haven, 1979), 1–5. *Black* and *mulatto* are almost exclusively somatic norm references. *Free colored* refers to status among nonwhite persons with some African descent. Not surprisingly, the free colored often tried to hide their African ancestry.

7. Jean-Baptiste Duterte, *Histoire général des Antilles habitées par les françois* (4 vols., Paris, 1667–71), 2:499, as quoted in Gwendolyn Hall, "Saint Domingue," in David Cohen and Jack P. Greene, eds., *Neither Slave Nor Free: The Freedmen of African Descent in the Slave Societies of the New World* (Baltimore, 1973), 173. See also Richard Pares, *War and Trade in the West Indies, 1739–1763* (Oxford, 1936), 256.

8. Shelby T. McCloy, *The Negro in the French West Indies* (Lexington, Ky., 1966), 62–65.

9. Quoted in Fick, *Making of Haiti,* 19. See also John Garrigus, "Blue and Brown: Contraband Indigo and the Rise of a Free Colored Planter Class in French Saint-Domingue," *The Americas* 50 (Oct. 1993): 233–63.

10. Quoted in Stein, *French Sugar Business,* 53. See also Léo Elisabeth, "The French Antilles," in Cohen and Greene, eds., *Neither Slave Nor Free,* 162; Martin Ros (Karin Ford-Treep, trans.), *Night of Fire: The Black Napoleon and the Battle for Haiti* (New York, 1994), 22–23. David Geggus notes: "The reasons behind this rising tide of racism are various. Prejudice and policy both played a part, most obviously in direct response to the increasing strength of the free coloureds. The policy of depressing the status of the free coloured also represented an attempt to erect a bulwark against the alarming growth in the number of slaves." Geggus, *Slavery, War, and Revolution,* 21.

An ordinance of 1778 forbade marriages between whites and free coloreds. The intent had less to do with preserving a color line than with preventing unions of political interest. As one minister wrote: "If, by means of these alliances the whites are able to fashion alliance with the free colored, the colony would be less vulnerable to royal authority and France would lose the strongest base of its commerce." Quoted in Gaston Martin, *Histoire de l'esclavage dans les colonies françaises* (Paris, 1948), 153.

11. On the puzzling rise of the free coloreds in Saint Domingue and their rapid decline in legal status after the mid-eighteenth century, evidence often used to explain why the free coloreds joined the revolution, Sidney Mintz cautions: "One might argue that the Saint Domingue experiment ended in revolution, precisely because the 'coloureds' wanted equal rights with the whites, and these were denied them. Not quite, however; the 'coloureds' were only able to dispute their treatment *because* they had been acknowledged, freed, protected and educated by their white fathers and grandfathers in the first place." Mintz, "Groups, Group Boundaries, and the Perception of Race," *Comparative Studies in Society and History* 13 (Oct. 1971): 445.

12. Quoted in C. L. R. James, *The Black Jacobins: Toussaint L'Ouverture and the San Domingo Rebellion* (New York, 1968; orig. pub., 1938), 63. My italics. Lower-class whites, Jonathan Brown writes, were "agitated by a thousand feelings, all originating in some vague notion that a period had arrived fraught deep with the richest hope and blessings for their own order." Brown, *The History and Present Condition of St. Domingo* (2 vols., London, 1971; orig. pub., 1837), 1:134.

13. Quoted in Martin, *Histoire de l'esclavage,* 164.

14. David Geggus, "Racial Equality, Slavery, and Colonial Secession During the Constituent Assembly," *American Historical Review* 94 (Dec. 1989): 1293–95.

15. Garragus, "Blue and Brown," 233–63; Craton, *Sinews of Empire,* 221; Geggus, "Racial Equality, Slavery, and Colonial Secession," 1288–1301. See also Charles Frostin, *Les révoltes blanches à Saint-Domingue aux xviie et xviiie siècles (Häiti avant 1789)* (Paris, 1975), 381.

16. Aimé Césaire, *Toussaint Louverture: La Révolution française et le problème colonial* (Paris, 1960), 97.

17. Quoted in James, *The Black Jacobins,* 76–77. "It was magnificent," wrote James, "but it was not abolition. It was only the word slavery Robespierre was objecting to—not the thing. All had agreed to leave that alone, though it was in all minds." Ibid., 77.

18. Quoted in Ros, *Night of Fire,* 27.

19. Quoted in Franklin Knight, *The Caribbean: The Genesis of a Fragmented Nationalism,* 2nd ed. (New York, 1988), 173.

20. Quoted in James H. Billington, *Fire in the Minds of Men: Origins of the Revolutionary Faith* (New York, 1980), 109.

21. Quoted in James, *Black Jacobins,* 82.

22. Quoted in Patrick Bellegarde-Smith, *Haiti: The Breached Citadel* (Boulder, Colo., 1990), 41. The uses of first rather than family names for these Haitian leaders is commonplace in Haitian historiography, as the last name among slaves was often the name of a plantation or was given by their owners.

23. James, *Black Jacobins,* 88. For the report of the special committee see Ralph Korngold, *Citizen Toussaint* (Boston, 1944), 71. See also Geggus, "The Haitian Revolution," in Knight and Palmer, eds., *The Modern Caribbean,* 29–30.

   Addressing Eugene Genovese's ascription of "bourgeois-democratic" to the Haitian Revolution, Geggus notes that before 1793 (when Toussaint rose to prominence), the commitment of revolutionary leaders to the overthrow of slavery was "rather ambiguous and rarely expressed in idealistic terms. It did not prevent them from selling slaves themselves, nor from seeking a compromise peace on more than one occasion. . . . Far from using bourgeois-democratic slogans, the rebels of 1791 identified not with those they contemptuously called 'les citoyens' but with the Counter-Revolution." Geggus, "Slave Resistance Studies and the Saint-Domingue Revolt," 21; see also 18–19; and Philip Curtin, "The Declaration of the Rights of Man in Saint-Domingue, 1788–1791," *Hispanic American Historical Review* 30 (May 1950): 157–75.

24. Quoted in Martin, *Histoire de l'esclavage,* 211. For a general survey of the migration of French colons to Jamaica, see Philip Wright and Gabriel Debien, *Les colons de Saint-Domingue passés à Jamaique (1792–1835)* (Guadeloupe, 1975), esp. 19–21.

   The participation of maroons in the insurrection is a matter of continuing scholarly debate. Carolyn Fick's observation about the dynamics of African, Creole, and maroon interaction in the making of the 1791 rebellion is apt: "To separate any one element from the others, as if they are by nature mutually exclusive, will invariably leave the vital questions about the revolutionary organization and capacities of the black masses perpetually unanswered." *Making of Haiti,* 95.

25. Ros, *Night of Fire,* 5–7.

26. Robin Blackburn, *The Overthrow of Colonial Slavery, 1776–1848* (London, 1988), 190–92. The fighting between whites and mulattoes, writes Martin Ros, "ended in unimaginable tragedies. White fathers strangled the bastard mulattoes whom they knew to be their own sons. Mulattoes murdered sleeping planters whom they believed to be their fathers." *Night of Fire,* 33.

   North Province in Saint Domingue lay to the north, but West Province lay to the *south* of North Province and *east* of South Province.

27. It was a dubious victory, as one colon sensed: "The enemy we must destroy in order to restore calm in the colony is too numerous and their means of defense too great for us to ever bring them back into submission; whichever way things turn out, our ruin is total. If we do not defeat and destroy the rebel slaves, we will all end up being slaughtered by these monsters, and by destroying them we destroy our fortunes. For it is in these slaves that our fortunes exist." Quoted in Fick, *Making of Haiti,* 156.

   In South Province, slave leaders reassured the whites that they had been misled by the mulattoes, some of whom owned slaves. Mulattoes had armed their slaves to advance mulatto interests, then joined the counterrevolution. This was a slave tactic to gain advantage, argues Carolyn Fick, as "the slaves were beginning to see clearly that the mulatto owners were no less a class enemy than their white masters." Ibid., 153.

28. Quoted in Robert Louis Stein, *Légér Félicité Sonthonax: Lost Sentinel of the Republic* (Rutherford, N.J., 1985), 83.

29. Jonathan Brown, *The History and Present Condition of St. Domingo* (2 vols., London, 1971; orig. pub., 1837, 2:143. See also David Nicholls, *Haiti in Caribbean Context: Ethnicity, Economy, and Revolt* (New York, 1985), 23–24. David Geggus explores the literature on slave resistance and the revolt of 1791 in "Slave Resistance Studies."

30. Althéa de Parham (trans. and ed.), *My Odyssey: Experiences of a Young Refugee from Two Revolutions, by a Creole of Saint-Domingue*, as quoted in Thomas Ott, *The Haitian Revolution, 1789–1804* (Knoxville, Tenn., 1973), 71.

31. Quoted in Ott, *The Haitian Revolution,* 72. News of the black revolt on Saint Domingue terrified Jamaica's planters, who called out the militia (now expanded to include rich and poor whites, free blacks, and mulattoes) and established committees of security in every parish. But Jamaica's white society was "bound together by racial solidarity and strengthened by a high degree of social mobility. It was Saint Domingue with its exceptionally diversified economy and large population of *petits blancs* that displayed an unusual amount of class tension." David Geggus, "Jamaica and the Saint-Domingue Slave Revolt, 1791–1793," *The Americas* 38 (Oct. 1981), 225.

32. James, *Black Jacobins,* 124.

33. Toussaint to the Minister of Marine, April 13, 1799, quoted in George F. Tyson, ed., *Toussaint L'Ouverture* (New York, 1973), 31. Toussaint addressed the black-colored issue forthrightly in 1795 when he warned blacks against traitorous men of color but added: "God forbid, however, that I confuse the Innocent ones with the guilty! No, my brothers, I am not prejudiced against any particular class; I know that there are men of color who are estimable and virtuous, irreproachable . . . to whom I accord my Esteem, my Friendship and my Confidence." Proclamation on the Villalte affair, March 1795, quoted in ibid., 32.

34. Quoted in ibid., 125. This was a disingenuous self-description, given the evidence of his own career. "There is a danger in overstressing the policies of Toussaint Louverture," observes David Geggus. "Partly because they were not the sole expression of the Haitian Revolution, and met with opposition from other of its leaders as well as from the mass of ex-slaves. But also because it is now known that Toussaint was not a slave at all when the revolt broke out, and had been free and a slaveowner for at least fifteen years." Geggus, "Slave Resistance Studies, 21."

35. Toussaint's often convoluted thinking about slavery, the plantation economy, and the place of Saint Domingue in the French empire can be followed in his correspondence. See Laurent, ed., *Toussaint L'Ouverture à travers sa correspondance.*

36. Stories about the slave insurrection and parallel fears of its impact had already reverberated throughout the Caribbean and even into the southern United States. Spanish authorities established a cordon of troops along the frontier with French Saint Domingue to prevent the "pestilence" from intruding into the Spanish portion of the island and implored Spanish subjects to assist beleaguered whites, thus reaffirming a "strong ethnic solidarity, a colonial solidarity, and a solidarity of class when confronting the Saint-Domingue slave rebellion." Alain Yacou, "Cube et la Révolution française," in Michel Martin and Alain Yacou, eds., *De la Révolution française aux révolutions creoles et nègres* (Paris, 1989), 19. My translation.

37. Knight, *The Caribbean*, 210–11.

38. Quoted in Manuel Moreno Fraginals (Cedric Belfrage, trans.), *The Sugarmill: The Socioeconomic Complex of Sugar in Cuba, 1760–1860* (New York, 1976), 28. See also Jeffrey J. Crow, "Slave Rebelliousness and Social Conflict in North Carolina, 1775–1802," *William and Mary Quarterly* 37 (Jan. 1980): 93–94.

39. James, *Black Jacobins*, 102–3.

40. Ott, *Haitian Revolution*, 81–82.

41. Blackburn, *Overthrow of Colonial Slavery*, 232–33. British losses in the Lesser Antilles between 1796 and 1800—killed, dying from disease, or discharged because of unfitness—reached forty thousand.
    Even in victory, British commanders faced a new kind of war in the Caribbean. As did their French enemies, they confronted heavy demands for slave labor from planters. Persuaded that white soldiers could not survive in the debilitating climate, they increased the numbers of slaves assigned to officers and free coloreds in arms. In the conquered colonies of Martinique, Saint Lucia, and Guadeloupe, the invading British encountered pockets of slaves engaged in guerrilla resistance. The solution, wrote one British officer, was a thousand-man corps of blacks and mulattoes to wage Britain's war in the West Indies, a struggle of "opposing Blacks to Blacks." Buckley, *Slaves in Redcoats*, 13.

42. Quoted in Ott, *Haitian Revolution*, 90. "Toussaint always had his officers give commands with their pistols in hand," Martin Ros states, commenting on Toussaint's command abilities. "Obedience was therefore always a matter of life or death. It was astonishing how he trained the blacks to take their ammunition, musket, sword, sabre and chopping knife wherever and whenever they went." Ros, *Night of Fire*, 59.

43. Ros, *Night of Fire*, 84–85. His other potential rivals had already departed the island. Jean François migrated to Spain in 1795 and assumed the governorship of Cádiz a few years later. He died a rich man. Biassou fled Saint Domingue and lived as an impoverished exile in the United States. He was killed in a tavern.

6 The Haitian Revolution

1. Maitland calculated the cost of maintaining an adequate force in Haiti at half a million pounds, twice the amount available from the British War Office. He speculated "whether what We now hold is worth that Sum Annually as affording protection to Jamaica. . . . I confess I . . . feel myself strongly inclined to say . . . the advantage to be derived is not equal to the Expence to be incurred." Quoted in Charles C. Tansill, *The United States and Santo Domingo, 1798–1873: A Chapter in Caribbean Diplomacy* (Baltimore, 1938), 28. For an account of those who fled to Jamaica see Philip Wright and Gabriel Debien, *Les colons de Saint-Domingue passés à la Jamaique, 1792–1835* (Extrait du Bulletin de Société de Guadeloupe, No. 26, 1975).

2. The often tangled account of British and U.S. relations with Toussaint may be explored in more detail in Bradford Perkins, *The First Rapprochement: England and the United States, 1795–1805* (Philadelphia, 1955). For the undeclared war between France and the United States, see Alexander DeConde, *The Quasi-War: The Politics and Diplomacy of the Undeclared War with France, 1797–1801* (New York, 1966).

3. Quoted in Martin Ros (Karin Ford-Treep, trans.), *Night of Fire: The Black Napoleon and the Battle for Haiti* (New York, 1994), 98.

4. Quoted in Carolyn Fick, *The Making of Haiti: The Saint Domingue Revolution from Below* (Knoxville, Tenn., 1991), 200. A French officer (General Kerverseau) wrote in

a report of 1796 that Rigaud's mulattoes "dram of acquiring power over the entire Caribbean territory from their base of attack in Haiti . . . [and] they are totally determined to take control of our Big Island." Quoted in Ros, *Night of Fire*, 107.

5. Quoted in Thomas Ott, *The Haitian Revolution, 1789–1804* (Knoxville, Tenn., 1973), 111. The revolt of 1791 had so devastated the Plaine du Nord that it had not recovered when the British left. A young British officer stationed there in 1797 wrote: "All was Desolation & misery, not an Inhabitant but had quitted his Habitation, & not an Habitation but what was destroyed & laid in Ruins. The revolted Negroes had carried Destruction wherever they had been, & as if to be revenged of their old Masters, out of the 240 Habitations that formerly embelished & formed the Beauty of this Rich Plain, not more than three Houses were left standing." Roger N. Buckley, ed., *The Haitian Journal of Lieutenant [Thomas Phipps] Howard, York Hussars, 17796–1798* (Knoxville, Tenn., 1975), 129–30.

6. Quoted in Ott, *Haitian Revolution*, 112. "The punishment of the North," wrote T. Lothrop Stoddard, "was frightful. The mulattoes and even free negroes were butchered *en masse;* the survivors were broken by torture and by conscription into black regiments where life was made one long agony. Toussaint characteristically announced the close of the massacres by a sermon to the surviving mulattoes of Le Cap on the Christian duty of pardoning one's enemies." Stoddard, *The French Revolution in San Domingo* (Westport, Conn., 1970; orig. pub., 1914), 280.

    United States aid to Toussaint, Rayford Logan argues, was largely dictated by international politics. In an undeclared war with France on the high seas, the U.S. government found Toussaint's separatist policies more agreeable to its interests than those of Rigaud. Logan, *The Diplomatic Relations of the United States with Haiti, 1776–1891* (Chapel Hill, N.C., 1941), 103.

7. Mats Lundahl, "Toussaint L'Ouverture and the War Economy of Saint Domingue, 1796–1802," in Hilary Beckles and Verene Shepherd, eds., *Caribbean Freedom: Economy and Society from Emancipation to the Present* (Kingston, Jamaica, 1993), 2–11.

8. Etienne Polverol, one of the French commissioners, had criticized the policy of forced labor in 1793 in a letter to Sonthonax: "Can you expect Africans to resume work by giving them liberty unless you first give them land, and by so doing create an incentive to labour which they did not possess before?" Quoted in Robert K. LaCerte, "The Evolution of Land and Labour in the Haitian Revolution, 1791–1820," in Beckles and Shepherd, eds., *Caribbean Freedom*, 43).

9. "Regulations Respecting Field Labor," October 12, 1800, quoted in George F. Tyson, ed., *Toussaint L'Ouverture* (New York, 1973), 52. For Toussaint's explanation of Sonthonax's expulsion see Toussaint to General Laveaux, May 22, 1798, in ibid., 46–49.

10. Quoted in Ralph Korngold, *Citizen Toussaint* (Boston, 1944), 200.

11. Quoted in Tyson, *Toussaint L'Ouverture*, 83; see also 56–64. When General Victoire-Emmanuel Leclerc instituted a French labor code in May 1802, he noted that Toussaint's plan was "a very good system. I wouldn't dare imagine any better system under the circumstances. I will, in fact, use it in its entirety." Quoted in Ros, *Night of Fire*, 128.

12. These descriptions of Toussaint's behavior are taken from the recollections of a French officer, Pamphile de LaCroix, in Tyson, *Toussaint L'Ouverture*, 81–85. See also Ros, *Night of Fire*, 142–50.

13. Tyson, introduction to *Toussaint L'Ouverture*, 13.

Alfred N. Hunt, *Haiti's Influence on Antebellum America: Slumbering Volcano in the Caribbean* (Baton Rouge, La., 1988), details these U.S. fears about Haiti. White southerners, alert to the contradictions in American professions of libertarian ideals and racial views, drew careful distinctions between black slavery and white freedom. Independence merely provided an opportunity to reinforce these prejudices. See Duncan Macleod, "Toward Caste," in Ira Berlin and Ronald Hoffman, eds., *Slavery and Freedom in the Age of the American Revolution* (Baltimore, 1983), 230–33; and Macleod, *Slavery, Race and the American Revolution* (Cambridge, 1974).

14. "Notes sur l'etat politique de Saint-Domingue," December 30, 1800, quoted in Stoddard, *French Revolution in San Domingo*, 291.

15. Fick, *Making of Haiti*, 206–9, 250.

16. Quoted in Winthrop Jordan, *White over Black: American Attitudes Toward the Negro, 1550–1812* (Chapel Hill, N.C., 1968), 381. A British official expressed similar sentiments to the British minister to the United States. "In looking at the present state of St. Domingo," he wrote, "the first of all Objects of Attention is the Security both of our West India Colonies, and of the Southern States of America, from the Effect which such circumstances may produce on the Slaves." Grenville to Liston, January 19, 1799, in Bernard Mayo, ed., *Instructions to the British Ministers to the United States, 1791–1812*, AHA *Annual Report, 1936* (Washington, D.C., 1941), 3:169–70. For the impact of the Haitian revolt on New York City blacks see Paul Gilje, *The Road to Mobocracy: Popular Disorder in New York City* (Chapel Hill, N.C., 1987), 147.

17. Albert Gallatin, *Annals of Congress* 10, 5th Cong. (Jan. 1799), quoted in Tyson, *Toussaint L'Ouverture*, 95–96. For Stevens's reports see "Letters of Toussaint Louverture and Edward Stevens, 1798–1800," *American Historical Review* 26 (Oct. 1910), 64–101, esp. 76–80, 93.

Secretary of State Timothy Pickering had expressed a different view to the U.S. minister to Great Britain, Rufus King, in March 1799: "We meddle not with the politics of the Island. T[oussain]t will pursue what he deems the interest of himself and his countrymen; he will probably declare the Island independent." Pickering to King, March 12, 1799, quoted in ibid., 104–5. A few months later, however, as Toussaint's wrangling with the British over the Maitland agreement heightened U.S. concerns, President John Adams chose a more prudent course: "Harmony with the English, in all this Business of St. Domingo is the thing I have most at heart. The Result of the whole is in my mind problematical and precarious." He added, "All the rest of the World knows as little what to do with him as he knows what to do with himself." Quoted in Tansill, *United States and Santo Domingo*, 69.

On U.S. fears of independence, the distinguished black historian Rayford Logan wrote: "It may be noted, in the beginning, that during the debates in Congress over the reopening of commerce with Saint Domingue no one apparently demanded recognition of the colony. On the other hand, even some Southern members envisaged without fear the establishment of independence." Logan, *The Diplomatic Relations of the United States with Haiti*, 78–79.

18. Ott, *Haitian Revolution*, 140–51. See also Carl Lokke, "Jefferson and the LeClerc Expedition," *American Historical Review* 33 (Jan. 1928): 322–23. The British, fearful of Toussaint's power, raised no obstacle to the French reconquest. Several of the French officers who had served with the British during the occupation of Saint Domingue departed with the retiring British forces to Jamaica. Elsewhere the Peace of Amiens provided for the restoration of all captured islands except Trinidad. British West

Indies planters approved, for they no longer had to compete with the produce of the conquered islands in home markets. Lowell Ragatz, *The Fall of the Planter Class in the British Caribbean, 1763–1833* (New York, 1963; orig. pub., 1928), 229.

19. Jefferson surmised that the "conquest of St. Domingo will not be short work. It will take considerable time to wear down a great number of soldiers." Quoted in Robert W. Tucker and David Hendrickson, *Empire of Liberty: The Statecraft of Thomas Jefferson* (New York, 1990), 128.

20. Quoted in Ott, *Haitian Revolution,* 153.

21. François Joseph Pamphile Lacroix, *Mémoires pour servir à l'historique de la révolution de Saint-Domingue* (2 vols., Paris, 1820), 2:153, as quoted in Ott, *The Haitian Revolution,* 154.

22. Lacroix, *Mémoires,* 2:164, as quoted in Ott, *Haitian Revolution,* 157; see also Ros, *Night of Fire,* 172.

23. C. L. R. James, *The Black Jacobins:* Toussaint L'Ouverture and the San Domingo Revolution (New York, 1968), 317; Toussaint, Aimé Césaire wrote in his adulatory biography, believed that time was his ally. "In time the enemy would acquire liabilities; in time the enemy would be unmasked, revealing his treacherous face to the people." Césaire, *Toussaint-Louverture: La Révolution française et le problème colonial* (Paris, 1960), 306. My translation.

24. Leclerc wrote to Bonaparte: "We have a false idea of the Negro. . . . We have in Europe a false idea of the country in which we have to fight and the men whom we fight against." Quoted in Eric Williams, *From Columbus to Castro: The History of the Caribbean, 1492–1969* (London, 1970), 271. On French casualties and desertions see the extract from a secret Spanish report in Eleazar Cordova-Bello, *La independencia de Haiti y su influencia en Hispanoamérica* (Caracas, 1967), 88–89.

25. Quoted in Cordova-Bello, *La independencia de Haiti* 90–91. See also Emilio Cordero Michel, *La evolución haitana y Santo Domingo* (Santo Domingo, D.R., 1974; orig. pub., 1968).

26. Gaston Martin, *Histoire de L'Esclavage dans les Colonies Françaises* (Paris, 1948), 246–47; Lyonel Paguin, *The Haitians: Class and Color Politics* (New York, 1983), 23.

27. Quoted in Jan Pachonski, *Poland's Caribbean Tragedy: A Study of Polish Legions in the Haitian War of Independence, 1802–1803* (Boulder, Colo., 1986), 68. Toussaint's removal offered no reassurance to the French, Leclerc wrote: "[For] here there are two thousand black leaders that must be removed" (quoted in Fick, *Making of Haiti,* 226). Equally somber assessments of the French military predicament appeared in Chef de l'Etat major [D'Henin], *Mémoire historique et politique sur la situation actuelle à la Colonie de St. Domingue* (July-Aug. 1803), copy in University of Florida Library.

28. James Stephen, *The Crisis of the Sugar Colonies; or, An Enquiry into the Objects and Probable Effects of the French Expedition to the West Indies . . .* (New York, 1969; orig. pub., 1802), 57; Robin Blackburn, *The Overthrow of Colonial Slavery 1776–1848* (London, 1988), 249.

29. Quoted in Pachonski, *Poland's Caribbean Tragedy,* 97.

30. Ibid., 112–13.

31. Lapoype to Rochambeau, July 17, 1803, in Rochambeau Papers, University of Florida.

32. Peter S. Chazotte, *Historical Sketches of the Revolution, and the Foreign and Civil War*

in the Island of St. Domingo, with a Narrative of the Entire Massacre of the White Population of the Island: Eyewitness Report (New York, 1840), 32–33, as quoted in Ott, *The Haitian Revolution,* 180–81.

33. Pachonski, *Poland's Caribbean Tragedy,* 225. For a spirited defense of the role of maroons in the achieving of independence, see Jean Fouchard, *Les marrons de la liberté* (Paris, 1972), 553–55.

34. Quoted in David Nicholls, *From Dessalines to Duvalier: Race, Colour, and National Independence in Haiti* (Cambridge, 1979), 37.

35. Frank Moya Pons, "Haiti and Santo Domingo," in Leslie Bethell, ed., *The Cambridge History of Latin America,* vol. 3, *From Independence to c. 1870* (New York, 1985), 247. See also Michel, *La revolución haitiana y Santo Domingo,* 78–79, 110–11.

36. Quoted in Nicholls, *From Dessalines to Duvalier,* 38.

37. Michel S. Laguerre, *The Military and Society in Haiti* (Knoxville, Tenn., 1993), 26–27; Hilary Beckles, "Divided to the Vein: The Problem of Race, Colour, and Class Conflict in Haitian Nation-Building, 1804–1820," in Beckles and Shepherd, eds., *Caribbean Freedom,* 494–503.

38. Cordovo-Bello, *La independencia de Haiti,* 258.

39. Charles MacKenzie, *Notes on Haiti Made During a Residence in That Republic* (2 vols., London, 1830), 2:145. See also Patrick Bellegarde-Smith, *Haiti: The Breached Citadel* (Boulder, Colo., 1990), 48–49; Bellegarde-Smith, *In the Shadow of Powers: Dantès Bellegarde in Haitian School Thought* (Atlantic Highlands, N.J., 1985), 14–15; William Harvey, *Sketches of Haiti: From the Expulsion of the French to the Death of Christophe* (London, 1971; orig. pub., 1827); and Brenda G. Plummer, *Haiti and the United States: The Psychological Moment* (Athens, Ga., 1992), 21.

40. For a survey of the successive land policies during and after the revolution see LaCerte, "Evolution of Land and Labour in the Haitian Revolution, 1791–1820."

41. Mark B. Bird, *The Black Man of Haytian Independence* (Freeport, N.Y., 1971; orig. pub., 1869), 94. The determination to resist any effort to reimpose slavery remained strong. With the restoration of the French monarchy in 1815, there occurred renewed calls for a reconquest of the island and the restoration of the slave economy. Pétion told the Haitians: "Your will is [to] be free and independent. . . . Haytions! Your security is in your arms!" Quoted in David Nicholls, "Haiti: Race, Slavery, and Independence," in Leonie Archer, ed., *Slavery and Other Forms of Unfree Labour* (2 vols., London, 1988), 1:229.

42. David Nicholls, *Haiti in Caribbean Context: Ethnicity, Economy, and Revolt* (New York, 1985), 94–95, 122.

43. Quoted in Nicholls, *From Dessalines to Duvalier,* 61. Boyer, a mulatto, tried to limit the shift to peasant agriculture with his rural code of 1826, which imposed severe controls on agricultural labor. The move was not successful, and plantation agriculture continued to decline. An unsympathetic visitor in that decade noted the low state of agriculture and the disappointing results of the free labor system. "On the estates of every individual connected with the government," he wrote, "all the labourers employed work under the superintendence of a military police, and it is on these properties alone that anything resembling successful agriculture exists in Hayti." James Franklin, *The Present State of Haiti* (London, 1971; orig. pub., 1828), 7–8.

44. Hunt, *Haiti's Influence on Antebellum America*, 3; see also Eugene Genovese, *From Rebellion to Revolution: African-American Slave Revolts in the Making of the New World* (New York, 1979), 46–49. On the economic condition of Haiti at the time of Boyer's assumption of power, see Frank Moya Pons, *La dominación haitana, 1822–1844*, 2nd ed. (Santiago de los Caballeros, D.R. 1972), 18–20.

45. Quoted in Bellegarde-Smith, *In the Shadow of Powers*, 8–9.

46. Quoted in Tansill, *United States and Santo Domingo*, 121.

47. Plummer, *Haiti and the United States*, 33.

48. Quoted in Bellegarde-Smith, *In the Shadow of Powers*, 9.

49. Quoted in Hilary Beckles, "Emancipation by War or Law?" in David Richardson, ed., *Abolition and Its Aftermath: The Historical Context, 1790–1816* (London, 1986), 98. See also Douglas Egerton, *Gabriel's Rebellion: The Virginia Slave Conspiracies of 1800* (Chapel Hill, N.C., 1993).

50. Quoted in David Brion Davis, *Revolutions: Reflecting on American Equality and Foreign Interventions* (Cambridge, Mass., 1990), 52–53.

51. David Geggus, "Haiti and the Abolitionists," in Richardson, ed., *Abolition and Its Aftermath*, 114–17, 122–25, 128–31; Geggus, "British Opinion and the Emergence of Haiti," in James Walvin, ed., *Slavery and British Society, 1776–1846* (Baton Rouge, La., 1982), 146–49.

52. Geggus, "Haiti and the Abolitionists," in Richardson, ed., *Abolition and Its Aftermath*, 132–33; Frank Moya Pons, "Haiti and Santo Domingo," in Bethell, ed., *Cambridge History of Latin America*, 3:250–51, 256–57. See also Pons, "The Land Question in Haiti and Santo Domingo: The Socio-Political Context of the Transition from Slavery to Free Labor, 1801–1843," in Moreno Fraginals, et al., eds., *Between Slavery and Free Labor*, 181–205.

53. Cedric J. Robinson, *Black Marxism: The Making of the Black Radical Tradition* (London, 1983), 324.

54. Quoted in Brenda Gayle Plummer, *Haiti and the Great Powers, 1902–1915* (Baton Rouge, La., 1988), 20.

55. Plummer, *Haiti and the United States*, 28–29.

56. Robert K. Lacerte, "Xenophobia and Economic Decline: The Haitian Case, 1820–1843," *Americas* 37 (April 1981): 500.

57. Plummer, *Haiti and the Great Powers*, 16–21; Plummer, *Haiti and the United States*, 24–27; Sidney Mintz, *Caribbean Transformations* (Chicago, 1974), 267–301.

58. Genovese, *From Rebellion to Revolution*, 89.

59. Quoted in Plummer, *Haiti and the United States*, 24.

7 Iberoamerica on the Eve of Revolution

1. Richard M. Morse, *New World Soundings: Culture and Ideology in the Americas* (Baltimore, 1989), 107.

2. Quoted in John Leddy Phelan, *The People and the King: The Comunero Revolution in Colombia, 1781*, as cited in John Lynch, ed., *Latin American Revolutions, 1808–1826: Old and New World Origins* (Norman, Okla., 1994), 42. For the impact of the expulsion of the Jesuits on Creole thinking, see Ricardo Donoso, "Bosquejo de una historia de la

independencia de América Española," in *El movimiento emancipador de Hispano-américa* (4 vols., Caracas, 1961), quoted in R. A. Humphreys and John Lynch, eds., *The Origins of the Latin American Revolutions, 1808–1826* (New York, 1965), 50.

3. Colin MacLachlan, *Spain's Empire in the New World: The Role of Ideas in Institutional and Social Change* (Berkeley, 1988), 90; see also Anthony Pagden, *The Uncertainties of Empire* (Aldershot, Hampshire, G.B., 1994), pt. xv: 2–3, 8–9; and Tulio Halperín-Donghi, *Historia de América Latina*, vol. 3: *Reforma y disolución de los imperios ibéricos* (Madrid, 1985), 51–52. On the reforms see Jean Sarrailh, *La España ilustrada de la segunda mitad del siglo xviii* (Mexico City, 1957); Richard Herr, *The Eighteenth Century Revolution in Spain* (Princeton, N.J., 1958); and John Fisher, *Government and Society in Colonial Peru: The Intendant System, 1789–1814* (London, 1970).

4. For assessments of the increased productivity in mining, see John Fisher, *Silver Mines and Silver Miners in Colonial Peru, 1776–1824* (London, 1977), 108–16; David Brading, *Haciendas and Ranchos in the Mexican Bajío: León, 1700–1860* (Cambridge, 1978), 174; for increases in commerce, see John Fisher, "Imperial 'Free Trade' and the Hispanic Economy, 1778–1796," *Journal of Latin American Studies* 11 (1981): 21–56; and Javier Cuenca Esteban, "Statistics of Spain's Colonial Trade, 1792–1820," *Hispanic American Historical Review* 61 (1981): 381–428; and for agricultural production, William Glade, *The Latin American Economies* (New York, 1969), 180–81.

5. John Lynch, *Spanish Colonial Administration, 1782–1810: The Intendant System in the Viceroyalty of the Rio de la Plata* (London, 1958), 287. See also ibid., 15, and Jacques Barbier and Herbert S. Klein, "Las prioridades de un monarca ilustrado: El gasto público bajo el reinado de Carlos III," *Revista de historia económica* 3 (1985): 473–95. On the unanticipated consequences of imperial reform, especially in their impact on administration, see H. García Chuecos, *Relatos y comentarios sobre temas de historia venezolana* (Caracas, 1957); Luis Navarro García, *Intendencias en Indias* (Seville, 1959); Bernard E. Bobb, *The Viceregency of Antonio Maria Bucareli in New Spain, 1771–1779* (Austin, 1962); and José Ots Capdequí, *Las instituciones del Nuevo Reino de Granada al tiempo de la independencia* (Madrid, 1958).

In part, suspicions about the Creoles stemmed not so much from beliefs that Creole officeholders were privileged and thus easily corrupted but from beliefs that their loyalty to the Crown was questionable. A mid-century report had reinforced this suspicion. Commenting on Peru, Jorge Juan and Antonio de Ulloa explained: "A situation arises peculiar to individuals who have not held other offices of this type away from their home areas. Once they find themselves elevated to a high post, they become vain and indiscreet. Their creole compatriots rally to their side." Juan and de Ulloa (John J. TePaske, ed.; TePaske and Bessie Clements, trans.), *Discourse and Political Reflections on the Kingdoms of Peru. Their Government, Special Regimen of Their Inhabitants, and Abuses Which Have Been Introduced into One and Another, with Special Information on Why They Grew Up and Some Means to Avoid Them* (Norman, Okla., 1978), 233–34.

Scholars now discount the older notion that the Creoles were systematically replaced with peninsulars in the bureaucracy from the beginning of Bourbon rule early in the eighteenth century. From the 1780s, however, as the economic condition of Spanish America noticeably improved, peninsulars began to supplant Creoles, arousing colonial complaints, "directed as much against the disruption of existing patterns of influence as against the principles involved." Stuart Schwartz, "State and Society," in Richard Graham and Peter Smith, eds., *New Approaches to Latin American History* (Austin, Tex., 1974), 34. See also Lynch, *Spanish Colonial Administration,* 20–21; Mark A. Burkholder and D. S. Chandler, *From Impotence to Authority: The*

Spanish Crown and the American Audiencias, 1687–1808 (Columbia, Mo., 1977), as cited in Lynch, ed., *Latin American Revolutions,* 56. On Creole-peninsular antagonism in Chile compare the views of Sergio Villalobos R., *Tradición y reforma en 1810* (Santiago, 1961), 100–104, who argues that Creole exclusion from office alienated the Creoles; and the assessment of another Chilean scholar, Jaime Eyzaguirre, *Idea y ruta de la emancipación* (Santiago, 1957), 52–58, who points out that the Spanish were responsive to Creole complaints, only to be met by heightened Chilean demands for patronage. Extracts from both books appear in Humphreys and Lynch, eds., *Origins of the Latin American Revolutions.*

6. The quotation of the Puebla priest is from Peggy Liss, *Atlantic Empires: The Network of Trade and Revolution, 1713–1826* (Baltimore, 1982) 91, but see also 85–95, 136–37; Alexander von Humboldt (Mary Dunn, ed.), *Political Essay on the Kingdom of New Spain* (New York, 1973; orig. pub., London, 1811), 73.

7. Juan and Ulloa, *Discourse on the Kingdom of Peru,* 243–44. See also Salvador de Madariaga, *The Rise of the Spanish American Empire* (New York, 1947), 128–29, 317–18.

8. John H. Coatsworth, "Patterns of Rural Rebellion," in Friedrich Katz, ed., *Riot, Rebellion, and Revolution: Rural Social Conflict in Mexico* (Princeton, N.J., 1988), 30. Coatsworth identifies six types of rebellion: slave insurrections, maroon wars, regional revolts, caste wars, Indian village uprisings, and plantation revolts. See also Anthony McFarlane, "Civil Disorders and Popular Protests in Late Colonial New Granada," *Hispanic American Historical Review* 64 (1984): 22–27; and McFarlane, "The Rebellion of the Barrios: Urban Insurrection in Bourbon Quito," in ibid. 69 (1989): 328–30. A classic study in this genre is William Taylor, *Drinking, Homicide, and Rebellion in Colonial Mexican Villages* (Stanford, 1979). For rebellion in the Andes, see the suggestive essays in Steve J. Stern, ed., *Resistance, Rebellion and Consciousness in the Andean Peasant World, 18th to 20th Centuries* (Madison, Wis., 1987), several of which offer provocative interpretations of Andean peasants' concepts of "space-time" and nation.

The role of economic, as opposed to racial or ethnic, factors in measuring elite status or social mobility in the eighteenth century has certainly been undervalued. See Robert McCaa, "Modeling Social Interaction: Marriage, Miscegenation and the Society of Castes in Colonial Spanish America," *Historical Methods* 15:2 (1982): 45–66. I nonetheless share James Lockhart's apprehension that "social science can bring in rigid concepts from a different historical context which . . . impede a fresh view of historical reality." *Latin American Research Review* 7:1 (1972): 33. See also Magnus Mörner, "Economic Factors and Stratification in Colonial Spanish America with Special Regard to Elites," *Hispanic American Historical Review* 63 (May 1983): 335–69.

9. Ramón Ruíz, *Triumph and Tragedy: A History of the Mexican People* (New York, 1992), 130–31.

10. Doris Ladd, *The Mexican Nobility at Independence, 1780–1826* (Austin, Tex., 1976), 118; see also Leon Campbell, "The Army of Peru and the Túpac Amaru Army," *Hispanic American Historical Review* 56 (1975): 31–57; Campbell, "The Social Composition of the Túpac Amaru Army," ibid., 61 (1981): 675–94; and Campbell, "Recent Research on Andean Peasant Revolts," *Latin American Research Review* 14 (1979): 3–49.

11. Scarlett O'Phelan Godoy, "El mito de la 'independencia concedida': Los programas políticos del siglo xviii y del temprano xix en el Perú y Alto Perú, 1730–1814," *Independencia y revolución* (2 vols., Lima, 1987), 2:157; MacLachlan, *Spain's Empire*

in the New World, 100–101. In the rebellion Indian behavior contrasted sharply with the stories of "submissive, patient, and docile individuals" from earlier times. Oscar Cornblit, "Levantamientos de masas en Perú y Bolivia durante el siglo xviii," in Cornblit, comp., *Túpac Amaru II,* 138; see also 166–67; Leon G. Campbell, "Ideology and Factionalism During the Great Rebellion, 1780–1782," in Stern, ed., *Resistance, Rebellion and Consciousness,* 133; Alberto Flores Galindo, "In Search of an Inca," in ibid., 202–4; and Galindo, *Buscando un Inca: Identidad y utopia en los Andes* (Lima, 1987).

12. On Brazilian defiance see Luis Henrique Dias Tavares, *História da sedicão intendada na Bahia em 1798: A "conspiracão do alfaites,"* (São Paulo, 1975); and Kenneth R. Maxwell, *Conflicts and Conspiracies: Brazil and Portugal, 1750–1808* (Cambridge, 1973).

13. Nils Jacobsen and Hans-Jürgen Puhle, eds., *The Economies of Mexico and Peru in the Late Colonial Period* (Berlin, 1986); Carlos Sempat Assadourian, *El sistema de la economía colonial* (Lima, 1982); D. A. Brading, *Miners and Merchants in Bourbon Mexico, 1763–1810* (Cambridge, 1978); and Lyman Johnson and Enrique Tandeter, eds., *Essays on the Price History of Eighteenth-Century Latin America* (Albuquerque, N.M., 1990).

14. Quoted in Jaime Eyzaguirre, *Ideario y ruta de la emancipación chilena* (Santiago, 1957), 61.

15. The intent of metropolitan efforts to gain control over the colonial economy, observe Stanley and Barbara J. Stein in a seminal essay, was to strengthen Spain's efforts to resist further embroilment in the Anglo-French struggle. Spanish metropolitan social elites had benefited from the income provided by Spanish America, but Spain yet lagged behind Great Britain in industrial development and remained dependent. Further exploitation of the colonies preserved the privileges of the traditional Spanish social order—something the French aristocracy understood—and explains why the Spanish looked to French administrative models for guidance. Stein and Stein, *The Colonial Heritage of Latin America: Essays on Economic Dependence in Perspective* (New York, 1970), 101–2. See also José Cuello, "The Economic Impact of the Bourbon Reforms and the Late Colonial Crisis of Empire at the Local Level: The Case of Saltillo, 1777–1817," *Americas* 44 (Jan. 1988): 301–24.

16. Indalecio Liévano Aguirre, *Los grandes conflictos sociales y económicos,* 5th ed. (2 vols., Bogotá, 1963), 2:525. In Valparaiso in 1802, William Shaler and Richard Cleveland listened to Creoles' indignant outbursts against Spanish economic machinations. See Simon Collier, *Ideas and Politics of Chilean Independence, 1808–1833* (Cambridge, 1967), 38–39.

17. Quoted in John Lynch, *Spanish American Revolutions, 1808–1826* (New York, 1973), 1. On colonial identity in Portuguese and Spanish America see Stuart Schwartz, "The Formation of Identity in Brazil," and Anthony Pagden, "Identity Formation in Spanish America," in Nicolas Canny and Anthony Pagden, eds., *Colonial Identity in the Atlantic World* (Princeton, N.J., 1987), 15–94.

18. Confronted with the social threat, Venezuelan whites insisted all the more on maintaining the color line. See Federico Brito Figueroa, *Estructura social y demográfica de Venezuela colonial* (Caracas, 1961), 77.

19. Quoted in Juan Marchena Fernández, "The Social World of the Military in Peru and New Granada," in John Fisher, Allan J. Kuethe, and Anthony McFarlane, eds., *Reform and Insurrection in Bourbon New Granada and Peru* (Baton Rouge, La., 1990), 58.

20. Sergio Villalobos R., Osvaldo Silva G., Fernando Silva V., and Patricio Estelle M., *Historia de Chile* (Santiago, 1974), 274; for a contemporaneous Chilean view see Manuel de Salas's statement before the minister of the exchequer (January 10, 1796), in Lynch, ed., *Latin American Revolutions,* 143–49, who summed up a widespread Creole sentiment when he wrote, "The kingdom of Chile is without doubt the most fertile in America and the most propitious for human happiness; yet in fact it is the most wretched of all the Spanish dominions. With scope for everything, it lacks the essentials, and imports products that it could easily export to others" (ibid., 144).

Lucas Alamán, the nineteenth-century Mexican historian and social conservative, expressed Creole animosities in *Historia de México desde los primeros movimientos que prepararon su Independencia en el año de 1808 hasta la época presente* (5 vols., Mexico City, 1985; orig. pub., 1850), 1, 13–14.

21. One of the Jesuit exiles, Juan Pablo Viscardo, in the 1798 pamphlet *Letter to the American-born Spaniards* reminded the alienated Creoles that their ancestors had gone to the New World "at their own cost, to gain themselves a new living and faced immense weariness and very great dangers. . . . The great success . . . gave them . . . a right which, even though it were not entirely justified, . . . to enjoy the fruits of their valour and their labours." Quoted in Mario Góngora (Richard Southern, trans.), *Studies in the Colonial History of Spanish America* (Cambridge, 1975), 31. See also the comments of Anthony Pagden in *Spanish Imperialism and the Political Imagination: Studies in European and Spanish-American Social and Political Theory, 1513–1830* (New Haven, 1990), 128–29.

22. Quoted in Kenneth Maxwell, *Pombal: Paradox of the Enlightenment* (Cambridge, 1995), 118. For a somewhat contrary view of the effect of the Pombaline reforms, see Claudio Véliz, *The Centralist Tradition in Latin America* (Princeton, N.J., 1980), 112–13.

23. In the conquest, virtually every Spanish immigrant could obtain land, so land ownership did not carry the same weight in denoting social status as in Spain. Since Indians were not landowners, race came to play a more important role as indicator of social status. I am grateful to my colleague Thomas Whigham for this observation.

24. Quoted in Lynch, *Spanish American Revolutions,* 22. The defensiveness of the Venezuelan white minority about racial mobility and the violent behavior of the castas were not atypical. "In every colony where whites were a clear minority, a similar siege mentality was exhibited; and in all colonies . . . endemic poverty and repression led to social and criminal banditry." D. McKinley Cantor, *Pre-revolutionary Caracas: Politics, Economy, and Society, 1777–1811* (Cambridge, 1985), 16. For a discussion of Iberoamerican kinship systems, see Diana Balmori, Stuart Voss, and Miles Wortman, *Notable Family Networks in Latin America* (Chicago, 1984), 30–33.

25. John Mawe, *Travels in the Interior of Brazil . . . Including a Voyage to the Rio de la Plata* (Philadelphia, 1816), 47–48.

26. Emilio Willems, "Social Differentiation in Colonial Brazil," *Comparative Studies in Society and History* 12 (1970): 31–49; Stuart Schwartz, "Elite Politics and the Growth of a Peasantry in Late Colonial Brazil," in A. J. R. Russell-Wood, *From Colony to Nation: Essays on the Independence of Brazil* (Baltimore, 1975), 138–39, 145–46. See also C. R. Boxer, *The Portuguese Seaborne Empire, 1415–1825* (New York, 1969), 119, who notes that "tension between [Brazilian-born and European-born] . . . should not be exaggerated. . . . There was much intermarriage between them, and many [European-born] . . . participated in the abortive plots and revolts which preceded the attainment of Brazilian independence."

27. Tulio Halperín-Donghi, *Historia contemporánea de América Latina*, 10th ed. (Mexico City, 1983), 40. "The steady progress in racial mixing," he writes, "had begun to undermine one of the basic principles of the social order, and increasingly complex caste lines were constructed by the colonial upper classes to maintain a hierarchy that was in danger of collapsing in confusion. The more complex caste system reinforced social distinctions no longer marked by economic differences, preventing the social ascent of urban lower-caste individuals through the army, the church, or the government and otherwise neutralizing the social consequences of wealth acquired by people of mixed blood." Halperín-Donghi (John Chasteen, trans.), *The Contemporary History of Latin America* (Durham, N.C., 1993), 19–20.

28. Manuel Abad y Queipo, "Estado moral y política en que se hallaba la población del virrenato de Nueva España en 1799," quoted in Lynch, *Spanish American Revolutions*, 23. See also Magnus Mörner, *Race Mixture in the History of Latin America* (Boston, 1967), 101–2; and George Reid Andrews, *The Afro-Argentines of Buenos Aires, 1800–1900* (Madison, Wis., 1980), 36–38.

29. Theda Skocpol, *States and Social Revolutions: A Comparative Analysis of France, Russia, and China* (Cambridge, 1979), 51; Jorge Domínguez, *Insurrection or Loyalty: The Breakdown of the Spanish American Empire* (Cambridge, Mass., 1980), 244–45, 254–55; Halperín-Donghi, *Historia contemporánea de América Latina*, 74. For a dissenting view of the success of Bourbon reforms, see Timothy Anna, *Spain and the Loss of America* (Lincoln, Neb., 1983), 12–13.

30. R. A. Humphreys and John Lynch, "The Emancipation of Latin America," in Instituto Panamericano de Geografía e Historia, *La emancipación latinoamericana: Estudios* (Mexico City, 1966), 10. See also John Lynch, "Intendants and Cabildos in the Viceroyalty of the Rio de la Plata, 1782–1810," *Hispanic American Historical Review* 35 (1955): 337–62; and Lyle N. McAlister, *The "Fuero Militar" in New Spain, 1764–1800* (Gainesville, Fla., 1957). McAlister's conclusion that the *fuero militar* in New Spain noticeably weakened civilian authority because it reinforced the military's corporate identity has inspired other scholars to investigate Bourbon military reforms in other regions of Spanish America. See Leon Campbell, *The Military and Society in Colonial Peru, 1750–1810* (Philadelphia, 1978), 238; and Allan J. Kuethe, *Military Reform and Society in New Granada, 1773–1808* (Gainesville, Fla., 1977). Even in New Spain, McAlister's assessment has been modified by the findings of Christon Archer in "To Save the King: Military Recruitment in Late Colonial Mexico," *Hispanic American Historical Review* 55 (1975): 226–50; and Archer, *The Army in Bourbon Mexico, 1760–1810* (Albuquerque, N.M., 1977).

31. "Representación que hizo la ciudad de México al rey D. Carlos III en 1771 sobre que los criollos deben ser preferidos á los europeos en la distribución y beneficios de estos reinos." Lynch, trans., *Latin American Revolutions*, 59.

32. Juan and Ulloa, *Discourse and Political Reflections on the Kingdoms of Peru*, 217, 218, 219.

33. Liss, *Atlantic Empires*, 68–74. The quotation is on page 74. For yet another assessment of the reforms and their consequences, see Colin MacLachlan, *Spain's Empire in the New World*, esp. 86–88. Charles III expelled the Jesuits, whom Juan and Ulloa thought praiseworthy (save for their accumulated wealth). In contrast, their portrait of a scandalous and licentious secular and regular clergy was devastating. Juan and Ulloa, *Discourse and Political Reflections on the Kingdoms of Peru*, 280–83, 314–15. Some orders, such as the Jesuits, favored segregation of Indians; others (among them the Franciscans) did not. On the yet disputed issue of whether or not Spanish

dominions in the New World were "colonies" or "kingdoms," see Magnus Mörner, *Region and State in Latin America's Past* (Baltimore, 1993), 5.

34. MacLachlan, *Spain's Empire in America,* 125–27. In the Mexican Bajío commerce and mining benefited merchants and mine owners but brought severe pressures on landowners. Brading, *Haciendas and Ranchos in the Mexican Bajío,* 115–18. For the Guadalajara region, see Eric Van Young, *Hacienda and Market in Eighteenth-Century Mexico: The Rural Economy of the Guadalajara Region, 1675–1820* (Berkeley, 1981), 139–68. *Contradiction* applied to the Mexican economy in the late eighteenth century, writes Van Young. "A considerable degree of economic expansion and prosperity was present, but also an increasing amount of rural proletarianization and impoverishment." Van Young, "The Age of Paradox: Mexican Agriculture at the End of the Colonial Period," in Nils Jacobsen and Hans-Juergen Puhle, eds., "The Economies of Mexico and Peru During the Late Colonial Period, 1760–1810," in Lynch, ed., *Latin American Revolutions,* 113. Except for those cases where they had access to European markets, as in Cuba and Venezuela, landowners received little benefit from Bourbon reforms. Eduardo Arcila Farías, *Economía colonial de Venezuela* (Mexico City, 1946), 379–80; Carlos Muñoz Oraá, *La sociedad venezolana frente a la intendencia* (Caracas, 1964), 24–25.

35. Both quotations are in Liss, *Atlantic Empires,* 143. See also Dauril Alden, *Royal Government in Colonial Brazil, with Special Reference to the Administration of the Marquis of Lavradio, Viceroy, 1769–1779* (Berkeley, 1968).

36. Véliz, *Centralist Tradition of Latin America,* 128.

37. John Fisher, "Commercial Relations Between Spain and Spanish America in the Era of Free Trade, 1778–1796," in Lynch, ed., *Latin American Revolutions,* 119.

38. Ibid., 126. See also Sergio Villalobos R., "El comercio extranjero a fines de la dominación española, *Journal of Inter-American Studies* 4 (1962): 517–44; Troy S. Floyd, "The Guatemalan Merchants, the Government, and the *Provincianos,* 1750–1800," *Hispanic American Historical Review* 41 (1961): 90–110; Arthur P. Whitaker, "Causes of Spanish American Wars of Independence: Economic Factors," *Journal of Inter-American Studies* 2 (1960): 132–39; and Pedro Santos Martínez, *Historia económica de Mendoza durante el virreinato, 1776–1810* (Madrid, 1961). For marxist interpretations see H. Ramírez Necochea, *Antecedentes económicos de la independencia de Chile* (Santiago, 1959); and Caio Prado Júnior, *Evolución política do Brasil e outros estudos,* 2nd ed. (São Paulo, 1957).

39. Robert Tucker and David Hendrickson, *The Fall of the British Empire* (Baltimore, 1982), 196–209; Bernard Bailyn, *Voyagers to the West: A Passage in the Peopling of America on the Eve of the Revolution* (New York, 1986), 29–30.
    What liberal Creoles saw in British America before the American Revolution was the benefits of seasoning and experience of those who ultimately led the separatist cause. Simón Bolívar lamented: "We were left in a state of permanent childhood." Quoted in R. A. Humphreys, "The Fall of the Spanish American Empire," in Humphreys and Lynch, eds., *Origins of Latin American Independence,* 139. See also Alfonso Armas Ayala, *Influencia del pensamiento venezolano en la revolución Hispanoamérica* (Caracas, 1970). In any event, they couched their political grievances not in the eighteenth-century Enlightenment thinkers nor the pamphleteers of the American Revolution, argues Carlos Stoetzer, but in the late Spanish Scholastic thought of Francisco Suárez, Luis de Molina, and Juan de Mariana. Stoetzer, *The Scholastic Roots of the Spanish American Revolution* (New York, 1979), 259. See also Tulio Halperín-Donghi, *Tradición política española e ideologia revolucarionaria de*

Mayo (Buenos Aires, 1961); Anthony McFarlane, "The Rebellion of the Barrios," in Fisher, Kuethe, and McFarlane, eds., *Reform and Insurrection in Bourbon New Granada and Peru*, 216–17; and John Leddy Phelan, *The People and the King: The Comunero Revolution in Colombia, 1781* (Madison, Wis., 1978), 79–88.

40. For an account of changing historiographical views on the impact of the Enlightenment on the independence movement in Latin America, see Charles C. Griffin, "The Enlightenment and Latin American Independence," in Arthur P. Whitaker, ed., *Latin America and the Enlightenment*, 2nd ed., (Ithaca, N.Y., 1961), 119–41. See also Jacques Barbier and Allan Kuethe, eds., *The North American Role in the Spanish Imperial Economy, 1760–1819* (Manchester, G.B., 1984); José Carlos Chiaramonte, ed., *Pensamiento de la Illustración: Economía y sociedad iberoamericanas en el siglo XVIII (Caracas,* 1979); and, especially, Liss, *Atlantic Empires.*

41. Quoted in D. A. Brading, *The First America: The Spanish Monarchy, Creole Patriots and the Liberal State, 1492–1866* (Cambridge, 1991), 597. For an account of Pradt's influence see Manuel Aguirre Elorriaga, *El abate de Pradt [Dominique Georges Frederic] en la emancipación hispanoamericana (1800–1830)* (Buenos Aires, 1946).

42. Quoted in Salvador de Madariaga, *The Fall of the Spanish American Empire* (London, 1947), 298–99. The Count of Aranda, reflecting on the difficulties confronting Charles III in governing his New World kingdoms in the aftermath of the American Revolution, advised the Spanish king to divide Spanish America into three kingdoms. Otherwise, Charles III would "never be able to conserve such vast possessions so far from Spain." Quoted in José Gabriel Navarro, *La revolución de agosto de 1809* (Quito, 1962), 5. Spain was a nation but it "did not become a nation-state during the colonial period." Margaret Crahan, "Spanish and American Counterpart," in Graham and Smith, eds., *New Approaches to Latin American History,* 67.

43. Quoted in Pagden, *Spanish Imperialism and the Political Imagination,* 8. See also Stanley Stein and Barbara Stein, *The Colonial Heritage of Latin America: Essays on Economic Dependence in Perspective* (New York, 1970), 20; Crahan, "Spanish and American Counterpart," in Graham and Smith, eds., *New Approaches to Latin American History,* 63; Sergio Villalobos R., *Tradición y reforma en 1810* (Santiago, 1961), 89–100; and Hernán Ramírez Necochea, *Antecedentes económicos de la independencia de Chile* (Santiago, 1959). Caio Prado Júnior applies a marxist analysis in concluding that Brazil's independence movement drew its strength from economic forces in *Evolucão política do Brasil e outros estudos* (São Paulo, 1957), 35–54.

44. The standard account is Lillian E. Fisher, *The Last Inca Revolt, 1780–1783* (Norman, Okla., 1966), but see also Scarlett O'Phelan Godoy, *Rebellioins and Revolts in Eighteenth Century Peru and Upper Peru* (Cologne, 1985); and Steve Stern, ed., *Resistance, Rebellion, and Consciousness in the Andean Peasant World, 18th to 20th Centuries* (Madison, Wis., 1987). The role of women in the Túpac Amaru rebellion, often overlooked or slighted in general accounts, provides further evidence of the nature of late colonial indigenous protest movements. Participation by women in this case was a familial undertaking, for the most part, but the movement included women members of the "native political hierarchy . . . backed by a large cadre of peasant women who exercised more traditional responsibilities." Leon G. Campbell, "Women and the Great Rebellion in Peru, 1780–1783," *The Americas* 42 (Oct. 1985), 190.

45. George Reid Andrews, "Spanish American Independence: A Structural Analysis," *Latin American Perspectives* 12 (Winter 1985): 117. See also Alberto Flores Galindo,

ed., *TúpacAmaru II, 1789: Sociedad colonial y sublevaciones populares* (Lima, 1976); Elizabeth Perry Pitzer, "The Moral Economy of the Andean World: A Comparison of the Cultural Context of the Taki Onqoy Rebellion with Resistance and Rebellion in the Eighteenth Century," *Southeastern Latin Americanist* 37 (Fall 1993): 22–36; Oscar Cornblit, "Society and Mass Rebellion in Eighteenth-Century Peru and Bolivia," in Raymond Carr, ed., *Latin American Affairs*, No. 22 (London, 1970); Jürgen Golte, *Repartos y rebeliones: TúpacAmaru y las contradicciones de la economía* (Lima, 1980), 116–17, 171–72, 192–93; Van Young, *Hacienda and Market in Eighteenth-Century Mexico*, 352; and Josep Fontana, "La crisis colonial en la crisis del antiguo regimen español," in Alberto Flores Galindo, ed., *Independencia y revolución, 1780–1840* (2 vols., Lima, 1987), 1:35.

46. Rafael Altimira, *Resumen histórico de la independencia de la América Española* (Buenos Aires, 1910), 18. On the sense of Creole national identity, the *conciencia de sí*, see Jorge Basadre, *La promesa de la vida peruana y otros ensayos* (Lima, 1958), 95–110. On the denigration of Spain in the literature of the independence movement, see Philip W. Powell, *Tree of Hate: Propaganda and Prejudices Affecting United States Relations with the Hispanic World* (New York, 1971), 114–15.

8 The Feared Revolution

1. John Lynch, *The Spanish American Revolutions, 1808–1826* (New York, 1973), 1. Jaime Rodríguez, *La independencia de la América Española* (Mexico City, 1996), assesses the revolutions in the context of Spanish politics. More succinct accounts are Jay Kinsbruner, *Independence in Spanish America: Civil Wars, Revolutions, and Underdevelopment*, 2nd ed., (Albuquerque, N.M., 1994); and the suggestive comparative assessment, Richard Graham, *Independence in Latin America: A Comparative Approach*, 2nd ed. (New York, 1994). *Latin American* is here used because in 1822 Brazil, which is part not of Spanish but of Latin America, achieved a bloodless independence.

2. Michael P. Costeloe, *Response to Revolution: Imperial Spain and the Spanish American Revolutions, 1810–1840* (Cambridge, 1986), 4–7. "Spain's position rested on a single, consistent policy; recognition of independence would not be granted" (ibid., 6). See also Timothy Anna, *Spain and the Loss of America* (Lincoln, Neb., 1983); Enrique de Gandía, *Napoleón y la independencia de América* (Buenos Aires, 1955); and William Spence Robertson, *France and Latin American Independence* (Baltimore, 1939).

3. O. Carlos Stoetzer, *The Scholastic Roots of the Spanish American Revolution* (New York, 1979), 156–57; Richard Morse, *New World Soundings: Culture and Ideology in the Americas* (Baltimore, 1989), 108–9. For an assessment of the Spanish crisis of 1808–1810 as the *determining* factor in the onset of radical views in Spanish America see P. Michael McKinley, *Pre-revolutionary Caracas: Politics, Economy and Society* (Cambridge, 1985), 146–47.

4. Quoted in Peggy Liss, "Creoles, the North American Example," in Jacques A. Barbier and Allan J. Kuethe, eds., *The North American Role in the Spanish Imperial Economy, 1760–1819* (Manchester, G.B., 1984), 19. See also McKinley, *Pre-revolutionary Caracas*, 135–36. This appears self-serving and opportunistic, but it demonstrated that Miranda grasped the psychological impact of Spanish reforms on the Creoles and the urgency that drove radical Creoles to believe in the "possibilities of insinuating their activities into the political development of society." What they wanted was limited, writes the Mexican historian Luís Villoro, "but if successful . . . , they would be able to transform the social order from a rigid, bureaucratically dominated structure into something they could change." Villoro, *La revolución de independencia*

(Mexico City, 1953), 36. See also Brian R. Hamnett, "The Economic and Social Dimension of Revolution in Mexico," *Ibero-Amerikanisches Archiv* (1980): 1–27.

Venezuelan conspirators of 1797 called for "the greatest harmony between whites, Indians, mestizos, and mulattoes, who should look upon each other as brothers in Christ equal under God, [and] who should attempt to be different only through merit and virtue" (quoted in Stoetzer, *Scholastic Roots of the Spanish American Revolution*, 145). The ideal of most Spanish-American revolutionaries, writes David Robinson, was the classic republican model that antedated eighteenth-century variations. See Robinson, "Liberty, Fragile Fraternity, and Equality: Assessing the Impact of French Revolutionary Ideals on Early Republican Spanish America," *Journal of Historical Geography* 16 (1990): 51–75.

5. Anthony Pagden, "Fabricating Identity in Spanish America," in *History Today* 42 (May 1992): 48–49. For a denunciation of Spanish duplicity, see Servando Teresa de Mier (Manuel Calvillo, comp.), *Cartas de un americano, 1811–1812* (Mexico City, 1987), 90–91.

6. Juan Uslar Pietri, *Historia de la rebelión popular de 1814* (Caracas, 1962), 16. Michael McKinley (*Pre-revolutionary Caracas*, 1–2) takes issue with the portrayal of a plantation economy profoundly damaged by metropolitan economic policy, arguing that prerevolutionary Venezuela was stable and prosperous and enjoyed a harmonious relationship with Spain. Although persuasive in its details, his analysis of prewar conditions cannot explain the racial and social violence in the colony after 1810.

7. Quoted in Lynch, *Spanish American Revolutions*, 192. On prerevolutionary Venezuela see Federico Brito Figuerora, *Historia económica y social de Venezuela* (2 vols., Caracas, 1966); Figuerora, *La estructura económica de Venezuela colonial* (Caracas, 1963); and Alexander von Humboldt, *Viaje a las regiones equinocciales del Nuevo Continente* (5 vols., Caracas, 1956), esp. vol. 2.

8. Coro's Creoles were ambitious and modern in their political and economic thinking, but memories of the uprising of black freedmen and slaves shook their anti-Spanish sensibilities. Jorge Domínguez, *Insurrection or Loyalty: The Breakdown of the Spanish American Empire* (Cambridge, Mass., 1980), 158–59. See also McKinley, *Pre-revolutionary Caracas*, 118–19, 124–25.

9. Miranda composed a declaration exhorting his countrymen to rise against "the oppressive unfeeling government which has obscured our finer qualities . . . but was never able to eradicate from our hearts those moral and civil virtues which a holy religion, and a regular code of laws, incorporated with our customs, and led to an honest and natural course of action." Quoted in John Sherman, *A General Account of Miranda's Expedition Including the Trial and Execution of Ten of His Officers* . . . (New York, 1808), 35–36. Some of the Americans, apparently, were persuaded that the U.S. government had sanctioned the expedition.

10. Quoted in McKinley, *Pre-revolutionary Caracas*, 145. "Without doubt," writes Tulio Halperín-Donghi, the "significance [of the pre-1810 outbursts and uprisings] has been magnified, first by the imperial officials eager to take credit for repressing them and later by historians seeking precursors of national independence movements." Halperín-Donghi (John Chasteen, trans.), *The Contemporary History of Latin America* (Durham, N.C., 1993), 44.

11. Henry A. Brackenridge, *Voyage to South America . . . in 1817 and 1818* (2 vols., Baltimore, 1819), 2:220. See Robert A. Humphreys, *Liberation in South America*,

1806–1807: The Career of James Paroissien (London, 1952), 1–15; Jorge Abelardo Ramos, *Revolución y contrarevolución en la Argentina* (Buenos Aires, 1957); and Tulio Halperín-Donghi, *Historia Argentina: De la revolución de la independencia a la confederación rosista* (Buenos Aires, 1989).

12. Mark Szuchman, "From Imperial Hinterland to Growth Pole: Revolution, Change, and Restoration in the Rio de la Plata," in Szuchman and Jonathan Brown, eds., *Revolution and Restoration: The Rearrangement of Power in Argentina, 1776–1860* (Lincoln, Neb., 1994), 14–16.

13. For "The Making of an Insurgent," see Manuel Belgrano, *Autobiografía*, 2:953–68, as translated by John Lynch in Lynch, ed., *Latin American Revolutions, 1808–1826; Old and New World Origins* (Norman, Okla., 1994), 258–62.

14. Quoted in William Spence Robertson, *Rise of the Spanish American Republics as Told in the Lives of Their Liberators* (New York, 1918), 157.

15. Quoted in George Reid Andrews, *The Afro-Argentines of Buenos Aires, 1800–1900* (Madison, Wis., 1980), 48.

16. Quoted in Halperín-Donghi, *Historia Argentina*, 58.

17. Tulio Halperín-Donghi, *Historia Contemporánea de América Latina*, 10th ed. (Mexico City, 1983), 126.

18. Tulio Halperín-Donghi, *Politics, Economics, and Society in Argentina in the Revolutionary Period* (Cambridge, 1975), 192–95, 197, 241–43.

19. Ibid., 206.

20. Washington Reyes Abadie, *Artigas y el federalismo en el Río de la Plata, 1811–1820* (Montevideo, 1990).

21. A Scots businessman, John Parish Robinson, explained his revolutionary style in J. P. and W. P. Robertson, *Letters on Paraguay* (2 vols., London, 1838), 1:336–37. See also Halperín-Donghi, *Politics, Economics, and Society in Argentina*, 208–11.

22. Robert K. Lowry to Secretary of State Robert Smith, November 30, 1810, in William Ray Manning, ed., *Diplomatic Correspondence of the United States Concerning the Independence of the Latin American Nations* (3 vols., New York, 1925), 2:1147.

23. Halperín-Donghi, *Historia contemporánea de América Latina*, 136–37; see also McKinley, *Pre-revolutionary Caracas*, 163.

24. Manifesto to the Nations of the World, Simón Bolívar, *Obras Completas*, ed. Vicente Lecuna and Esther Barret de Nazaris (3 vols., Havana, 1950), 3:574. See also Caracciolo Parra Pérez, *Historia de la Primera República de Venezuela* (2 vols., Caracas, 1959).

25. Uslar Pietri, *Historia de la rebelión popular de 1814*, 8–9.

26. Alexander Scott to Secretary of State James Monroe, November 16, 1812, in Manning, ed., *Diplomatic Correspondence of the United States Concerning the Independence of the Latin American Nations*, 2:1160. For unflattering commentary on Bolívar's participation in Miranda's arrest see the account by his chief of staff, Gen. H. L. V. Ducoudray-Holstein, *Memoirs of Simón Bolívar . . .* (Boston, 1829), 28–31. Miranda died in a Spanish prison.

27. "Memorial to the Citizens of New Granada by a Citizen of Caracas," December 15, 1812, in Bolívar (Vicente LeCuna, comp. Lewis Bertrand, trans. Harold Bierck, ed.),

Selected Writings of Bolívar (2 vols., New York, 1952), 1:18. The "Memorial" was printed in pamphlet form in the following year.

28. Lorenzo de Zavala, *Ensayo histórico desde 1808 hasta 1830* (2 vols. in one, Mexico City, 1985; orig. pub., 1845), 1:31. Hugh Hamill, *The Hidalgo Revolt: Prelude to Mexican Independence* (Westport, Conn., 1981; orig. pub., 1966), 44–45, points out that "indio" on the eve of the revolution was not an ethnological but a social designation— a downtrodden, underprivileged, and impoverished person.

29. Lyle McAlister, "Social Structure and Social Change in New Spain," *Hispanic American Historical Review* 43 (May 1963): 364.

30. D. A. Brading, "Government and Elite in Late Colonial Mexico," *Hispanic American Historical Review* 53 (Aug. 1973): 397; see also 392–93. For a parallel study in social psychology see Domingue O. Mannoni's study of twentieth-century Madagascar, *Prospero and Caliban: The Psychology of Colonization*, 2nd ed. (New York, 1964). See also William B. Taylor, *Landlord and Peasant in Colonial Oaxaca* (Stanford, 1972), 141–42, 251; and Brian R. Hamnett, "The Economic and Social Dimension of the Revolution of Independence in Mexico, 1800–1824," *Ibero-Amerikanisches Archiv* 6 (1980): 1–27.

Spanish merchants had greater advantages in dealing with the Spanish bureaucracy, wrote Ramón Flores Caballero, but the Creoles dominated mining, agriculture, and cattle-raising and were richer. Spaniard and Creole rarely divided over economic issues, though it was evident the former depended on the metropolis, the latter, the colony. See Flores Caballero (Jaime Rodríguez, trans.), *Counterrevolution: The Role of the Spaniards in the Independence of Mexico, 1804–1838* (Lincoln, Neb., 1974; orig. pub., Mexico City, 1969), 8–9, 18–19.

31. Enrique Florescano, "Antecedents of the Mexican Independence Movement: Social Instability and Political Discord," in Robert Detweiler and Ramón Ruíz, eds., *Liberation in the Americas: Comparative Aspects of the Independence Movements in Mexico and the United States* (San Diego, 1978), 71, notes: "In any society, even the most equitable in the distributions of the dividends of the social production, the process of accelerated development produces imbalances or alterations of a greater or lesser degree."

In the late eighteenth century, the Crown began to address some of the more debilitating social inequities. The corporatist social structure, based on estates, corporate entities, and juridical inequality, weakened somewhat; social identification and status based on economic role or class strengthened. Lyle McCalister, "Social Structure and Social Change in New Spain," *Hispanic American Historical Review* 43 (May 1963): 360–70. See also Eric Van Young, "Islands in the Storm: Quiet Cities and Violent Countryside in the Mexican Independence Era," *Past and Present: A Journal of Historial Studies* 118 (Feb. 1988): 130–55; Colin MacLachlan and Jaime Rodríguez, *The Forging of the Cosmic Race: A Reinterpretation of Colonial Mexico* (Berkeley, 1980); Doris Ladd, *The Mexican Nobility at Independence, 1780–1826* (Austin, Tex., 1976); and John Kicza, "The Great Families of Mexico: Elite Maintenance and Business Practices in Late Colonial Mexico City," *Hispanic American Historical Review* 62 (1982): 429–57.

32. Quoted in Hugh Hamill, Jr., *The Hidalgo Revolt: Prelude to Mexican Independence* (Gainesville, Fla., 1966), 113. On the social and economic conditions in Bajío, see Eric B. Wolf, "The Mexican Bajío in the Eighteenth Century," *Middle American Research Institute Publications* 17 (1955): 177–200; and Brian R. Hamnett, *Roots of Insurgency: Mexican Regions, 1750–1824* (Cambridge, 1986), esp. 6–23. Hamnett makes a persuasive case for the regional dimension of the Mexican war for independence.

33. Hamnett, *Roots of Insurgency,* 16. The archbishop of the diocese of Mexico warned that the Hidalgo rebellion violated Christ's teachings. See Genaro García, ed., *El clero de México: La guerra de independencia,* in vol. 9 of *Documentos inéditos o muy raros para la historia de México* (Mexico City, 1906), 12–15.

Historians of the Hidalgo revolt sometimes draw a sharp distinction between what Hidalgo commenced in 1810 and what Iturbide finished in 1821. On the one side are those who argue the case for the Hidalgo revolt as the alpha of the independence movement and Iturbide's declaration as its omega. What such linear thinking obscures, however, is what such contemporaries as Lucas Alamán recognized: the liberty championed by Hidalgo was a cry for liberation from *los de abajo;* the independence proclaimed by Iturbide represented a fundamental understanding among Spanish and Creole elites. See Hugh Hamill, "Was the Mexican Independence Movement a Revolution?" in Josefina Vázquez and Richard B. Morris, eds., *Dos revoluciones: México y los Estados Unidos* (Mexico City, 1976); 50–51; Edmundo O'Gorman, "La aparición histórica de la nación mexicana," in ibid., 38–41; and Luís Villoro, "Comentario" in ibid., 72–75; idem., Villoro, *La revolución de independencia* (Mexico City, 1953); and Villoro, *El proceso idelológico de la revolución de independencia* (Mexico City, 1967).

34. John Tutino, *From Insurrection to Revolution in Mexico: Social Bases of Agrarian Violence, 1750–1940* (Princeton, N.J., 1986), 354–55; Hamnett, *Roots of Insurgency,* 202–7. See also Eric Van Young, "Moving Toward Revolt: Agrarian Origins of the Hidalgo Rebellion in the Guadalajara Region," in Friedrich Katz, ed., *Riot, Rebellion, and Revolution: Rural Social Conflict in Mexico* (Princeton, N.J., 1988), 185. Hidalgo offered a command to Agustín de Iturbide, who alertly chose to serve in the counterrevolution because "I was persuaded that his plans were poorly conceived and would produce nothing but disorder, blood, and destruction." Quoted in Lucas Alamán, *Historia de México desde los primeros movimientos que preparon su Independencia en el año de 1808 hasta la época* (5 vols., Mexico City, 1985; orig. pub., 1850), 2:212.

35. Quoted in Robertson, *Rise of the Spanish American Republics,* 88.

36. Alamán, *Historia de México,* 1:437. Antonio López de Santa Anna, assigned to the royalist army in June 1811 and dispatched to Veracruz, was similarly jarred, as he later remembered the "coarse people committing all kinds of excesses in the name of the insurrection." López de Santa Anna, *Mi historia, militar y política, 1810–1874* (Mexico City, 1905), 2.

37. Pedro García, *Con el cura Hidalgo en la guerra de independencia* (Mexico City, 1982), 45–46.

38. Hidalgo, Manifesto, in [Mexico], *Documentos histórico relativos a la independencia nacional* (Mexico City, 1872), 10; Eric Van Young, "Islands in the Storm," *Past and Present* 118 (Feb. 1988): 133, 140. See also Hamnett, *Roots of Insurgency,* 16–21; MacLachlan and Rodríguez, *The Forging of the Cosmic Race,* 318–19. The rebel newspaper, *El Desperador Americano,* appealed to these "noble Americans and virtuous Creoles . . . to open their eyes to their true interests and not be frightened by the sacrifices and privations that accompany all revolutions. . . ." No. 1, December 20, 1810, quoted in J. M. Miquel y Verges, *La independencia y la prensa insurgente* (Mexico City, 1941), 49. In Guadalajara, the insurgent government summarily executed several hundred peninsulars. See José Ramírez Flores, *El gobierno insurgente en Guadalajara, 1810–1811* (Guadalajara, 1969), 95–110.

For an assessment of Hidalgo's position on the agrarian question, see José Mancisador, *Hidalgo y la cuestión agraria* (Mexico City, 1944), 30–32.

39. Villoro, *Revolución de independencia*, 88.

40. Quoted in MacLachlan and Rodríguez, *Forging of the Cosmic Race*, 325.

41. "Manifesto del congreso de Chilpantzingo al declarar la independencia," in [Mexico], *Documentos de la Guerra de Independencia* (Mexico City, 1945), 19–20; Morelos to Creoles fighting with the gachupines, February 23, 1812, in Ernesto Lemoine Villicaña, *Morelos: Su vida revolucionaria a través de sus escritos y otros testimonios de la época* (Mexico City, 1965), 195; Lynch, *Spanish American Revolutions*, 314. See also Hamnett, *Roots of Insurgency*, 142–49; Morelos, Decree, October 13, 1811, in Antonio Arriaga, comp., *Morelos: Documentos* (Morelia, Michoacán, 1965), 99–100. Hidalgo's decree abolishing slavery (December 6, 1810) prescribed death for slaveowners who did not comply.

Morelos's determination not to wage a struggle along racial or class lines was admirable, but these divisions failed to explain the character of the insurgency as much as its fragmentation. Neither Hidalgo nor Morelos proved capable of preventing the fractionalism that sapped the movement and transformed it into chaotic patterns of localized conflict. Christon Archer, "Banditry and Revolution in New Spain," *Bibliotheca Americana* 1 (1982): 59–88. The royalist commander, Félix Calleja, was similarly frustrated by Europeans who looked after their own interests, expecting others to do their fighting. See Hamill, "Was the Mexican Independence Movement a Revolution?" in Vázquez and Morris, eds., *Dos revoluciones*, 57.

42. Arriaga, comp., *Morelos: Documentos*, 33–35; Ricki Shultz Janicek, "The Development of Early Mexican Land Policy: Coahuila and Texas, 1810–1825" (Ph.D. diss., Tulane University, 1985), 51–52.

43. Domínguez, *Insurrection or Loyalty*, 199–200.

44. Nettie Lee Benson, "Comparison of the American Independence Movements," in Vázquez and Morris, eds., *Dos revoluciones*, 121; Decreto Constitucional . . . América Mexicana, Apatzingan, October 22, 1814, in México, *Documentos de la Guerra de Independencia*, 31–97.

45. Quoted in Alamán, *Historia de México*, 4:356.

46. Florencia E. Mallon, *In Defense of Community in Peru's Central Highlands: Peasant Struggle and Capitalist Transition, 1860–1940* (Princeton, N.J., 1983), 51. See also Scarlett O'Phelan Godoy, "El mito de la 'independencia conecida,'" in Flores Galindo, comp., *Independencia y revolución, 1780–1840* (2 vols., Lima, 1987), 1:196–99; and Charles Arnade, *Emergence of the Republic of Bolivia* (Gainesville, Fla., 1957), 50–51.

47. Thomas Blossom, *Nariño: Hero of Colombian Independence* (Tucson, Ariz., 1967); Manuel José Forero, *Camilo Torres* (Bogotá, 1960).

48. Quoted in Blossom, *Nariño*, 109; Indalecio Liévano Aguirre, *Los grandes conflictos sociales y económicos de Nuestra Historia*, 5th ed. (2 vols., Bogotá, 1973; orig. pub., 1964), 670.

49. Liévano, *Los grandes conflictos*, 2:836–37; see also 636–37, 676–77, 806–7. Pasto's hostility to Nariño's republican ideology was only partially explained by the reality of castas' identifying with the royalist cause. The region had a long history of opposition to the intrusions of centralist power. See Brian Hamnett, "Popular Insurrection and Royalist Reaction," in John Fisher, Allan J. Kuethe, and Anthony McFarlane, eds., *Reform and Insurrection in Bourbon New Granada and Peru* (Baton Rouge, La., 1990), 302–5, 310–11, 324–26.

50. Liévano, *Los grandes conflictos*, 2:636–37.

51. "Proclamation to the People of Venezuela," June 15, 1813 in Bolívar, *Selected Writings of Bolívar* 1:31–32.

The best summation of social and economic themes in the independence movements is Charles C. Griffin, "Economic and Social Aspects of the Era of Spanish American Independence," *Hispanic American Historical Review* 29 (May 1949): 170–87, expanded in a collection of essays, *Las temas sociales y económicas en la época de la independencia* (Caracas, 1962).

52. Bolívar, *Selected Writings of Bolívar,* 1:40–41, 63 ("Address Before the Caracas Assembly," January 2, 1814); McKinley, *Pre-revolutionary Caracas,* 171.

For more on these years in the independence movement in Venezuela see Parra Pérez, *Historia de la Primera República de Venezuela;* Parra Pérez, *Mariño y la independencia de Venezuela* (5 vols., Madrid, 1954–57); Parra and Pérez, *Causas de infidencia* (2 vols., Caracas, 1960). As expected, Bolívar as subject dominates the literature on the Venezuelan independence movement. Of the many biographies, Gerhard Masur, *Simón Bolívar,* rev. ed., (Albuquerque, N.M., 1969), is the most balanced in English. A classic psychological portrait, much denounced among Bolivarian hagiographers, is Salvador Madariaga, *Bolívar* (New York, 1969).

53. Quoted in Lynch, *The Spanish American Revolutions,* 203.

54. Liévano, *Los grandes conflictos,* 2:847; Domínguez, *Insurrection or Loyalty,* 178; Uslar Pietri, *Historia de la rebelión popular de 1814,* 97–98, 99. Germán Carrera Damas explores Boves's social base in *Boves: Aspectos socioeconómicos de su acción histórica,* 2nd rev. ed. (Caracas, 1968).

55. Uslar Pietri, *Historia de la rebelión popular de 1814,* 128; Stephen K. Stoan, *Pablo Morillo and Venezuela, 1815–1820* (Columbus, Ohio, 1974), 51.

56. Daniel Florencio O'Leary (Robert F. McNerney, trans. and ed.), *Memorias del General Florencio O'Leary: Narración* (Austin, Tex., 1970), 69; Domínguez, *Insurrection or Loyalty,* 179; Magnus Mörner, *Race Mixture in the History of Latin America* (Boston, 1967), 81. Miguel Izard, *El miedo a la revolución: La lucha por la libertad en Venezuela, 1777–1830* (Madrid, 1979), as the title suggests, reinforces the argument that Venezuela's Creole elite wanted to avoid a revolution from below. It should be followed by a reading of Germán Carrera Damas, *La crisis de la sociedad colonial venezolana* (Caracas, 1976). For more on the "war to the death" and racial issues in Venezuela, see Robert Sutherland, *Un amigo de Bolívar en Haiti* (Caracas, 1969); and Rufino Blanco Fombona, *Bolívar y la Guerra a Muerte, Epoca de Boves, 1813–1814* (Caracas, 1942).

57. Uslar Pietri, *Historia de la rebelión popular de 1814,* 163; see also Stoan, *Pablo Morillo,* 56–57.

58. Uslar Pietri, *Historia de la rebelión popular de 1814,* 94–95, 164.

9   *The Price of Victory*

1. Juan Uslar Pietri, *Historia de la rebelión popular de 1814* (Caracas, 1962), 100; Manuel Forero, *Camilo Torres* (Bogotá, 1960), 115. One of those executed was Camilo Torres, whose decapitated head the Spanish affixed to a pole. Morillo took Bogotá without a struggle in early May 1816. In desperation a small band of Creoles led by Francisco de Paula Santander fled to the Llanos of Casanare. By the end of 1816, Morillo informed the monarch, the reconquista of New Granada had crushed the rebellion, save for isolated resistance in the outlying provinces. See Daniel Florencia O'Leary (Robert F. McNerney, Jr., ed. and trans.), *Bolívar and the War of Independence* (Austin, Tex., 1970), 155; Thomas Blossom, *Nariño: Hero of Colombian Independence* (Tucson, Ariz.,

1967), xxvii–xviii; Jane M. Rausch, *Tropical Plains Frontier: The Llanos of Colombia, 1531–1830* (Albuquerque, N.M., 1984), 173–74.

2. Tulio Halperín-Donghi (John C. Chasteen, trans.), *The Contemporary History of Latin America* (Durham, N.C., 1993), 58.

3. Quoted in Stephen K. Stoan, *Pablo Morillo and Venezuela, 1815–1820* (Columbus, Ohio, 1974), 72.

4. Quoted in Uslar Pietri, *Historia de la rebelión popular de 1814,* 195; Halperín-Donghi, *Contemporary History of Latin America,* 64–65.

5. "Reply of a South American to a Gentleman of [Jamaica]," September 6, 1815, in Simón Bolívar (Vicente Lecuna, comp., Harold Bierck, ed., Lewis Bertrand, trans.), *Selected Writings of Bolívar,* (2 vols., New York, 1952), 1:104–5. In the final passages of the Jamaica letter, Bolívar laid claim as a founding father of hemispheric unity, though he meant by that term a union of those Spanish colonies fighting a war of independence.

6. Quoted in Magnus Mörner, *Race Mixture in the History of Latin America* (Boston, 1967), 85.

7. "Address Delivered at the Inauguration of the Second National Congress of Venezuela in Angostura," February 15, 1819, in Bolívar, *Selected Writings of Bolívar* 1:194.

8. Robin Blackburn, *The Overthrow of Colonial Slavery, 1776–1848* (London, 1988), 344–47; Stoan, *Pablo Morillo,* 212–13.

9. Quoted in Jorge Domínguez, *Insurrection or Loyalty: The Breakdown of the Spanish American Empire* (Cambridge, Mass., 1980), 197. See also Uslar Pietri, *Historia de la rebelión popular de 1814,* 100.

10. Bolívar, "Address at Angostura," February 15, 1819, in Bolívar, *Selected Writings of Bolívar* 1:175–76.

11. Ibid., 179–80.

12. Bolívar to Gen. F[rancisco] de P[aula] Santander, April 20, 1820, ibid., 222–23.
   The Haitian war of independence offered a disturbing reminder, he wrote Santander a month later: "Our path has been determined—to draw back means weakness and general ruin for all. We must triumph by the road of revolution and no other. The Spaniards will not kill the slaves; they will kill the masters, and then all will be lost" (Bolívar to Santander, May 30, 1820, ibid., 229).

13. Of the condition of his fierce plainsmen and their struggle, Páez wrote: "Only God knows what we suffered. . . . Never will our children be able to imagine at what price independence was achieved." Páez, *Autobiografía* (2 vols., New York, 1946; orig. pub., 1869), 97. Páez's memoirs are less reliable, however, than those of the foreigner, Daniel O'Leary, *Bolívar and the War of Independence* (Austin, Tex., 1970).

14. Virtually all the chronicles of the ill-fated band of British legionnaires who arrived on the north coast in 1817 and 1818 to join the patriot cause depict a ghastly conflict. Undisciplined soldiers, some no more than thirteen or fourteen years of age, clothed in coarse fragments, with buffalo hide as shoes and knives or clubs as weapons, subsisted on mules' flesh, fruit, and dried corn. They trod behind mounted officers wearing a blanket with a hole cut out for the head. In battle, their lethargic behavior gave way to a bravery that dumbfounded veterans of the Napoleonic wars. In victory, they were devoid of compassion, killing their prisoners and stripping the bodies. One

English legionnaire, recruited in 1817, recalled a battleground outside Angostura where a royalist garrison had made a final stand: "[It was evident] that they had been dispatched by their conquerors in cold blood, after being made prisoners, and left unburied amongst the killed of the Patriots, to feed the wild beasts and . . . black vultures." C. Brown, *Narrative of the Expedition to South America* (London, 1819), 97. Another, George Laval Chesterton, *A Narrative of the Proceedings in Venezuela . . .* (London, 1820), 66, wrote of royalist prisoners stripped and bound and speared in the base of the skull until dead. See also H. L. V. Ducoudray-Holstein, *Memoirs of Simón Bolívar . . .* (Boston, 1829), 58–59; James Hackett, *Narrative of the Expedition which sailed from England in 1817 to Join the South American Patriots* (London, 1818), 52–57.

15. Brian Hamnett, "Popular Insurrection and Royalist Reaction," in John Fisher, Allan J. Kuethe, and Anthony McFarlane, eds., *Reform and Insurrection in Bourbon New Granada and Peru* (Baton Rouge, La., 1990), 319–21.

16. Jaime Duarte French, *Bolívar, Libertador; Santander, Vicepresidente* (Bogotá, 1993), 83; Stoan, *Pablo Morillo*, 184–85.

17. John Lynch, *Caudillos in Spanish America, 1800–1850* (Oxford, 1992), 99. Bolívar complained to Antonio Nariño: "Colombia, governed by the sword of its defenders, is a military camp rather than a body social" (quoted in ibid.).

18. Quoted in ibid., 101.

19. To the Editor, *The Royal Gazette,* Kingston, Jamaica, September 28, 1815, in Bolívar, *Selected Writings of Bolívar,* 1:123; Anthony Pagden, *Spanish Imperialism and the Political Imagination: Studies in European and Spanish-American Social and Political Theory, 1513–1830* (New Haven, 1990), 138–39. The U.S. Constitution had been a model for that of Venezuela's first republic, the "foolish republic," but it had collapsed into civil strife and counterrevolution.

20. In part, the problems confronted by the Buenos Aires revolutionaries were economic, as financial commitments exceeded the resources of the state and prompted the revolutionary cadres to centralize their authority and the provinces to resist. In this confrontation lay one of the persistent dilemmas in postrevolutionary Argentina— unitarism versus federalism—where economic issues dominated political debate. A parallel problem brought on by the financial crisis was the uncertain relationship between the revolutionary leaders and the social elites, whose loyalties to the revolution remained suspect. See Tulio Halperín-Donghi, *Politics, Economics, and Society in Argentina in the Revolutionary Period* (Cambridge, 1975), 236–38; and Miron Burgin, *The Economic Aspects of Argentine Federalism, 1820–1850* (Cambridge, Mass., 1946), 16–17.

21. Halperín-Donghi, *Politics, Economics, and Society,* 262–63.
    In the province of Salta, the revolution relied on a Creole landowner and officer, Martín Güemes, whose background and talents typified the caudillo. With his rural base, he was able to recruit an army from the province and rule Salta virtually unhampered. Güemes was alternately populist and conservative: from 1815 until his death six years later, he indulged his gaucho followers by permitting plundering of selected estates and won the backing of wealthy estancieros by exempting their properties from the ravaging of his men. Governments in Buenos Aires saw in caudillos such as Güemes a less costly method of fighting a war. Inevitably, Argentina paid a price for such a strategy. In La Rioja, the porteños identified an even more formidable caudillo ally, Facundo Quiroga, the "Tiger of the Pampas," who rounded up a gaucho army for the war on the northwest frontier and kept it supplied by using

another force to plunder estates of his choosing. Lynch, *Caudillos in Spanish America,* 37–39; see also Tulio Halperín-Donghi, "El surgimiento do los caudillos en el marco de la sociedad rioplatense postrevolucionaria," *Estudios de Historia Social* 1 (1965): 121–49; Roger Haigh, *Martín Güemes: Tyrant or Tool?* (Fort Worth, 1968), 2–5; and Richard Slatta, *Gauchos and the Vanishing Frontier* (Lincoln, Neb., 1983), 11.

22. David Bushnell, *Reform and Reaction in the Platine Provinces, 1810–1852* (Gainesville, Fla., 1983), 17; George R. Andrews, *The Afro-Argentines of Buenos Aires, 1800–1900* (Madison, Wisc., 1980), 59. In the beginning of the *rescate* program, whereby slaves sold to the government to become soldiers earned their freedom, Buenos Aires's slaveowners enthusiastically participated. But their revolutionary ardor quelled, and many took to petitioning the government for exemption or even risked criminal penalty by taking their slaves into the interior. By 1816 the revolutionary government was confiscating any male slave otherwise eligible for military service. (Ibid., 116–17) Black soldiers were assigned to segregated units, though in fact they were integrated with a few whites. The numbers of black males who served were disproportionately large when compared with the number of blacks in the entire population, which has fueled speculation that commanders assigned them to more hazardous duty. "Let it stand to Argentina's credit," writes the historian of the Afro-Argentine, "that there is no evidence of such thought or practice in the country's military history." Ibid., 121.

23. John Robertson (brother of William Parish Robertson) visited the camp of Artigas and found "His Excellency the Protector" "seated on a bullock's skull, on the mud floor of his hut, eating beef off a spit, and drinking gin out of a cow horn! He was surrounded by a dozen officers in weather-beaten attire, in similar positions and similarly occupied. . . . All were smoking, all gabbling. The Protector was dictating to two secretaries, who occupied . . . the only two dilapidated chairs in his hovel." Quoted in Desmond Gregory, *Brave New World: The Rediscovery of Latin America in the Early 19th Century* (New York, 1993), 12.

24. Quoted in Henry M. Brackenridge, *Voyage to South America . . . in 1817 and 1818* (2 vols., Baltimore, 1819), 1:257. See also Lynch, *Caudillos,* 43, citing Mitre, *Historia de Belgrano y de la independencia argentina,* 6th ed. (4 vols., Buenos Aires, 1927), 1:256.

25. William Miller to John Quincy Adams, July 13, 1821, in William Manning, ed., *Diplomatic Correspondence of the United States Concerning the Independence of the Latin American Nations* (3 vols., New York, 1925), 3:2179. See also Halperín-Donghi, *Politics, Economics, and Society,* 286–87; María Saenz Quesada, *Los estancieros* (Buenos Aires, 1980); and L. S. de Touron, N. de la Torre, and J. G. Rodríguez, *La revolución agraria artiguista* (Montevideo, 1969).

26. Richard Alan White, *Paraguay's Autonomous Revolution, 1810–1840* (Albuquerque, N.M., 1978), summarizes the case for Dr. Francia's Paraguay as a "social revolution," but see the persuasive demurral in Thomas Whigham, *The Politics of River Trade: Tradition and Development in the Upper Plata, 1780–1870* (Albuquerque, N.M., 1991), 22–29.

27. Simon Collier, *Ideas and Politics of Chilean Independence, 1808–1823* (Cambridge, 1967), 4–5.

28. Ibid., 226; see also 362–63; and Jaime Eyzaguirre, "La conducta política del grupo dirigente chileno durante la guerra de independencia," in Universidad de Chile, Facultad de Ciencias Jurídicas y Sociales, *Estudios de Historia de las Instituciones Políticas y Sociales* (1967): 227.

29. Quoted in William B. Stevenson, *History and Descriptive Narrative of 20 Years Residence in South America* (3 vols., London, 1825), 3:277.

30. Eyzaguirre, "La conducta política del grupo dirigente," 251; Stephen Clissold, *Bernardo O'Higgins and the Independence of Chile* (New York, 1968), 207–217; Mary L. Felstiner, "Kinship Politics in the Chilean Independence Movement," *Hispanic American Historical Review* 56 (Feb. 1976): 58–81.

31. Christon Archer, "The Counterinsurgency Army and the Ten Years' War," in Jaime Rodríguez, ed., *The Independence of Mexico and the Creation of the New Nation* (Los Angeles, 1989), 102–5.

32. Lucas Alamán, *Historia de México desde los primeros movimientos que preparon su Independencia en el año hasta la época* (5 vols., Mexico City, 1985; orig. pub., 1850), 4:723. For assessments of the nuances of rural insurgency in Mexico see William B. Taylor, "Bandits and Insurrections: Rural Unrest in Central Jalisco, 1790–1816," in Friedrich Katz, ed., *Riot, Rebellion, and Revolution: Rural Social Conflict in Mexico* (Princeton, 1988), 205–46; Enrique Semo, ed., *Historia mexicana: Economía y lucha de clases* (Mexico City, 1978), 189–99; and Joel S. Migdal, *Peasants, Politics, and Revolution: Pressures Toward Political and Social Change in the Third World* (Princeton, N.J., 1975), 254–60.

33. *El clamor de la justicia de los antiguos patriotas titulados insurgentes . . .* (Mexico, 1822). Among the warring insurgents and royalists were women. Their impact, especially in the rebel cause, belied their relatively small numbers. They reconnoitered villages, delivered messages, spied, and, in several encounters, fought. See Janet R. Kentner, "The Socio-Political Role of Women in the Mexican War of Independence, 1810–1821" (Ph.D. diss., Loyola University of Chicago, 1975).

34. Brian Hamnett, *Roots of Insurgency: Mexican Regions, 1750–1824* (Cambridge, 1986), 208–9; Ramón Flores C. (Jaime Rodríguez, trans.), *Counterrevolution: The Role of the Spaniards in the Independence of Mexico, 1804–1838* (Lincoln, Neb., 1974), 57–58. One of the peripatetic rebel leaders, Fray Servando Teresa de Mier, was in Havana en route to Philadelphia when he learned of the Plan of Iguala and the naming of Iturbide as emperor. He denounced it: "We want no more of monarchy and emperors. . . . They have eyes but cannot see . . . the needs of their people . . . ; they have ears but hear nothing but . . . lies." *Memoria política-instructiva enviada desde Filadelfia . . .* (Philadelphia, 1821), 39–40.

35. Quoted in Timothy Anna, *The Mexican Empire of Iturbide* (Lincoln, Neb., 1989), 39. "A final, and probably decisive, element in the allure of the Plan of Iguala was its strong appeal to the masses. The speed with which the plan swept the country, the euphoria of the triumph, and the fact that Iturbide himself was propelled almost irresistibly toward the throne by popular acclaim all suggest such a conclusion" (ibid., 9).

36. Luís Villoro, *La Revolución de independencia: Un ensayo de interpretación* (Mexico City, 1953), 211. See also Jaime Rodríguez, "From Royal Subject to Republican Citizen," in Rodríguez, ed., *The Independence of Mexico and the Creation of the New Nation* 40–43; and Josefina Vázquez, *Tropiezos para establecer un nuevo estado, 1821–1848* (Mexico City, 1976), 56–68.

37. For the independence movement in Peru see Rubén Vargas Ugarte, *Historia del Perú: Emancipación (1809–1825)* (Buenos Aires, 1958); Daniel Valcarcel, *Rebeliones indígenas* (Lima, 1946); Juan José Vega, *La emancipación frente al indio peruano* (Lima, 1958); and Alipio Valencia Vega, *El indio en la independencia* (La Paz, 1962).

38. "Reply of a South American to a Gentleman of this Island [Jamaica]," September 6, 1815, in *Selected Writings of Bolívar,* 1:105.

39. San Martín wrote: "My soul would never be satisfied with a victory obtained at the cost of spilling American blood; I desire a peaceful victory, fruit of irresistible necessity." San Martín to Torre Tagle, January 19, 1821, quoted in Lynch, *Spanish American Revolutions,* 174. See also R. A. Humphreys, ed., "James Paroissien's Notes on the Liberating Expedition to Peru," *Hispanic American Historical Review* 31 (1951):254–68.

40. Captain Basil Hall, *Extracts from a Journal Written on the Coasts of Chili, Peru, and Mexico in the Years 1820, 1821, and 1822* (London, 1824), I, 222–23, 226.

41. Lynch, *Caudillos,* 53.

42. San Martín went into European exile and died in 1850. On the Guayaquil interview see Vincente Lecuna, *La entrevista de Guayaquil* (Madrid, 1917); and Lecuna, "Bolívar and San Martín at Guayaquil," *Hispanic American Historical Review* 31 (1951), 369–93; and Gerhard Masur, "The Conference of Guayaquil," ibid., 189–229.

43. Bolívar to Sucre, May 24, 1823, *Selected Writings of Bolívar,* 2:373. Peru's arrogant Creoles, wrote the special agent of the United States, John Prevost, wanted to rid themselves of the Spanish without "augmenting an [i]nfluence that might endanger their privileges and their [s]way." Prevost to Secretary of State John Quincy Adams, March 13, 1823, in Manning, ed., *Diplomatic Correspondence,* 3:1638.

44. Quoted in Lynch, *Spanish American Revolutions,* 272. See also Jorge Basadre, *Historia de la República de Perú,* 6th ed. (16 vols., Lima, 1968), 1:76.

45. Bolívar to Santander, January 6–7, 1825, in Bolívar, *Selected Writings of Bolívar,* 2:462.

46. Quoted in Fredrick Pike, *The United States and Latin America: Myths and Stereotypes of Civilization and Nature* (Austin, Tex., 1992), 69.
    This sentiment angered some of the visitors to revolutionary South America, among them the special U.S. emissary H. H. Brackenridge, who wrote: "Persons who have never seen a Southern American are in the habit of condemning them all by the wholesale, as stupid, depraved, and worthless." "Letter on South American Affairs," in Brackenridge, *Voyage to South America,* 2:325. In 1818, as Brackenridge toured the revolutionary scene, Jefferson expressed to John Quincy Adams his belief that their "dangerous enemy is within their own breasts. Ignorance and superstition will chain their minds and bodies under religious and military despotism." He added: "It is our duty to wish them independence and self-government, because they wish it themselves; and they have the right, and we none, to choose for themselves, and I wish, moreover, that our ideas may be erroneous, and theirs prove well-founded." Quoted in Robert W. Tucker and George Frederickson, *Empire of Liberty: The Statecraft of Thomas Jefferson* (New York, 1990), 253.

47. Frank Safford, "Politics, Ideology, and Society in Post-Independence Spanish America," in Leslie Bethell, ed., *Cambridge History of Latin America,* vol. 3, *From Independence to c. 1870* (Cambridge, 1985), 347–422; Domínguez, *Insurrection or Loyalty,* 222–25.

48. Speech, January 20, 1816, *Annals of Congress* (14th Cong., 1st Sess.), 727. Randolph may have been ignorant of the profound intellectual influence of Francisco Suárez (1548–1617), who had synthesized neo-Thomist thought and bequeathed to the Spanish-American liberators a political philosophy more relevant to their experience

than the work of John Locke. North American revolutionaries had absorbed Locke's argument about natural rights, sovereignty, and just government; they justified their cause on the putative right of revolution against unjust government. Suárez's doctrine, however, led to sharply differing conclusions. Suárez distinguished between natural law, which was general and always right, and conscience, which represented the human application of law. As did Locke, he accepted the belief that sovereignty resides with the people. At this intellectual juncture, however, Latin and North Americans sharply divided. The latter believed that government could be perfected or, in practical terms, could be both authoritative and functional, its legitimacy derived from consensus (expressed by the people at the ballot box) and sustained by just laws. See Richard Morse, "The Heritage of Latin America," in Louis Hartz, ed., *The Founding of New Societies* (New York, 1964), 157; and Morse, *New World Soundings,* 102–3. For other psychocultural interpretations of Spanish-American political culture in the nineteenth century see Francisco García Calderon, *Latin America: Its Rise and Progress* (New York, 1913); and Lionel Cecil Jane, *Liberty and Despotism in Spanish America* (London, 1929).

49. Quoted in Arthur Whitaker, *United States and the Independence of Latin America, 1800–1830* (New York, 1964; orig. pub., 1941), 334. On the domestic political implications of Monroe's message see Ernest R. May, *The Making of the Monroe Doctrine* (Cambridge, Mass., 1975).

50. Charles Francis Adams, ed., *Memoirs of John Quincy Adams* (12 vols., Philadelphia, 1874–77), 5:176, as quoted in Lester D. Langley, *America and the Americas: The United States in the Western Hemisphere* (Athens, Ga., 1989), 41. On Adams as a continental imperialist see the useful collection edited by Walter LaFeber, *John Quincy Adams and American Continental Empire* (Chicago, 1965).

51. "The success of government . . . requires the acceptance of fictions, requires the willing suspension of disbelief, requires us to believe that the emperor is clothed even though we can see that he is not. Government requires make-believe. . . . Make believe that the people *have* a voice or make believe that the representatives of the people *are* the people." Edmund S. Morgan, *Inventing the People: The Rise of Popular Sovereignty in England and America* (New York, 1988), 13. Such fictions are fundamental in the early years of a new country. Intellectuals who articulated Argentine identity from the 1820s to mid-century, argues Nicholas Shumway, provided a "mythology of exclusion rather than a unifying national ideal, a recipe for divisiveness rather than consential pluralism. This failure to create an ideological framework for union helped produce what novelist Ernesto Sábato has called 'a society of opposers' as interested in humiliating each other as in developing a viable nation united through consensus and compromise." Shumway, *The Invention of Argentina* (Berkeley, 1991), x–xi.

52. Quoted in Pike, *United States and Latin America,* 67. Some years later, as faraway Argentina sank into the caudillo rule of Juan Manuel de Rosas, the brilliant Argentine man of letters Domingo Sarmiento (himself from the interior provinces) employed a similar dialectic in depicting Argentine history in the 1830s and 1840s as "civilization and barbarism." Domingo Sarmiento (Mrs. Horace Mann, trans.), *Life in the Argentine Republic in the Days of the Tyrants: Or, Civilization and Barbarism* (New York, 1868).

53. Captain Charles Stuart Cochrane, *Journal of a Residence and Travels in Colombia, During the Years 1823 and 1824* (New York, 1971; orig. pub., London, 1825), 245.

10 *Tocqueville's America*

1. Alexis de Tocqueville (Henry Reeve, trans.), *Democracy in America*, 4th ed. (2 vols., New York, 1845).

2. Edward Pessen, *Jacksonian America: Society, Personality, and Politics* (Urbana, Ill., 1985), 77–81. Until the late nineteenth century, when dramatic changes wrought by the corporation compelled them to come up with new formulations, Americans believed that political, not economic, systems explained inequities in wealth distribution—a theory axiomatically derived from "the labor theory of property or value, the political economy of aristocracy, the laws of primogeniture and entail, and the population-to-land ratio." James Huston, "The American Revolutionaries, the Political Economy of Aristocracy, and the American Concept of the Distribution of Wealth, 1765–1900," *American Historical Review* 98 (Oct. 1993): 1080.

3. "I know of no country," Tocqueville wrote, "in which there is so little true independence of mind and freedom of discussion as in America." Quoted in Clement Eaton, *The Leaven of Democracy: The Growth of the Democratic Spirit in the Time of Jackson* (New York, 1963), 487.

   For a recent assessment of this topic from a comparative perspective see the essays in Byron Shafer, ed., *Is America Different? A New Look at American Exceptionalism* (Oxford, 1991), esp. Seymour Martin Lipset, "American Exceptionalism Reaffirmed," 1–45.

4. Quoted in John J. Johnson, *A Hemisphere Apart: The Foundations of United States Policy Towards Latin America* (Baltimore, 1990), 45. Gordon Wood concludes: "What happened in America in the decades following the Declaration of Independence was after all only an extension of all that the revolutionary leaders had advocated. White males had taken only too seriously the belief that they were free and equal with the right to pursue their happiness. Indeed, the principles of their achievement made possible the eventual strivings of others—black slaves and women—for their own freedom, independence, and prosperity." Wood, *The Radicalism of the American Revolution* (New York, 1992), 368. This passage provoked denunciation from social historians, who observed that the American Revolution *denied* the benefits of revolution to black slaves and women and thus set back rather than accelerated their quest for participating in the revolution's benefits. Achievement of these benefits required a struggle.

5. Joyce Appleby, *Capitalism and a New Social Order: The Republican Vision of the 1790s* (New York, 1984), 5, and 46–53; Appleby, *Liberalism and Republicanism in the Historical Imagination* (Cambridge, Mass., 1992), 208–9, 256–57, 268–69, 272–75; and Ronald Formisano, "Deferential-Participant Politics: The Early Republic's Political Culture, 1789–1840," *American Political Science Review* 68 (1974): 473–87. The conflictual character of politics inevitably shifted, gradually but perceptibly, from individual to faction and then to party. See the essays in Lance Banning, ed., *After the Constitution: Party Conflict in the New Republic* (Belmont, Calif., 1989). For a suggestive essay on the influence of the War of 1812 on the making of a liberal nation see Steven Watts, *The Republic Reborn: War and the Making of Liberal America, 1790–1820* (Baltimore, 1987).

6. Tocqueville, *Democracy in America*, 1:322.

7. Quoted in Michael Kammen, *A Season of Youth: The American Revolution and the Historical Imagination* (New York, 1978), 45. See also Michael Lienesch, *New Order of*

the Ages: Time, the Constitution, and the Making of Modern America (Princeton, N.J., 1988), 204–6.

8. Quoted in Stephen Thernstrom, *Poverty and Progress: Social Mobility in a Nineteenth Century City* (Cambridge, Mass., 1964), 63. See also Ralph Lerner, "Commerce and Character: The Anglo-American as a New Model Man," *William and Mary Quarterly* 36 (Jan. 1979): 10; Lawrence Friedman, *The Republic of Choice* (Cambridge, Mass., 1990), 22–27; and Tocqueville, *Democracy in America*, 1:54–55.

9. Seymour Drescher, *Dilemmas of Democracy: Tocqueville and Democratization* (Pittsburgh, 1968), 257. Harriet Martineau, a contemporary traveler in Tocqueville's America, wrote disparagingly of its modern democratic man: "There is fear of vulgarity [in the United States], fear of responsibility; and above all, fear of singularity." From *Society in America* (New York, 1837), as quoted in Seymour M. Lipset, *The First New Nation: The United States in Historical and Comparative Perspective* (New York, 1963), 107.

10. Quoted in Edward Pessen, *Riches, Class, and Power Before the Civil War* (Lexington, Mass., 1973), 151. See also Pessen, *The Log-Cabin Myth: The Social Backgrounds of the Presidents* (New Haven, 1984), 58–59. "Popular ideology notwithstanding," Pessen writes, "the era of the common man was remarkable above all for how few rich men were in fact descended of common folk." Pessen, "The Egalitarian Myth and the American Social Reality: Wealth, Mobility, and Equality in the Era of the Common Man," in Pessen, ed., *The Many-Faceted Jacksonian Era: New Interpretations* (Westport, Conn., 1977), 19.

11. "Public office," writes Gordon Wood, "could no longer be regarded merely as a burden that prominent gentlemen had an obligation to bear. . . . Government officials were no longer to play the role of umpire; they were no longer to stand above the marketplace and make disinterested impartial judgments about what was good for the whole society." Wood, *Radicalism of the American Revolution*, 294.

12. Quoted in Robert Wiebe, *The Opening of American Society: From the Adoption of the Constitution to the Eve of Disunion* (New York, 1984), 349. See also Wood, *Radicalism of the American Revolution*, 294–99; Pessen, *Jacksonian America*, 97–99; Peter B. Knupfer, *The Union as It Is: Constitutional Unionism and Sectional Compromise, 1787–1861* (Chapel Hill, N.C., 1991), 18–19, 104–5; Major Wilson, *Space, Time, and Freedom: The Quest for Nationality and the Irrepressible Conflict* (Westport, Conn., 1974), 50–53, 74–77, 92–93; and Robert Remini, *The Legacy of Andrew Jackson* (Baton Rouge, La., 1988), 12–13. On the political culture of Jacksonian America see Harry L. Watson, *Liberty and Power: The Politics of Jacksonian America* (New York, 1990); Lee Benson, *The Concept of Jacksonian Democracy: New York as a Test Case* (Princeton, N.J., 1961); Ronald P. Formisano, *The Birth of Mass Political Parties: Michigan, 1827–1861* (Princeton, N.J., 1971); Joel H. Silbey, *The American Political Nation, 1838–1893* (Stanford, Calif., 1991); and, especially, John William Ward, *Andrew Jackson: Symbol for an Age* (New York, 1955).

13. Marc Egnal, *A Mighty Empire: The Origins of the American Revolution* (Ithaca, N.Y., 1988), 328–37.

14. Jack E. Eblen, *The First and Second United States Empires: Governors and Territorial Government, 1784–1912* (Pittsburgh, 1968), 2–5. Paul Rahe makes the case for Jefferson and Madison as "market-oriented" expansionists in the purchase of Louisiana, pursued as a means of "guaranteeing to the farmers already resident in the Ohio Valley the opportunity to transport their crops for export down the Mississippi

through the port of New Orleans." Rahe, *Republics Ancient and Modern: Classical Republicanism and the American Revolution* (Chapel Hill, N.C., 1992), 734.

15. Quoted in Robert W. Tucker and David Hendrickson, *Empire of Liberty: The Statecraft of Thomas Jefferson* (New York, 1990), 160. See also 126–27. Though he characterized earlier territorial government as the "despotic oligarchy without one rational objective," he was "ambivalent" about the organization of Louisiana's first government (quoted in Eblen, *First and Second United States Empires*, 145). In 1821, even as the political rancor over the admission of Missouri as a slave state made Jefferson's observations about expansionism seem naive, he remained confident about the benefits: "I still believe that the Western expansion of our confederacy will ensure its duration, by overruling local factions, which might shake a smaller association." Quoted in John R. Nelson, Jr., *Liberty and Property: Political Economy and Policymaking in the New Nation, 1789–1812* (Baltimore, 1987), 139.

16. George Dargo, *Jefferson's Louisiana: Politics and the Clash of Legal Traditions* (Cambridge, 1975), 171, 174.

17. Quoted in D. W. Meinig, *The Shaping of America: A Geographical Perspective on 500 Years of History*, vol. 2: *Continental America, 1800–1867* (New Haven, 1993), 17; see also 23.

18. Quoted in David Weber, *The Spanish Frontier in North America* (New Haven, 1992), 299; see also 296–99.

19. Quoted in Stuart Bruchey, *The Wealth of a Nation: An Economic History of the United States* (New York, 1988), 32; Henry Nash Smith, *Virgin Land: The American West as Symbol and Myth* (Cambridge, Mass., 1950), 53; and 56–57. See also Peter Charles Hoffer, *Liberty or Order: Two Views of American History from the Revolutionary Crisis to the Early Works of George Bancroft and Wendell Phillips* (New York, 1988), 188–91, which relates the westerner's tension over the price of "progress."
The Panic of 1819 had a further depressing effect, as it coincided with the abandonment of installment payments for public land purchases. In 1820, the minimum size for public land fell to eighty acres (at $1.25 per acre) but required the $50 purchase price in cash. Few could afford this. As public land sales plummeted from five million acres in 1819 to 750,000 two years later, westerners complained about such restrictive measures. By contrast, Mexico's offerings to empresarios willing to settle in Texas were generous. "Mexico," a Missouri editor sneered, "does not think of getting rich by land speculation, digging for lead, or boiling salt water, but by increasing the number and wealth of her citizens." Quoted in Eugene C. Barker, *Mexico and Texas, 1821–1835* (New York, 1965; orig. pub., 1928), 18.

20. Quoted in Peter S. Onuf, *Statehood and Union: A History of the Northwest Ordinance* (Bloomington, Ind., 1987), 146.

21. Eblen, *First and Second United States Empires*, 317–18.
On the frontier mobility meant not only horizontal but vertical movement on the social scale. Unlike the East, writes Ray Allen Billington, a distinguished historian of the American West, communities in the West had "self-sustaining family units [that] made unnecessary the graded social structure essential in compact communities where each group performed functions indispensable to the good of the whole." Billington, "The Frontier in American Thought and Character," in Archibald Lewis and Thomas McGann, eds., *The New World Looks at Its History* (Austin, Tex., 1963), 88. Pedigree or family name carried less social clout in the West, yet acquired wealth or the display of manners befitting a plantation family back in Virginia or South Carolina prompted some to claim they were "well-born." Malcolm Rohrbaugh, *The*

Land Office Business: The Settlement and Administration of American Public Lands, 1789–1837 (New York, 1968), 299.

Two books portray the diversity and circumstance of western migrants. In Joan Cashin, *A Family Venture: Men and Women on the Southern Frontier* (New York, 1991), the venturer is more often the restless son in an elite plantation family, trapped in a declining seaboard economy, who is determined to prove his manliness by breaking the bonds of kinship. Michael Allen, *Western Rivermen, 1763–1861: Ohio and Mississippi Boatmen and the Myth of the Alligator Horse* (Baton Rouge, La., 1990), depicts a world that had its share of opportunists (Moses Austin and James Wilkinson) and the proverbial Kentucky boatmen but was largely dominated by hardworking, dirty, and often violent older men who frequented the dives and whorehouses of the river towns and particularly young, unmarried, and poor (among them Abraham Lincoln). Most numerous were the French-Canadians, many of whom were of Indian-European ancestry.

22. Quoted in Barker, *Mexico and Texas*, 6. In the late 1820s, as U.S. pressures on Mexico to sell Texas roused the Mexican government to curtail immigration, the exuberant Senator Thomas Hart Benton proudly validated his sarcasm when he declared: "The western people have a claim from the laws of God and nature to the exclusive possession of the entire valley of the Mississippi" (quoted in ibid., 44). A Mexican official attributed such vigorous expansionism to more secular instincts: "Instead of armies, battles, or invasions . . . , these men lay hands on means which, if considered one by one, would be rejected as slow, ineffective, and at times palpably absurd." General Mier y Terán to the minister of war, November 14, 1829, in Barker, *Mexico and Texas*, 8–9. See also William E. Weeks, *John Quincy Adams and American Global Empire* (Lexington, Ky., 1992).

23. Barker, *Mexico and Texas*, 148; see also 82–83, 144–45. Statistics on Texas's population are from ibid., 21. For a different perspective on Texan-Mexican relations see Vicente Filísola, *Memorias para la historia de la guerra de Tejas* (2 vols., Mexico City, 1849), 2: 170–71, 222–25; Dirk Raat, *Mexico and the United States: Ambivalent Vistas* (Athens, Ga., 1992), 4–7; and Samuel Lowrie, *Culture Conflict in Texas, 1821–1835* (New York, 1932).

24. See Paul D. Lack, *The Texas Revolutionary Experience: A Political and Social History, 1835–1836* (College Station, Tex., 1992). The Mexican consul in New Orleans wrote: "With a determination to arouse the city's inhabitants in favor of their cause, [the Texans] carried out their designs in public meetings and in the press." Consul to Sec. Foreign Relations, Jan. 8, 1836, in Mexico, Archivo de Relaciones Exteriores, L-E-1060, pp. 120–21.

For the diplomatic background, see the relevant chapters in David Pletcher, *The Diplomacy of Annexation: Texas, Oregon, and the Mexican War* (Columbia, Mo., 1973); Carlos Bosch García, *Historia de las relaciones entre México y los Estados Unidos, 1819–1848* (Mexico City, 1961); and Gene Brack, *Mexico Views Manifest Destiny, 1821–1846* (Albuquerque, N.M., 1975).

25. Gregory Dowd, *A Spirited Resistance: The North American Indian Struggle for Unity, 1745–1815* (Baltimore, 1992), 117. For a brilliant exposition of this theme see Frederick B. Pike, *The United States and Latin America: Myths and Stereotypes of Civilization and Nature* (Austin, Tex., 1992), esp. chs. 1 and 3. See also Francis Paul Prucha, *American Indian Policy in the Formative Years: The Indian Trade and Intercourse Acts, 1790–1834* (Cambridge, Mass., 1962).

26. Joyce Appleby, *Capitalism and a New Social Order: The Republican Vision of the 1790s* (New York, 1984), 101; Dale Van Every, *The Disinherited: The Lost Birthright of the American Indian* (New York, 1976), 17–19.

27. Joel Martin, *Sacred Revolt: The Muskogees' Struggle for a New World* (Boston, 1991), 124–25, 173. Theda Purdue (applying the construct of Albert Memmi in *The Colonizer and the Colonized*) argues that the Cherokees assimilated not from conviction but by imitation. "From initial contact with whites to the American Civil War," Perdue writes, "the Cherokees gradually developed a severe case of this same social schizophrenia." *Slavery and the Evolution of Cherokee Society, 1540–1866* (Knoxville, Tenn., 1979), xiii; see also 54–57; and Tom Hatley, *The Divided Paths: Cherokees and South Carolinians Through the Era of Revolution* (New York, 1993), 232–41.

28. Alden T. Vaughn, "From White Man to Redskin: Changing Anglo-American Perceptions of the American Indian," *American Historical Review* 87 (Oct. 1987): 952. See also Oren Lyons, et al., *Exiled in the Land of the Free: Democracy, Indian Nations, and the U.S. Constitution* (Santa Fe, N.M., 1993). For Jefferson's ambivalent views about Indians see Ronald Takaki, *Iron Cages: Race and Culture in 19th-Century America* (New York, 1990), 56–65.

29. Quoted in Arthur Ekirch, *Man and Nature in America* (New York, 1963), 24. See also Richard Slotkin, *The Fatal Environment: The Myth of the Frontier in the Age of Industrialization, 1800–1890* (New York, 1985), 110.

  As on other controversial decisions made by Jackson, Robert Remini offers a partial rebuttal to those who uniformly condemn Jackson's role in Indian removal: "Although the Whigs pummeled the Democrats for their unconscionable theft of Indian property and inhuman disregard of Indian life and safety, nevertheless they pursued Jackson's identical policy when they themselves came into office and had the opportunity of reversing or halting that policy." *Legacy of Andrew Jackson*, 81. "The key to understanding Jackson's attitude toward the Indian is not hatred but paternalism." Remini, *Andrew Jackson and the Course of American Empire, 1767–1821* (New York, 1977), 337. See also Michael P. Rogin, *Fathers and Children* (New York, 1975).

30. Eugene Genovese, *The World the Slaveholders Made: Two Essays in Economic Interpretation* (New York, 1969), 132–33. Sylvia Frey observes: "The degree to which racist ideology pervaded southern society is strikingly apparent in the treatment of free blacks. . . . The idea that blackness was itself prima facie evidence of inferiority, if not of slave status, reached its apotheosis in the quarter century after the Revolution in a cluster of court cases involving legislative formulations of the natural rights philosophy." Frey, *Water from the Rock: Black Resistance in the Revolutionary Age* (Princeton, N.J., 1991), 240. See also Gary Nash, *Race and Revolution* (Madison, Wis., 1990), 48–49.

  The impact of slave labor on the southern economy was already a sharply debated issue among contemporaries and remains one among modern students, largely because of the entanglement of the twin factors of new land for cotton production and the strength of slave institutions. See Peter Temin, "Free Land and Federalism" in Shafer, ed., *Is America Different?*, 79–80; Robert W. Fogel and Stanley L. Engerman, *Time on the Cross: The Economics of American Negro Slavery* (Boston, 1974); and Gavin Wright, *The Political Economy of the Cotton South: Households, Markets, and Wealth in the Nineteenth Century* (New York, 1978). Fred Bateman and Thomas Weiss, *A Deplorable Scarcity: The Failure of Industrialization in the Slave Economy* (Chapel Hill, N.C., 1981), observe: "Southerners were 'different,' but they were not economic masochists. Markets functioned not perfectly but adequately through the nation in this less harried nineteenth-century world" (163). More important for the slaveholders' dominance and prestige was the usefulness of slavery and material acquisitiveness as a utilitarian means for preserving the South's hierarchical social structure. "Slavery established the basis of the planter's position and power. It measured his affluence, marked his status, and supplied leisure for social graces and aristocratic duties." Eugene Genovese, *The Political Economy of Slavery: Studies in the Economy and Society of the Slave South* (New York, 1965), 29. See also Frey, *Water from the Rock*, 243, 328–29.

31. Wiebe, *Opening of American Society,* 339. "This racism," William Cooper Jr. notes, "also made believable an ideology that placed all whites on an equal social and political level." Cooper, *Liberty and Slavery: Southern Politics to 1860* (New York, 1983), 249. His observation must be qualified, however, as Bill Cecil-Fronsman points out in a study of antebellum North Carolina, where "common whites . . . certainly did not always believe that they lived in a fair social order. . . . The planter class's hegemony was real, but it was also limited." Cecil-Fronsman, *Common Whites: Class and Culture in Antebellum North Carolina* (Lexington, Ky., 1992), 6.

32. George M. Frederickson, *The Black Image in the White Mind: The Debate on Afro-American Character and Destiny* (New York, 1971), 19.

33. Tocqueville, *Democracy in America,* 1:364. See also Fredrickson, *Black Image in the White Mind,* 6–11; Dwight W. Hoover, *The Red and the Black* (Chicago, 1976), 112–13; Takaki, *Iron Cages,* 110–13, 126–27; and Alexander Saxton, *The Rise and Fall of the White Republic: Class Politics and Mass Culture in Nineteenth-Century America* (London, 1990), 68–69.

For the racist dynamics of U.S. continental expansionism see Thomas Hietala, *Manifest Destiny: Anxious Aggrandizement in Late Jacksonian America* (Ithaca, N.Y., 1985), esp. 134–35, 260–61. In his study of mulattoes, Joel Williamson validates Tocqueville's observation. Free Negroes and (if native-born) free mulattoes "were not yet seen as a threat in the lower South. They not only were tolerated, they were in some ways valued" because . . . fearful whites prudently imposed stringent controls upon their black slaves, and they looked to their mulatto kin for help." *New People: Miscegenation and Mulattoes in the United States* (New York, 1980), 15–16.

Freed blacks who were reluctant to move to Sierra Leone, Haiti, Jamaica, or Trinidad were apt to emigrate to the Canadas instead. Though slavery remained legal throughout British America until 1833, the freed U.S. slave or fugitive was generally well-treated by Canadians. Confronted with a much larger immigration in the late twenties and early thirties, writes Robin Winks in his study of blacks in Canada, "they were less certain of their liberal sentiments. . . . Paradoxically, many of the Negro arrivals were showing a distressing ambivalence toward their adopted country. They asserted their loyalty and their love for the Crown, and many served in the armed forces, voted, and acquired property. Yet, when given an opportunity, many returned to the United States." Robin Winks, *The Blacks in Canada* (New Haven, 1971), 143.

34. Kenneth McNaught, *The Pelican History of Canada* (London, 1969), 60–69; J. M. Bumsted, "The Cultural Landscape of Early Canada," in Bernard Bailyn and Philip Morgan, eds., *Strangers in the Realm: Cultural Margins of the First British Empire* (Chapel Hill, N.C., 1991), 390–91.

35. M. L. Hansen and J. B. Brebner, *The Mingling of Canadian and American Peoples* (New Haven, 1937), 1:98–107; Klaus Eugene Knorr, *British Colonial Theories, 1570–1850* (Toronto, 1968; orig. pub., 1944), 269–71.

36. McNaught, *History of Canada,* 56–59, 76–79, 84–87; William J. Eccles, *France in America* (New York, 1972), 248–49; Hansen and Brebner, *Mingling of Canadian and American Peoples,* 115–19. French-Canadian patriots won an initial victory and then were repulsed. Mackenzie's rebels attacked Toronto and were driven from the city by a makeshift force of government volunteers. Mackenzie took refuge among sympathizers in Buffalo and, with several hundred American sympathizers, prepared

to renew the conflict. The commotions on the border precipitated an international incident when local British officials dispatched a raiding party that attacked and sank a rebel vessel, the *Caroline*, berthed on the U.S. side of the Niagara. For the diplomatic settlement of this affair, see Kenneth R. Stevens, *Border Diplomacy: The Caroline and McLeod Affairs in Anglo-American–Canadian Relations, 1837–1842* (Tuscaloosa, Ala., 1989).

37. Quoted in Ekirch, *Man and Nature in America*, 36.

38. Quoted in William Appleman Williams, "The Age of Mercantilism: An Interpretation of the American Political Economy," *William and Mary Quarterly* 15 (Oct. 1958): 434; Wood, *Radicalism of the American Revolution*, 313. See also Appleby, *Liberalism and Republicanism*, 316–23.

   The historiographical debate on Jeffersonian thought—essentially, a quarrel about whether to place Jefferson in the political lineage of classical republicans or among that of liberals—remains spirited and is probably irreconcilable. Lance Banning (who identifies with the former) alertly reminds us that "liberal ideas were only part of their [Revolutionary Americans'] inheritance [and] . . . that Jeffersonians could never be wholly comfortable with the increasingly complexity and privatization of American life." "Jeffersonian Ideology Revisited: Liberal and Classical Ideas in the New American Republic," *William and Mary Quarterly* 43 (June 1986): 12.

39. Wiebe, *Opening of American Society*, 216.

40. John Agnew, *The United States in the World Economy* (Cambridge, 1987), 39–41; William N. Parker, *Europe, America, and the Wider World: Essays on the Economic History of Western Capitalism*, vol. 2, *America and the Wider World* (New York, 1991), 14–15; James O. Henretta, *The Evolution of American Society, 1700–1815: An Interdisciplinary Analysis* (Lexington, Mass., 1973), 184–85; Allan Kulikoff, "The Transition to Capitalism in Rural America," *William and Mary Quarterly* 46 (Jan. 1989): 129–30; and Richard Bushman's essay in James Henretta, ed., *Transformation of Early American History: Society, Authority, and Ideology* (New York, 1991), 252–53.

   Economic historians dispute the triggering mechanism for the impressive growth of the U.S. economy over a long period of time. The earliest model was the export-based, or staple model, incorporated by Douglas C. North in *The Economic Growth of the United States, 1790–1860* (Englewood Cliffs, N.J., 1961). According to this model, exports (after 1815, the English demand for southern cotton; after 1843, for midwestern grains) broke down the subsistence economy and drew U.S. producers and laborers into the marketplace. Income from southern cotton went to the midwest to pay for food, and southern and midwestern consumers in turn purchased manufactures from northeastern industrialists. Structuralists demur about the apparent lack of suitable alternatives to this model and argue that it downplays the significant role of alternative factors, particularly in the internal economy. See Stanley Engerman and Robert E. Gallman, "U.S. Economic Growth, 1783–1860," *Research in Economic History* 8 (1983): 26–29, and the observations of William G. Staples in *Castles of Our Conscience: Social Control and the American State, 1800–1985* (New Brunswick, N.J., 1991), 20–21.

41. Thomas C. Cochran, *Frontiers of Change: Early Industrialism in America* (New York, 1981), 9.

42. Quoted in Eaton, *Leaven of Democracy*, 38. See also Banning, *Jeffersonian Persuasion*, 302; Joseph Blau, ed., *Social Theories of Jacksonian Democracy* (Indianapolis, 1954), 25–28; and Robert Remini, *Andrew Jackson and the Course of American Freedom*,

1822–1832 (New York, 1981), 34–38. Remini finds Jackson's devotion to states' rights, his harsh critique of strong central government, and his passionate nationalism "strange [and] seemingly contradictory" but explains that "Jackson exuded a brand of national that was total and fanatical in its embrace of the concept of an indivisible confederation of states. This patriotic and nationalist fervor undoubtedly took shape and form in his youth." Remini, *The Legacy of Andrew Jackson*, 11. A more precise reason, I believe, lay in Jackson's understanding of the distinction between *nation-state* and its sustaining economic philosophy of liberalism on the one hand and *nation*, which derived its strength from qualitative sentiments and feelings.

43. Richard D. Brown, "The Emergence of Urban Society in Rural Massachusetts," *Journal of American History* 61 (June 1974): 45.

44. Henretta, *Evolution of American Society, 1700–1815*, 194–97. But industrialization did not impede the "process of democratization," writes Seymour Drescher; "the phenomena of social mobility and the supremacy of the masses in America were the decisive facts of American life, and they simply canceled out all hierarchical and inegalitarian tendencies." *Dilemmas of Democracy*, 72.

45. Michel Chevalier, "The Factory Girls of Lowell," extracted from *Society, Manners, and Politics in the United States* (Boston, 1839), cited in Eaton, *Leaven of Democracy*, 411; Nancy F. Cott, *The Bonds of Womanhood: 'Women's Sphere' in New England, 1780–1835* (New Haven, 1977), 2–3, 20–21, 58–61; E. P. Thompson, "Time, Work-Discipline, and Industrial Capitalism," *Past and Present* 38 (1967): 56–79.

46. Quoted in J. R. Pole, *Pursuit of Equality in American History* (Berkeley, 1978), 135. Their living standards were certainly higher than those of New York City's rising numbers of welfare families and working poor—those who performed menial unskilled tasks, had no permanent employment, and competed with arriving Irish immigrants for low-wage jobs. See Raymond A. Mohl, *Poverty in New York, 1783–1825* (New York, 1971), 28–29. As their economic situation worsened, white laborers became more violent in their antipathies toward free blacks. For three days in July 1834 in New York City, where black institutions had suffered harassment for years, "lower and middling classes who detested abolitionists and blacks" ravaged black churches and the properties of abolitionist sympathizers. They were driven by fears of amalgamation and competition of freed persons, but overshadowing and subsuming both issues . . . was the concern over the development of a black subcommunity." Paul A. Gilje, *The Road to Mobocracy: Popular Disorder in New York City, 1763–1834* (Chapel Hill, N.C., 1987), 163.

For a general discussion of the racial dynamic in the growth of the labor movement see David R. Roediger, *The Wages of Whiteness: Race and the Making of the American Working Class* (New York, 1991); and Saxton, *Rise and Fall of the White Republic.*

47. Stuart Blumin, *The Emergence of the Middle Class: Social Experience in the American City, 1760–1900* (Cambridge, 1989), 78–81, 111–12, 136–37; Gilje, *Road to Mobocracy*, 176–77; Jonathan A. Glickstein, *Concepts of Free Labor in Antebellum America* (New Haven, 1991).

48. Carl Degler, *At Odds: Women and the Family from the Revolution to the Present* (New York, 1980), 8–9; Wiebe, *Opening of American Society*, 265–67.

Though the Jacksonian era had its share of the arbitrary, coercive social reformer, Lawrence Kohl observes, "what is remarkable about the age was its reluctance to exercise power, its insistence that the best way to bring order to society was to allow the enlightened self-interests of a free populace to order themselves." Kohl, "The

Concept of Social Control and the History of Jacksonian America," *Journal of the Early Republic* 5 (Spring 1985): 31.

49. Rowland Berthoff, *An Unsettled People: Social Order and Disorder in American History* (New York, 1971), 204–5; 218–19, 244–45, 254–55. See also Wiebe, *Opening of American Society*, 230–31, 288–89; Blumin, *Emergence of the Middle Class*, 192–95; and, for a general account, Clifford S. Griffin, *Their Brothers' Keepers: Moral Stewardship in the United States, 1800–1865* (New Brunswick, N.J., 1960).

50. William C. Mitchell, *The American Polity: A Social and Cultural Interpretation* (New York, 1962), 11–17; Blumin, *Emergence of the Middle Class*, 192–93.

51. Wilson, *Space, Time, and Freedom*, 8–9. See also Fred Somkin, *Unquiet Eagle: Memory and Desire in the Idea of American Freedom, 1815–1860* (Ithaca, N.Y., 1967), who delineates the ways in which the pursuit of material "desires" ultimately dissipated the strength of communal "memories."

11 Bolívar's America

1. Alexis de Tocqueville (Henry Reeve, trans.), *Democracy in America*, 4th ed. (2 vols., New York, 1845), 1:349.

The judgment of Sanford Mosk on the condition of Latin America appears unduly harsh but merits quoting: "When the Latin-American colonies gained their independence in the nineteenth century, the semifeudal system of landholdings and social classes was not at all disturbed. . . . New individuals rose to power during and after the conflict, some nominal legal changes were made with respect to the status and treatment of Indians, but nothing was altered in the fundamental institutions of Latin America by the movement for independence." Mosk, "Latin America vs. the United States," in Lewis Hanke, ed., *Do the Americas Have a Common History? A Critique of the Bolton Theory* (New York, 1964), 10.

2. Quoted in Arthur Preston Whitaker, *The United States and the Independence of Latin America, 1800–1830* (New York, 1964; orig. pub., 1941), 335–36; see also 181. The comments of Adams are from Peggy Liss, *Atlantic Empires: The Network of Trade and Revolution, 1713–1826* (Baltimore, 1982), 124. See also Whitaker's suggestive essay, *The Western Hemisphere Idea: Its Rise and Decline* (Ithaca, N.Y., 1954); and Harry Bernstein, *Making an Inter-American Mind* (Gainesville, Fla., 1961), 20–23, 34–35, 78–79. In revolutionary Buenos Aires, U.S. emissary Henry M. Brackenridge found French translations of Benjamin Franklin's works, Thomas Paine's *Common Sense*, the Declaration of Independence, and George Washington's Farewell Address.

Bolívar's failure to become "another Washington" was, in the eyes of North Americans, the result of his inability to curb his passionate Latin nature. "Incapable of subjecting his own passions to control even as he fought for independence, Bolívar in the course of the struggle liberated outward symbols of passion and primitivism: he freed the slaves of Latin America . . . and established a close alliance with the tumultuous blacks and mulattoes of Haiti. . . . Washington had the sense . . . to retain his slaves . . . [and] unlike Bolívar did not entertain utopian dreams about the speedy incorporation of Indians into the political and social mainstream." Fredrick Pike, *United States and Latin America: Myths and Stereotypes of Civilization and Nature* (Austin, Tex., 1992), 64–75.

3. Bolívar to Santander, March 11, 1825, in Simón Bolívar (Vicente Lecuna, comp.; Harold Bierck, ed.; Lewis Bertrand, trans.), *Selected Writings of Bolívar* (2 vols., New York, 1951), 2:484. "Never were we as badly off as present. . . . [Under Spain] we enjoyed positive and tangible benefits, whereas today we have dreams bordering on

illusion, hope feeding upon the future, and disillusionment forever tortured with the bitterness of reality." Bolívar, "A Panoramic View of Spanish America" (1829), in ibid., 747. The comments about Mexico, the United States, Haiti, and Colombia are in ibid., 1:306, 307.

Using the experience of the long wars of independence as his reference, Tulio Halperín-Donghi observes: "Among the changes brought by independence, the negative consequences stood out: the debasement of civil administration, a tendency to chronic upheaval, and heavy-handed governmental repression of an armed and politically mobilized populace, leaving insurgency as the only recourse." Halperín-Donghi (John Chasteen, trans.), *The Contemporary History of Latin America* (Durham, N.C., 1993), 85–86.

4. Halperín-Donghi, *Contemporary History of Latin America*, 94.

5. "After liberty," he wrote in 1818, immigration "would be the most effective means . . . of creating a homogeneous, industrious, and moral people [and] the one solid foundation for Equality, Liberty, and consequently prosperity of a nation." Quoted in Tulio Halperín-Donghi, *El espejo de la historia: Problemas argentinos y perspectivas hispanoamericanas* (Buenos Aires, 1987), 196. A contemporary concluded: "[Rivadavia] lacked the patience to let his [decrees] soak in; he had no respect for time nor customs and even less for popular concerns. The people were not ready to see so much light all at once." Tomás de Iriarte, *Memorias* (12 vols., Buenos Aires, 1945), 3:31. See also Nicholas Shumway, *The Invention of Argentina* (Berkeley, 1991), 82–85, 100–101, 112–13; David Bushnell, *Reform and Reaction in the Platine Provinces, 1810–1852* (Gainesville, Fla., 1983), 20–23, 44–45; and Ricardo Piccirilli, *Rivadavia y su tiempo* (2 vols., Buenos Aires, 1943).

6. Miron Burgin, *The Economic Aspects of Argentine Federalism, 1820–1852* (Cambridge, Mass., 1946), 108–9; Shumway, *Invention of Argentina*, 112–16.

7. Poinsett to Secretary of State Martin Van Buren, March 10, 1829, in William R. Manning, *Diplomatic Correspondence of the United States Concerning the Independence of Latin American Nations* (3 vols., New York, 1925), 3:1674. See also Stanley C. Green, *The Mexican Republic: The First Decade, 1823–1832* (Pittsburgh, 1987), 52–63, 88–91; Lucas Alamán, *Historia de México desde los primeros movimientos que prepararon su Independencia en el año de 1808 has la época presente* (5 vols., Mexico City, 1985; orig. pub., 1850), 5:517; and Harold Sims, *The Expulsion of Mexico's Spaniards, 1821–1836* (Pittsburgh, 1990), 10–11.

8. Bolívar to Santander, August 20, 1825, *Selected Writings of Bolívar*, 2:499. See also John J. Johnson, *A Hemisphere Apart: The Foundations of United States Policy Toward Latin America* (Baltimore, 1990), 75–76.

9. Quoted in Louis Pérez Jr., *Cuba and the United States: Ties of Singular Intimacy* (Athens, Ga., 1990), 36–37. On the issue of Cuban *independence*, Secretary of State Henry Clay expressed a view compatible with Bolívar's: "If Cuba were to declare itself independent," Clay warned, "the amount and character of its population render it improbable that it could maintain its independence. Such a premature declaration might bring about a renewal of those shocking scenes, of which a neighboring island was the afflicted theatre" (quoted in ibid., 42).

10. Quoted in ibid., 38. See also Knight, *Slave Society in Cuba*, 16–17, 20–21.

11. Tulio Halperín-Donghi, *The Aftermath of Revolution in Latin America* (New York, 1973), 26–34. On racial categories in postindependence Venezuela see Magnus Mörner, *Region and State in Latin America's Past* (Baltimore, 1993), 33–35.

12. Quoted in Winthrop R. Wright, *Café con Leche: Race, Class, and National Image in Venezuela* (Austin, Tex., 1990), 28; see also 32–33, and Halperín-Donghi, *Aftermath of Revolution in Latin America*, 24–39.

These fears did not diminish Bolívar's and Santander's commitment to eventual emancipation, however, "By this means the colored race would come to see that its objectives were attained by peaceful means, and would give up any thought of seeking long overdue justice by force of arms." David Bushnell, *The Santander Regime in Gran Colombia* (Newark, Del., 1954), 173.

13. Edward L. Cox, *Free Coloreds in the Slave Societies of St. Kitts and Grenada* (Knoxville, Tenn., 1984), 145.

Early in the century, James Stephen had succinctly expressed the case for amelioration when he wrote: "It would be monstrous to maintain that the Mother Country has no right to correct by wholesome laws, evils by which she is exposed to such costly demands for protection and relief. It would be to say, that the planter has a right to raise and maintain at pleasure on his own land a nuisance pestiferous to the vital resources of the empire; and that Parliament has no right to enter and abate it." Stephen, *The Crisis of the Sugar Colonies; or, An Inquiry in the Objects and Probable Effects of the French Expedition to the West Indies; and Their Connection with the Colonial Interests of the British Empire* (New York, 1969; orig. pub., 1802), 140.

14. As the slaves often said, "you brown man hab no country . . . only de neger and buckra hab country." Quoted in William A. Green, *British Slave Emancipation: The Sugar Colonies of the Great Experiment, 1830–1865* (Oxford, 1976), 34.

15. David Brion Davis, *Slavery and Human Progress* (New York, 1984), 181; Michael Craton, *Testing the Chains: Resistance to Slavery in the British West Indies* (Ithaca, N.Y., 1982), 242–44.

Michael Craton has turned abolitionists' logic on its head: slave rebelliousness acted noticeably on British leaders and on metropolitan opinion. Slave leaders took advantage of the opportunities offered by antislavery agitation to fashion their own agenda, and slaves themselves received Christian teaching from naive missionaries, transforming it "to their own needs and ends, making it an instrument of political as well as spiritual change." Craton, "Slave Culture, Resistance and the Achievement of Emancipation in the British West Indies, 1783–1838," in James Walvin, ed., *Slavery and British Society, 1776–1846* (Baton Rouge, La., 1982), 103.

For an assessment of the infuriating complexities of slave society and rebellion in Demerara, see Emilia Viotti da Costa, *Crowns of Glory, Tears of Blood: The Demerara Slave Rebellion of 1823* (New York, 1994), esp. 24–25, 34–35, 78–79.

16. Mary Turner, *Slaves and Missionaries: The Disintegration of Jamaican Slave Society, 1787–1834* (Bloomington, Ind., 1982), 48–49, 148–51, 159–63, 200–1.

17. Quoted in Philip Curtain, *Two Jamaicas* (Cambridge, Mass., 1955), 87. See also Green, *British Slave Emancipation*, 112–13.

18. Quoted in Craton, "Slave Culture, Resistance, and Emancipation," in Walvin, ed., *Slavery and British Society*, 122.

19. "Laws only served to burden the weak without restraining the strong. . . . Our America can only be ruled through a well-managed, shrewd despotism." Bolívar to Santander, July 8, 1826, *Selected Writings of Bolívar*, 2:623–24; Bolívar to General Daniel O'Leary, September 13, 1829, in ibid., 739.

Bolívar alternated between calumnious outbursts against his enemies, real and imagined, and despair over the elusive goal of unity. After the decisive victory over

Spanish forces at Ayacucho, he had warned his ally Santander of the dangers from within: "Every day I am more convinced that it is necessary to provide a guarantee for our existence. I foresee civil war and disorder breaking out in all directions. . . . I see my native gods consumed by domestic fire" (Bolívar to Santander, January 6–7, 1825, in ibid., 461). His notion of republic was a contradictory fusing of the modern notions of liberty and ancient practices; in the ideal society, the state existed "to make men good, and consequently happy." Quoted in Anthony Pagden, *Spanish Imperialism and the Political Imagination: Studies in European and Spanish-American Social and Political Theory, 1513–1830* (New Haven, 1990), 146. Such a society required a strong, perhaps even a despotic, leader—thus the inappropriateness of the North American political model.

20. Quoted in Desmond Gregory, *Brute New World: The Rediscovery of Latin America in the Early 19th Century* (New York, 1993), 109.

21. Bolívar to Páez, April 12, 1828, *Selected Writings of Bolívar,* 2:689. Bolívar had neglected to dwell on "Montesquieu's main argument—that all political arrangements must be adapted to the culture and the climate of the communities for which they are intended—which showed a sensitivity . . . to the degree to which even the most virtuous of societies depends for its creation and survival upon its prior cultural constitution." Pagden, *Spanish Imperialism and the Political Imagination,* 149.

22. Pagden, *Spanish Imperialism and the Political Imagination,* 148. See also "Reply to a Gentleman of [Jamaica]," September 6, 1815, *Selected Writings of Bolívar,* 1:115; Halperín-Donghi, *El espejo de la historia,* 115; and Halperín-Donghi, *Aftermath of Revolution in Latin America,* 132.

23. Quoted in John Lynch, *The Spanish American Revolutions, 1808–1826* (New York, 1973), 293.

24. I have relied principally on John Lynch, *Caudillos in Spanish America, 1800–1850* (Oxford, 1992); see also Félix Luna, *Los caudillos* (Buenos Aires, 1976); Fernando Díaz Díaz, *Caudillos y caciques: Antonio López de Santa Anna* (Mexico City, 1972); John Lynch, *Argentine Dictator: Juan Manuel de Rosas, 1829–1852* (Oxford, 1981); Ralph Lee Woodward, Jr., *Rafael Carrera* (Athens, Ga., 1993); Laureano Vallenilla Lanz, *Obras completas,* vols. 1: *Cesarismo democrático* (Caracas, 1983); and R. B. Cunninghame Graham, *José Antonio Páez* (London, 1929).

25. Quoted in Robert Gilmore, *Caudillism and Militarism in Venezuela, 1810–1910* (Athens, Ohio, 1964), 25. See also Richard Morse, *New World Soundings: Culture and Ideology in the Americas* (Baltimore, 1989), 111–16; and Morse, "The Heritage of Latin America," in Louis Hartz, ed., *The Founding of New Societies* (New York, 1964), 123–77, which is rightly considered a seminal assessment of Latin American political culture. There are two fundamental problems with the cultural explanation of nineteenth-century Spanish American political history, Frank Safford observes. The first has to do with its "excessively static" view, "as if Spanish culture, once crystallized at some point in the distant past, never underwent significant change afterward." A second is the relative neglect of the "role of geographic, economic, and social structural factors in destabilizing political systems, and in permitting their stabilization." Safford, "Politics, Ideology, and Society," in Leslie Bethell, ed., *The Cambridge History of Latin America,* vol. 3: *From Independence to c. 1870* (Cambridge, 1985), 417.

On the political condition of postrevolutionary Mexico see Luis Villoro, *El proceso ideológico de la revolución de independencia,* 2nd ed. (Mexico City, 1967). Charles Arnade has described the creation of independent Bolivia as the "product of sixteen long years of revolution, war, and intrigue. . . . Its immediate creators deserved to be despised rather than praised." Arnade, *The Emergence of the Republic of Bolivia* (Gainesville, Fla., 1957), 205.

26. Halperín-Donghi, *Aftermath of Revolution in Latin America*, 2–24; Henry M. Brackenridge, *Voyage to South America . . . in 1817 and 1818* (2 vols., Baltimore, 1819), 2:281, 282.

"One way nations demonstrate the strength and geographical extent of their power," Barbara Tenenbaum argues in reviewing the discordant and violent history of Mexico during its first quarter-century after independence, "is through their ability to impose and collect taxes." Tenenbaum, *The Politics of Penury: Debts and Taxes in Mexico, 1821–1856* (Albuquerque, N.M., 1986), xiii. The issue of state finance in assessing the survival of early republican government, a topic of subsumed but critical importance, has yielded a more abundant scholarship in the history of the early U.S. republic than in that of Latin America. Conflicts between liberals and Conservatives over ideology, development, religion, or other salient matters have too often distracted modern scholars from the primacy of taxes and budgets in the Latin American experience of governance. See also Burgin, *Economic Aspects of Argentine Federalism;* Bushnell, *Santander Regime in Gran Colombia;* Tulio Halperín-Donghi, *Guerra y finanzas en los origenes del estado argentino, 1791–1850* (Buenos Aires, 1982); Malcolm Deas, "The Fiscal Problem of Nineteenth-Century Colombia," *Journal of Latin American Studies,* 14 (1982): 287–328; and Vincent Peloso and Barbara Tenenbaum, eds., *Liberals, Politics, and Power: State Formation in Nineteenth-Century Latin America* (Athens, Ga., 1996).

27. Poinsett to Secretary of State Henry Clay, October 12, 1825, in Manning, ed., *Diplomatic Correspondence,* 3:1639; Green, *The Mexican Republic: The First Decade,* 83.

John Johnson may distort reality with the comment that "the liberators turned upon the liberated." Johnson, *The Military and Society in Latin America* (Sanford, 1964), 25. As Tulio Halperín-Donghi reminds us, the "role of the army within the new social structure was as ambiguous as its position therein." *Aftermath of Revolution in Latin America,* 24. See also Gregory, *Brute New World,* 178–81.

28. Gilmore, *Caudillism and Militarism in Venezuela,* 124–33; Alain Rouquié (Paul Sigmund, trans.), *The Military and the State in Latin America* (Berkeley, 1987), 52; Johnson, *Military and Society in Latin America,* 32–35.

29. "In the early decades after independence the veteran officers constituted a consensus group, but not a closely organized pressure group in the modern technical sense. They were virtually unanimous on one subject. They had created the Venezuelan state, and therefore they should lead and control it." Gilmore, *Caudillism and Militarism in Venezuela,* 11. See also Halperín-Donghi, *Aftermath of Revolution in Latin America,* 21–25.

30. David Bushnell and Neill Macaulay, *The Emergence of Latin America in the Nineteenth Century* (New York, 1988), 34. See also Bushnell, *Reform and Reaction in the Platine Provinces,* 3–4; and Charles A. Hale, *Mexican Liberalism in the Age of Mora, 1821–1853* (New Haven, 1968). The geographical locus of power was another fundamental issue. Inspired by the North American model, an early generation of liberals inclined toward federalism as a means of dissipating central authority, but these "imaginative federal schemes, the audacious liberal constitutions, and courageous attempts at decentralization had one thing in common. . . . They were all tried, but none worked." Claudio Véliz, *The Centralist Tradition of Latin America* (Princeton, N.J., 1980), 151.

31. Safford, "Politics, Ideology, and Society," in Bethell, ed., *Cambridge History of Latin America*, 3:384–85, 404–7; see also Safford, "Bases of Political Alignment in Early Republican Spanish America," in Richard Graham and Peter H. Smith, eds., *New Approaches to Latin American History* (Austin, Tex., 1974), 71–111; and Safford, "Social Aspects of Political Alignment in 19th Century Spanish America: New Granada, 1825–1850," *Journal of Social History* 5 (Spring 1972): 344–70.

32. Quoted in E. Bradford Burns, *The Poverty of Progress: Latin America in the Nineteenth Century* (Berkeley, 1980), 11.

    "The elites believed that 'to progress' meant to recreate their nations as closely as possible to their European and North American models," Burns explains in a suggestive reinterpretation of nineteenth-century Latin American history. "They felt they would benefit from such a recreation, and by extension they assumed that their nations would benefit as well. They always identified (and confused) class well-being with national welfare" (ibid., 9).

33. Travel accounts of the 1820s and 1830s offer graphic descriptions of depopulation and physical devastation. Roaming about Venezuela in the 1830s, John Hawkshaw wrote: "Houses and streets are empty. Farms and cultivated estates are left to go back to a state of nature; and weeks of rank vegetation are covering up what once were scenes of productiveness and prosperity." John Hawkshaw, *Reminiscences of South America* (London, 1838), 38.

    On economic issues see Halperín-Donghi, *Aftermath of Revolution in Latin America*, 46; and especially Stanley Stein and Barbara Stein, *The Colonial Heritage of Latin America: Essays on Economic Dependence in Perspective* (New York, 1970), 134–35. This brief but powerfully argued book is perhaps the most persuasive statement of the dependentista view of Latin American modernization. In a sharp rebuttal, D. C. M. Platt has written: "The takeoff point in the economic relationship between Latin America and the outside world was not 1810, nor 1820, nor any of the next three decades. These were years of modest expansion, not of radical change." Platt, *Latin America and British Trade, 1806–1914* (London, 1972), 3.

    Dependency as an explanation for Latin America's twentieth-century condition had its greatest impact among scholars in the 1970s, but its utility as a theoretical construct remains hotly debated. The literature is vast. A good beginning is the discussion by Tulio Halperín-Donghi, Robert Packenham, Marcelo Cavarozzi, and Christopher Chase-Dunn in *Latin American Research Review*, 17 (1982): 115–71. See also C. R. Bath and D. D. James, "Dependency Analysis of Latin America: Some Criticisms, Some Suggestions," ibid. 11 (1976): 3–54; and Ronald H. Chilcote, "Dependency: A Critical Synthesis of the Literature," *Latin American Perspectives* 1 (1974): 4–29. For the nineteenth-century aspects of dependency, see D. C. M. Platt, "Dependency in Nineteenth-Century Latin America: An Historian Objects," in ibid., 15 (1980): 112–30; and the reply by Stanley Stein and Barbara Stein, "D. C. M. Platt: The Anatomy of Autonomy," in ibid., 131–43. On the influence of foreign merchants see the seminal article by Eugene Ridings, "Foreign Predominance Among Overseas Traders in Nineteenth-Century Latin America," in ibid., 20 (1985): 3–27; and the responses by Carlos Marichal, in ibid., 21 (1986): 145–50; and D. C. M. Platt, "Wicked Merchants and Macho Entrepreneurs: Shall We Grow up Now?" in ibid., 151–53.

34. Argentina and Central America are two such places. The history of rural development in each is often viewed retrogressively from the late nineteenth century to the first decades of independence. Analyzing from this perspective, historians have sometimes concluded that the undeniable existence of *latifundium* and plantation, the weakness of the rural middle class, and the parallel making of a rural underclass

in the later era must have resulted from statist policies aimed at destroying democratic, self-sufficient, and premodern communities. See, for example, Lynch, *Argentine Dictator: Juan Manuel de Rosas,* 92–101; and Richard Slatta, *Gauchos and the Vanishing Frontier* (Lincoln, Neb., 1983), 100–111. In actuality, the patterns of rural development were more complicated. Jonathan Brown has concluded "that export growth fostered the subdivision of older landholdings as well as settlement of new land." Brown, "The Bondage of Old Habits in Nineteenth-Century Argentina," *Latin American Research Review* 21 (1986): 7.

Undeniably, El Salvador's coffee *finqueros* benefited tremendously from the government's rapid dismantling of communal land ownership in the 1880s, but this choice, with all its damning implications for El Salvador's campesinos, had less to do with the government's earlier policies toward communal and small-scale farming than with the abrupt decision of a planter-dominated regime "to abolish any aspect of man's ownership, use or settlement of the land that hindered the rapid establishment of coffee plantations." David Browning, *El Salvador: Landscape and Society* (Oxford, 1971), 174. For Costa Rica's different experience see Lowell Gudmonson, *Costa Rica Before Coffee: Economy and Society on the Eve of the Export Boom* (Baton Rouge, La., 1986), 151–52.

On the influence of the postindependence family, see Diana Balmori, Stuart Voss, and Miles Wortman, *Notable Family Networks in Latin America* (Chicago, 1984), 38–41. For social aspects of postindependence politics see the important article by Frank Safford, "Social Aspects of Political Alignments in Nineteenth-Century Spanish America: New Granada, 1825–1850," *Journal of Social History* 5 (Spring 1972): 350.

35. Bushnell and Macaulay, *Emergence of Latin America in the Nineteenth Century,* 44.

36. Quoted in Halperín-Donghi, *Aftermath of Revolution in Latin America,* 59. See also Roberto Cortés-Conde, *The First Stages of Modernization in Spanish America* (New York, 1974), 5–6, 156–57.

37. Paul Gootenberg, *Between Silver and Guano: Commercial Policy and the State in Postindependence Peru* (Princeton, N.J., 1989), 6.

For largely favorable judgments of Paraguay's early years see Richard Alan White, *Paraguay's Autonomous Revolution, 1810–1840* (Albuquerque, N.M., 1978); and John Hoyt Williams, *The Rise and Fall of the Paraguayan Republic, 1800–1870* (Austin, Tex., 1979). For a critical assessment see Thomas Whigham, *The Politics of River Trade: Tradition and Development in the Upper Plata, 1780–1870* (Albuquerque, N.M., 1991).

38. Whigham, *Politics of River Trade,* 29. "Francia was neither a Bonapartist, nor a popular, proto-socialist revolutionary, nor the founder of an alternative development model for Paraguay. He governed his country along patrimonial lines, like a skillful Bourbon administrator. Francia strictly regulated trade so as to strengthen his regime, but he left alone the basic fabric of Paraguayan society" (ibid., 199). See also John Hoyt Williams, "Paraguayan Isolation Under Dr. Francia: A Reevaluation," *Hispanic American Historical Review* 52 (Feb. 1972): 102–22.

39. Gootenberg, *Between Silver and Guano,* 139; see also 10–11, 66–67, 138–41. "Protectionists were disguised Hapsburgs; free traders were latter-day Bourbons, revolutionary modernizers hopelessly outgunned in Peru. In this view, Peruvian nationalism actually retarded the development of a modern state and its economic institutions, which arrived long overdue in the 1850s. . . . Rather than resisting neocolonialism in their efforts to fend off foreigners and liberals, Peruvian nationalists were actually resuscitating the oldest and most venerable version of colonial society" (ibid., 155).

40. "Emancipation," wrote Halperín-Donghi, "appeared more than anything to be an event in which the chaos endemic but contained in the old colonial order not only burst forth but was amplified by new confusions." Halperín-Donghi, *Historia de América Latina*, vol. 3: *Reforma y disolución de los imperios ibéricos* (Madrid, 1985), 188.

41. David A. Brading, *The First America: The Spanish Monarchy, Creole Patriots, and the Liberal State, 1492–1867* (Cambridge, 1991), 623–24. "In [gaucho] society," wrote Sarmiento, "where mental culture is useless or impossible, where no municipal affairs exist, where, as there is no public, the public good is a meaningless word, the man of unusual gifts, striving to exert his faculties, takes with that design the means and the paths which are at hand. The gaucho will be a malefactor or a military chief, according to the course which things are taking at the moment when he attains celebrity." Sarmiento, *Life in the Argentine Republic*, in Robert G. Keith, ed., *Haciendas and Plantations in Latin American History* (New York, 1977), 188.

42. Quoted in Shumway, *Invention of Argentina*, 119. See also Lynch, *Caudillos*, 90–93; and Kevin Kelly, "Rosas and the Restoration of Order Through Populism," in Mark D. Szuchman and Jonathan Brown, eds., *Revolution and Restoration: The Rearrangement of Power in Argentina, 1776–1860* (Lincoln, Neb., 1994), 208–39.

43. Quoted in Burgin, *Economic Aspects of Argentine Federalism*, 159.

44. Sarmiento, *Facundo*, quoted in Shumway, *Invention of Argentina*, 151. See also Burns, *Poverty of Progress*, 20–23.

45. Rosas, *Mensaje*, December 31, 1835, quoted in Lynch, *Caudillos*, 249.

46. Lynch, *Caudillos*, 156–59. For a different view of Rosas see Bushnell, *Reform and Reaction in the Platine Provinces*, 60–65.

47. Quoted in Brading, *First America*, 641. For a depressing view of Mexico's postindependence condition by two contemporaries of otherwise contrary political views see Alamán, *Historia de México*, 5:566; and the comments of Fray Servando Teresa de Mier, who had lived in Philadelphia in the early years of the Mexican war for independence. Anticipating Tocqueville, Mier acknowledged that the United States had achieved "social perfection" because its inhabitants were "a new people, homogeneous, industrious, diligent, enlightened and full of social virtues, educated as a free nation." Mexicans, however, were "an old people, heterogeneous, without industry, hostile to work, who wish to live off public office like the Spaniards, as ignorant in the general mass as our fathers, and rotten with the vices that derive from the slavery of three centuries" (quoted in Brading, *The First America*, 599, 600).

48. Lynch, *Caudillos*, 120–21; Florencia Mallon, *Peasant and Nation: The Making of Postcolonial Mexico and Peru* (Berkeley, 1994), 144.

49. Quoted in Lynch, *Caudillos*, 324. When Santa Anna rode into the capital in 1832, the chronicler Bustamante wrote despondently: "If Hidalgo could have imagined this farce would he have uttered the Grito de Dolores?" Quoted in Brading, *First America*, 643.

50. Díaz D., *Caudillos y caciques* 345. See also Jan Bazant, "Mexico from Independence to 1867," in Bethell, ed., *Cambridge History of Latin America*, 3:436–37; Michael P. Costeloe, "Federalism to Centralism in Mexico: The Conservative Case for Change, 1834–1835," *The Americas* 45 (Oct. 1988): 173–85.

51. Wilfred H. Callcott, *Santa Anna: The Story of an Enigma Who Once Was Mexico* (Hamden, Conn., 1964), 126.

52. Tenenbaum, *The Politics of Penury,* 44–46; Nelson Reed, *The Caste War of Yucatán* (Stanford, Calif., 1964).

53. Jan Bazant, "Spanish America After Independence," in Bethell, ed., *Cambridge History of Latin America,* 3:444–49.

54. Russell H. Fitzgibbon has summarized the political circumstances of the early republics in almost apocalytic phrases: "The turbulence of the time, the lack of experience in democratic self-government, the uncertainty that Spain or some other European state would not again plant an alien flag over much of Latin America, the physical facts of a general frontier rawness and an absence of adequate transportation, all these and other factors scarcely permitted any other condition to prevail." Fitzgibbon, "The Process of Constitution Making in Latin America," *Comparative Studies in Society and History* 3 (Oct. 1960): 2. See also the classic interpretation by Glen Dealy, *The Latin Americans: Spirit and Ethos* (Boulder, Colo., 1992.

55. Halperín-Donghi, *Aftermath of Revolution in Latin America,* 42–43, 114–19, 123–25, 130–35; Balmori, Voss, and Wortman, *Notable Family Networks in Latin America,* 24–25, 34–43.

12 The Americas at 1850

1. Judith Shklar, *After Utopia: The Decline of Political Faith* (Princeton, N.J., 1957), 23–31. "Tocqueville saw in American individualism not so much the virtues of pluralism as the perils of an amorphous society, a society of uniformed sameness in which the individual loses strength of character and independence," John Diggins observes, "[but if] liberal individualism asserted the sovereignty of the individual over himself, it liberated man only by abrogating all authority of custom and tradition. Yet authority does not simply disappear. In a democratic culture the more power is weakened the more its sphere is widened until society itself becomes the seat of power and authority." Diggins, "The Three Faces of Authority in American History," in Diggins and Mark E. Kann, eds., *The Problem of Authority in America* (Philadelphia, 1981), 28.

A short time before his death, contemplating the legacy of the revolutions of 1848, Tocqueville wrote: "The French Revolution begins again, for it is always the same. . . . Must we simply end up in that intermittent state of anarchy which is the well-known, chronic, and incurable malady of old peoples?" Quoted in Seymour Drescher, "'Why Great Revolutions Will Become Rare': Tocqueville's Most Neglected Prognosis," *Journal of Modern History* 64 (Sept. 1992): 448–49.

2. Thomas C. Holt, *The Problem of Freedom: Race Labor and Politics in Jamaica and Britain, 1832–1938* (Baltimore, 1991), 6, 39; Eric Hobsbawm, *Age of Revolution, 1789–1848* (Cleveland, 1962), 237. See also Joshua Miller, *The Rise and Fall of Democracy in Early America, 1630–1789* (University Park, Penn., 1991), 12–13; Gary Gerstle, "The Protean Character of American Liberalism," *American Historical Review* 99 (Oct. 1994): 1046; John Diggins, *The Lost Soul of American Politics: Virtue, Self-Interest, and the Foundations of Liberalism* (New York, 1984), 4–5. On the harsh social consequences of modern liberal development, see John Hall, *Liberalism: Politics Ideology, and the Market* (Chapel Hill, N.C., 1987), 193. For a devastating critique of liberal progress in late-nineteenth-century Latin America, see E. Bradford Burns, *The Poverty of Progress: Latin America in the Nineteenth Century* (Berkeley, 1980), esp. 5–17. See also E. Bradford Burns and Thomas Skidmore, with an introduction by Richard Graham, *Elites, Masses, and Modernization in Latin America, 1850–1930* (Austin, Tex., 1979).

3. Eric Hobsbawm, *Nations and Nationalism Since 1780: Programme, Myth, Reality* (Cambridge, 1990), 36–40. The equation of nationhood, nationalism, and

modernization raised other issues yet debated by historians and historical sociologists. In the 1940s, Carlton J. H. Hayes and Hans Kohn identified nationalism with ideas, not social constructs, though both acknowledged that nationalism accompanied the emergence of a middle class. Their successors reversed the process, identifying nationalism with the dramatic social and economic transformation that defined the modern nation-state. Nationalism was thus determined by the elements that characterize the modern nation. See Ernest Gellner, *Nations and Nationalism* (Ithaca, N.Y., 1983); Benedict Anderson, *Imagined Communities: Reflections on the Origin and Spread of Nationalism* (New York, 1991); and Liah Greenfield, *Nationalism: Five Roads to Modernity* (Cambridge, Mass., 1992). Greenfield has returned to the older view that nationalism is closely linked to a sense of national identity and sovereignty. English nationalism, then, held the scattered English people together. Once the English in North America became convinced that traditional English national ideals could be preserved only through separation, they chose independence. Ibid., 412–13. This is a less precise definition of nationalism than that offered by Gellner, who defines *nationalism* as "primarily a political principle" and "a theory of political legitimacy, which requires that ethnic boundaries should not cut across political ones" (Gellner, *Nations and Nationalism*, 1). Alex Inkeles and David H. Smith make the explicit connection between modernization and nationhood when they posit that "nation building and institution building are only empty exercises unless the attitudes and capacities of the people keep pace with other forms of development." Inkeles and Smith, *Becoming Modern: Individual Change in Six Developing Countries* (Cambridge, Mass., 1974), 3.

4. Though more evident in Europe than in the New World, deep ideological fissures now divided national and social revolutionaries: the latter, echoing the egalitarian credos of the French Revolution, invoked the Enlightenment's universalist thought; the former invoked romantic attachment to nation, however vaguely defined. James H. Billington, *Fire in the Minds of Men: Origins of the Revolutionary Faith* (New York, 1980), 146–47.

In the case of the United States, continentalism reinforced strong racialist beliefs. "By 1850 American expansion was viewed . . . less as a victory for the principles of free democratic republicanism than as evidence of the innate superiority of the American Anglo-Saxon branch of the Caucasian race." Reginald Horsman, *Race and Manifest Destiny: The Origins of American Racial Anglo-Saxonism* (Cambridge, Mass., 1981), 1.

5. Hobsbawm, *Age of Revolution*, 198–99. We now know what the mid-nineteenth-century world only dimly perceived: "There is no inevitable secular line of human history, which guarantees that every successive phase be progress over every previous phase." Immanuel Wallerstein, *Geopolitics and Geoculture: Essays on the Changing World-System* (Cambridge, 1991), 106.

6. Quoted in Steven Topik, "Brazil and Mexico Compared, 1888–1910," in Joseph Love and Nils Jacobsen, eds., *Guiding the Invisible Hand: Liberalism and the State in Latin America* (New York, 1988), 119.

7. Horsman, *Race and Manifest Destiny*, 3.

8. "What preoccupied the thoughts of major statesmen from Jackson to Lincoln," writes John Diggins, "was not so much the political duty of the citizen as the economic opportunity of the worker and entrepreneur. Whether Jackson attacked the Bank of the United States or Lincoln the slave system of the South, both leaders did much to bring into politics the labor theory of value. The Lockean principle that property is the outcome of human exertion was anathema to conservative Whiggism and Southern

political economy alike, where property was regarded as prior to labor" (*Lost Soul of American Politics*, 14). See also David M. Potter, *The Impending Crisis: 1848–1861* (New York, 1976), 196–97; Mark Summers, *The Plundering Generation: Corruption and the Crisis of the Union, 1849–1861* (New York, 1987), xii–xv; Major Wilson, *Space, Time, and Freedom: The Quest for Nationality and the Irrepressible Conflict* (Westport, Conn., 1974), 34–35, 184–87, 236–37; and Eric Foner, *Free Soil, Free Labor, Free Men: The Ideology of the Republican Party Before the Civil War* (New York, 1995; orig. pub., 1970), xx–xxi, 310–11, 316–17.

9. Diggins, *Lost Soul of American Politics*, 232.

10. Robert Wiebe, *Opening of American Society: From the Adoption of the Constitution to the Eve of Disunion* (New York, 1984), 250–51, 255–56. For a different perspective, see Leonard White, *The Jacksonians: A Study in Administrative History, 1829–1861* (New York, 1954), esp. 506–9.

11. Daniel Boorstin, *The Americans: The National Experience* (New York, 1965), 272–73, 418–27.

12. Quoted in Mark Summers, *The Plundering Generation: Corruption and the Crisis of the Union, 1849–1861* (New York, 1987), 5.

13. David M. Potter notes: "The antislavery and nativist groups frequently avoided a contest with one another for the good reason that both appealed to the same elements in the population. It may seem paradoxical in the later twentieth century to say that the same people who opposed the oppression of a racial minority also favored discrimination against a religious minority." Potter, *The Impending Crisis, 1845–1861* (New York, 1976), 251. See also 240–41; and Arthur A. Ekirch, Jr., *The Civilian and the Military* (New York, 1956), 72–73, 86–87. Irish, German, and Hungarian immigrants, denied jobs in their new homeland, joined filibustering expeditions to find employment. See Robert May, "Young American Males and Filibustering in the Age of Manifest Destiny: The United States Army as Cultural Mirror," *Journal of American History* 78 (Dec. 1991): 863.

14. The Adams quotation is from Joyce Appleby, ed., *Materialism and Morality in the American Past: Themes and Sources, 1600–1860* (Reading, Mass., 1974), 422; that of Lincoln is cited in Ralph Lerner, *Revolutions Revisited: Two Faces of the Politics of the Enlightenment* (Chapel Hill, N.C., 1994), 93. "The fundamental issue," writes Barrington Moore, Jr., "became more and more whether the machinery of the federal government should be used to support one society [the Northeast and the West] or the other [the South]" Moore, *Social Origins of Dictatorship and Democracy* (Boston, 1967), 136.

15. Roy F. Nichols, *The Disruption of American Democracy* (New York, 1948), 344.

16. Seymour Drescher, "British Way, French Way: Opinion Building and Revolution in the Second French Slave Emancipation," *American Historical Review* 96 (June 1991): 709–34; Franklin Knight, *The Caribbean: The Genesis of a Fragmented Nationalism*, 2nd ed. (New York, 1988), 167.

17. See Luís Martínez-Fernández, "Caudillos, Annexationism, and the Rivalry Between Empires in the Dominican Republic, 1844–1874," *Diplomatic History* 17 (Fall 1993): 576–77.

18. Following a prolonged Dominican guerrilla insurrection, the Spanish abandoned the island in 1865. In the postwar years, U.S. penetration of the Dominican Republic rapidly increased and, in 1870, the Grant administration negotiated an annexation

treaty with a compliant Dominican government. It failed after a withering assault by Charles Sumner in the U.S. Senate.

19. Brenda G. Plummer, *Haiti and the United States: The Psychological Moment* (Athens, Ga., 1992), 43.

20. See Basil Rauch, *American Interest in Cuba, 1848–1855* (New York, 1948); C. Stanley Urban, "The Africanization of Cuba Scare, 1853–1855," *Hispanic American Historical Review* 37 (Feb. 1957): 29–45; Lester D. Langley, *The Cuban Policy of the United States: A Brief History* (New York, 1968), ch. 2; Robert May, *The Southern Dream of Tropical Empire, 1854–1861* (Baton Rouge, La., 1973); and Heminio Portell Vilá, *Narciso López y su época* (3 vols., Havana, 1930–1958).

21. Quoted in Pérez, *Cuba and the United States*, 48–49; Luís Martínez-Fernández, *Torn Between Empires: Economy, Society, and Patterns of Political Thought in the Hispanic Caribbean, 1840–1878* (Athens, Ga., 1994), 148–49.

22. Quoted in Pérez, *Cuba and the United States*, 52.

23. Thomas Holt, *The Problem of Freedom: Race, Labor, and Politics in Jamaica and Britain, 1832–1938* (Baltimore, 1991), 48–49; Robert Miles, *Capitalism and Unfree Labour: Anomaly or Necessity?* (London, 1987), 88–91; Herbert S. Klein and Stanley L. Engerman, "The Transition from Slave to Free Labour: Notes on a Comparative Economic Model," in Manuel Moreno Fraginals, Frank Moya Pons, and Stanley Engerman, eds, *Between Slavery and Free Labor: The Spanish-Speaking Caribbean in the 19th Century* (Baltimore, 1985), 255–68; Peter C. Emmer, "The Price of Freedom," in Frank McGlynn and Seymour Drescher, eds., *The Meaning of Freedom: Economics, Politics, and Culture After Slavery* (Pittsburgh, 1992), 34–37; Stanley Engerman, "The Economic Response to Emancipation," in ibid., 54–57.

Clearly, as William Green points out, conflict persisted, but imposing a theoretical dialectic on the Caribbean in the nineteenth century diminishes the reality of a region where "struggles were multi-faceted, diverse, interregional, even intercontinental; they involved differing culture groups, racial groups, economic groups, political, religious, philanthropic and administrative groups whose loyalties and alliances shifted as issues and circumstances changed." Green, "The Creolization of Caribbean History: The Emancipation Era and a Critique of Dialectical Analysis," in Hilary Beckles and Verene Shephard, eds., *Caribbean Freedom: Society and Economy from Emancipation to the Present* (Kingston, Jamaica, 1993, 35–36. See also Robin Blackburn, *The Overthrow of Colonial Slavery, 1776–1848* (London, 1988), 538–39; and Arthur L. Stinchcombe, *Sugar Island Slavery in the Age of Enlightenment: The Political Economy of the Caribbean World* (Princeton, 1995), who explains why freedom often resulted in new forms of social control over the emancipated slaves.

24. Mintz, "Panglosses and Pollyannas," in McGlynn and Drescher, eds., *The Meaning of Freedom*, 246–51, 254–55; Holt, *Problem of Freedom*, xxii–xxiii. See also O. Nigel Bolland, "The Politics of Freedom in the British Caribbean," in McGlynn and Drescher, eds., *The Meaning of Freedom*, 113–15, 120–21, 126–29, 132–33, 142–43.

25. William A. Green, *British Slave Emancipation: The Sugar Colonies and the Great Experiment, 1830–1865* (Oxford, 1976), 402–5; Michael Craton, *Sinews of Empire: A Short History of British Slavery* (Garden City, N.Y., 1974), 282–83; Mavis C. Campbell, *The Dynamics of Change in Slave Society: A Sociopolitical History of the Free Coloreds of Jamaica, 1800–1865* (Rutherford, N.J., 1976), 366–68; Gad Heuman, *Between Black and White: Race, Politics, and the Free Coloreds in Jamaica, 1792–1865* (Westport, Conn., 1981), 192–94; Michael Smith, *Culture, Race, and Class in the Commonwealth*

Caribbean (Mona, Jamaica, 1984), 137–38; Elso Goveia, *Slave Society in the British Leeward Islands at the End of the Eighteenth Century* (New Haven, 1965), 332.

26. Quoted in Holt, *Problem of Freedom,* 277; see also 266–67.

27. Phillip D. Curtin, *Two Jamaicas* (Cambridge, Mass., 1955), 101–3, 176–77, 194–95; Holt, *Problem of Freedom,* 298–301, 306–9.

28. Quoted in Halperín-Donghi, *Aftermath of Revolution in Latin America,* 128; see also Frank Safford, "Politics, Ideology, and Society," in Leslie Bethell, ed., *The Cambridge History of Latin America* (Cambridge, 1985), 390–91; and Nicolás Sánchez-Albornoz (W. A. R. Richardson, trans.), *The Population of Latin America* (Berkeley, 1974), 146–51.

The historiographical debate on the long-term implications of Latin American modernization under the mid-nineteenth-century liberal regimes can be traced in Stein and Stein, *Colonial Heritage of Latin America,* 126–38, who make comparisons with U.S. economic development; and Bushnell and Macaulay, *Emergence of Latin America in the Nineteenth Century,* 180–92. Latin Americanists disagree over whether or not the European economic links with regional elites constituted neocolonialism or a new "colonial pact," as Tulio Halperín-Donghi maintains. "Despite the underlying cogency of this argument," warns Carlos Marichal, "it tends to place the emphasis on the impact of external rather than internal factors. The growth of foreign trade and the renewed flows of foreign capital did impel adoption of a new model of economic growth, but the ruling groups in each Latin American nation decisively influenced how the model was formulated and implemented." Marichal, *A Century of Debt Crisis in Latin America from Independence to the Great Depression* (Princeton, N.J., 1987), 70–71.

29. Tulio Halperín-Donghi, *El espejo de la historia: Problemas argentinos y perspectivas hispanoamericanas* (Buenos Aires, 1987), 28. See also Florencia Mallon, "Economic Liberalism: Where We Are and Where We Need to Go," in Joseph Love and Nils Jacobsen, eds., *Guiding the Invisible Hand: Economic Liberalism and the State in Latin American History* (New York, 1988), 177–79.

Richard Graham explains how the cloning of British modernizing ideas and forces onto mid-nineteenth-century Brazil incorporated the country into the international economy but did not fundamentally alter the traditional society and its values in *Britain and the Onset of Modernization in Brazil, 1850–1914* (Cambridge, 1968), 8–9, 16–17, 18–21, 24–27. See also Emilia Viotti da Costa, *The Brazilian Empire: Myths and Realities* (Chicago, 1985), 54–55.

30. See Lowell Gudmondson and Héctor Lindo-Fuentes, *Central America, 1821–1871: Liberalism Before Liberal Reform* (Tuscaloosa, Ala., 1995), esp. 4–7, 86–89, 104–5.

31. See the authoritative biography by Ralph Lee Woodward, Jr., *Rafael Carrera and the Emergence of the Republic of Guatemala, 1821–1871* (Athens, Ga., 1993); and his earlier study, "Social Revolution in Guatemala: The Carrera Revolt," in *Applied Enlightenment: Nineteenth Century Liberalism* (New Orleans, 1972), 43–70. On the liberal experiment in Guatemala, see William J. Griffith, *Empires in the Wilderness: Foreign Colonization and Development in Guatemala, 1834–1844* (Chapel Hill, N.C., 1965); and Miles Wortman, *Government and Society in Central America, 1680–1840* (New York, 1982), 247–49.

32. Gudmondson and Lindo-Fuentes, *Central America,* 30–31, 72–74. E. Bradford Burns chronicles the demise of folk culture in Nicaragua in *Patriarch and Folk: The Emergence of Nicaragua, 1798–1858* (Cambridge, Mass., 1991).

33. Gudmondson and Lindo-Fuentes, *Central America*, 38–39, 42–43.

34. Quoted in William Sater, *Chile and the United States: Empires in Conflict* (Athens, Ga., 1990), 22.

35. Quoted in Comisión de Investigación Histórico de la Campaña de 1856–57, *Documentos relativos a la guerra contra los filibusteros* (San José, Costa Rica, 1956), 64.

36. On the shaping of political alignments in Latin America in the nineteenth century see Frank Safford, "Bases of Political Alignment," in Richard Graham and Peter Smith, eds., *New Approaches to Latin American History* (Austin, Tex., 1974), 74–111. For the Central American case, see the essay by Lowell Gudmondson in Gudmondson and Lindo-Fuentes, *Central America*, 108–11.

37. W. Dirk Raat, *Mexico and the United States: Ambivalent Vistas* (Athens, Ga., 1992), 75; Charles Hale, "The War with the United States and the Crisis in Mexican Thought," *The Americas* 14 (Oct. 1957): 153–73; and Hale, *Mexican Liberalism in the Age of Mora, 1821–1853* (New Haven, 1968), 302–3.

38. Barbara Tenenbaum, *The Politics of Penury: Debts and Taxes in Mexico, 1821–1856* (Albuquerque, N.M., 1986), 143; see also Florencia Mallon, *Peasant and Nation: The Making of Postcolonial Mexico and Peru* (Berkeley, 1994), 154–57, 174–75. Compare the assessments of Walter V. Scholes, *Mexican Politics During the Juárez Regime, 1855–1872* (Columbia, Mo., 1957), and Richard Sinkin, *The Mexican Reform, 1855–1876: A Study in Nation Building* (Austin, Tex., 1979). Their enemies, rightfully denounced for their machinations and their intriguing with European monarchists, nonetheless shielded Mexico's indigenous peoples from the destructive patterns of modernization. Ultimately, they would become the victims of the nation's late-nineteenth-century progress.

39. David Bushnell, *Making of Modern Colombia: A Nation in Spite of Itself* (Berkeley, 1993), 92–95, 101–9; William P. McGreevey, *An Economic History of Colombia, 1845–1930* (Cambridge, 1971), 74–77, 95–96, 139–40; and Frank Safford, *The Ideal of the Practical: Colombia's Efforts to Form a Technical Elite* (Austin, Tex., 1976), 15–17.

40. John Lynch, *Caudillos in Spanish America, 1800–1850* (Oxford, 1992), 312–15; Robert P. Matthews, *Violencia rural en Venezuela, 1840–1858: Antecedentes socioeconómicos de la Guerra Federal* (Caracas, 1977).

41. David Bushnell, *Reform and Reaction in the Platine Provinces, 1810–1852* (Gainesville, Fla., 1983), 102–3.

42. Tulio Halperín-Donghi, "Liberalism in Argentina," in Love and Jacobsen, eds., *Guiding the Invisible Hand*, 100–111; Susan Calvert and Peter Calvert, *Argentina: Political Culture and Instability* (Pittsburgh, 1989), 6–7, 60–63. See also Jonathan Brown, "The Bondage of Old Habits in Nineteenth-Century Argentina," *Latin American Research Review* 21 (1986): 3–31; and the sobering judgment of Nicholas Shumway, *The Invention of Argentina* (Berkeley, 1991), 164–67.

43. Quoted in Bushnell and Macaulay, *Emergence of Latin America in the Nineteenth Century*, 115. See also Sater, *Chile and the United States*, 10–11; and Halperín-Donghi, *Espejo de la historia*, 68–69.

44. Quoted in Sater, *Chile and the United States*, 21.

45. Quoted in Maurice Zeitlein, *The Civil Wars in Chile, or The Bourgeois Revolutions That Never Were* (Princeton, N.J., 1984), 36; see also 68–70.

46. Hobsbawm, *Nations and Nationalism Since 1780*, 10–11.

Index